Tragedy's End

Tragedy's End

*Closure and Innovation
in Euripidean Drama*

FRANCIS M. DUNN

New York   Oxford
Oxford University Press
1996

Oxford University Press

Oxford   New York
Athens   Auckland   Bangkok   Bogata   Bombay
Buenos Aires   Calcutta   Cape Town   Dar es Salaam
Delhi   Florence   Hong Kong   Istanbul   Karachi
Kuala Lumpur   Madras   Madrid   Melbourne
Mexico City   Nairobi   Paris   Singapore
Taipei   Tokyo   Toronto

and associated companies in
Berlin   Ibadan

Copyright © 1996 by Francis M. Dunn

Published by Oxford University Press, Inc.
198 Madison Avenue, New York, New York 10016

Oxford is a registered trademark of Oxford University Press

Library of Congress Cataloging-in-Publication Data
Dunn, Francis M.
Tragedy's end : closure and innovation in Euripidean drama /
Francis M. Dunn.
p.   cm.
Includes bibliographical references and index.
ISBN 0-19-508344-X
1. Euripides—Criticism and interpretation.   2. Greek drama
(Tragedy)—History and criticism.   3. Originality (Aesthetics)
4. Closure (Rhetoric)   5. Rhetoric, Ancient.   I. Title.
PA3978.D86   1996
882'.01—dc20   95-14997

1 3 5 7 9 8 6 4 2

Printed in the United States of America
on acid-free paper

In memory of
my mother Pamela
and my brother Nicholas

———————————

Preface

In one sense, this book marks the end of a long road that began at a performance of *Hamlet*; why, I had to ask myself, does the playwright end with a stage full of corpses? Is this an easy and economical way to close the performance or is there something about Hamlet's internal and external conflicts that can only be resolved in a paroxysm of blood? Such questions led me to write a dissertation on the deus ex machina and other formal closing devices in Euripides, to read and think about problems of closure in the novel and in literary theory, to write articles on plot and closure in various plays of Euripides, and finally to undertake the present study of closure and generic innovation in Euripidean drama. In another sense, this book stands at a crossroads. Classical scholars have long been perplexed both by Euripides' fondness for the deus ex machina and by his increasing partiality for what can only be called nontragic plots. By addressing closure not just as the end of a performance but as an organization of the plot, we shall find that the issues of formal closure and of generic innovation are interrelated in ways that will shed light on both. And as the study of closure becomes more important in classical studies, and theoretically much more varied in other literary disciplines, I hope that my focus in this work upon plot and generic expectations will contribute to an ongoing dialogue involving scholars in classics, drama, and literary studies more generally. Finally, to some extent this book marks a detour and a new beginning. I found myself intrigued by the questions of time and narrative raised in chapter 5, and I suspect that these reflections, like that performance of *Hamlet* many years ago, may be the beginning of another interesting road.

My argument relies upon frequent citation from Euripides and other dramatists. In quoting from Euripides, Aeschylus, and Sophocles, I include both the Greek text and my own translation; I hope that readers will find the translation readable yet reasonably faithful to the language of the original. The Greek text follows the Oxford editions of Denys Page (Aeschylus), Hugh Lloyd-Jones and Nigel Wilson (Sophocles) and James Diggle (Euripides), except as indicated in the notes.

Every traveler incurs many debts of friendship and hospitality, and this journey has been no different. My greatest debt is to John Herington, who graciously and patiently read drafts of the dissertation, articles, and chapters of the manuscript, saving me from many errors and providing unfailing support and encouragement. I am grateful to the President's Fund for the Humanities at Northwestern University, which allowed me the time to get this project underway, and I am pleased to acknowledge the helpful comments of the two readers for Oxford University Press. Many friends and colleagues kindly read earlier versions of individual chapters, especially Deborah Roberts, Bridget Murnaghan, Helene Foley, David Konstan, and Michael Halleran. And above all, the generous support of my wife and children made every step worthwhile.

Santa Barbara, California   F. M. D.
August 1995

Contents

Tragedy's End

1

Introduction

All tragedies are finished by a death,
All comedies are ended by a marriage;
The future states of both are left to faith.
BYRON, *Don Juan*

The Tragic End

Near the beginning of his history of the Persian Wars, Herodotus tells a parable about
ends. Croesus, the king of Lydia, was at the height of his wealth and power when
Solon the wise Athenian visited his court. The rich oriental king entertained the simple
Athenian in lavish style, gave him a tour of his treasuries, and then asked him who
was the happiest man on earth. Solon disappointed Croesus by naming an Athenian,
Tellus, who was fortunate enough to have lived in a prosperous city with fine sons
and healthy grandchildren, and who died a brave death in battle that was rewarded
with public burial on the battlefield. When Croesus in annoyance asked who came in
second, Solon told the story of Cleobis and Biton, who performed a remarkable feat
of strength and piety and then died at the height of their glory. The king became angry
that the wise Athenian was not impressed with his own good fortune, so Solon patiently explained the famous Greek paradox that no man is happy before he is dead:
the wealth or happiness we enjoy today may be lost tomorrow, and only the man
whose fortune remains to the end can truly be called happy. "One must look at the
end of each thing and see how it will turn out," Solon concluded, "for god often gives
men a glimpse of happiness and then destroys them entirely."[1] To Croesus, this talk
about ends was foolish and he sent Solon away, but events that followed proved Solon
correct: with a similar false confidence in his own power and in the meaning of an
oracle, Croesus attacked Persia, only to lose his empire, his city, and apparently his
life. Croesus was taken prisoner and placed on a pyre by Cyrus, king of the Persians,
and there he remembered how Solon had said that no one could be happy while still
alive. Only in suffering his own disastrous reversal did he recognize the importance
of waiting for the end.

This is one of Herodotus' most memorable stories, and one that portrays with
special clarity the tragic end: only through suffering a terrible reversal does the protagonist reach understanding, and only at the end is full or complete understanding
possible. To have its full effect, however, the tragic end must transform: it is not

enough for the foolish king to realize his error; his end must bring enlightenment to those who witness it. So Herodotus goes on to tell how Croesus called out the name of Solon, how Cyrus asked the meaning of these cries from the pyre, and how, as the flames were crackling around him, Croesus explained to the Persian king the lesson he had learned from Solon. Cyrus was moved by this drama: "considering that he himself was mortal and was burning alive another mortal who had been as prosperous as himself, and also fearing retribution and realizing that nothing was stable in human affairs, he changed his mind and ordered that the flames be extinguished at once."[2] Finally, in order to impress the meaning of the end as fully upon his own audience as Croesus did upon Cyrus, Herodotus concludes with a miracle: the fire was burning too strongly to be extinguished, but when Croesus realized that Cyrus was so moved by his story, he prayed to Apollo, who sent rain from a clear sky and put out the blaze.

This tragic end to the career of Croesus gives an effective end to this section of the *Histories*, which has digressed in the intervening fifty chapters to report various episodes from Athenian, Spartan, and Scythian history. In providing narrative coherence, it also provides a moral or didactic end, proving in the destruction of Croesus that Solon was right and that Athenian wisdom is superior to barbarian wealth that eventually destroys itself. The tragic end of Croesus thus serves as a model for the *Histories* as a whole, which will show at much greater length both the contrast between Greek wisdom and Persian self-indulgence and the proof of this contrast in the victory of the Greeks against the overwhelming numbers of the Persian army. The end of Croesus, which is so clear and so persuasive, anticipates the similar end to a much longer and more rambling story.[3]

Yet the end of Croesus, which is so important to the narrative of Herodotus, was shrewdly deconstructed by Aristotle:

> Must no one at all, then, be called happy while he lives; must we, as Solon says, see the end? Even if we are to lay down this doctrine, is it also the case that a man *is* happy when he is *dead*? Or is not this quite absurd, especially for us who say that happiness is an activity? But if we do not call the dead man happy, and if Solon does not mean this, but that one can then safely *call* a man blessed, as being at last beyond evils and misfortunes, this also affords matter for discussion; . . . for though a man has lived blessedly until old age and has had a death worthy of his life, many reverses may befall his descendants . . . it would also be odd if the fortunes of the descendants did not for *some* time have *some* effect on the happiness of their ancestors.[4]

How can dead men profit from having reached the end? If we cannot be happy while alive, what sort of happiness do we attain when dead? Herodotus finesses this problem with a clever sleight of hand. Only because this is clearly the end for Croesus does his own realization have authority; only because this is truly the end do Cyrus and the audience share in this fuller understanding. At the same time, this is not the end. The drama of Croesus is over, but his life continues; he is saved by the rain and later becomes a counselor to Cyrus and an advisor to Cambyses before silently slipping from the narrative; his death is never reported. Only because this is *not* the end can Croesus live to learn from his mistakes, and only because he lives to reach a new understanding can others share vicariously in the transforming power of the (apparent) end. The tragic end described by Herodotus is thus inherently paradoxical; full understanding comes only at the end, while a real or absolute end does not allow room for understanding to take place.

Solon's warning about the importance of the end is a favorite theme in Greek tragedy. Andromache, for example, proclaims that "one must never call a mortal happy until he dies and you can see what his last day is like before he goes below" (χρὴ δ' οὔποτ' εἰπεῖν οὐδέν' ὄλβιον βροτῶν, / πρὶν ἂν θανόντος / τὴν τελευταίαν ἴδης / ὅπως περάσας ἡμέραν ἥξει κάτω, *Andromache* 100–102) and the sentiment is repeated in eight other plays.[5] Greek tragedy also shares with Herodotus a fondness for contriving ends that are not really ends, bringing a protagonist to the end at which a life can be judged happy or unhappy, yet somehow leaving ample room for the protagonist and his peers and his audience to work out the meaning(s) of that end. In Aeschylus' *Persians* the destruction of Xerxes could not be more complete: a messenger reports his crushing defeat in the Battle of Salamis, the ghost of his father describes this reversal as divine punishment for his crimes, and the play ends with a lament as the king and the chorus rend their clothes in mourning. Yet for all the funereal spectacle, Xerxes survives, if only to appreciate the enormity and the meaning of his loss. In Sophocles' *Oedipus the King*, Oedipus discovers his past crimes of incest and parricide and learns that he is the cause of the present plague, and by the end of the play he has lost his wife, his sight, and his city—an end that the chorus considers worse than death (1367–68). Yet only because he lives can the blind man see what the proud king had been unable to see. The pattern seems quintessentially Sophoclean, repeated in *Antigone* (in which Creon survives, crushed and chastened) and varied in *Ajax* and *Oedipus at Colonus*, in which the hero *does* reach his mortal end in death, and therefore fails to reach the tragic end of understanding, leaving peers and audience to debate and struggle with the meaning of his end.[6] Of special interest is *Women of Trachis*, in which Deianeira challenges conventional wisdom in the very first lines of the play:

> There is an old saying current among men,
> that you cannot learn if a mortal life
> is good or bad for one, before a man dies;
> but as for me, I know before I die
> that my life is a burden and full of misfortune.

> Λόγος μέν ἔστ' ἀρχαῖος ἀνθρώπων φανεὶς
> ὡς οὐκ ἂν αἰῶν' ἐκμάθοις βροτῶν, πρὶν ἂν
> θάνη τις, οὔτ' εἰ χρηστὸς οὔτ' εἴ τω κακός·
> ἐγὼ δὲ τὸν ἐμόν, καὶ πρὶν εἰς Ἅιδου μολεῖν,
> ἔξοιδ' ἔχουσα δυστυχῆ τε καὶ βαρύν. 1–5

The old saying certainly comes true for her husband Heracles, who returns triumphant from his latest conquest only to be poisoned by his jealous wife. It is true also for Deianeira, despite her protest, since her past sufferings will not compare with mistakenly killing her husband and then taking her own life in shame and grief. Yet the tragic end, Heracles' gruesome death in the poisoned robes, is again a contrived end, since his slow agony will not result in death until after the play is finished. This ending involves a double contrivance. First, as in other examples, the playwright postpones the hero's death, allowing Heracles to reflect upon his own tragic end. But second, in doing so he removes from the play a very different end: according to most versions of the legend, Heracles will become a god, and this reversal *after* death would completely alter our assessment of his life. *Women of Trachis* derives its tragic effect in large part from Sophocles' careful contrivance of an end, his invention of a crucial point that, like the capture of Croesus, *seems* to be the end from which we can properly decide whether a life has been happy or not. Yet the contrivance is exposed by the poet's gesture of excluding from the drama a miraculous end that will overturn the hero's apparent end upon the pyre, and will reverse the way in which we apply that old saying.[7]

Greek tradition ascribed to Solon the paradox that no one can be happy before he dies, and in Herodotus, in Aeschylus, and especially in Sophocles, this paradox describes the tragic end, in which the final destruction of the protagonist brings to him and to those who witness his drama a new and authoritative understanding. Yet however natural this end seems, it remains a fiction. Neither Herodotus in his *Histories* nor Aeschylus in *Persians* draws attention to this contrivance,[8] but Sophocles does so in various ways. In *Ajax* and *Oedipus at Colonus,* the hero's death shifts the burden and the problem of reflection onto others; *Women of Trachis* begins by rejecting the old saying and ends by excluding from the action the untragic end of apotheosis; and in *Oedipus the King* the chorus tells Oedipus that it would have been better to die rather than live in blindness (1367–68), eliciting a long speech in which Oedipus justifies his decision to live and rationalizes the choice of self-mutilation as his appropriate end (1369–1415). Euripides, however, will dramatize the artificial nature of the end without relying upon the paradigm of the tragic end.

Gestures and Genres

In Euripides we find relatively little interest in the hero's end. The protagonist is usually a man (Ion) or a woman (Andromache) or a reunited couple (Helen and Menelaus, Orestes and Iphigenia) with a future full of travels and adventures, and the end of the play, as we shall see, tends to be not the end of a single action, but a pause in a continuous and endless story. Only two extant plays, *Hippolytus* and *Bacchant Women,* reach their climax at or soon after the death of the protagonist, but neither Hippolytus nor Pentheus finds belated understanding in the manner of Croesus. Hippolytus does not learn from his own career and unhappy death, although he is instructed in the ways of gods by Artemis, and Pentheus is dismembered offstage, pleading that his mother not kill him for his mistakes, but leaving Agave literally and metaphorically to put things together as she reassembles the corpse of her son. If there are hints or ingredients of the tragic end, these are parceled out among various characters or scenes. When the action leaves a character crushed like Oedipus, it is not a protagonist who is destroyed but her opponent: in *Medea* Jason loses his bride, his new city, and his children, and in *Hecuba* Polymestor must watch his children being murdered before he himself is blinded. When the hero himself is crushed with a terrible fit of madness in *Heracles,* we find that this is not an end at all, but one more episode in a long career that will continue in new and uncharted directions once the play is over.

To some extent the tragic end is ignored, discarded as irrelevant in a larger story that has no end. And to some extent it is subverted, fragmented among different characters and thus unable to provide a coherent pattern for the action. Its place is taken by something very different. For the rhetorically and morally persuasive end of a hero, Euripides substitutes a flourish of formally persuasive closing gestures. *Hippolytus* ends not with a truth discovered by the hero but with a god on the machine explaining what has happened; the play reaches a convincing end not with the death of its protagonist but with the intervention and command of a deus; the meaning of what has happened is not gathered from reflection upon a hero's successes and failures, but is recited in a convenient moral by the departing chorus. With disconcerting clarity or *sapheneia,* the complex, subjective process of closure is analyzed into a set of discrete and objective devices, yet as we shall see, this blaze of clarity leaves the process of closure all the more uncertain.[9]

These curious closing gestures raise many questions of interpretation. How do we "read" this new and more formal rhetoric of closure? How does this rhetoric shape our response to individual plays? And what do we make of the fact that such a rhetoric is preferred or required? It is the end, after all, that defines the whole both prospectively and retrospectively. Looking forward from the beginning of a work, the expectation of a certain end or a certain kind of end gives the reader or viewer the basic framework, the map and compass as it were, with which to navigate the work, and looking backward, a recognition of how this end has or has not been reached makes clearer the nature of this particular journey. It is clearly untrue that every tragedy ends with a death, just as it is not the case that every comedy ends with a marriage, but insofar as it is possible to map the terrain and the expectations of either genre, the shape of the drama cannot be divorced from its end. Sophoclean tragedy, for example, creates for itself generic boundaries that are distinguished in equal measure by the "heroic temper" of its protagonist and by the tragic end that he embraces. The comedies of Aristophanes likewise mark out for themselves both the "comic hero" and the riotous triumph he wins for himself.[10] And because there was no precedent for his brand of historical prose, Herodotus had to appropriate—and make it clear that he was appropriating—the tragic end as a defining feature of his drama on the war between East and West. It follows that the formal end of Euripidean drama, with its predictable deus ex machina, aetiology, and choral "tag," evades the boundaries of dramatic genre. It creates a pattern of closure that is as flexible and consistent as the Sophoclean hero and his tragic end, but because the pattern is strictly formal, it avoids giving shape or direction to the action itself.

This absence of generic bearings is at the heart of the problem of reading Euripides. The lack of bearings is recognized in a negative manner by Ann Michelini, who describes Euripidean drama as an anti-genre, a drama defined by its rejection of Sophocles. And it is recognized in a more positive manner by the eclectic mix of categories ("mythological tragedy," "tragédie manquée," "romantic tragedy," and so on) into which D. J. Conacher divides the plays.[11] But the former ties Euripides too closely to the rejection of a single model, while the latter too easily associates him with categories that did not yet exist.[12] Because Euripidean drama avoids being marked or defined by the tragic end, it is radically free to create its own boundaries; tragedy placed in limbo, cut free from its familiar bearings, may choose to plot an entirely new course.

My argument consists of three separate movements. In Part I, I examine the closing gestures developed by Euripides, and explore the gap these create between formal or extra-dramatic signals of the end on the one hand, and the absence of completeness or a convincing end to the dramatic action on the other. I discuss familiar and controversial features of Euripidean technique, such as the deus ex machina, the aition or closing aetiology, and the choral "tag" or exit lines of the chorus, as well as less commonly noted features such as the closing prophecy and the speech of acquiescence.[13] Yet I regard these not as isolated problems, but as part of a larger rhetoric of closure that tends to allow and encourage a more open articulation of the plot. In Part II, I turn to the uses of this rhetoric, exploring large-scale variations in these gestures in *Hippolytus, Trojan Women,* and *Heracles,* and showing how these variations go beyond a formalization of closure to subvert the very notion of an appropriate end. The figures or tropes of repetition, reversal, and erasure directly challenge familiar expectations of dramatic coherence by organizing events in ways that run, often with powerful effect, against the grain of the tragic end. Finally, in Part III, I argue that new tropes of closure and new ways of organizing the plot make possible new contours and new ends for Greek drama. Fuller readings of three late plays, *Helen, Orestes,* and *Phoenician Women,* show how they introduce into tragedy the fortuitous logic of romance, the contradictory impulses of tragicomedy, and the prosaic course of narrative; both the end and the logic of tragedy become irrelevant as drama explores entirely new forms.

Closure and Criticism

Parts of my argument revisit familiar problems in Euripides: the role of the deus ex machina, the relevance and authenticity of the choral exit, and the function of the closing aetiologies. And parts of my argument revisit the interpretation of individual plays, whether familiar like *Hippolytus,* relatively unfamiliar like *Orestes* and *Phoenician Women,* or acknowledged "problem plays" like *Trojan Women* and *Heracles.* I hope that by returning to these features and these plays from a new perspective, we can resolve some long-standing questions in Euripidean drama, or (to put it less positivistically) come to see that they are not the problems we thought they were. The deus and the choral "tag," for example, may be seen not as discrete problems but as related devices in a formal rhetoric of closing gestures. And the unusually regular design of *Hippolytus* and the notoriously episodic design of *Trojan Women* may be seen as revising, in two different ways, the expectation of a formally satisfying end. I also hope that in tracing the connections between closing gestures and dramatic innovation, and by devoting attention to the ways in which dramatic plots realize their ends, we will better understand the generic license or openness that informs some of Euripides' most original dramas.

It will be evident, here and in what follows, that my discussion is neither theoretical (by which I mean that it does not advance a new theory about closure) nor theory driven (by which I mean that it does not apply a specific theory about closure in reading Euripides), although I gladly make use of more theoretical studies, especially Peter Brooks and Mikhail Bakhtin on plot and narrative.[14] But it needs to be pointed out that the study of closure is, in an important way, atheoretical. The objects of this study are remarkably varied, from the endings of certain poems (Barbara Herrnstein Smith on sonnets) to the rhetorical goal in certain forms of fiction (David Richter on the fable or apologue) to the need for a quasi-religious transformation in the Western novel (Frank Kermode on the apocalyptic impulse).[15] "Closure" has been understood in equally varied ways as the more or less formal devices and patterns that bring a work to an end (Smith on the sonnet, Marianna Torgovnick on the novel), as the aesthetic coherence that a work strives for or rejects (Murray Krieger and Robert Adams, respectively), or as some totalizing meaning available in religious faith, imperial power, or patriarchal authority, to which a literary work may or may not subscribe (see, for example, Kermode, David Quint, and Rachel Blau DuPlessis).[16] Any survey of approaches to closure at once becomes a survey of critical interests and approaches. Is order something within a work or text and if so, is the task of the critic to describe how such order is realized (as in New Criticism) or to show that such order is impossible (as in deconstruction)? Is order something outside a work or text and if so, is the task of the critic to show how the work obeys the hierarchies of power and gender, or to show how it resists such hierarchies? The study of closure, in other words, is atheoretical in that the "closure" of a work, the way in which it constructs or rejects order, may be defined and interpreted from any theoretical perspective.[17]

The chapters that follow are primarily concerned with the internal order of a work and with the relation between formal closing devices and the loosening of generic constraints. In thinking about questions of closure, I am most indebted to the seminal works of Smith and Kermode, and in trying to describe how Euripidean plots play with desire for an end and with a more open construction of events, I am most indebted to Brooks and Bakhtin. Most of these critics, and most scholars who have written on closure, are concerned with narrative closure and with nineteenth- and twentieth-century fiction. This is not just because the novel has a privileged place in modern literature and criticism, but because this genre, in its programmatic allegiance to a continually unfolding story (whether we explain this by invoking the secular time of Kermode or the unfinalizability of Bakhtin), raises the problem of closure in a particularly insistent manner. I suspect that the peculiar problem of closure in the novel will not have close parallels elsewhere, and that as scholars turn to other periods and other genres, different and more local issues will come to the fore.[18] In the present study however, we will find that the work of a playwright anticipates the novel both in its insistent concern with the problem of closure, and in the particular form of narrative openness it explores.[19] The nature of this dramatic innovation is described in the chapters that follow, while the intellectual and cultural context of this innovation is another story.

I

Closing Gestures

A good novel depends on a "happy ending," on a distribution at the last of prizes, pensions, husbands, wives, babies, millions, appended paragraphs, and cheerful remarks.

HENRY JAMES

2

Curtain: The End of Performance

> The end has always begun.
> DERRIDA

Perhaps because they are so uncertain and so provisional, endings seem anxiously to demand validation; they want gestures to confirm that this is the proper place to end. There are, as we shall see, many different ways of lending formal or cultural authority to the ending, but the simplest and most familiar is confirmation that the performance is over. As a movie comes to an end, the strings strike up their coda, the credits begin to roll, and finally the house lights come up. The plot of a novel comes to an end as we turn the last few pages of the book and finally reach a blank space inscribed "The End." A manuscript will advertise its own conclusion with the flourish of a *koronis* ("hook" or "crow's beak") or with a grander declaration such as τέλος εὐριπίδου ἑκάβης ("End of Euripides' *Hecuba*") or *vergili maronis georgicon liber IIII explicit* ("Book Four of Virgil's *Georgics* is ended"). And a modern play will confirm that the performance is over when the curtain falls, the house lights come up, and members of the cast line up to take their bows.

Greek drama was different. The outdoor theater had no curtain and no lights, and so far as we know the actors did not come back onstage to receive applause; the only confirmation that the show had ended was the exit of the actors and the chorus. This emptying of the stage was a familiar signal that the play was over—a signal that might be exploited in interesting ways, as when actors and chorus exit after less than 400 lines in Euripides' *Helen*, prematurely ending the action and preparing for the second, comic prologue in which the gatekeeper drives Menelaus from the palace.[1] But whereas the *koronis* and the curtain are external markers, signals from outside the action that confirm the work has come to an end, the same is not true of the emptied stage. The departure of characters and chorus requires plausible motivation *within* the plot, and the need for such motivation seems to impose on Greek tragedy a stricter sense of closure. At the end of *Trojan Women*, the stage is left empty because now the surviving women of Troy must depart with the herald to a life of slavery. At the end of *Eumenides*, the acting area is emptied as the characters, the chorus, a second chorus of attendants, and perhaps the audience as well[2] march from the theater in a grand civic procession. In either case, the emptying of the stage is a natural part of the drama's end.

The same is not true of the modern stage. Lights and curtain are extra-dramatic devices that announce that the performance is over by intervening between action and audience, reimposing a visual and physical boundary between them. This is not to say that the curtain has a life of its own. It presumably falls only when the action has reached a suitable or appropriate conclusion. Yet precisely because it offers external and independent confirmation of the end, it has the ability to signal an end even when the action is unfinished. *The Bald Soprano*, for example, ends by starting over again, with Mrs. Martin (or Mrs. Smith) again reciting the menu of her English supper; only the curtain or a fade-out allows the play to end here, and saves us from watching a second enactment of the plot. This the Greek stage cannot do. By emptying the stage of actors and chorus, the playwright can produce a false and premature ending, but he cannot lower the curtain on an action that is still in progress, or signal an end where the plot is ready to start again.

Nevertheless, something very like this was invented by Euripides, who created a "curtain" for the ancient theater, signals outside the action that confirmed the performance was over. His clearest "curtain" is the choral exit.

Exeunt Omnes

There are obviously many different ways of emptying the stage, and Euripides' innovation consisted in finding and refining one particular method that shares the effect of a curtain or a *koronis*. Euripides gives the last words not to an actor but to the chorus, and he sets these words not in dialogue or song but in marching rhythm. These closing words are general and gnomic rather than directed to a specific situation, and they refer implicitly or explicitly to the end of the performance. Both in developing this device and in repeating the device from one play to the next, the playwright finds a gesture appropriate to the provisional nature of endings.

Electra, for example, concludes with an interesting exchange between the gods on the machine, Castor and Pollux, and the mortals below, Orestes and Electra, but after Castor hints at events to come, it is the chorus of women that has the last word:

> Farewell; and whichever mortal is able to
> fare well, and is troubled by no calamity,
>   leads a blessed life.
>
> χαίρετε· χαίρειν δ᾿ ὅστις δύναται
> καὶ ξυντυχίᾳ μή τινι κάμνει
>   θνητῶν εὐδαίμονα πράσσει.   1357–59

The chorus and its members often take part in events of the play, but nevertheless in Greek tragedy generally, and in Euripides in particular, it tends to be somewhat detached, more often responding to and commenting upon events rather than actively participating in them. Because the chorus stands partly outside the action, because it has an extra-dramatic perspective, it can intervene to moralize upon mortal calamity and good fortune without threatening the dramatic illusion. Its role is therefore analogous to that of Shakespeare's clown Feste, who both participates in and reflects upon the action, and who sings the closing lines of *Twelfth Night*:[3]

A great while ago the world begun,
With hey, ho, the wind and the rain;
But that's all one, our play is done,
And we'll strive to please you every day.

Euripides' practice of always giving the last lines to the chorus[4] enhances what we might call visual closure: after the exit of the three actors and any extras, the spectacle of the departing chorus—with their numbers, elaborate costume, and choreography—will give an appropriate climax to the emptying of the stage at the end of the drama. But it also gives those lines to a voice that is able to signal from without the end of the performance.

This "curtain" is made more effective by the choice of meter. Typically, the final scene is spoken in iambic trimeter, while the closing lines of the chorus are delivered in anapestic dimeter. The Greek iambic line, like Shakespeare's pentameter, has a flexible cadence that is closest to that of everyday speech and is regularly used in dialogue; as Aristotle points out, "we often speak iambs in conversation with one another" (*Poetics* 1449 a.26–27). The anapestic dimeter, however, has an insistent, marching rhythm best suited to emphatic entrances and exits (◡◡−◡◡−/◡◡−◡◡−). Both lines admit a number of variations and substitutions, but a crucial difference is that variations in the trimeter shift the cadence (e.g., spondee for iamb) while variations in the dimeter strictly preserve its rhythm (eg., dactyl for anapest). The striking up of this chanted, marching meter, probably accompanied by the flute, is a cue to cast and to spectators that the time has come to empty the stage.[5] Of the surviving plays of Euripides, only two do not end with the chorus chanting anapests. At the end of *Ion*, the rhythm changes to trochaic tetrameter (a "recitative" meter, like the anapestic dimeter, that indicates a higher emotional register and that was accompanied by the flute), and the last four lines are chanted in this meter by the departing chorus.[6] *Trojan Women*, however, ends with a lyric exchange between Hecuba and the chorus, a musical number sung in a highly resolved iambic lyric meter; if the chorus members do speak the last two lines of the play,[7] they do so not by striking up marching anapests, but by completing the song and repeating its rhythm from the preceding strophe. I shall return to this unusual ending later.

It is not the anapestic meter alone that allows the words of the chorus to signal the end of the performance, but the change from dialogue to anapests, as well as the brevity of these parting words. The rhyming couplet that often ends the Shakespearean speech or scene creates a sense of finality by closing off the forward movement of the preceding lines with a distinct and self-contained metrical unit:[8]

Till then sit still, my soul: foul deeds will rise,
Though all the earth o'erwhelm them, to men's eyes.   *Hamlet* I.ii

In the same way, a brief passage of no more than five anapestic lines usually closes off the iambic dialogue at the end of Euripides' plays and gives a self-contained metrical shape to the gesture of emptying the stage. One choral exit is slightly longer: in *Iphigenia among the Taurians,* the chorus has a total of ten lines—seven typical lines of conclusion followed by a three-line prayer for victory. And in three plays—*Medea, Orestes,* and *Bacchant Women*—the actors have already shifted into anapests when the chorus concludes with a brief formulaic prayer or moral. An interesting departure from the usual pattern is *Electra*. Here, after Castor delivers his speech from the machine, Orestes and Electra engage the god in dialogue for sixty-five lines—all in anapests—before the play ends and the chorus departs reciting the three lines quoted previously. The effect is that of a colossal tease. The deus has given his speech, the anapests begin, and we expect the stage to empty, but instead the action drags on, and the characters insist upon asking the god impertinent questions. How could it be right to murder one's mother? How could Apollo command Orestes to perform such a deed? Then, instead of welcoming the god's prophecies, they lament the future and their impending separation until the god cuts them off (1342), dismisses the characters, and delivers his own concluding moral (1354–56); only now, after the ending has signally failed, does the chorus give the cue to depart.

If the metrical shape of these closing lines helps to mark an end to the performance, so too does their content. In fact the final anapests usually include a generalizing moral and thus indicate not only that the performance is over, but that the action is complete: only from an intelligible whole can one abstract a point or lesson. This lesson is most clearly tied to the action when it is most provisional, when it gives one character's personal or subjective response to events. At the end of *King Lear*, for example, the Duke of Albany reflects on what has happened from his own perspective:

> The weight of this sad time we must obey;
> Speak what we feel, not what we ought to say.
> The oldest hath borne most: we that are young,
> Shall never see so much, nor live so long.

A more general or universal reflection, however, responds less directly to the action and gives an extra-dramatic cue that the play is finished. At the end of *The Beggar's Opera*, for example, the beggar's moral is not so much a hard-won lesson of the drama as it is a farewell to the audience:

> But think of this Maxim, and put off your Sorrow,
> The Wretch of To-day, may be happy To-morrow.[9]

Closing morals in Euripides tend to universal and extra-dramatic reflection. There is nothing like the Duke of Albany's personal response to events, which has its closest parallel not in Euripides but in Sophocles, in the final lines of *Oedipus the King*:[10]

> Dwellers in your native Thebes, look upon this Oedipus
> who knew the famous riddle, a mighty man
> whose fortunes a citizen viewed without envy,
> to such a tide of dread calamity he came.

So being mortal, one should look to that final
day, considering no one happy before
he passes life's limit untroubled by grief.

ὦ πάτρας Θήβης ἔνοικοι, λεύσσετ', Οἰδίπους ὅδε,
ὃς τὰ κλείν' αἰνίγματ' ᾔδει καὶ κράτιστος ἦν ἀνήρ,
οὗ τις οὐ ζήλῳ πολιτῶν καὶ τύχαις ἐπέβλεπεν,
εἰς ὅσον κλύδωνα δεινῆς συμφορᾶς ἐλήλυθεν.
ὥστε θνητὸν ὄντ' ἐκείνην τὴν τελευταίαν ἔδει
ἡμέραν ἐπισκοποῦντα μηδέν' ὀλβίζειν, πρὶν ἂν
τέρμα τοῦ βίου περάσῃ μηδὲν ἀλγεινὸν παθών.   1524–30

The closest Euripides comes to such particular reflection is in *Hippolytus*, but even
here the chorus describes the universal suffering and tears of all the citizens and
concludes with a gnomic proverb:

To all citizens in common this suffering
came unexpectedly.
Many tears will fall like oars,
for the reputations of the mighty
    most deserve lamentation.

κοινὸν τόδ' ἄχος πᾶσι πολίταις
ἦλθεν ἀέλπτως.
πολλῶν δακρύων ἔσται πίτυλος·
τῶν γὰρ μεγάλων ἀξιοπενθεῖς
    φῆμαι μᾶλλον κατέχουσιν.   1462–66

Euripides prefers morals so general that they might fit anywhere, as in the final lines
of *Ion* ("For in the end the good get what they deserve, / and the evil, born evil, would
never prosper," ἐς τέλος γὰρ οἱ μὲν ἐσθλοὶ τυγχάνουσιν ἀξίων, / οἱ κακοὶ δ', ὥσπερ
πεφύκασ', οὔποτ' εὖ πράξειαν ἄν), and above all in the formulaic moral that concludes five different plays (*Alcestis, Medea, Andromache, Helen*, and *Bacchant
Women*):[11]

Many are the shapes of divinity,
and the gods fulfill many things surprisingly.
What was expected has not been accomplished,
and for the unexpected god found a way.
    That is how this affair turned out.

πολλαὶ μορφαὶ τῶν δαιμονίων,
πολλὰ δ' ἀέλπτως κραίνουσι θεοί·
καὶ τὰ δοκηθέντ' οὐκ ἐτελέσθη,
τῶν δ' ἀδοκήτων πόρον ηὗρε θεός.
    τοιόνδ' ἀπέβη τόδε πρᾶγμα.

The gnomic quality of such reflections does not offer up the truth or the lesson of a
particular drama; instead it is a general or generic cue that the play is over and that

the time has come to reflect upon it as we may. The cue from chorus to audience is spelled out in the final line of this repeated passage: "That is how this affair turned out" (τοιόνδ᾽ ἀπέβη τόδε πρᾶγμα).

The other common theme of the choral exit is departure and farewell. This closing motif, like sunset or sleep, may suggest a natural conclusion to the action, but it may also serve as a curtain, emptying the stage whether or not the action is complete. At the end of *Julius Caesar*, victory in battle coincides with departure from the stage:

> So, call the field to rest; and let's away,
> To part the glories of this happy day.

while, at the other extreme, the ineffectual decision to leave underscores the incompleteness of the action at the end of *Waiting for Godot*:

> Vladimir: Well? Shall we go?
> Estragon: Yes, let's go.
> *They do not move.*[12]

In Euripides, the theme of departure does indeed motivate the emptying of the stage, but often as a prelude to new events that will follow. At the end of *Heracles*, the old townsmen return to their homes, while Heracles begins a new journey to Athens. When the women of Troy leave behind their burning city, they also turn to a new life of slavery in Greece. The chorus in *Hecuba* departs to the harsh necessity of life as a slave:

> Go to the harbor and the tents, friends,
> who must endure the hardships of
>   masters; for necessity stands firm.
>
> ἴτε πρὸς λιμένας σκηνάς τε, φίλαι,
> τῶν δεσποσύνων πειρασόμεναι
>   μόχθων· στερρὰ γὰρ ἀνάγκη.   1293–95

And when the chorus of Athenians departs at the end of *Children of Heracles*, it does so accompanied by attendants who will carry out the disturbing execution of Eurystheus:

> I agree. Go, attendants;
> to the rulers
>   our affairs shall be pure.
>
> ταὐτὰ δοκεῖ μοι. στείχετ᾽ ὀπαδοί.
> τὰ γὰρ ἐξ ἡμῶν
>   καθαρῶς ἔσται βασιλεῦσιν.   1053–55

Departure, in other words, functions in these plays not as an end but as a pause or hiatus; it empties the stage between actions or episodes just as the curtain might intervene between them. Like the generalizing moral, it suggests that the play is over without necessarily confirming that it is complete, but whereas the moral provides an extra-dramatic cue from chorus to audience, the words of departure—στείχωμεν (let's go), ἴτε (go!), χαίρετε (farewell)[13]—cloak this cue in theatrical metaphor, suggesting also the departure of actors from the stage. And when members of the chorus together call out "Good-bye" (*Electra* 1357, *Ion* 1619, *Iphigenia among the Taurians* 1490), this metaphor is most transparent.[14]

In Euripides' closing lines, natural closing themes such as reflection and departure are pushed in a new direction, becoming as much as possible external cues that the performance is over. The other theme of these passages needs no such push. At the end of *Iphigenia among the Taurians, Phoenician Women,* and *Orestes* we find an appeal to Nike or Victory that is unabashedly extra-dramatic, praying that the play will win first prize in the dramatic contest:

> O most holy Victory,
> embrace my life
> > and do not cease crowning me.

> ὦ μέγα σεμνὴ Νίκη, τὸν ἐμὸν
> βίοτον κατέχοις
> > καὶ μὴ λήγοις στεφανοῦσα.

The *plaudite* or request for applause is a familiar feature of comedy[15] in which an actor stands aside from the performance and asks the audience to show its approval, as Volpone himself does at the end of Jonson's *Volpone, or the Fox*:

> The seasoning of a play is the applause.
> Now, though the fox be punished by the laws,
> He yet doth hope there is no suff'ring due
> For any fact which he hath done 'gainst you.
> If there be, censure him; here he doubtful stands;
> If not, fare jovially, and clap your hands.[16]

The lines in Euripides are addressed to a personified Victory rather than to the spectators or the ten judges, but otherwise they play exactly the same role. Of course, the invitation for applause or victory naturally *follows* the curtain, and in two of these three plays, the appeal to Nike is preceded by a form of the choral exit. In *Iphigenia among the Taurians*, the chorus recites in anapests its farewell to the other characters and to the god on the machine before addressing Nike:[17]

> Go with good fortune, blessed now
> > that your fate has been rescued.
> But holy both among immortals
> and mortals, Pallas Athena,
> I will do as you command.
> For I have heard report most pleasant
> > and unexpected.
> O most holy Victory . . .

ἴτ᾽ ἐπ᾽ εὐτυχίᾳ τῆς σῳζομένης
   μοίρας εὐδαίμονες ὄντες.
ἀλλ᾽, ὦ σεμνὴ παρά τ᾽ ἀθανάτοις
καὶ παρὰ θνητοῖς, Παλλὰς Ἀθάνα,
δράσομεν οὕτως ὡς σὺ κελεύεις.
μάλα γὰρ τερπνὴν κἀνέλπιστον
   φήμην ἀκοαῖσι δέδεγμαι.
ὦ μέγα σεμνὴ Νίκη . . .   1490–97

Likewise in *Phoenician Women* Oedipus describes in recitative tetrameters how he has become an exile and delivers a universal moral ("For being mortal one must endure the gods' necessity," τὰς γὰρ ἐκ θεῶν ἀνάγκας θνητὸν ὄντα δεῖ φέρειν, 1763) before the chorus appeals for victory (1764–66). The end of *Orestes* is an interesting exception. The final spectacular scene with Apollo on the machine, Orestes on the palace roof, and Menelaus attacking the doors (discussed in chapter 10) closes first with anapests in which Apollo dismisses the others and returns to the unreal world of gods and of Helen, and then with the words of the chorus:[18]

APOLLO: Go now on your journey, honoring
          Peace, the most beautiful god. I shall
          bring Helen to the palace of Zeus
          reaching the pole of bright stars
          where she will sit next to Hera and
          Hebe the wife of Heracles, a god herself
          always honored in men's libations,
          and with the Dioscuri, sons of Zeus,
              will rule the salt sea for sailors.
CHORUS: O most holy Victory . . .

Απ.   ἴτε νυν καθ᾽ ὁδόν, τὴν καλλίστην
      θεῶν Εἰρήνην τιμῶντες· ἐγὼ δ᾽
      Ἑλένην Ζηνὸς μελάθροις πελάσω,
      λαμπρῶν ἄστρων πόλον ἐξανύσας,
      ἔνθα παρ᾽ Ἥρᾳ τῇ θ᾽ Ἡρακλέους
      Ἥβῃ πάρεδρος θεὸς ἀνθρώποις
      ἔσται σπονδαῖς ἔντιμος ἀεί,
      σὺν Τυνδαρίδαις τοῖς Διὸς ὑγρᾶς
          ναύταις μεδέουσα θαλάσσης.
Χο.   ὦ μέγα σεμνὴ Νίκη . . .   1682–91

In Apollo's instruction to depart (1682) and in the closing anapests of the chorus, we have ingredients of the choral exit, but there is no "curtain." The god ascends the starry pole to rejoin the blissful immortals, and the chorus stands aside to ask for favorable votes, but for those left onstage—the mortal throng of Orestes and Electra, Pylades and Hermione, Menelaus and his army—there is no moral or farewell, no concluding gesture to empty the stage or mark an end to the performance.

At this point I want to return to the conditions of dramatic performance, since these raise questions about our analogy between the *plaudite* of comedy and Euripides' prayer for victory. In the Greek theater, plays were produced on a single occasion in competition for the prize awarded to one of three playwrights; hence the interest not in applause but in victory, both in Euripides and in Aristophanes, who appeals for victory at the end of *Acharnians*, *Birds*, *Lysistrata*, and *Ecclesiazusae* (see note 15). The crucial difference between Aristophanes and Euripides, however, is that comedies were produced as individual plays, while the tragic playwright competed with a set of three tragedies and a satyr-play. Aristophanes will naturally place his victory cry τήνελλα καλλίνικος at the end of *Acharnians*, but where will Euripides place w\ mevga semnh; Nivkh" At the end of the satyr-play? After the third tragedy? After the play that will make the deepest impression? We do not know. The only surviving satyr-play, *Cyclops*, has no prayer for victory at the end, and no standard choral exit, while the "pro-satyric" *Alcestis* ends not with a prayer to Nike but with the formula πολλαὶ μορφαὶ τῶν δαιμονίων.[19] Of the three plays that end with a prayer for victory, none can be placed within its tetralogy.[20] And of the surviving third-place tragedies, *Trojan Women* concludes abruptly with responding lyrics in the antistrophe, while *Bacchant Women* (produced posthumously and perhaps without a satyr-play) ends with the πολλαὶ μορφαί exit lines. Less important than the problem of placing this appeal for victory is recognition that in the tragic contest the boundaries of performance were fluid. Even if the four plays were unrelated in theme, the end of one marks not an end but a pause, the vibrant lull of an intermission between one-act plays that were somehow to be viewed and judged as a group.[21] If the stage lacked a physical curtain, it also lacked a conceptual one, since the performance was not really over until the end of the satyr-play. This makes the Euripidean "curtain" all the more curious: Why devise a gesture to signal the end of the performance *before* the end, when the tetralogy is suspended but not finished?

Innovation at the End

I want to come back to this question by asking a different one: How did the other tragedians empty the stage? How original was Euripides? Judging from the small number of surviving plays,[22] Aeschylus had a very different technique. There are no repeated passages in Aeschylus, and no consistent form or theme. The closing lines may be spoken by the chorus, by a character, or by a special chorus of attendants.[23] They are just as often sung in lyric as chanted in anapests,[24] and they range greatly in length, from one line in *Persians* to fifty-nine lines in *Suppliant Women*. Only rarely do the closing lines summarize events,[25] and never do they abstract a moral; in four cases they allude to departure,[26] but there is no farewell (χαίρετε), such as we find in Euripides, and no prayer for victory. Instead, four plays end with songs of lament or celebration, a natural form of closure not found in Euripides.[27] In fact, only the ending of *Libation Bearers* bears comparison with the regular choral exit favored by Euripides:

> Good luck, then; and looking on you kindly
> may god guard you with good fortune.
>> This is now the third storm
>> blowing against the royal house

which has been fulfilled.
First began wretched
childeating troubles;
second the royal sufferings of a man:
the general of the Greeks died
slain in his bath;
and now a third has come, a savior
from somewhere, or shall I call it death?
Where will it be accomplished, where will it cease
and slumber—the strength of destruction?

ἀλλ᾿ εὐτυχοίης, καὶ σ᾿ ἐποπτεύων πρόφρων
θεὸς φυλάσσοι καιρίοισι συμφοραῖς.
ὅδε τοι μελάθροις τοῖς βασιλείοις
τρίτος αὖ χειμὼν
πνεύσας γονίας ἐτελέσθη.
παιδοβόροι μὲν πρῶτον ὑπῆρξαν
μόχθοι τάλανες,
δεύτερον ἀνδρὸς βασίλεια πάθη,
λουτροδάκτος δ᾿ ὤλετ᾿ Ἀχαιῶν
πολέμαρχος ἀνήρ,
νῦν δ᾿ αὖ τρίτος ἦλθέ ποθεν σωτήρ,
ἢ μόρον εἴπω;
ποῖ δῆτα κρανεῖ, ποῖ καταλήξει
μετακοιμισθὲν μένος ἄτης;   1063–76

A relatively short passage is chanted by the chorus in anapests (except the first two lines spoken in trimeters), beginning with a farewell and summarizing events of the two preceding plays; it differs from Euripidean endings only in its slightly greater length and in its closing questions that look forward to the third play of the trilogy. The ending that has most in common with those of Euripides, with many of the same closing gestures, does not conclude the trilogy, and in fact suggests a high degree of continuity with the play to follow. Whereas many years go by between the end of *Agamemnon* and the beginning of *Libation Bearers*, only a brief interval and a change of scene separate *Libation Bearers* from *Eumenides*. This continuity is reinforced by Orestes' incipient frenzy (1023–25) and by his vision of the Furies (1048–50), which together create an almost seamless flow of action from the end of one play to the beginning of the next. Although our sample is small, this continuity between plays is without parallel.[28] As the action moves from Argos to Delphi, the division between plays is largely formal or artificial, a scene-change that involves no break or interruption in the action of the trilogy. In producing this effect, Aeschylus used exactly those devices that Euripides later employed to create his independent curtain—or (less anachronistically) Euripides regularly gave his single tragedies an ending that resembles the formal break or pause between parts of the *Oresteia*. The end of this performance is almost as arbitrary as that of *The Bald Soprano*.

The endings in Sophocles adhere much more closely than those of Aeschylus to a regular pattern. Among his surviving plays, the closing lines are always, or nearly always, spoken by the chorus[29] and are relatively short, ranging from three to seven lines in length.[30] All are in anapests with the exception of *Oedipus the King*, which (like *Ion*) concludes with chanted tetrameters, and all except *Philoctetes* include some form of summary or moral.[31] The chief differences are that in Sophocles the choral exit rarely involves a change in meter, rarely mentions departure, and never includes a prayer for victory.[32] His exit lines are therefore less abrupt than those of Euripides, since preceding anapests prepare the audience for the exit of the chorus, nor do they draw attention to themselves as theatrical gestures, since they avoid expressions of farewell or appeals for victory. Even themes common to the two playwrights are employed differently by Sophocles. *Philoctetes*, for example, ends with words of departure:

> So let us all go together,
> once we have prayed to the nymphs of the sea
>   to preserve our return.

> χωρῶμεν δὴ πάντες ἀολλεῖς,
> Νύμφαις ἁλίαισιν ἐπευξάμενοι
>   νόστου σωτῆρας ἱκέσθαι.   1469–71

Actors and chorus all depart for Troy, where the designs of the Greeks will eventually succeed. This success may carry a price of sacrilege, as Heracles warns (1440–41), but there is nothing uncertain about the end of the performance: "all together" they leave the stage. Contrast this with the endings of *Children of Heracles*, *Hecuba*, or *Trojan Women*, where departure directly entails new troubles. The moral in Sophocles likewise tends to be more closely dependent on the action. Even the moral in *Ajax*, which comes closest to gnomic universality, draws a lesson from the hero's experience:

> There are many things mortals understand
> when they see them; but before seeing no one is prophet
>   of what the future will bring.

> ἦ πολλὰ βροτοῖς ἔστιν ἰδοῦσιν
> γνῶναι· πρὶν ἰδεῖν δ᾽ οὐδεὶς μάντις
>   τῶν μελλόντων ὅ τι πράξει.   1418–20

The mention of sight refers not only to human knowledge in general, but also to the madness of Ajax, in which he mistook animals for generals and failed to see Athena plotting against him, and the uncertain future refers both to the sudden onset of madness and to the uncertain verdict on honors that will be accorded him. Contrast this with the universal moral of *Ion* or *Helen*.

It would be easy to read the differences among the playwrights as a familiar story of rise and decline: the fertile genius of Aeschylus multiplying means of ending, Sophocles' sublime sense of form favoring the provisional closure of choral anapests, and Euripides, the shallow virtuoso, creating from this an empty and formal "tag." But rather than adopt, or reverse, such a model, I want to emphasize instead the manner in which Euripides divorces plot from performance. If Sophocles, in signaling the end of the performance, reinforces the fact that the action is complete,[33] for Euripides the end of the performance is an arbitrary pause, one that not only interrupts the staging of a tetralogy in the dramatic contest, but interrupts the enactment of dramatized events. The performance will continue with a tragedy or satyr-play on a different subject, and the characters of the plot will continue with another phase of their lives; the curtain only marks a pause.

This sense that the action continues, unbounded and unboundable, is an important feature of Euripidean drama to which I return in chapter 5. But the more clearly an action is continuous, the more it requires a purely formal gesture of closure, one that concludes the performance but nothing else. It follows that the choral exits usually regarded as least authentic and least interesting are those that best exemplify Euripides' approach to closure. A total of eight different plays end with a "formulaic" exit passage repeated elsewhere; *Alcestis, Medea, Andromache, Helen*, and *Bacchant Women* all end with the general moral "Many are the shapes of divinity . . ." (although the first of the five lines is different in *Medea*), while *Iphigenia among the Taurians, Phoenician Women* and *Orestes* all end with the prayer for victory, "O most holy Victory . . ." The formal nature of these endings, which in a sense opens up their possibilities, has met resistance from many critics; once the lines are cloned, after all, what is their relevance to a given play? One response is to cut them out. J. A. Hartung argued that "a poet such as Euripides would surely have been capable of putting something special and personal in the mouth of the chorus" and suggested that the repeated exit lines might be later interpolations.[34] W. S. Barrett went further, arguing that if these eight are not genuine, "the tail-pieces of the other nine must also come under suspicion,"[35] and the most recent editor of Euripides follows his lead.[36] However, the case for the interpolation of these exit passages has no textual foundation[37] and rests upon the critic's judgment whether such repetition is dramatically appropriate. A second response is to deny significance to the repeated endings. Thus Godfried Hermann wrote on the ending of *Bacchant Women*:[38]

> Surely, as happens in the theater when the actors have finished their parts, there was such a noise of people getting up and leaving that they could scarcely hear what the chorus would say at the end of the play. As a result, little attention was paid to those lines of the chorus.

But why write lines designed not to be heard? And if the clatter of the audience drowned out these lines, it would also drown out lines certainly meant to be heard, such as the appeal for victory in the dramatic contest. The logic of Barrett's argument requires that if we remove the repeated endings, we must remove them all; the logic of Hermann's argument requires that if repeated endings are meaningless, all of them are.[39]

Many defenders of the formulaic endings start from the same premise, namely that they must have a dramatic significance to justify their presence. Johann Mewaldt, for example, argued that every play expressed Euripides' constant worldview, and "every myth he presented was for him a new confirmation of his general view of God, world and man"; *Alcestis, Helen*, and *Bacchant Women* therefore conclude with the same "signature" of the poet, the same "personal seal of authenticity."[40] B. R. Rees argues instead for thematic relevance and tries to show that the πολλαὶ μορφαί ending is appropriate to each of the five tragedies in its reference to "the unpredictability of the ways of God with men," and is especially appropriate to *Medea*, where the absence of a divine epiphany is reflected in a different first line (πολλῶν ταμίας Ζεὺς ἐν Ὀλύμπῳ, "Zeus in Olympus dispenses many things").[41] And Franz Mayerhoefer suggests that the repeated endings draw attention to the poet's originality, arguing that ἀέλπτως refers not to events that surprise the characters, but to innovations that surprise the audience (a reading hard to extract from πολλὰ δ' ἀέλπτως κραίνουσι θεοί, "the gods accomplish many things in a manner unforeseen").[42]

But rather than reject lines deficient in dramatic meaning, or rescue them by trying to find meaning in them, we need to revise our premises. As Deborah Roberts points out, the last words need not be charged with special meaning:[43]

> In a play by Shaw, for example, the fall of the curtain reveals that the end is the end and the last words are last; it thus gives these last words, by its apparent arbitrariness, the weight we associate with a person's dying words, cut off by death. But in a play by Sophocles, it is the last words themselves which reveal that the end is the end and that they are the last words; they thus resemble the ritualized words of a priest at a death-bed.

The closing anapests should be read less for significant content than as a gesture or ritual of closure. But as we have seen, the three playwrights are different, and the formulaic lines in particular are only found in Euripides. For Sophocles, the gesture *is* significant, just as the words a priest recites endow the moment of death with ritual completeness: the departure of the chorus is a formality, but a formality that confirms the outcome of the plot. In *Alcestis* or *Helen*, however, the departure of the chorus is self-consciously formal, a ritual that opens up the possibility that it lacks the proper force of ritual, a gesture that plays at being empty. As we shall see, this emptied or formalized "curtain" that ends the performance has analogues in several other closing gestures employed by Euripides.

3

Machine: Authorizing an End

> Help, neighbors! Come here, come here!
> My master is rising into the air
> like a horseman on a dung beetle!
>
> ARISTOPHANES, *Peace*

The credits begin to roll, the curtain falls, or the curl of a *koronis* adorns the page, and we are reassured that the performance has ended or that the book is finished. But is such a gesture necessary? Or is a mere gesture sufficient? If the drama is complete, then surely the gesture is an empty one: formal but redundant confirmation that the action has been wrapped up in a satisfactory manner. However, if the action remains open, then the gesture is ironic, like Ionesco's curtain or Estragon's decision to go: not an agent of closure but an informer that betrays the work's incompleteness. In either case we have, or seem to have, an opposition between form and content, between the "internal" completeness or incompleteness of the action and the "external" flourishes that advance or subvert this closure. This opposition shifts the question of closure from the outside to the inside, from the empty gestures of the stage to the "real" completeness of the plot or action that these gestures may or may not endorse. Once we turn our attention from the outside to the inside, and try to judge the completeness of the action, the question seems to have a simple answer: the deus ex machina, the god on the machine, enters at the end to tie up loose ends, resolve all problems, and guarantee that the action is complete. But in so doing, the deus formalizes the closure of the plot and turns this reassuring ending into yet another gesture. The opposition between inside and outside, meaning and gesture, collapses and renders closure deeply problematic.

The formalized closure provided by the deus is relatively violent and dangerous. Curtain, *koronis*, and "Finis" are innocuous markers, simply confirming the end of the performance, but more drastic measures are required to wrap up the plot and bring it to a convincing end. At the end of *The Beggar's Opera*, for example, when it turns out that the entertaining musical will end with the hero being hanged, the author himself, the beggar who wrote the opera, steps in to write a different and more satisfactory ending:

PLAYER: Why then, Friend, this is a down-right deep Tragedy. The Catastrophe is
manifestly wrong, for an Opera must end happily.

BEGGAR: Your Objection, Sir, is very just; and is easily remov'd. For you must allow, that in this kind of Drama, 'tis no matter how absurdly things are brought
about.—So—you Rabble there—run and cry a Reprieve—let the Prisoner be brought
back to his Wives in Triumph.

PLAYER: All this we must do, to comply with the Taste of the Town.[1]

Such intervention in the content, in the events of the play, is much less common than
the intervention of a curtain in its form or staging, and it suggests that things are more
seriously amiss. It is an index of crisis, a signal that the action is somehow so wrong
that nothing else can correct it. It is also an apparent signal of the playwright's loss
of control: it seems that because he has failed to keep the plot in check and has
allowed the catastrophe to go wrong, he or a divine surrogate must step in to produce a satisfactory end. According to the comic poet Antiphanes, the deus ex machina
covers up the incompetence of tragic poets:[2]

> when they don't know what to say,
> and have completely given up on a play,
> just like a finger they lift the machine
> and the spectators are satisfied.
> There is none of this for us . . .
>
> ‹ἔπειϑ᾽ ὅταν μηθὲν δύνωντ᾽ εἰπεῖν ἔτι,
> κομιδῇ δ᾽ ἀπειρήκωσιν ἐν τοῖς δράμασιν,
> αἴρουσιν ὥσπερ δάκτυλον τὴν μηχανήν,
> καὶ τοῖς θεωμένοισιν ἀποχρώντως ἔχει.
> ἡμῖν δὲ ταῦτ᾽ οὐκ ἔστιν . . .   fr. 189.13–17 *PCG*

Power and authority are therefore crucial issues, both in the author's failure to keep
the plot under control, and in his belated attempt to correct it. Equally important, as
we shall see, is the issue of propriety, of willingness or ability to conform to generic
or cultural norms, and to comply with the "taste of the town." But again this closing
gesture is paradoxical. The particular form of the deus in Euripides, and the almost
mechanical reproduction of this figure from one play to the next, contains and
domesticates it. Rather than a violent intervention to address a dangerous crisis, the
deus ex machina is often a reassuring and unthreatening figure, one whose comforting gestures leave open at the end the question of how tragedy should end.

   Before turning to particular ways in which the deus authorizes an end to the action, I must begin with a definition. The term *deus ex machina* (in Greek, θεὸς ἀπὸ
μηχανῆς), whether in scholarly or colloquial usage, has freely been used to describe
everything from divine intervention to a surprising turn of events.[3] In Euripides,
however, the term can and should be used much more narrowly. "Deus ex machina"
literally means "god from the machine," referring to his or her entrance through the
air upon some form of crane. We might reasonably limit use of the term to divine
entrances that make use of this stage property, but for many plays the surviving text
does not indicate whether or not it was used.[4] These texts do indicate, however, a
remarkably consistent pattern: nine plays by Euripides end with the entrance of a

god who issues a command, explains what has happened or resolves an impasse, and foretells the future. I call this regular epilogue and its speaker a "deus" or "deus ex machina" even if we cannot show that a crane or machine was used. One borderline case I often include as a deus: the surprising entrance on the palace roof by Medea, a mortal with divine prerogatives who departs on the Sun god's chariot with the help of a crane. I shall mention for comparison other epilogues that share one or more features with the deus (e.g., 'demonic epiphanies' in *Hecuba* and *Children of Heracles*)[5] without describing these as examples of the deus ex machina. So regular are the formal features of the deus that I shall deal with two of these—a prophecy of events yet to come and an aetiological explanation of a name or institution— separately in following chapters.

In this chapter, I shall look more closely at the entrance and intervention of the deus, asking in particular how the deus goes about concluding the action and in what sense this intervention is formalized. The example of *The Beggar's Opera* shows that there are many different ways of stepping in to wrap up the ending. There the author, the beggar-poet, breaks into the action and rewrites it, substituting a reprieve for the hanging of MacHeath in a light-hearted, almost capricious manner. In Euripides, as we shall see, it is a god who both belongs and does not belong to the action who intervenes, without an overt breach of dramatic illusion, and doing less to alter events than to interpret them to characters and audience. In Shakespearean drama we often find an epilogue speaker who neither alters nor interprets the action, but simply promotes its reception by the public. In *As You Like It*, the actor who played Rosalind steps out of the action to court the spectators:

> It is not the fashion to see the lady the epilogue; but it is no more unhandsome than to see the lord the prologue. If it be true that good wine needs no bush, 'tis true that a good play needs no epilogue; yet to good wine they do use good bushes, and good plays prove the better by the help of good epilogues. What a case am I in then, that am neither a good epilogue, nor cannot insinuate with you in the behalf of a good play! I am not furnished like a beggar, therefore to beg will not become me: my way is, to conjure you. . . . If I were a woman I would kiss as many of you as had beards that pleased me, complexions that liked me, and breaths that I defied not; and, I am sure, as many as have good beards, or good faces, or sweet breaths, will, for my kind offer, when I make curtsy, bid me farewell.

The epilogue is entirely irrelevant to the plot, and the gratuitous nature of this appeal is driven home by a double conceit: the epilogue speaker says that a good play needs no epilogue, and in flirting with male spectators, he reminds them that he is only dressed as a woman. Far from trying to alter or correct the play, the epilogue speaker enters in order to solicit approval and applause, even as he exposes his meretricious designs.

It is worth noting that in Gay and in Shakespeare the play itself is exposed or unmasked; the intervention at the end lays bare the role of the author in writing the drama, or that of the actor in impersonating its characters. This is not true in Euripides, at least not true to the same extent. The god who enters, Athena or Apollo or Thetis, is not a thespian but a familiar inhabitant of the legendary past, one that literature regularly represented as interfering in mortal affairs, ever since the Olympians took opposing sides in the Trojan War, and Athena and Poseidon meddled in the home-coming of Odysseus. Of course, the distinction is not absolute. The deus may in fact be a surrogate for the poet, a convenient divinity smuggled in, as Antiphanes implies, to do his dirty work for him. Likewise in *The Beggar's Opera*, it is not really the author, John Gay, who steps in to issue MacHeath's reprieve, but his surrogate the beggar, a factitious author first introduced in the prologue. Nevertheless an important difference remains: whereas the epilogue speaker in Gay and Shakespeare explicitly breaks the dramatic illusion by exposing an actor or author, the deus in Euripides is a more conventional participant in the action; if there is a breach in dramatic illusion, it is only implied.

This difference has something to do with tragic decorum. The comic stage generally likes to play with removing masks, whether exposing the male actor playing a woman in Shakespeare, or revealing the author of the play in the parabasis of Aristophanes.[6] Tragedy does not allow such liberties, and if Euripides goes further in this direction than his predecessors, he is careful not to go too far.[7] But aside from this negative constraint, the deus allows Euripides to play a double game, introducing at the end a figure within the plot who enters from outside it, a god who suddenly and unexpectedly invades the mortal realm. This double game is peculiarly Euripidean. It would be impossible, for example, on the stage of Aeschylus, where gods and mortals may rub shoulders with one another (as in *Eumenides*), and where divinities may make up the chorus (e.g., *Cabiri, Nereids, Prometheus Unbound*) or the entire cast (*Prometheus, Psychostasia*).[8] Euripides, however, strictly reserves the action of the play for mortals, allowing gods to appear, if at all, in the prologue and epilogue that frame it.[9] Nor would this game be possible if the god who enters as deus has already made an appearance in the prologue. But in Euripides' surviving plays the prologue speaker is never the same as the epilogue speaker,[10] and the god's introduction at the end marks the first incursion of this privileged figure—who might therefore betray the role of the author as a god in Homer or Aeschylus would not. This role of the deus as authorial figure is reinforced in two ways. The god within the action regularly delivers an extended prophecy, foretelling, for example, Electra's marriage to Pylades, Orestes' exile and trial in Athens, and the arrival of Menelaus from Troy (*Electra* 1249–87); so the deus in a sense writes or narrates a sequel to the plot. And just as regularly the god explains names or institutions familiar to the audience, revealing, for example, that a city in Arcadia will be named for Orestes (*Electra* 1275); so the learned deus presents the audience with a just-so story (on prophecy and aetiology, see the following chapters).

To see how this ambiguous figure brings the action to an end, I turn to two sets of attributes. The first, gestures of authority, help to establish the privileged position of the deus, and his or her power to bring events to a close. The second, gestures of efficacy, register the god's effectiveness in concluding the action.

Gestures of Authority

A most effective, and most theatrical, way to underscore the superior power and knowledge of the epilogue speaker is by use of the machine, or μηχανή. We cannot be sure exactly what this property looked like, but we do know that it allowed gods to make an impressive entrance or exit through the air, sometimes depositing an entering actor on the roof of the skene-building and sometimes holding him suspended in midair. (Whereas the modern stage uses a harness attached to the actor, the machine seems to have been a platform for actors to stand on, raised and lowered by a crane behind the skene-building.)[11] The effect of the μηχανή is registered in the reactions of the chorus when Thetis appears at the end of *Andromache*:

> Ah, ah!
> What is happening? What godly presence
> is this? Women, look! watch!
> Some divinity is crossing the pearly
> heavens and landing on the horse-rich
>   plains of Phthia!

> ἰὼ ἰώ·
> τί κεκίνηται, τίνος αἰσθάνομαι
> θείου; κοῦραι, λεύσσετ᾽ ἀθρήσατε·
> δαίμων ὅδε τις λευκὴν αἰθέρα
> πορθμευόμενος τῶν ἱπποβότων
>   Φθίας πεδίων ἐπιβαίνει.   1226–30

We cannot be sure that every deus arrived by machine; comments such as these indicate an aerial entrance or exit in several plays (*Andromache, Electra, Ion, Orestes*; compare *Medea*),[12] but in other cases it is possible that the god simply appeared standing on the roof of the skene-building. The standing epiphany would be less spectacular, but it still creates an effective contrast between mortals at ground level and gods above.[13] In the "double epiphany" at the end of *Orestes*, both the palace roof and the machine are used in this way: Menelaus at ground level is startled by the triumphant entrance of Orestes on the roof, and then Orestes is surprised in turn by Apollo's sudden entrance on the machine.[14]

The spectacular effect of the god's entrance upon the machine[15] is sometimes reinforced by exclamations from the chorus. We have seen the reaction of the chorus at the end of *Andromache*, and there are similar expressions of awe and amazement at the entrance of Athena in *Ion* (1549–52), and at the entrance of the Dioscuri in *Electra*:[16]

> But here above the roof of the house
> we see some divinities or heavenly
> gods, for this is no mortal path!
> But why do they come in full
>   sight to mortals?

> ἀλλ᾽ οἵδε δόμων ὑπὲρ ἀκροτάτων
> φαίνουσί τινες δαίμονες ἢ θεῶν
> τῶν οὐρανίων· οὐ γὰρ θνητῶν γ᾽
> ἥδε κέλευθος. τί ποτ᾽ ἐς φανερὰν
>   ὄψιν βαίνουσι βροτοῖσιν;   1233–37

Of course, when the deus appears suddenly with no exclamation, it does not follow that the entrance was less impressive or that the machine was not used;[17] it may be that surprise is of the essence (*Medea*), or that the urgency of the situation requires that the god should have the first word (*Suppliant Women, Iphigenia among the Taurians, Helen, Orestes*). In *Hippolytus*, this verbal expression of awe is postponed; the clumsy Theseus has no words of recognition for Artemis, who must wait for proper acknowledgement until the dying Hippolytus is brought onstage: "Ah! Breath of divine fragrance! Even in my misfortune I sense you and my body is lightened, for the goddess Artemis is here" (1391–93).

Entrance on high and expressions of awe reinforce the god's stature and authority; so too does a proclamation of identity. Artemis in *Hippolytus* may enter unannounced, but this does not prevent her from commanding attention and proclaiming to Theseus her name and pedigree:

> You the well-born son of Aegeus,
> I command you to listen.
> I Artemis, daughter of Leto, speak to you.

> σὲ τὸν εὐπατρίδην Αἰγέως κέλομαι
> παῖδ᾽ ἐπακοῦσαι·
> Λητοῦς δὲ κόρη σ᾽ Ἄρτεμις αὐδῶ.   1282–85

The deus regularly begins with a self-introduction of this sort, establishing her or his divine authority from the start.[18] In *Helen* (1643–45) and *Orestes* (1625–26) an urgent command precedes this formal introduction, while in *Andromache* it is more personal. God above and mortal below are in this case woman and husband as well, but she still proclaims her identity and divine lineage as daughter of Nereus:

> Peleus, remembering our marriage long ago,
> I Thetis am here, leaving the house of Nereus.
> And first of all in these present evils
> I advise you not to bear things hard.

> Πηλεῦ, χάριν σοι τῶν πάρος νυμφευμάτων
> ἥκω Θέτις λιποῦσα Νηρέως δόμους.
> καὶ πρῶτα μέν σοι τοῖς παρεστῶσιν κακοῖς
> μηδέν τι λίαν δυσφορεῖν παρήνεσα.   1231–34

Finally, a god's own power and prestige are further reinforced by the larger order he or she represents, the authority of Zeus or the designs of fate that warrant or legitimate this divine intervention. Thetis concludes her speech to Peleus by saying, "You must endure what has been fated; that is what Zeus wills" (τὸ γὰρ πεπρωμένον / δεῖ σ᾽ ἐκκομίζειν, Ζηνὶ γὰρ δοκεῖ τάδε, *Andromache* 1268–69). In *Orestes*, a command from Zeus authorized Apollo's rescue of Helen (1633–34), and in *Helen*, the appeals to a larger authority become a refrain: "you rage for a marriage that was never fated" (οὐ γὰρ πεπρωμένοισιν ὀργίζῃ γάμοις 1646), "but we are weaker than both fate and the gods, to whom it seemed well this way" (ἀλλ᾽ ἥσσον᾽ ἦμεν τοῦ πεπρωμένου θ᾽ ἅμα / καὶ τῶν θεῶν, οἷς ταῦτ᾽ ἔδοξεν ὧδ᾽ ἔχειν 1660–61), "this is the will of Zeus" (Ζεὺς γὰρ ὧδε βούλεται 1669).

This final gesture of authority is potentially most significant. Given the jealous and independent nature of Euripides' gods, a divine epiphany does not guarantee a satisfactory ending: the god may have full authority to proclaim an end, but what if he or she is acting from partisan or selfish motives? The assurance that the deus is acting in accord with the larger purposes of Zeus and the fates would seem to make the resolution of the action more intelligible. So it is worth noting that these assurances are largely formulaic. In the examples just given, "you must endure what has been fated" or "this is the will of Zeus" are conventional platitudes rather than signs of a grand design, while the command of Zeus invoked by Apollo (Zeus authorized him to save Helen's life) has little to do with the characters onstage. And in *Electra*, as Orestes and Electra struggle to make sense of what has happened, Castor's answer rings especially hollow:

> And Phoebus, Phoebus—but he's my lord, so I
> am silent; although wise he prophesied unwisely to you.
> One must approve what's done, and in the future
> do what Fate and Zeus ordained for you.

> Φοῖβος δέ, Φοῖβος—ἀλλ᾽ ἄναξ γάρ ἐστ᾽ ἐμός,
> σιγῶ· σοφὸς δ᾽ ὢν οὐκ ἔχρησέ σοι σοφά.
> αἰνεῖν δ᾽ ἀνάγκη ταῦτα· τἀντεῦθεν δὲ χρὴ
> πράσσειν ἃ Μοῖρα Ζεύς τ᾽ ἔκρανε σοῦ πέρι.   1245–48

Here is an obvious hierarchy of power: mortals appealing to demigods (Castor and Pollux) who answer to an Olympian (Apollo) who is subject in turn to Fate and Zeus. But if Castor cannot explain or condone what his own master Apollo has prophesied, there is little reason to take seriously his warnings that mortals must obey Fate and Zeus.

The god has all it takes to authorize an end: name and pedigree, imprimatur of Zeus or Fate, and a privileged entrance on high. But are these sufficient, or are they the empty trappings of authority? Does divine authority really bring an end?

Gestures of Efficacy

We might say that the answer, again, is easy: the god's effectiveness in wrapping up the plot is clearly signaled in three ways. The first and most emphatic is the command with which the deus intervenes in the action. In her first words onstage, Artemis says to Theseus, "I command you to listen" (*Hippolytus* 1282–83), and every surviving deus likewise begins with a command to mortals.[19] But what is the effect of this command? Often the entering god does nothing more than call for attention: "I command you to listen," Artemis says to Theseus; "Listen to these words," says Athena to Theseus (*Suppliant Women* 1183); "Hear me, child of Agamemnon," Castor proclaims to Orestes (*Electra* 1238); "Listen to my words," says Athena to Thoas (*Iphigenia among the Taurians* 1436). A similar appeal is couched in negative terms in *Ion*, "Do not flee; I am no enemy" (1553), while Thetis more gently urges Peleus to set aside his grief before she launches into her speech (*Andromache* 1233–34).

Only in three plays does the god begin with a command to action. In *Iphigenia among the Taurians*, the command to listen (1436) is followed at once with a more direct injunction to Thoas (παῦσαι διώκων, "stop chasing" 1437); in *Helen,* the very first words of the Dioscuri enjoin Theoclymenus from killing his sister (ἐπίσχες ὀργάς, "restrain your anger" 1642); and in *Orestes*, Apollo begins by commanding Menelaus not to storm the palace (Μενέλαε, παῦσαι, "stop, Menelaus" 1625). But in the first two cases, the action is already complete when the deus intervenes. In *Iphigenia among the Taurians*, Iphigenia and Orestes have set sail on seas made calm by Poseidon when Athena enters, and the threats of Thoas will not alter the outcome, and in *Helen*, Menelaus and Helen have killed the Egyptians and made their escape when the Dioscuri appear before Theoclymenus. In each case, the sideshow of deus and barbarian king ratifies the conclusion with a demonstration of divine authority but without a meaningful intervention by the god. Only in *Orestes* does the god's command alter the course of events. As Orestes prepares to kill Hermione and fire the palace, and Menelaus prepares to attack the palace and kill the conspirators, Apollo commands them both to stop (1625–28) and resolve their quarrel (νείκους τε διαλύεσθε 1679): Orestes must remove his knife from Hermione's neck and marry her, while Menelaus, instead of putting Orestes to death, must make him king of Argos. The divine command has a direct and tangible effect only when the result it produces is least plausible.

Injunctions issued later by the god also tend to be empty gestures. The speech of the deus may be punctuated with a command to listen (*Andromache* 1238, *Ion* 1570), while the god's forecast of the future is often cast as a command, as when Orestes is told: "when you come to Athens, embrace the holy image of Athena" (*Electra* 1254–55).[20] Less rhetorical but no more tangible in its effect is the parting instruction intended to ratify events onstage. Since the Athenians recovered the bodies of the Argive soldiers, Athena leaves instructions for an oath of friendship (*Suppliant Women* 1185–90); since Ion's mother has been found, Athena reminds her to name him heir at Athens (*Ion* 1572–73); and since the body of Neoptolemus has been brought onstage, Thetis reminds his grandfather to give him burial (*Andromache* 1240). In each case, the command will be realized in the future, and rather than intervening in the action, it gives formal confirmation to what has happened. In *Hippolytus*, a similar command is realized onstage when Hippolytus forgives his father (1442). He does so not because he was ordered to by Artemis (1435), not because a god has intervened and made him do it; as critics have noted, the point is that the young man displays a kindness or humanity that the god cannot.[21]

If the god's authority is squandered upon empty and ineffectual commands, there are many different ways this can happen; the irony of a god commanding mortals to do what she cannot and will not do (*Hippolytus*) is an interesting example. It might be instructive to explore such variations in detail, but I simply note a general distinction. In earlier plays, the god's command, however empty, tends to suggest completeness—reconciliation (*Hippolytus*), burial (*Andromache*), and treaty (*Suppliant Women*)—while in later plays it tends to halt an ongoing action (by Thoas, Theoclymenus, or Orestes) and thus remove a threat to closure. The emphasis, in other words, is more negative and its effect is more open-ended; we shall find the same is true of other closing gestures.

The second sign of the god's effectiveness is the explanation of what has happened, by which the god's privileged knowledge can resolve remaining doubts and render events of the play intelligible. The explanation, like the command, is a sign both of the god's authority and of the drama's insufficiency: only an action that is somehow unresolved will require a god to correct it or to explain it. In some cases this privileged account does not go very far, as when Thetis reveals that "all men must die" (*Andromache* 1271–72), Artemis explains to Theseus that "gods punish evil men" (*Hippolytus* 1340–41), Athena tells Creusa that "gods will have their way in the end" (*Ion* 1614–15), and so on.[22] Some explanations are slightly more useful, explaining to a stupid or stubborn character what the audience already knows. Thus Athena must explain to the barbarian king Thoas that Apollo sent Orestes to bring back his sister (*Iphigenia among the Taurians* 1437–41b);[23] the Dioscuri must remind the Egyptian Theoclymenus that Hermes brought Helen to Egypt for safekeeping (*Helen* 1646–55), and Athena must persuade the stubborn and skeptical Ion that he is—as the priestess has already shown—the son of Apollo (*Ion* 1559–62). Other explanations are essentially irrelevant. In *Orestes* (1639–42) and *Electra* (1278–83), the deus explains that the gods started the Trojan War to reduce overpopulation,[24] and in *Orestes*, Apollo goes on to explain how Helen made her surprising escape earlier in the play: "I saved her and snatched her from your sword, thus commanded by father Zeus" (ἐγώ νιν ἐξέσωσα χὺπὸ φασγάνου / τοῦ σοῦ κελευσθεὶς ἥρπασ᾽ ἐκ Διὸς πατρός, 1633–34). In *Electra*, Castor is about to provide a more useful explanation of all that has happened by letting Orestes know why the oracle told him to kill his mother—but at this crucial moment the god cuts himself off: "and Phoebus, Phoebus—but he's my lord, so I am silent; although wise he prophesied unwisely to you" (1245–46).

Only in *Hippolytus* does the god's explanation of past events play a more substantial role in resolving the action. Artemis explains to Theseus at considerable length (1282–1341) Phaedra's love for Hippolytus, the role of the nurse, Phaedra's false accusation, the hasty curse of Theseus, and the responsibility of Aphrodite. After the entrance of Hippolytus, she repeats her explanation of Aphrodite's role to the dying boy (1400–6) before concluding with a forecast of the future (1416–39). Some explanation may be needed to undeceive Theseus and to allow him to forgive his son, but why at such length and why at the hands of a god? (Seneca and Racine, for example, allow a repentant Phaedra to reveal the truth herself.) The intervention of the deus does double duty, summarizing what has happened for the benefit of Theseus, who was absent for most of the play, and also revealing to Theseus and his son the hidden agenda of Aphrodite (announced to the audience but not to the characters by Aphrodite in the prologue). This apparently exhaustive explanation goes too far and not far enough. Artemis is so eager to assign responsibility for what has happened that she leaves us with a surfeit of conflicting accounts. She demonstrates the justice of Hippolytus (1298–99, 1307), as well as the nobility and innocence of Phaedra (1300–1, 1305), the guilt of Theseus (1320), and the responsibility of Aphrodite (1327). But if Aphrodite is to blame then Theseus may be excused (δείν᾽ ἔπραξας, ἀλλ᾽ ὅμως / ἔτ᾽ ἔστι καί σοι τῶνδε συγγνώμης τυχεῖν 1325–26, 1334–37), and if

Hippolytus is innocent, then Phaedra is guilty of a terrible deceit (ψευδεῖς γραφὰς ἔγραψε καὶ διώλεσεν / δόλοισι σὸν παῖδ᾽ 1311–12). We might try to resolve these conflicting judgements, but the deus does not help us do so. Artemis has no stake in a fair assessment of blame or in truth for its own sake; she has her own axe to grind. Her long speech to Theseus is intended not to enlighten him but to make him squirm— to let the one who caused the death of Hippolytus suffer also: "Hear, Theseus, how your evils stand, and if I gain no advantage, at least I will hurt you" (1296–97; compare 1313–14). In the remainder of the scene the deus exonerates Theseus and Phaedra, as well as Hippolytus, and instead blames Aphrodite (1327, 1400, 1406). But rather than explaining the ways of gods to men, this exposé of Aphrodite serves to rescue herself from embarrassment (1331–34), and to justify the revenge she is plotting against her rival:

> Not even beneath the gloom
> of earth shall Aphrodite's willful anger
> hurtle against you unavenged,
> thanks to your good and pious heart.
> With my own hand and these relentless
> arrows I will be avenged on one of hers,
> whatever mortal is most dear to her.

> οὐ γὰρ οὐδὲ γῆς ὑπὸ ζόφον
> θεᾶς ἄτιμοι Κύπριδος ἐκ προθυμίας
> ὀργαὶ κατασκήψουσιν εἰς τὸ σὸν δέμας,
> σῆς εὐσεβείας κἀγαθῆς φρενὸς χάριν·
> ἐγὼ γὰρ αὐτῆς ἄλλον ἐξ ἐμῆς χερὸς
> ὃς ἂν μάλιστα φίλτατος κυρῇ βροτῶν
> τόξοις ἀφύκτοις τοῖσδε τιμωρήσομαι.   1416–22

In the one play of Euripides in which divine explanation plays the greatest part in resolving the action, the god offers not a single authoritative account but a series of accounts vitiated by contradictions and ulterior motives. Between human folly and divine spite we find many reasons but no reliable, privileged explanation.[25]

A third sign of the god's effectiveness in concluding the action is the acceptance or endorsement of the command and explanation by the actors onstage. At the end of *Suppliant Women*, for example, Athena delivers from the machine a series of instructions binding Argos to Athens, and Theseus responds by endorsing what she has said:

> My Lady Athena, I will obey your words,
> for you set me straight so I will not err.

> δέσποιν᾽ Ἀθάνα, πείσομαι λόγοισι σοῖς·
> σὺ γάρ μ᾽ ἀπορθοῖς ὥστε μὴ ᾽ξαμαρτάνειν.   1227–28

Almost every deus is greeted with a similar gesture of acceptance, even if the god's command is largely rhetorical or the explanation is conventional. "Queen Athena," replies Thoas in *Iphigenia among the Taurians*, "only a fool would hear these godly words and not believe" (ἄνασσ᾽ Ἀθάνα, τοῖσι τῶν θεῶν λόγοις / ὅστις κλύων ἄπιστος, οὐκ ὀρθῶς φρονεῖ, 1475–76); after Apollo's spectacular intervention at the end of *Orestes*, Orestes exclaims "Prophet Apollo, what oracles! You weren't a false prophet; you spoke the truth" (1666–67); and even Peleus answers his wife Thetis at the end of *Andromache* with formal words of acquiescence: "I end my grief as you command, goddess, and I will go to the dales of Pelion to bury him [Neoptolemus]" (1276–77). Here and elsewhere (*Hippolytus* 1442–43, *Ion* 1606–7, *Helen* 1680–81) the gesture is a signal that the god's intervention has served its purpose. The gesture is somewhat different in *Bacchant Women*, in which Dionysus concludes his fragmentary speech by telling Cadmus that he must go into exile and will be turned into a snake. Cadmus responds not with a speech of acceptance but with an exchange in stichomythia (1344–51), in which he admits his guilt and acknowledges the god's power to punish mortals, but appeals in vain for more lenient treatment. The gesture plays a double role, confirming the authority of Dionysus and his right to demand worship, while questioning the manner in which he has used this authority.

Finally, in *Electra*, the speech of the Dioscuri is greeted not with acceptance but with interrogation as Orestes and Electra[26] question the conduct both of the Dioscuri and of Apollo:

> Since you are both gods and brothers
> of this dead woman, how
> did you not keep this doom from the house?

> πῶς ὄντε θεὼ τῆσδέ τ' ἀδελφὼ
> τῆς καπφθιμένης οὐκ ἠρκέσατον
> Κῆρας μελάθροις;   1298–1300

> What kind of Apollo, what sorts of oracles
> ordained that I be murderous to my mother?

> τίς δ' ἔμ' Ἀπόλλων, ποῖοι χρησμοὶ
> φονίαν ἔδοσαν μητρὶ γενέσθαι;   1303–4

The deus, however, simply responds with riddles and platitudes ("necessity led where it must, and the unwise cries of Apollo's tongue" 1301–2;[27] "common deeds, common fates, and a single ancestral ruin crushed you both" 1305–7), leaving Orestes and Electra to share their grief together and make their sad farewells. In this case (and here alone) the gesture that normally deflects the problem of the god's intervention with a formal endorsement is replaced by questions that draw attention to the problem: How can it be right to kill one's mother? What can any god do or say to make it right?

The example of *Electra* can and should remind us that the gestures that accompany the deus vary considerably from one play to the next (interesting examples of such variation will be explored in part II). It is worth noting also that Euripides' later plays tend to differ from earlier ones. In general, when a god intervenes to resolve the action, its purpose is in some way to create or to restore order. In the earlier plays, this project is positive in emphasis: Artemis reconciles Hippolytus to his father Theseus, Thetis arrives to commemorate Neoptolemus and to console her husband

Peleus, and Athena establishes a lasting concord between the Argive suppliants and the Athenians who came to their aid. In the later plays, the god's purpose is essentially negative: rather than actively attempting to dispose and order the affairs of the drama, the deus intervenes only to remove a threat or obstacle to order. Thus in *Electra* and *Ion* the god seeks to appease the persistent doubts and dissatisfactions of the protagonist, while in *Iphigenia among the Taurians, Helen,* and *Orestes* the goal is to neutralize the opposition of Thoas and Theoclymenus or to defuse the conflict between Orestes and Menelaus. Also, in later plays, the intervention of the deus becomes more overtly inadequate. In *Electra*, the god makes a loyal effort to make sense of the oracle and matricide, but fails; in *Helen*, the god is superfluous as Helen and Menelaus continue on their adventures while the deus settles a dispute between Theoclymenus and his sister; and in *Orestes*, the god imposes an ending that is clearly implausible, turning a disastrous showdown into a double wedding. There are other variations as well, but for my purposes the differences are less significant than the similarities—the formal gestures, spectacular entrance, rhetorical command, and trite explanation that betray the god's inability to intervene in a more than formal manner. This consistently formalized deus stands in clear contrast to what we find in Aeschylus, in Sophocles, and even in some other plays of Euripides.

Other Interventions

We tend to think of the deus ex machina as typically Euripidean, and with good reason: neither Aeschylus nor Sophocles makes much use of the device. The closest thing to a deus in the surviving plays of Aeschylus is the entrance of Athena in *Eumenides*: the goddess enters near the end of the trilogy to decide the case of Orestes and resolve the conflict between Apollo and the Furies.[28] Because the case is so difficult to decide (Is the matricide of Orestes justifiable when undertaken at the command of Apollo, and to avenge the murder of his father the king?), the intervention of a god is required, and in the process of helping to resolve this dispute, Athena provides an aetiology for the court of the Areopagus and the shrine of the Eumenides.[29] Yet this is far from a deus ex machina as we find it in Euripides. Athena is onstage for nearly two-thirds of the play (651 out of 1047 lines). It can hardly be called a divine epiphany when she enters to mediate a dispute among gods, and her role in the resolution is ambiguous. Does Athena herself resolve the conflict by casting the deciding vote? Or is the action resolved not by divine fiat but by the human, civil institution of trial by jury?

The final play of the trilogy involves a search among various possible means of resolution. At the end of *Libation Bearers*, Orestes, pursued by furies, left for Delphi to be purified by Apollo. The expectation that Apollo's divine authority will resolve the action is reinforced by the opening scene of *Eumenides*, in which the Pythia traces the authority of Apollo's oracle back to Themis and to Earth her mother (1–8). This image of an eternal order is suddenly overturned as the priestess crawls out of the temple in horror at the monstrous creatures inside. Apollo can order the Furies to leave his temple, but he cannot overrule them in the case of Orestes, and he therefore defers to Athena, sending Orestes as a suppliant to Athens. The conflict between

Apollo and the Furies will be decided by Athena not because her power or authority transcends theirs, but because she is an equal whose wisdom they trust. Yet the effectiveness of her settlement is qualified by her reliance upon threats (826–28) and bribes (804–7), and most significantly by her refusal to decide the issue herself, entrusting the case instead to a jury of citizens. In a sense we have come full circle, returning from the divine to the human plane and leaving resolution of the action to the civic institutions of Athens; at the same time, of course, the jurors are evenly divided, and Athena must cast the deciding vote. There is thus in *Eumenides* no figure comparable to a deus ex machina, although the whole play in a sense takes us on a search for someone able to authorize an end. The end result is somewhat uncertain and ambiguous, forcing us to wonder how successfully Athena or the jury has resolved events, but this is entirely different from the formal and mannered intervention of the deus.

The situation is quite different with Sophocles, who employs a full-scale deus ex machina in *Philoctetes* and may have used the deus in other lost plays.[30] Since the only surviving example is from the end of Sophocles' career, it is likely that his use of the deus was influenced by poets such as Euripides.[31] In *Philoctetes*, Heracles intervenes at the last minute to rescue the scheme of Odysseus and return the action to the familiar account of legend: Philoctetes and Neoptolemus must return to Troy with Heracles' bow, where Philoctetes will be cured of his wound, and the two young heroes will bring about the sack of Troy. As in Euripides, the deus begins by issuing a command (μήπω γε 1409; repeated in 1417, σὺ δ᾿ ἐμῶν μύθων ἐπάκουσον), identifying himself (1411–12), invoking the authority of Zeus (τὰ Διός τε φράσων βουλεύματά σοι 1415), and announcing his own divine stature (ἀθάνατον ἀρετὴν ἔσχον, ὡς πάρεσθ᾿ ὁρᾶν 1420), before launching into a prophecy of events to come (1423–40). There is no explanation of past events; this prophecy is enough to reinforce the command and to secure the acceptance of Philoctetes (1445–47) and Neoptolemus (1448). This forceful intervention has its closest parallel in the *Orestes* of Euripides. In each play, the action is about to make a surprising departure from the familiar legend, when a god intervenes to return events to their traditional course. In each case, the intervention is abrupt and troubling and seems to negate or overturn a prior ending that had already been reached: the departure for Greece of Neoptolemus and Philoctetes in Sophocles, and the triumphant entry of Orestes in Euripides.[32] In other words, not only is this Sophoclean deus similar to those of Euripides, with all the formal gestures of command, divine authority, and mortal acceptance, but it resembles the most extreme intervention in Euripides, in which the god reverses the situation onstage.

However, the epiphany of Heracles in *Philoctetes* differs in several ways from the Euripidean deus ex machina, suggesting a different intent in Sophocles. First, for all the divine authority of Heracles, his intervention does not juxtapose the mortal and divine realms. Heracles has now joined the gods, but it was as a mortal that Philoctetes befriended him and as a mortal that he gave the bow to Philoctetes in gratitude. This act of mutual friendship is a premise of the entire plot and is visually represented onstage by the bow and the struggle to possess it. When Heracles enters to resolve the impasse, his authority stems from the fact that the bow is his and that he (as a mortal) gave it to Philoctetes; this authority is further reinforced by the fact that he, like Philoctetes, has endured great troubles and hardships (1418–19). The effect at the end is of an off-stage character finally making his belated entrance; his presence has constantly been felt through allusion, through the presence of the bow, and through analogies between the stories of Philoctetes and Heracles,[33] but only at the end can the hero be seen and heard directly (φάσκειν δ᾽ αυδὴν τὴν Ἡρακλέους / ἀκοῇ τε κλύειν λεύσσειν τ᾽ ὄψιν 1411–12). This is not so much the incursion of a god into mortal affairs as the entrance of a mortal agent, the owner of the bow and the friend of Philoctetes, now decked out in the trappings of a deus.

If Sophocles' deus does not arrive from outside the action, the role he plays is also less extraneous. As we have seen, the deus in Euripides usually intervenes in a formal manner, commanding silence or halting the empty fulminations of a Thoas or Theoclymenus. The exception is *Orestes*, in which the god resolves a real impasse but does so in an implausible manner, replacing both the triumphant escape of Orestes and his death at the hands of Menelaus and the Argives with a third ending altogether, the traditional exile of Orestes, and the marriages of Electra to Pylades and Orestes to Hermione. Heracles in *Philoctetes* also resolves a real impasse in a manner that is not entirely plausible, but he does so within the premises of the plot. The entire drama has revolved around whether or not Philoctetes will go to Troy. In this regard, the play is exceedingly simple: either he will or he won't, and the play is a series of attempts to persuade him, by deception, force, friendship, and finally by divine command. There is something artificial about bringing in the god where all else has failed, but at least the god simply tips the balance: Philoctetes wavered before ("What shall I do? How can I reject his advice when he treats me like a friend?" 1350–51), and now a deus decides the issue. In *Orestes*, however, Apollo negates the action onstage, sweeping away both dramatic alternatives, Orestes' victory and escape, or his death at the hands of the Argives. Interpretation of *Philoctetes* has rightly drawn attention to the "Euripidean" nature of its ending;[34] but we should also be aware that the intervention of Heracles is less formal or gratuitous than the usual deus. In fact, we might emphasize not the debt of Sophocles' deus to Euripides but the way in which Sophocles has revised or corrected his younger rival. If the deus has a place onstage, Sophocles seems to say, it is not to scatter gestures of closure and give the action a specious sense of completeness; let the deus really resolve a crucial issue. Divine intervention then leaves us with a problem, but a different one. Sophocles leaves us wondering why only Heracles can persuade Philoctetes; Euripides leaves us wondering what purpose is served by his flourish from the machine.

Our scanty remains of Greek tragedy make generalization risky, but it is reasonably clear that neither Aeschylus nor Sophocles used the deus ex machina as a regular closing device, and it is likely that Aeschylus never used the device at all, although the search for an agent able to untie the knot of the *Oresteia* may well have influenced later authors. The single extant example in *Philoctetes* suggests that Sophocles experimented with the deus late in his career, but also that he used it in a different way, not to advance a largely formal resolution, but to focus upon a real and precarious one.

If Euripides has a model, it is to be found not in drama but in epic, in Athena's intervention to end the battle between Odysseus and the suitors' relatives in the last book of the *Odyssey*. Now that the story is over, now that Odysseus has returned and the suitors have been punished, a new conflict is introduced, as in *Helen*, prompting the entrance of a god to resolve the impasse. Athena, like a Euripidean deus, intervenes with a command, inspires awe in those who see her, and ratifies with a truce the warring parties' acceptance of her dispensations. The similarities are obvious, but so too are the differences: Athena does not enter from outside the narrative, but has long inhabited it both as a god and as Odysseus' fellow conspirator, and the divine intervention, here aided by Zeus' thunderbolt, is not an index of crisis but a recurring motif seen earlier when Zeus sends Hermes to Calypso, when Hermes brings moly to Odysseus, and when Poseidon turns the ship of the Phaeacians to stone. The battle with the suitors' relatives, provoked by the angry Eupeithes, is nevertheless somewhat gratuitous, and its resolution by Athena seems contrived, thus pointing to the problem of narrative closure: the apparent end of the plot with the deaths of the suitors cannot really be the end, since the newly returned king must somehow negotiate his place among the other people of Ithaca. This problem of closure in the public and political sphere has a counterpart in the personal sphere: Odysseus' reunion with his wife and family cannot really be the end for the wandering hero, but as Teiresias told Odysseus (and as he tells Penelope), he will go on further travels until he reaches people with no knowledge of the sea. Only then, in some remote place at some remote time, will he finally allay the anger of Poseidon and clear the way for a peaceful death. Just as the entrance of Athena anticipates the Euripidean deus, the prophecy of Teiresias anticipates the Euripidean prophecy of events to follow, and although Teiresias stands at the center, not the end, of the epic, his forecast likewise reminds the audience that the end of this poem will not really be the end of the story.

There is a curious contrast between the novelty of the deus that Euripides brings onstage and the venerable prototypes that we find in the *Odyssey*. If Euripides borrowed from Homer, he also created for the Athenian stage a striking innovation with no precedent in Aeschylus or in Sophocles. His debt therefore consists in turning to a poem of remarkable narrative sophistication,[35] adapting devices that convey the provisional nature of narrative closure and creating a figure whose spectacular, and spectacularly formalized, entrance throws open the problem of concluding the plot.

It is worth noting, to conclude this section, that despite Euripides' relatively consistent approach in his use of the deus ex machina, a few plays stand somewhat apart. In nine of his extant plays, Euripides uses a deus ex machina, while in three early plays he concludes with a related device that I call the "demonic epiphany." In *Medea*, *Children of Heracles*, and *Hecuba*, the epilogue is marked by a new presence, a human character who assumes unusual power and authority; in each case this figure, who is somehow more than human, destabilizes the ending by portraying a passion that the drama cannot contain. Medea comes closest to playing the part of a god on the machine. At the end of the play, as Jason besieges the palace doors determined to rescue his children, Medea suddenly appears on the roof above, commands him to stop, explains that she will bury them in Corinth, and finally departs upon the machine, carried off in the chariot of her divine grandfather, the sun. Medea, like a deus, foretells the future (the death of Jason, 1386–88) and offers an aetiology (rites for the children, 1382–83), and like a god, she inflicts ferocious and uncompromising revenge.[36] Medea's consuming passion—which destroys her friends and family, alienates the sympathetic chorus, and eventually renounces her own human nature—

makes a spectacle of transgressing all bounds: she does violence to the norms of human conduct and violates the norms of drama.[37] The demonic epiphany literally embodies Medea's inhuman fury, which cannot be contained on the human stage.

In the other two plays, the excessive passion of the protagonist elicits from the antagonist an expression of superhuman authority. In *Children of Heracles*, Alcmene finally prevails over Eurystheus her persecutor, who is defeated in battle and captured by the Athenians. But rather than showing Athenian moderation, Alcmene is driven by her sufferings to demand the unjust murder of Eurystheus in revenge. Yet Alcmene's violent transgression is suddenly and unexpectedly answered by Eurystheus, who acquiesces in his death and foretells that his place of burial will protect Athens from descendants of the children of Heracles. In foretelling the future, offering an aetiology, and using his special authority to effect a resolution, Eurystheus approaches the stature of a deus. But he does not intervene from outside the action; rather, Alcmene's excessive passion elicits a spectacular conversion of her antagonist, turning the hated king into an almost supernatural savior. In *Hecuba*, the queen's uncontainable suffering, driven beyond all bounds by the murders of Polydorus and Polyxena, similarly spills over into a terrible revenge against Polymestor. Hecuba's brutality in blinding Polymestor and killing his children likewise transforms the shameless tyrant into a prophet of destruction. With superhuman authority worthy of a deus, he foretells the deaths of Hecuba and Agamemnon, offers an aetiology for a promontory near Troy, and corrects the vengeful triumph of Hecuba. Violent passion alters and transforms, and excessive, uncontainable passion can transform human subjects into voices of divine authority. In *Medea*, the woman's ← passion transforms her into something like a deus, while in the other two plays the epiphany is displaced: as too much suffering turns Alcmene or Hecuba from victim into avenger, it is the new victim and past oppressor who finds a privileged voice.

In these plays, passion that cannot be contained transforms a mortal vessel into a figure of divine authority; the "demonic epiphany" is a signal that the human action onstage can no longer contain its own terrifying energies. Yet as the playwright becomes less interested in these plays of passion, he stages a different problem and a different kind of epiphany. The problem will no longer be passion that cannot be contained, but a plot that cannot be closed or contained by the bounds of the drama. The epiphany that signals and confirms this crisis will not arise from characters within the action, but will intrude from a privileged sphere outside it.

Bending the Rules

By contrast with the series of divine and human authorities in *Eumenides* and with the human credentials of Sophocles' Heracles and of Euripides' demonic epiphanies, the Euripidean deus ex machina is clearly defined as a figure outside the action, belonging to a different realm, and intervening in a formal manner. The formal qualities of the deus have troubled scholars ever since A. W. Verrall, who drew attention to

the singular stiffness, formality, frigidity, and general artlessness which often appear in [Euripides'] opening and conclusion. The final scenes in particular, the *coups de*

théâtre with which the action is wound up or cut short, have almost always a conventionality of manner, a perfunctory style . . . [that contrasts] with the originality, terse-
ness, energy, and passion displayed in other parts of the work.[38]

But for Verrall, and for the critics who took up his challenge, the problem of the deus
was one of reason versus piety, and the perfunctory intervention of the deus was a
signal, variously understood, of the gulf between men and gods. Those who give
greater precedence to the secular action of the play (e.g., Verrall, Nicolà Terzaghi,
Kurt von Fritz) will see the formal intervention of the deus as a direct or indirect
critique of the gods and of myth.[39] Those who give precedence to the divine frame,
however (e.g., Andreas Spira, Anne Burnett, David Kovacs), will read the same
intervention as a reprimand designed to chasten erring mortals.[40] A third, more interesting, approach is that of Wieland Schmidt, who regards the conflict between
divine and human action as aporetic, challenging viewers to make sense of a problem that cannot be resolved.[41] There is much to be said for Schmidt's argument,
especially in *Ion* or *Electra*, where divine authority is a locus of debate throughout
the play. But the same formal or mannered deus is found in many other plays—
in plays such as *Hippolytus* and *Bacchant Women* in which the god's authority is never
in doubt, in a play such as *Suppliant Women* with its strong political interest, as well as
in many plays now lost (e.g., Hermes in *Antiope*, Dionysus in *Hypsipyle,* and Athena
in *Erechtheus*).[42] So whatever the playwright's views on traditional religion, we need
to take a new approach, examining the deus as one among several closing gestures
in Euripides and paying attention to what we might call the rhetoric of closure.[43]

   The choral exit and the deus ex machina both formalize closure, introducing external signals that the performance is finished or the action is complete. As such, both
are disruptive: lowering the curtain to end the play or landing onstage to tie up the
plot. And both disruptions betray apparent problems in the play: an unfinished performance and an incomplete plot. We might conclude that the gestures serve to
disguise or conceal these problems, creating the illusion of an ordered whole. As
H. D. F. Kitto observes:

> The real end of the story . . . neither makes a satisfactory dramatic close nor completes
> the poet's idea. . . . Therefore, in the absence of a logical climax, there must be more
> or less of deliberate contrivance in the ending; a feeling of finality has to be created.
> To meet this difficulty was the function of the *Deus ex machina.*"[44]

I suggest instead that the disruptive deus serves to expose this incompleteness, and
as I shall argue in the final chapters, this disruption goes deeper, challenging not just
the aesthetic unity of the play, but the privileged role of tragedy as a literary and
cultural model. The god on the machine is the most spectacular agent of this subversion, and I conclude by noting that this Euripidean invention may have performed
its job too well: in the Western dramatic tradition, the deus is rarely found, and then
not in tragedy but in comedy, where it again performs a subversive role.

   These descendants of the deus are few and far between, but they share an important feature with one another and with Euripides: they mark not just a lack of completeness in the plot itself, but a loss of bearings in the drama as a whole that threat-

ens to violate literary and cultural norms. The earliest surviving comic deus is the final entrance of Jupiter in Plautus' *Amphitryo*, the only extant Roman comedy based on a plot from tragedy, and the only one that dares to portray the adultery of a married woman.[45] If the mythical and tragic plot gives the playwright this unprecedented license to challenge Roman tabu, it also rescues him at the last minute from this dangerous game. At the end of the play, after Amphitryon discovers he has been cuckolded and righteously threatens to kill everyone in the house, it is the mythical god Jupiter who restores the happy ending required by comedy, commanding Amphitryon to love his wife as before and promising him eternal fame through his stepson's deeds (1135–43). Only the deus can hold in check this dangerous and unusual play with adultery.

Perhaps the most famous and most controversial "deus" in comedy is the officer of the king who rescues Orgon at the end of *Tartuffe*. In this remarkable play, Molière turns his comic demon inside out. Whereas the obsessions of a Harpagon or an Alceste destroy the character from within, rendering him both ridiculous and essentially harmless, Tartuffe's obsession with status and power spins out of control, threatening to overturn the entire social and political order. Comedy is thus upstaged by satire, which becomes most dangerous and unsettling when Tartuffe deals his final blow by arresting Orgon. In this extreme situation, the tables are suddenly and unexpectedly turned when the king's officer arrests Tartuffe instead.[46] Only this double agent of king and author can restore order to the realm and propriety to the drama.

The Beggar's Opera more boldly confuses the boundaries among comedy, satire, and burlesque, as this "pastoral among the whores and thieves" lampoons high society and its pretensions, while also mocking the current vogue of Italian opera.[47] This witty travesty of the contemporary scene becomes most subversive just as it approaches a moral conclusion, for if MacHeath must pay for his crimes, countless members of the upper classes should hang as well:

> Since Laws were made for ev'ry Degree,
> To curb Vice in others, as well as me,
> I wonder we han't better Company,
> Upon *Tyburn* Tree![48]

At this point, as MacHeath is carried off to execution, the sobering finale carries a very real threat for "better" criminals—until the beggar-poet resolves the crisis by rescuing both the protagonist and the comedy:

> Your Objection, Sir, is very just; and is easily remov'd. For you must allow, that in this kind of Drama, 'tis no matter how absurdly things are brought about.—So—you Rabble there—run and cry a Reprieve—let the Prisoner be brought back to his Wives in Triumph.

More recent versions of the deus ex machina include adaptations of Plautus and Gay in Brecht's *Threepenny Opera* and Giraudoux's *Amphitryon 38*. Both reinforce the artificial and theatrical quality of the deus, Brecht by insisting that the reprieve be announced by an actor on horseback,[49] and Giraudoux by casting Jupiter as a stage manager calling the cues for actors, lights, curtain, and audience:

And we must all disappear, gods to our zeniths, extras to your cellars. And you, audience, must file out without a word, with an affectation of total indifference. Now let
Alcmena and her husband appear one last time, alone in a circle of light, where my
arm will be seen no more save as a pointer in the direction of happiness; and now, on
this couple which no adultery has touched nor ever will, which will never know the
taste of sinful kisses, now, to enclose this glade of fidelity in a wall of velvet, now,
curtains of the night, who for nearly an hour have held back—now fall.[50]

In Euripides, the deus is equally theatrical, making its spectacular landing upon the
palace roof, and it is equally dangerous, drawing attention not just to a local problem
of closure (How can this plot reach an end?) but to a broader problem of genre (How
has the drama embraced issues or questions that it is not equipped to resolve?). Seen
in this light, Euripides' regular use of the deus ex machina is remarkable. Where later
playwrights use the deus only rarely to test and expose the limits of their work, for
Euripides this is not the exception but the rule. If the tragedian, as Antiphanes claims,
can use the deus as a convenient gesture to keep the audience happy and safely reaf-
firm the taste of the town, this is only because he also insists on challenging and
subverting its beliefs and assumptions.

4

Vestige: Traces of the Past

> Over Greek locales and the body of their ancient legends, Euripides swims
> and sails like a bead upon a sea of quicksilver.
>
> GOETHE

The most obvious closing gestures in Euripidean drama are the choral exit and the deus ex machina. They are also the most controversial: choral exits are frequently considered spurious, while the spectacular deus invites sharply conflicting interpretations. These visible and problematic gestures, as I have argued, are specifically formal answers to the basic questions of dramatic closure: how to end the performance and how to conclude the action. I turn now, in this chapter and the next, to further closing gestures that are less visible but every bit as important: the aition and the concluding prophecy regularly spoken by the deus ex machina (or by another figure playing a similar role). In so doing, we not only get a closer and more detailed look at Euripidean endings, but approach the problem of closure from a different angle. Choral exit and deus ex machina, after all, address what we might call the minimum formal requirements of closure: in one way or another, the stage must be emptied and the action must end. Aetiology and prophecy, however, explore continuities that might resist such closure: the historical and the narrative continuum enacted by the drama. It would perhaps be convenient to bring in again the contrast between form and content, arguing that these continuous threads are the content or matter that dramatic form attempts to shape or confine. This neo-Aristotelian model certainly has its uses (as we shall see in the following chapter). But its emphasis upon the continuum as stuff to be shaped or moulded does not give sufficient weight to the nature or logic of this continuum.

Unlike modern drama, Greek tragedy was essentially historical: it reenacted episodes from the past. For us, the past of myth and legend is radically different from the "factual," recorded past of history, and both are entirely different from the invented, factitious events portrayed in drama. Greeks in the fifth century, however, did not share our clear distinction between "myth" and "history." The Battle of Marathon and the Trojan War differed less in kind than in distance; both were "real" or historical events in the recent or not-so-recent past. And in describing this past, tragedy was less an exercise of the imagination than a reenactment of a shared, public history.[1] Hence the striking differences in staging. Modern drama is understood to be a fiction, requiring the spectators—even in ostensibly "historical" plays—to accept as "real" situations they know are factitious, and in the modern theater, a private, dark interior and illumined stage invite the individual to a personal exercise of the imagination. Greek tragedy, however, requires the audience to accept the present staging as a reenactment of the past; and in the ancient theater, a performance outdoors, on a state holiday and before all the people of the city, invites the spectators to witness a replaying of their common past.[2]

In what ways does the drama define or mark out the distance between past and present? There are many possibilities, but Euripides regularly ended his plays with a clear and explicit marker. The aition, or closing aetiology, spells out the connection between past and present by showing that events of the play survive in some specific way into the present world of the audience. Medea, for example, announces from the palace roof that the murder of her children will be commemorated in the future by rites performed in Corinth:

> in the land of Sisyphus
> I shall establish for the future a holy
> festival and rites for this impious murder.

> γῇ δὲ τῇδε Σισύφου
> σεμνὴν ἑορτὴν καὶ τέλη προσάψομεν
> τὸ λοιπὸν ἀντὶ τοῦδε δυσσεβοῦς φόνου.   *Medea* 1381–83

In *Iphigenia among the Taurians*, Athena explains to Orestes that a statue of Artemis at Halae will be named for his adventures among the Taurians:

> [when you come to Halae]
> build a shrine there and set up the statue,
> named for the Taurian land and for the troubles
> you suffered wandering around Greece
> goaded by Furies; mortals in future will sing
> of this as the goddess Artemis Tauropolos.

> ἐνταῦθα τεύξας ναὸν ἵδρυσαι βρέτας,
> ἐπώνυμον γῆς Ταυρικῆς πόνων τε σῶν,
> οὓς ἐξεμόχθεις περιπολῶν καθ᾽ Ἑλλάδα
> οἴστροις Ἐρινύων. Ἄρτεμιν δέ νιν βροτοὶ
> τὸ λοιπὸν ὑμνήσουσι Ταυροπόλον θεάν.   1453–57

Only because tragedy is "historical" in the sense I have described, can the aition play a meaningful role at the end, connecting the enacted past to the spectators' present. Yet nothing *demands* the presence of an aition; there are many ways in which this connection may be articulated, and other gestures that may (or may not) be deployed.

If the aition is Euripides' individual approach to a peculiar feature of Greek tragedy, it is not unique. In Western drama, the late medieval mystery play is also "historical" insofar as it reenacts the "factual" past of the Bible, and it also offers interesting parallels to Euripidean aetiologies. In the Chester cycle, for example, *Noyes Fludd* ends with God's promise to Noah:

My bowe betwene you and mee
in the fyrmamente shalbe,
by verey tokeninge that you may see
that such vengeance shall cease.
The man ne woman shall never more
be wasted by water as hath before . . .
Where clowdes in the welkyn bynne,
that ylke bowe shalbe seene,
in tokeninge that my wrath and teene
shall never thus wroken bee.[3]

The rainbow shown to Noah is the origin of the rainbows we see today, and this aetiology connects the dramatic action with the world of the audience, inviting the spectator to share the lesson delivered to Noah. In this case, the connection between past and present is not made explicit, and the difference between them is less pronounced. Because God's covenant implicitly embraces not only the dramatic Noah but also the extra-dramatic spectator, the play's closure becomes all-embracing and metaphorical: actors and audience are likewise redeemed by the transforming authority of God's word. At the end of the Chester *Nativity*, however, the expositor explicitly connects past and present in a closing reference to the contemporary church of St. Mary, or Ara Caeli, at Rome:

Lordings, that this is verey
by verey synge knowe yee maye;
for in Rome in good faye,
thereas this thinge was seene,
was buyld a church in noble araye—
in worship of Marye, that sweete maye—
that yett lastes untyll this daye,
as men knowe that there have binne.
. . . the church is called St Marye.
The surname is Ara Caeli,
that men knowe nowe well therby
that this was fullye trewe.[4]

In this version of the nativity, when Christ is born in Bethlehem, the emperor Octavian at Rome sees a vision of the newborn baby and his virgin mother; inspired by this vision, the emperor orders his subjects to worship the child, thus founding the Roman Catholic Church. The story of Octavian's vision and the evidence of the Ara Caeli are essential links between the biblical account of the nativity and the familiar institution of the church. The explicit connection between past and present (and between East and West) joins a contemporary institution to the biblical authority of Christ's birth, even as it acknowledges their distance and their difference: Saint Mary's church is merely a vestige of biblical truth, a part that attempts to indicate the whole.

These two examples from the Chester cycle connect past to present in different ways, and the Greek tragedians likewise found different ways of representing such a link. One possible approach is to ignore the issue, avoiding comment on the relation between past and present and treating the dramatic action as self-contained or self-sufficient. This is the usual procedure of Sophocles, whose plays seem both more "organic" and more fictional because they do not overtly link the viewers' present to the enacted past. Both Aeschylus and Euripides, however, draw attention to this historical continuum, although they do so in different ways. Aeschylus, as we shall see, uses aetiologies at various points in his plays to include the present within the reenacted past, while Euripides uses explicit closing aetiologies to mark the distance between them and to set aside the present as a vestige of the past. The aition in Euripides, in other words, is interesting for the way in which it divides, as well as the way in which it joins.

In looking more closely at this ambivalent gesture, I shall define *aition* (for my purposes[5]) as an aetiology occurring at the end of a play and explicitly connecting the plot with the world of the audience. Such *aitia* are found in every complete Euripidean ending with the exceptions of *Alcestis, Trojan Women,* and *Phoenician Women*[6] (there is a lacuna in *Bacchant Women,* and the ending of *Iphigenia at Aulis* is not genuine[7]) and are always spoken by a deus ex machina or a similar figure. Each of these features, as we shall see, helps to define the distance between past and present. One should note that although most aitia are explanations of names or institutions, the converse is not true. When Xuthus calls the young man Ion because he saw him coming out (ἐξιόντι, *Ion* 661–62), this is not an aition since the etymology involves no connection between enacted events and the contemporary world.[8]

Joining and Dividing

Euripidean aetiologies almost always occur at the end of a play, and in this position, they can most clearly articulate the distance between past and present. From this vantage, for example, we can look back to the dramatic problem of Ion and his lineage and forward to the Athenian Empire that claims him as its founder; we look back to the human protagonist and forward to the name that is all that survives of him:

> And the children born
> in turn from [Ion's children] at the fated time
> will colonize the island states of the Cyclades
> and the mainland coasts, giving strength
> to my land; on either side of the strait
> they will inhabit the two continents, Asia
> and Europe; and they will be famous, called
> Ionians thanks to this man's name.

> οἱ τῶνδε δ᾽ αὖ
> παῖδες γενόμενοι σὺν χρόνῳ πεπρωμένῳ
> Κυκλάδας ἐποικήσουσι νησαίας πόλεις
> χέρσους τε παράλους, ὃ σθένος τἠμῇ χθονὶ
> δίδωσιν· ἀντίπορθμα δ᾽ ἠπείροιν δυοῖν
> πεδία κατοικήσουσιν, Ἀσιάδος τε γῆς
> Εὐρωπίας τε· τοῦδε δ᾽ ὀνόματος χάριν
> Ἴωνες ὀνομασθέντες ἕξουσιν κλέος. *Ion* 1581–88

The aition that closes the play is a bridge of sorts that carries us over from the past of Athenian legend to the present extent of the city's power. And in so doing, it not only marks out the thread that connects them, but signals the gap to be crossed from the young man of the play to present-day Ionians. Not every closing aetiology has this effect; God's promise to Noah does not divide past from present, but implies that there is no difference between Noah's rainbow and those seen by the specta-tors—nor between his contract with Noah and his contract with members of the audience. In Euripides, however, the closing aetiology suggests a difference of kind: a young boy searching for identity (Ion) versus a collective name for Greeks allied to Athens (Ionians), or a young man trapped in a cycle of revenge (Orestes) versus a small town in the Peloponnese:[9]

> As for you,
> Orestes, you must exceed this country's bounds
> and live a round year on Parrhasian soil.
> There, named for your exile, Azanians
> and Arcadians will call it Oresteion.

> σὲ δ᾽ αὖ χρεών,
> Ὀρέστα, γαίας τῆσδ᾽ ὑπερβαλόνθ᾽ ὅρους
> Παρράσιον οἰκεῖν δάπεδον ἐνιαυτοῦ κύκλον·
> κεκλήσεται δὲ σῆς φυγῆς ἐπώνυμον
> Ἀζᾶσιν Ἀρκάσιν τ᾽ Ὀρέστειον καλεῖν.   *Orestes* 1643–47

It is therefore unusual, and worth noting, that two aetiologies in Euripides occur before the end of the play. In one, Aphrodite explains how a temple in Athens was named for Hippolytus (*Hippolytus* 29–33);[10] as I argue in a later chapter, this aition in the prologue contributes to a more general sense of premature closure, marking off past from present before the play has even begun. The second exception is dou-bly interesting: in the middle of *Iphigenia among the Taurians* (951–60), Orestes, a mortal, explains how his reception in Athens will give rise to the festival of the Choes; I suggest below that this out-of-place aition serves to confuse the distinction between the world of the plot and that of the audience.

To mark the connection between past and present requires a figure whose privi-leged knowledge extends beyond the bounds of the drama. This may be a god, as in *Noyes Fludd*, or a narrator, as in the *Nativity*, and in Euripides is usually a deus ex machina. When a narrator delivers the aition, he stands outside the dramatic action and addresses the spectators directly, collaborating with them in imagining or con-structing a link between past and present. Such a figure, standing in the world of the viewer and commenting upon the performance, establishes a clear divide between them. A god, however, may take part in the action, as he does in *Noyes Fludd*, and speak with the same authority to actors and audience. If his words have the same or similar meaning for Noah and spectator, the divide disappears and one realm is merely an extension of the other. The deus stands somewhere in between. The god is a char-acter within the play who maintains the dramatic illusion, but by appearing only at the end upon the roof or the machine, he or she stands partly outside the action and speaks more directly to the viewer. As a result, the deus who delivers the aition speaks with two voices, foretelling for the hero events he does not understand, while explaining a name or institution already familiar to the audience.

If the deus is a figure within the drama who stands partly outside it, like the Chester cycle's expositor, the same is true of plays that conclude with a demonic epiphany. In *Children of Heracles*, Eurystheus mentions the oracle foretelling that his tomb will protect Athens from invaders (1028–36), and in *Hecuba*, Polymestor repeats Dionysus' prophecy of her transformation into a dog and her death at a place called Kynossema, or Dog's Tomb (1265–73). This ability to connect the action to events known only to the audience reinforces the privileged stature of the condemned Eurystheus and the blinded Polymestor as somehow divine or authorial figures. Medea takes on a similar role with greater violence. After killing her own children in order to make her husband suffer, she usurps from Jason the right and duty of burying the children, and she usurps divine prerogative by establishing rites in their honor:

> No! I shall bury them with this hand,
> taking them to Hera Akraia's shrine
> lest one of their enemies dishonor them,
> tearing up their tombs; and in the land of Sisyphus
> I shall establish for the future a holy
> festival and rites for this impious murder.

> οὐ δῆτ, ἐπεί σφας τῇδ᾽ ἐγὼ θάψω χερί,
> φέρουσ᾽ ἐς Ἥρας τέμενος Ἀκραίας θεοῦ,
> ὡς μή τις αὐτοὺς πολεμίων καθυβρίσῃ
> τυμβοὺς ἀνασπῶν· γῇ δὲ τῇδε Σισύφου
> σεμνὴν ἑορτὴν καὶ τέλη προσάψομεν
> τὸ λοιπὸν ἀντὶ τοῦδε δυσσεβοῦς φόνου.   *Medea* 1378–83

Something very like an aition is spoken by another mortal, Theseus, who enters at the end of *Heracles* to persuade Heracles not to commit suicide, promising that after he dies, shrines and festivals in Athens will honor him (1331–33). As we shall see (chapter 8), Theseus plays an ambiguous role, and the aition is part the assurance of a deus, part the promise of a friend.

An intriguing exception is the passage in the middle of *Iphigenia among the Taurians*, in which Orestes reports that his reception at Athens will give rise to the festival of the Choes (951–60). This aition clearly and explicitly connects events involving the dramatic character with rites familiar to members of the audience. Yet unlike the demonic figures mentioned above (or even Theseus the savior), the mortal Orestes has nothing that would give him knowledge of rites outside the drama, or allow him to connect one world to the other. Some critics respond to this anomaly by simply deleting the lines.[11] There may be less drastic remedies. At this point in the play, the reunion between Orestes and Iphigenia brings together two stories, the fantastic account of Iphigenia's rescue from Aulis, spirited off among the exotic Taurians, and the story of Orestes' exile and trial immortalized by Aeschylus. As these stories come together to form a new plot, Orestes rewrites his own past, telling us that the end of Aeschylus' trilogy was not the end after all: after his trial and acquittal in Athens, the Furies were still not satisfied, but hounded him again until Apollo told him to bring back the statue of Artemis from the Taurians (968–78). This rewriting of Aeschylus and of the aition that concluded *Eumenides* is accompanied with a new and perhaps original aition for the festival of the Choes.[12] The result is a peculiar form of distancing: between Euripides' Orestes and the familiar version of Aeschylus is a gap or divide as clearly marked as the divide between spectator and Orestes. A similar technique is the use of an aition in the prologue of *Hippolytus* to mark the distance between the first and second versions of the play (see chapter 6).

Perhaps the most characteristic feature of the Euripidean aition is the explicit connection between the mythical plot and the world of the audience. The narrator in the Chester *Nativity* makes such a link by addressing the spectators ("Lordings, that this is verey . . .") and overtly connecting events of the play to the contemporary setting ("that yett lastes untyll this daye, / as men knowe that there have binne"). In Euripides, the aition is spoken by a deus who does not address the audience directly, but nevertheless clearly refers to the world outside the drama. At the end of *Orestes*, for example, Apollo speaks to a character within the drama (σὲ δ᾽ αὖ χρεών, / Ὀρέστα, "as for you, Orestes"1643–44) even as he explains a commemorative name that will be spoken in the future (Ἀζᾶσιν Ἀρκάσιν τ᾽ Ὀρέστειον καλεῖν, "Azanians and Arcadians will call it Oresteion" 1647) and that belongs to the world of the audience rather than the drama. Polymestor is engaged in a heated and rapid exchange with Hecuba when he connects her transformation and death to a landmark that has meaning only for the spectators:[13]

POLYMESTOR:	You'll become a dog with fiery eyes . . .
HECUBA:	Will I end my life there, or will I live?
POLYMESTOR:	You will die, and your tomb will be named—
HECUBA:	Do you mean some charm for my form?
POLYMESTOR:	A wretched Dog's Tomb, landmark for sailors.

Πο.	κύων γενήσῃ πύρσ᾽ ἔχουσα δέργματα . . .	
Εκ.	θανοῦσα δ᾽ ἢ ζῶσ᾽ ἐνθάδ᾽ ἐκπλήσω βίον;	
Πο.	θανοῦσα· τύμβῳ δ᾽ ὄνομα σῷ κεκλήσεται—	
Εκ.	μορφῆς ἐπῳδὸν μή τι τῆς ἐμῆς ἐρεῖς;	
Πο.	κυνὸς ταλαίνης σῆμα, ναυτίλοις τέκμαρ.	*Hecuba* 1265, 1270–73

This explicit connection with the world of the audience distinguishes the aition from other forms of allusion. Occasionally an aetiological allusion looks beyond the world of the drama without connecting it to the world of the audience. In the prologue of *Trojan Women*, Poseidon mentions the future fame of the Trojan horse (πρὸς ἀνδρῶν ὑστέρων κεκλήσεται / δούρειος ἵππος, "it shall be called by later men the Wooden Horse," 13–14), but the Trojan Horse was already famous when Odysseus reached Scheria (*Odyssey* 8.492–515), so we are not dealing with a link to the world of the spectator.[14] Likewise in *Alcestis*, the chorus looks forward to songs in memory of Alcestis (445–54) without situating these songs in the contemporary world.[15]

The connection between past and present is usually accompanied by phrases (such as τὸ λοιπόν, "in the future"; κεκλήσεται, "shall be named"; and ἐπώνυμος, "named for") that clearly point to the world of the viewers, even as they acknowledge its distance from events of the play. In fact, such phrases are a regular, formal index of separation found with almost every aition.[16] There is an interesting case where this formulaic connection between past and present is not spelled out. At the end of *Andromache*, Thetis explains the origin of the well-known tomb of Neoptolemus at Delphi:

> The dead son of Achilles here, you must
> take to the Pythian hearth and bury,
> a disgrace for Delphi, so his tomb may announce
> the violent murder of Orestes' hand.

> τὸν μὲν θανόντα τόνδ' Ἀχιλλέως γόνον
> θάψον πορεύσας Πυθικὴν πρὸς ἐσχάραν,
> Δελφοῖς ὄνειδος, ὡς ἀπαγγέλλῃ τάφος
> φόνον βίαιον τῆς Ὀρεστείας χερός·   1239–42

Why does Thetis not state explicitly that the tomb will be known "to mortals in the future" as a memorial to Orestes' violence? For good reason: Euripides' audience knew the tomb as a testament to the hybris of Neoptolemus (who came to Delphi demanding that Apollo atone for the death of his father, Achilles[17]); Euripides is free to alter its meaning in this play, but he cannot claim that his new version is common knowledge (on novel aetiologies, see discussion later in this chapter).

Placed at the end of the play, spoken by a deus or similar figure, and making an explicit connection between the past enacted in the drama and the present of the spectators, the aition draws attention to the gap or divide that it attempts to bridge. Does this mean that the gesture is futile? How does Euripides represent or reinterpret the connection between cultural past and present? At least in the surviving plays, there are two distinct patterns: present ritual may commemorate those who have died, or figures from the past may live on through their names. Yet both patterns tend to attenuate the connection they establish and in some cases to suggest that the connection is a factitious one.

A Slender Thread

The aition often commemorates the death of a character in the play, pointing to a tomb or rites of mourning that serve as a memorial in the contemporary world, and which afford consolation or atonement for the character's death. Thus Medea's children have been cruelly murdered, but they are remembered forever in the rites at Corinth, and Hippolytus, despite his tragic death, will always receive tribute from the young women of Trozen. In this form, the aition is a very effective closing device. The plot reaches a natural conclusion with the character's death, the significance of this death is suggested by its commemoration, and the connection between past death and present rites includes the audience in remembering and reflecting upon this end. An interesting parallel is the pair of commemorative statues at the end of *Romeo and Juliet*:[18]

MONTAGUE: For I will raise her statue in pure gold;
            That while Verona by that name is known,
            There shall no figure at such rate is known,
            As that of true and faithful Juliet.
CAPULET: As rich shall Romeo's by his lady's lie,
            Poor sacrifices of our enmity!

The tragic action reaches its conclusion with the deaths of the two lovers and is reified in twin statues at the end: the tragic beauty of the drama and the lesson it conveys have a tangible counterpart in the golden statues that will likewise move and inspire their viewers. The suggestion that the action, like a well-wrought sculpture, is complete and self-sufficient is possible only because Shakespeare's memorials are fictional and entirely contained within the drama. In Euripides, however, reference to a contemporary memorial familiar to the audience places the objective token of completeness outside the drama, sundering the end in death from its completion in ritual. A good illustration is the death of Hippolytus.

As the young man lies dying onstage, Artemis foretells the Trozenian rites that will honor the hero after his death:[19]

> You who have suffered so much, I will give you
> for your sufferings great honor in the city
> of Trozen: unmarried girls before they wed
> will cut their hair for you, harvesting
> throughout long time a great sorrow of tears.
> You will always be musically remembered
> by virgins, and Phaedra's love for you
> will never fall silent or nameless.

> σοὶ δ᾽, ὦ ταλαίπωρ᾽, ἀντὶ τῶνδε τῶν κακῶν
> τιμὰς μεγίστας ἐν πόλει Τροζηνίᾳ
> δώσω· κόραι γὰρ ἄζυγες γάμων πάρος
> κόμας κεροῦνταί σοι, δι᾽ αἰῶνος μακροῦ
> πένθη μέγιστα δακρύων καρπουμέναι.
> ἀεὶ δὲ μουσοποιὸς ἐς σὲ παρθένων
> ἔσται μέριμνα, κοὐκ ἀνώνυμος πεσὼν
> ἔρως ὁ Φαίδρας ἐς σὲ σιγηθήσεται.   1423–30

At the end of the play Hippolytus dies, Aphrodite's plan of revenge is complete, and the hero's sufferings will be remembered in the bridal customs of Trozen. This effective closure is reinforced by the aition, which offers in ritual a tangible counterpart to the content of the drama. As we shall see, this effective aetiology is unusual: only in *Hippolytus* does the aition commemorate the death of the protagonist in the course of the drama—thus resuming or reenacting the tragic action. Yet this is only a promise made to console the dying Hippolytus, a promise that from the characters' perspective must remain unfulfilled. From the viewer's perspective, however, the shrine of Hippolytus at Trozen and the rites performed there are objective facts, and the gesture of the deus succeeds in joining dissimilar things: the god's consolation of a favorite and current practice in another city. The tribute offered by Montague is a parallel to, or a metaphor for, the respectful response of the audience, while Artemis challenges the viewer to make the connection between part and whole, between the hero's suffering and the vestige preserved in ritual. As we shall see in chapter 6, the gap between dramatic consolation and ritual vestige is further signaled by the absence of the thread connecting them: there is no mention of Hippolytus' death, no preparations are made or mentioned for his funeral, and even the rites promised by Artemis make no mention of burial.

Yet *Hippolytus* is an exception; usually the connection between plot and commemoration is even less straightforward. When the aition promises ritual honor for one who has died, this is frequently for a minor character rather than the protagonist: the unnamed children of Medea, the secondary figure Neoptolemus in *Andromache*, or the Seven who died before the play begins in *Suppliant Women*. If not displaced on lesser figures, it is postponed to the future. All other aitia that honor the dead commemorate a character who is still alive at the end of the play: the condemned Eurystheus who foretells his own death in *Children of Heracles*, the death of Hecuba foretold by the blinded Polymestor, and the death of Iphigenia at Brauron foretold by Athena in *Iphigenia among the Taurians*.[20] These gestures of commemoration may be marginalized further. In *Hecuba*, the name Kynossema does double duty, remembering Hecuba's transformation into a dog, as well as her future death; in *Suppliant Women*, the aition is more concerned with the treaty between Athenians and Argives than with the seven pyres; and in *Iphigenia*, Athena dwells at length on the exile of Orestes before alluding, as an afterthought, to his sister's death. The potential role of the aition in bodying forth the tragic action is thus undermined by the gap between dramatic death and ritual vestige, and in most cases is further compromised by reference to a future death or to the death of a secondary figure.

The aition may also commemorate a living character who will give a place or a people its name; this figure will thus outlive the action of the play, surviving, in name, to the present day. Orestes in his future exile will give his name to a town in Arcadia, and Ion and Creusa through their children will give names to the tribes of Athens and the races of Greece. There is a fundamental difference between the two types of aetiology.[21] Whereas rites for the dead seek to reassure us that the end in death is complete and appropriate, names of the living reassure us that the hero lives on far beyond the end of the drama. One suggests completeness while the other suggests continuity. They also establish different sorts of connection between past and present. As *Romeo and Juliet* and *Hippolytus* suggest, there is or may be an equivalence between action and vestige, between a hero's tragic death and the present memorial that bears witness to it. The name, however, does not pretend to equivalence. In certain contexts, a name carries with it power over the person named; Polyphemus, for example, can only curse Odysseus when he knows his name. But even so, it is the sign and not the thing, and this lack of equivalence is stressed in Euripidean aetiologies. A small town, Oresteion, preserves a trace of Orestes' name; an epithet of Artemis, Tauropolos, is a relic of Iphigenia's journey among the Taurians. The aition marks the distance and the difference between the contemporary world and a mythical past that survives only in fossilized traces.

This slender thread between past and present is often spun out further by placing the link between them outside the drama, in a sequel. The town Oresteion, for example, preserves Orestes' name not because of anything he does in the play, but because in the wanderings that will follow once the play is over, Orestes will spend time in Arcadia as an exile (*Orestes*) or a settler (*Electra*). In *Ion*, this further remove is also one of lineage: the four tribes will be named not for Ion but for sons he will father in the future, while Dorians and Achaeans will be named for future children of Creusa. In *Helen*, the thread is spun out in a different direction. The Dioscuri explain to Helen that an island will be named for her:

> And where Maia's son first anchored you
> when he carried you off from Sparta through heaven
> and stole your body so Paris could not marry you—
> I mean the stretch of island guarding Acte—
> mortals in future will call this Helene
> since he took you stolen from the house.

> οὗ δ᾽ ὥρμισέν σε πρῶτα Μαιάδος τόκος
> Σπάρτης ἀπάρας τὸν κατ᾽ οὐρανὸν δρόμον,
> κλέψας δέμας σὸν μὴ Πάρις γήμειέ σε,
> φρουρὸν παρ᾽ Ἀκτὴν τεταμένην νῆσον λέγω,
> Ἑλένη τὸ λοιπὸν ἐν βροτοῖς κεκλήσεται,
> ἐπεὶ κλοπαίαν σ᾽ ἐκ δόμων ἐδέξατο. 1670–75

Here the deus refers not to future wanderings but to the past, and in particular to an episode seventeen years before the beginning of the play, when Paris first abducted Helen (or rather her phantom) and Hermes carried the real Helen to Egypt; Hermes apparently made a rest stop on the way to Egypt, and a minor island therefore bears the name Helene.

Both classes of aetiologies, those that commemorate the dead and those that preserve the names of the living, tend to attenuate the connection between past and present. But there is also a difference between the two classes, one that coincides to a large degree with differences between earlier and later plays. There are several changes in Euripides' style commonly placed at or soon after 420 B.C.E.,[22] which thus distinguish an earlier group of plays (*Alcestis, Medea, Children of Heracles, Hippolytus, Andromache, Hecuba,* and *Suppliant Women*) from a later group (*Electra, Heracles, Trojan Women, Iphigenia among the Taurians, Ion, Helen, Phoenician Women, Orestes, Bacchant Women,* and *Iphigenia at Aulis*). As we have seen, plays in the earlier group tend to commemorate a character's death with a tomb or funeral rites, while those in the later group tend to preserve the name of a living character and more often involve a sequel to the plot. Later plays also may include multiple aetiologies, either because more than one character is to be remembered (Orestes and Iphigenia in *Iphigenia among the Taurians,* Ion and his various descendants in *Ion*) or because a single character is to be remembered in several ways (Orestes at Athens and in Arcadia in *Electra*). Of course, the division is not a strict or absolute one. Among plays of the former group, Kynossema in *Hecuba* is both a memorial for Hecuba's death and a name recording her transformation into a dog, and *Suppliant*

Women devotes much more space to the aition commemorating the treaty with the Argives than it does to memorials for the fallen Seven. Among the latter group, Theseus alludes at the end of *Heracles* both to shrines named for Heracles while he is alive and rites in his honor after he dies, and *Iphigenia among the Taurians* includes both a shrine named for Iphigenia's travels and a rite remembering her future death. We might add a different combination in *Electra*, where aitia that close the play by recalling the resolution of *Eumenides* (1265–69) are supplemented by a new aition that looks forward to a town named for Orestes (1273–75). The aition in early plays tends to commemorate the death of a character, but this gesture of completeness, already displaced onto minor characters or postponed to the future, is combined in a transitional period with others that more openly advertise continuity, while in late plays, the aition simply preserves a name into the future. This is to generalize from a small sample, making no attempt to reconstruct an aition in *Bacchant Women*,[23] but there is nevertheless a marked shift of emphasis toward continuity and toward a nominal connection between past and present.

Finally, the thread between past and present may appear more slender if we are made aware of its factitious nature. Aetiology in general is often part fact and part fiction. We know why the camel has a hump, but we enjoy the just-so story because it creates an engaging, if fictional, explanation. Or we may have no idea *why* the camel has a hump, but we enjoy the explanation and need not take too seriously our narrator's claim that the evidence of the hump proves the story true. The Chester *Nativity* offers a novel account of how the Roman Catholic Church began with Octavian's dream and produces as evidence the Ara Caeli in Rome. Apparently, the *Oresteia* does likewise, giving a new account of the origin of Athenian judicial process in the trial of Orestes and offering as evidence the court of the Areopagus.[24] In each case, the explanation works not because it is known to be true, but because it *ought* to be true, because it is religiously or politically appropriate. Euripides goes further. Instead of finding a new explanation for a known institution, he sometimes invents the institution itself. *Children of Heracles*, for example, ends with Eurystheus foretelling his place of burial "beside divine Athena Pallenis" (just outside Athens) where his tomb will help protect the city from invaders (1030–36). Tradition often placed Eurystheus' tomb near Sciron's Rocks in Megara, and less often at Thebes, while Athenian writers favored a version in which his head was buried in Marathon and his body at Gargettus.[25] Euripides' account is unique and apparently his own invention; its factitious nature seems to be signaled by the implausible gesture of having the king captured at Sciron's Rocks and then brought to Marathon, thus coopting these familiar burial sites, and is reinforced when Eurystheus prohibits libations or sacrifices at his tomb (1040–41), acknowledging that this burial site is unknown. *Suppliant Women* is more complex, ending with Athena's forecasts that a buried knife will enforce the treaty between Athens and Argos (1205–9) and that a shrine will honor the fallen Seven (1210–12). Both aetiologies are fictional. As far as we can tell, the buried knife was invented by Euripides, as was the anachronistic treaty it seals, while the shrine for the Seven is a curious innovation. Tradition generally placed the burial of the Seven at Thebes, although Athenian authors pointed to their tombs at Eleusis as proof of Athenian help in recovering the dead. Yet Euripides makes no mention of the Seven Mounds and says instead that after cremation the remains were returned to Argos; the sanctuary at Eleusis (τεμένη 1211) is therefore a cenotaph.[26] These inventions play a complex political game, first inserting into the familiar, patriotic story of Athens and the Seven the concrete yet fictitious detail of a treaty between Athens and Argos; then undermining the ideological importance of this myth by denying that the Seven were buried at Eleusis. There are similar, if less striking, innovations in *Medea* and *Iphigenia among the Taurians*,[27] and one could argue that the factitious nature of earlier aitia anticipates the overt contrivance of place-names that predominates in later plays.

Culture and Text

I began by emphasizing the special status of tragedy as the public reenactment of a shared past and of the aition as an overt marker of the link between that past and the world of the audience. Yet in *Suppliant Women*, which reenacts a past unusually close to the present (situated in nearby Eleusis, with the Athenian hero Theseus in the leading role, in a story that served to demonstrate Athenian virtue), the aition draws attention to ways in which the link between past and present is or may be fabricated. The paradox is not unique to this play. In general the aition, rather than simply situating the play in the same continuum as contemporary culture, draws attention to the ways in which both are reinvented. These observations may be placed in clearer relief by comparing Euripidean practice with that of Aeschylus and Sophocles, and by reviewing some interpretations of the aition.

In Aeschylus, we find several recognizable aitia, but these are neither as common nor as consistent in form as those of Euripides. In the latter part of *Prometheus*,[28] the Titan's lengthy speech to Io includes two aetiological explanations, the first for the name Bosporus, or "Cow-crossing," and the second for the Ionian Sea:

> At the narrow gates of the lake, you will reach
> the Cimmerian isthmus, which you must leave
> stoutheartedly and cross the Maiotic channel.
> Mortals shall tell forever the great story
> of your crossing, and it will be named for this
> the Bosporos.

> ἰσθμὸν δ᾽ ἐπ᾽ αὐταῖς στενοπόροις λίμνης πύλαις
> Κιμμερικὸν ἥξεις, ὃν θρασυσπλάγχνως σε χρὴ
> λιποῦσαν αὐλῶν᾽ ἐκπερᾶν Μαιωτικόν.
> ἔσται δὲ θνητοῖς εἰσαεὶ λόγος μέγας
> τῆς σῆς πορείας, Βόσπορος δ᾽ ἐπώνυμος
> κεκλήσεται.   729–34

> Goaded from there along the seaside
> road, you flew to the great gulf of Rhea
> and were stormed back in reverse course.
> In time to come, the inlet of the sea
> will be called Ionian, you may be sure,
> a memorial of your crossing for all mortals.

ἐντεῦθεν οἰστρήσασα τὴν παρακτίαν
κέλευθον ᾖξας πρὸς μέγαν κόλπον Ῥέας,
ἀφ' οὗ παλιμπλάγκτοισι χειμάζῃ δρόμοις·
χρόνον δὲ τὸν μέλλοντα πόντιος μυχός,
σαφῶς ἐπίστασ', Ἰόνιος κεκλήσεται,
τῆς σῆς πορείας μνῆμα τοῖς πᾶσιν βροτοῖς.   836–41

In each case, the legendary world is explicitly connected with place-names familiar to the audience, using formulaic language very similar to that of Euripides (θνητοῖς εἰσαεὶ ... ἐπώνυμος / κεκλήσεται 732–34, and χρόνον δὲ τὸν μέλλοντα ... κεκλήσεται ... βροτοῖς 839–41). These aetiologies are delivered by Prometheus, who has a privileged knowledge of the future, but they are based upon the past and future wanderings of Io, rather than upon the action of the drama, and they occur neither at the end of a play nor in the final play of a trilogy. It seems to me that the result is to draw the viewers into the dramatic conflict: if Prometheus can accurately describe to Io the contemporary world outside the drama, then he can also challenge the superior power and knowledge of Zeus himself.

In the *Oresteia*, however, two aetiologies play an important role in the ending. In the course of Orestes' trial, Athena explains the origins both of the court of the Areopagus and of the worship of the Eumenides near the Acropolis:

Hear my decree, people of Athens,
as you decide the first trial for bloodshed.
In future for the host of Aegeus this
will always be a court of judges.

κλύοιτ' ἂν ἤδη θεσμόν, Ἀττικὸς λεώς,
πρώτας δίκας κρίνοντες αἵματος χυτοῦ.
ἔσται δὲ καὶ τὸ λοιπὸν Αἰγέως στρατῷ
αἰεὶ δικαστῶν τοῦτο βουλευτήριον.   *Eumenides* 681–84

Advancing time shall win more honor
for these citizens, and you shall have
an honored place by the house of Erechtheus,
and from processions of men and women shall have
more than you could from all mankind.

οὐπιρρέων γὰρ τιμιώτερος χρόνος
ἔσται πολίταις τοῖσδε, καὶ σὺ τιμίαν
ἕδραν ἔχουσα πρὸς δόμοις Ἐρεχθέως
τεύξῃ παρ' ἀνδρῶν καὶ γυναικείων στόλων
ὅσ' ἂν παρ' ἄλλων οὔποτ' ἂν σχέθοις βροτῶν.   853–57

The first is a clearly stated aition with formulaic language (τὸ λοιπόν 683, αἰεί 684) that connects the trial in progress with the recently reformed court of the Areopagus. The second is less clearly drawn, offering a shrine in Athens as an inducement to appease the Furies. But both are spoken by a god who presides over the conclusion like a deus ex machina, and both play a role in closure. The reference to contemporary institutions leads the spectator out of the mythic world at the end of the trilogy, while establishing a new significance and authority for the Areopagus and the shrine of the Furies. The contrast between past and present worlds, however, is not as clearly drawn as in Euripides. There the deus or equivalent figure delivers the aition after the action is complete; the result is a sharp contrast between the preceding enactment and the contemporary perspective introduced by the aition. In *Eumenides*, however, the "deus" is onstage for more than half the play, and the finale tends to mingle the worlds of drama and audience rather than juxtapose them. The first aition is followed by the casting of ballots, which fulfills the aition by inaugurating the judicial functions of the Areopagus. The second aition is a promise, or bribe, which is accepted in the following scene, where the Furies bless Athens and Athena grants them power (916–55). The impression that the stage action blends into the present world of contemporary Athens (rather than simply anticipating it) is reinforced as Athena and the chorus sing the city's praises, and as the procession of escorts calls upon the audience to join them: "Show honor, all you people! . . . Cry out now in song!" εὐφαμεῖτε δὲ πανδαμεί. . . . ὀλολύξατε νῦν ἐπὶ μολπαῖς (1039, 1043).[29]

Despite some important similarities, the closing aitia in the *Oresteia* are used to very different effect than in Euripides. Unfortunately, we cannot know how, if at all, Aeschylus used aetiologies to conclude other trilogies. The only other extant play that concludes its trilogy, the *Seven against Thebes*, has no aition, and reconstructions that have been offered for lost trilogies are purely speculative.[30] From *Prometheus* and *Eumenides*, it seems safe to say that the Euripidean aition has a precedent in Aeschylus, but that the earlier playwright probably used the device less frequently and (so far as we can tell) used it to incorporate the world of the viewer into the trilogy, rather than to mark a difference or distance between them.[31]

In Sophocles, there are no surviving aitia at all. Two passages allude to the world outside the drama. In *Ajax*, the chorus advises Teucer to bury his father quickly, "where he shall have a spacious tomb, ever remembered by men," ἔνθα βροτοῖς τὸν ἀείμνηστον / τάφον εὐρώεντα καθέξει (1166–67). The spectator may be reminded of the surviving tomb of Ajax,[32] but the advice to build a lasting memorial contains only an allusion rather than an explicit connection to the world of the audience. Likewise in *Women of Trachis*, Lichas tells Deianeira that Heracles is alive in Euboea, "where he marks out altars and fruitful rites for Kenaian Zeus," ἔνθ᾽ ὁρίζεται / βωμοὺς τέλη τ᾽ ἔγκαρπα Κηναίῳ Διί (237–38). This may allude to a known temple in Euboea[33] without making a specific reference to the contemporary world.

The closest thing to an aition in Sophocles comes near the end of *Oedipus at Colonus*, as Oedipus describes to Theseus the place where he will die:

> Untouched by a guide, I myself shall show
> at once the place where I must die.
> Tell this never to any man, neither
> where it is hidden nor in what area. . . .
> Thus you will inhabit this city without fear
> for Theban men.

χῶρον μὲν αὐτὸς αὐτίκ᾽ ἐξηγήσομαι,
ἄθικτος ἡγητῆρος, οὗ με χρὴ θανεῖν.
τοῦτον δὲ φράζε μήποτ᾽ ἀνθρώπων τινί,

μήθ᾽ οὗ κέκευθε μήτ᾽ ἐν οἷς κεῖται τόποις· . . .
χοὔτως ἀδῇον τήνδ᾽ ἐνοικήσεις πόλιν
σπαρτῶν ἀπ᾽ ἀνδρῶν.   1520–23, 1533–34

The implication is that the tomb of Oedipus will survive into the world of the audience and will (like the tomb of Eurystheus in *Children of Heracles* or the buried knife in *Suppliant Women*) protect Athens from invading enemies. But a connection with the contemporary world is never spelled out. There is no reference to the future (τὸ λοιπόν, αἰεί, etc.) that might establish such a link, and rather than appealing to a familiar name or place in the manner of an aition, Sophocles makes it clear that the site of Oedipus' death is unknown.[34] The private and mystical atmosphere is entirely different from an appeal to public knowledge of civic institutions, and the secret tomb could be considered a variation upon, or reversal of, the Euripidean aition, since the mantic hero announces that his impending death and burial will remain *unknown* to future generations. Sophocles does not offer a precedent for the Euripidean aition, since *Oedipus at Colonus* was produced after Euripides' death. This one example that comes closest to an aition has a very different effect, emphasizing the intensely personal meaning of the ending, rather than connecting it to the larger world of the audience.

Euripidean aitia seem to have a precedent not in Sophocles but in Aeschylus, and especially in *Eumenides*. Euripides, however, used aitia much more commonly and consistently,[35] and with a different emphasis. Rather than drawing the viewer into the world of the trilogy, Euripides marks out the distance between text and culture and between the past reenacted onstage and the traces of that past in the present world. The aition, in other words, lies somewhere in between the two poles of rhetoric and ritual that critics have assigned it. These critical poles can help to situate the aition in general and to frame discussion of the complex aetiology at the end of *Iphigenia among the Taurians*.

Interpretation of the aition as ritual begins with the obvious fact that a god (or mortal) may ordain the establishment of a religious cult or rite. At the end of *Hippolytus*, Artemis announces the ritual lament for Hippolytus that will be performed by women in Trozen, and at the end of *Iphigenia among the Taurians*, Athena instructs Orestes to establish the shrine to Artemis Tauropolos at Halae; in *Medea*, the mortal Medea likewise promises that rites will be established in Corinth to honor the murdered children. If we add tombs that have some religious association (those of Neoptolemus at Delphi in *Andromache* and of the Seven at Eleusis in *Suppliant Women*) and similar examples that may be fictional or allusive (the tomb of Eurystheus at Pallene in *Children of Heracles* and festivals honoring Heracles in *Heracles*), we can begin to argue that the aition has a special connection with ritual. In the historical model of ritualists such as Albrecht Dieterich, tragedy evolved from ritual, and the aition is a vestige that betrays those beginnings;[36] members of the Cambridge school went further, arguing with Gilbert Murray that tragedy preserves and reenacts its original religious function:

> For the play is, with the rarest and most doubtful exceptions, essentially the enactment of a ritual, or rather of what the Greeks called an *aition*—that is, a supposed historical

event which is the origin or "cause" of the ritual. Thus the death of Hippolytus is the *aition* of the lamentation-rite performed at the grave of Hippolytus. . . . The tragedy, as ritual, enacts its own legendary origin.[37]

Yet many aetiologies have nothing to do with ritual. Several are clearly invented, and most appear only in Euripides, the playwright furthest removed from the "origins" of tragedy.

Recent criticism has revived the anthropological approach, emphasizing not the evolution of tragedy from ritual, but their homology as social and civic structures: tragedy, like ritual, helps to define the individual's place in the social order. The closing aetiology makes this homology explicit, drawing attention, as Helene Foley argues, to the similarity between drama and rite: "The conclusions of Euripides' plays in particular insistently link myth and actual cult practice, often stressing the origins of cult in sacrificial deaths and demanding that the audience make connections between tragic violence and daily experiences of sacrifice."[38] Foley shows that the plots of *Bacchant Women* and *Iphigenia at Aulis* in many ways reenact ritual sacrifice, while Pietro Pucci argues that Medea's murder of her children draws upon the complex and ambivalent place of violence in Athenian ritual.[39] Yet these more sophisticated studies, in looking not for evolutionary vestiges but for a common discourse of drama and culture, are less interested in the aition and its uses.

The other general approach is to look at the aition's rhetorical uses, and in particular at how it secures the approval of the spectators. As Andreas Spira argues, it serves to make the drama more real and believable: "Perhaps one should view aetiology and prophecy instead as a kind of πιθανόν. They connect the dramatic action with shrines, cult practices or mythical memories which are the living and concrete present day for the spectator, and thus make it believable."[40] This implies that the aition is superficial, a closing attempt to win approval that (like the prayer for victory) is not essential to the drama. Critics such as Albin Lesky and Max Pohlenz see it as programmatic, a "purely superficial" vestige that allows the artistic and humanistic playwright to show that the "gods had become irrelevant to the inner structure of his tragedy."[41] For H. D. F. Kitto, however, aetiologies are simply marks of closure: "whatever may be the psychological explanation, it is clear that when an aition turns up the play is over. It reinforces our feeling of finality, and is used when a play does not reach an Aristotelian end but merely stops."[42] As we have seen, there is some truth to this; closing markers in Euripides often betray a lack of completeness. But plays most often credited with Aristotelian completeness (*Medea* or *Hippolytus*) also have emphatic aitia, while those that most arguably do not end but merely stop (*Trojan Women* and *Phoenician Women*) have none at all. In fact, the shift toward more open-ended aitia (from earlier aitia that commemorate a character's death and burial to later ones that promise that a character's name will live on) follows a similar change from plots that are relatively complete (the death of Hippolytus or the recovery and cremation of the Seven) to those which remain somehow open-ended (Ion, Xuthus, and Creusa must live together in Athens, and Orestes, Hermione, and Menelaus must patch up their differences).

This shift in emphasis brings us back to the contrast between ritual and rhetoric. If earlier plays tend to conclude with rituals and tombs that suggest cultural continuity from past to present, later plays close instead with words that offer a nominal link between text and audience. Yet the ritual vestige is also rhetorical, just as the name preserves a cultural thread. The manner in which ritual and rhetoric usurp one another is played out most fully at the end of *Iphigenia among the Taurians*. Here, Athena's lengthy speech incorporates several aetiologies. She begins by telling king Thoas to call off his pursuit of Orestes and Iphigenia since Apollo sent Orestes on this mission, and since they have already escaped the king's soldiers (1435–45). Then Athena turns to Orestes (who remains offstage) and tells him to take the Taurian statue of Artemis to Halae in Attica (1446–52) and build a shrine for it there:

> Build a shrine there and set up the statue,
> named for the Taurian land and for the troubles
> you suffered wandering around Greece
> goaded by Furies; mortals in future will sing of this as
> the goddess Artemis Tauropolos [TaurianWandering].

> ἐνταῦθα τεύξας ναὸν ἵδρυσαι βρέτας,
> ἐπώνυμον γῆς Ταυρικῆς πόνων τε σῶν,
> οὓς ἐξεμόχθεις περιπολῶν καθ᾽ Ἑλλάδα
> οἴστροις Ἐρινύων. Ἄρτεμιν δέ νιν βροτοὶ
> τὸ λοιπὸν ὑμνήσουσι Ταυροπόλον θεάν.   1453–57

In Halae, Orestes must also institute a ritual to commemorate the human sacrifices that the Taurians performed for Artemis:

> And establish this custom: when people feast,
> for your slaughter let someone hold the blade
> at a man's neck, and let him draw blood
> in ritual so the goddess may be honored.

> νόμον τε θὲς τόνδ᾽· ὅταν ἑορτάζῃ λεώς,
> τῆς σῆς σφαγῆς ἄποιν᾽ ἐπισχέτω ξίφος
> δέρῃ πρὸς ἀνδρὸς αἷμά τ᾽ ἐξανιέτω,
> ὁσίας ἕκατι θεά θ᾽ ὅπως τιμὰς ἔχῃ.   1458–61

But Iphigenia must continue on to Brauron, where she will serve Artemis and will be honored with offerings after her death:[43]

> But you, Iphigenia, must serve the goddess
> at the holy steps of Brauron; there you
> will die and be buried, and they will bring you
> offerings of fine-woven robes that women
> leave in the house when their lives are crushed
> in childbirth.

> σὲ δ᾽ ἀμφὶ σεμνάς, Ἰφιγένεια, κλίμακας
> Βραυρωνίας δεῖ τῇδε κληδουχεῖν θεᾷ·
> οὗ καὶ τεθάψῃ κατθανοῦσα, καὶ πέπλων
> ἄγαλμά σοι θήσουσιν εὐπήνους ὑφάς,
> ἃς ἂν γυναῖκες ἐν τόκοις ψυχορραγεῖς
> λίπωσ᾽ ἐν οἴκοις.   1462–67

Finally, in an allusion to the end of *Eumenides*, Athena reminds Orestes that since she cast the deciding vote in his favor, defendants will by custom always be acquitted when the votes are even (1469–72).

The first aetiology connects the wanderings of Orestes enacted in the drama to an epithet under which Athenians worshipped Artemis at Halae. The link between drama and cult is purely verbal and is in some sense factitious. Leaving aside the problem of etymology (the epithet was usually derived from ταῦρος, "bull"[44]), Brauron and Sparta both laid claim to the wooden statue brought to Greece by Iphigenia,[45] so viewers would at least be aware that this third claim need not be true. Since the statue at Brauron had been carried off to Susa by the Persians,[46] Euripides (or someone he follows) may have soothed Athenian pride by claiming that the real statue was not in Brauron but nearby at Halae and had been stolen from barbarians. The next aition explains not a name but a rite: the shedding of human blood at a feast for Artemis. Yet there is no evidence that such a rite was ever performed.[47] The drama constantly plays with the fiction of human sacrifice, first claiming that the sacrifice at Aulis did not take place; then presenting an Iphigenia who takes revenge for this near-sacrifice by performing human sacrifice herself—yet making it clear that barbarians, not she, perform the act, and finally staging another non-sacrifice in which Orestes is nearly killed. This fiction in ritual form is answered by an apparently fictitious ritual, and a legendary past that avoided sacrifice lives on, we are told, in the actual spilling of blood. The third aition comes closer to Athenian practice. There is no indication that robes of women who died in childbirth were offered to Iphigenia at Brauron, but wool and clothing were among the items dedicated to Artemis Brauronia on the Acropolis and also, perhaps, to Artemis at Brauron.[48] There is no evidence for offerings to Iphigenia, no evidence that offerings were associated with childbirth, and no reason to suppose that the offerings were posthumous. We thus have two faulty connections: one between Euripides' aition and what little we know of contemporary practice,[49] and the other between Euripides' aition and events of the play. The offering of robes, after all, commemorates not what happened among the Taurians, but what we are told will happen much later at Brauron, and it does so inappropriately, remembering not the sacrifices Iphigenia (nearly) suffered and inflicted, but the dangers of childbirth she never knew. Finally, the aition for acquittal with even votes takes us back to the very different version enacted by Aeschylus, and to this play's repeated reminders that the end of the story in *Eumenides* was not really the end: the trial at Athens did *not* appease the Furies, Orestes had to go back to Apollo, and the god prescribed another trial of atonement (77–92, 285–94, 940–78). Euripides overtly revises Aeschylus with a sequel that is largely invented[50] and is certainly less relevant (How does bringing a statue of Artemis to Athens cleanse the Argive of matricide?) and that draws attention to this revision with an afterthought on the trial at the Areopagus.

At the end of the performance, as the audience takes leave of the enacted past, the aition offers the promise of a stable, objective, and familiar end in the contemporary world. Yet it fails to deliver such an end, not just by marking the gap between past and present, but by confusing them. If rhetoric becomes ritual and culture becomes text, as they do in *Iphigenia*, then neither is a stable ground that will serve to secure the other.

5

Postscript: Outside the Frame

"An epilogue," Garp wrote, "is more than a body count. An epilogue, in the disguise of wrapping up the past, is really a way of warning us about the future."

JOHN IRVING, *The World According to Garp*

Greek tragedy, unlike many other forms of drama, presumes a historical and cultural continuum that embraces both the events enacted onstage and the viewers themselves, and the Euripidean aition overtly complicates this thread. Yet the drama implies (or seems to imply) another more essential continuum: the thread of events that constitute the plot. And insofar as the drama raises questions about the end of this thread, it brings us back to the issues of form versus content and of artistic invention.

Any narrative genre must grapple (it would seem) with the problem of choosing an end. How does the author decide where to begin and end the story? How does she or he choose, from the countless events of history or the infinite possibilities of fiction, what to enact or tell? And how do readers or spectators know that this is the end? Do they recognize that lives and events continue and that no retelling will embrace them all? The problem (as stated) assumes a contrast between form and content, between the infinite continuum and the finite story that tries to contain it, or between the real world of human experience and the contrivance of narration. This problem and this implied contrast are my point of departure in discussing closing prophecies in Euripides. It does not follow that my reading requires or depends upon the validity of this (Aristotelian) contrast; as I hope to show, the problem is one that some texts pose with greater or lesser insistence, and in various ways.

Aristotle says that the action should be a whole, with a beginning, a middle, and an end that is "followed by nothing else."[1] Although he does not say as much, he implies that the author will choose to dramatize an action that he finds to be already whole or complete, rather than take a given action and charm or wrestle it into the shape of a whole. Quite different is Henry James's neo-Aristotelian claim that although endings do not exist, the artist must try to convince us that they do: "Really, universally, relations stop nowhere, and the exquisite problem of the artist is eternally but to draw, by a geometry of his own, the circle within which they shall happily *appear* to do so."[2] But Aristotle and James do agree on this: the spectator or reader should be convinced that the end is the end and should not expect more to follow. This process of selection or sleight of hand is by no means the rule. Modern drama, for example, may openly frustrate the viewer's expectation that the end will be followed by nothing else. In his epilogue to *The Good Woman of Setzuan*, Bertolt Brecht goes out of his way to remind the viewer that this is not the end:

> It is for you to find a way, my friends,
> To help good men arrive at happy ends.
> *You* write the happy ending to the play!
> There must, there must, there's got to be a way![3]

A less alienating approach is simply to suggest that the action continues. This is a favorite device in nineteenth-century fiction, in which the author adds a postscript sketching the future careers of the protagonists. George Eliot's epilogue to *Middlemarch* begins by explaining why we are not satisfied to stop at the end: "Every limit is a beginning as well as an ending. Who can quit young lives after being long in company with them, and not desire to know what befell them in their afteryears? For the fragment of a life, however typical, is not the sample of an even web."[4] Whereas Eliot offers an apologia for the conventional epilogue, Charles Dickens laments that he is "required to furnish an account" of the aftermath and offers an epilogue to the *Pickwick Papers* only under protest: "In compliance with this custom—unquestionably a bad one—we subjoin a few biographical words, in relation to the party at Mr. Pickwick's assembled."[5]

Euripides, like Eliot or Dickens, cannot leave behind the continuing stories of his protagonists. At the end of *Andromache*, for example, the goddess Thetis announces to Peleus that Andromache will go to Molossia and will marry Helenus, her son's descendants will succeed one another as kings of Molossia, and Peleus will become immortal and will join Thetis in the house of Nereus (1243–62). But unlike Eliot or Dickens, Euripides is breaking with convention when he offers such a sequel. There are no parallels in Greek tragedy for his use of the dramatic epilogue and no more than partial parallels—to my knowledge—in the Western dramatic tradition. In comedy, the epilogue speaker addresses the audience with an apology or request for applause rather than the announcement of a sequel, and hints of the future at the end of Shakespeare's histories tend simply to connect one play to another (e.g., part 1 of *Henry VI* to part 2, or *Henry V* to the trilogy on Henry VI). The closest Shakespeare comes to such a technique is in *Richard II* in which the king's remorse includes a brief anticipation of the Crusades ("I'll make a voyage to the Holy Land, / To wash this blood off from my guilty hand") and *Henry VIII* in which Cranmer's eulogy of the king includes a prophetic paean to Elizabeth and James:[6]

> Wherever the bright sun of heaven shall shine,
> His honour and the greatness of his name
> Shall be, and make new nations. He shall flourish,
> And, like a mountain cedar, reach his branches
> To all the plains about him; our children's children
> Shall see this, and bless heaven.

Modern drama occasionally ends with a more straightforward announcement of a sequel, but as a rule such epilogues stand outside the drama. *Pygmalion* is followed by an essay in which Shaw argues that Eliza will marry Freddy rather than Higgins and goes on to criticize the conventions of romance; the essay describes the couple's future life in some detail, but it is not a part of the dramatic performance. Arthur Miller adds a much shorter postscript to *The Crucible*, sketching for the reader, but not for the theater audience, the aftermath of the trial in Salem. There are closer parallels to Euripidean epilogues in film, in which a narrator's voice or a scrolling text reveals the later careers of the protagonists. As in Euripides and the novel, such an epilogue stands at least partly outside the action and possesses a special authority—not the divine stature of a deus or the reflective distance of a novel's author, but the objectivity of a chronicle. In each case, the epilogue does not simply continue the action but allows it to resurface in a different and "truer" genre, whether legend, history, biography, or documentary. The parting of the ways redefines the action. If characters and events have a life of their own no longer contained by the plot, we must now view them not as parts of an artistic whole but as constituents of a more formless and realistic continuum.

The sequel therefore has an alienating role, transplanting events from the familiar confines of artistic reenactment to a more uncertain realm of unshaped experience. In modern genres such as the novel or film, this estrangement is heightened by our ignorance of what the future may hold for these fictional characters, even as the epilogue is typically banal, comforting, and predictable. In Euripides, however, the future course of the legend is generally familiar to the audience, while the end of the play renders problematic the means by which a character will reach or navigate that future.[7]

Tying and Untying

The Euripidean epilogue is a prophecy at the end of the play usually delivered by a deus ex machina that describes events subsequent to the action. A forecast of this kind occurs in every extant Euripidean ending, except those of *Alcestis*, *Trojan Women*, and *Phoenician Women*, and helps to create or reinforce a distinction between the end of the dramatic performance and the continuity of events portrayed.

The narration of events to follow distinguishes the concluding prophecy both from the closing aetiology and from other uses of prophecy. Aition and concluding prophecy both allude to a future beyond the drama, but the aition is more explicitly extra-dramatic. The aition connects two distinct worlds, past and present, inside and outside the drama, drawing attention to the gap between them. The concluding prophecy, however, simply extends the course of events. In *Orestes*, for example, Apollo explains that Orestes will now go into exile for a year in Arcadia before standing trial for matricide at the Areopagus in Athens, marrying Hermione, and ruling as king at Argos. Yet because the prophecy extends the story and because the reenactment cannot contain the continually unfolding legend, we are made aware of the dramatic illusion and its limitations. The narration of a sequel to the plot also distinguishes the concluding prophecy from other uses of prophecy. Whether delivered by a god in the prologue (e.g., Aphrodite in *Hippolytus*) or by a prophet within the action (Teiresias in *Phoenician Women*), the prophecy anticipates how the plot will pro-

ceed, arousing interest in whether, and how, these goals will be realized.[8] The concluding prophecy, on the other hand, describes events that lie entirely outside the
play; rather than arousing suspense within the drama, it removes uncertainty from
the sequel.

The concluding prophecy, like the aition, requires a speaker with privileged knowledge of events outside the play. This will usually be a deus ex machina, but may also
be a human with special access to the future (Medea, Theseus, Eurystheus, and
Polymestor). The liminal status of this figure corresponds to the liminal status of the
sequel itself. Just as the sequel is both a necessary part of the story and an appendage
added to it, the divine or human speaker is both a character within the action and a
voice from outside it. In the novel, the epilogue speaker is liminal in a different way:
the author continues to narrate events, but does so now in his or her own voice. In
each case, the deus figure or the author of the novel renegotiates the work's authority. By displaying her persona as narrator, George Eliot reminds us that the work is
a fiction, but by describing the sequel in her own voice, she bears witness to the cred-
ibility of this narrative. An epiphany of Apollo or Athena compromises the independence and completeness of the human action, even as the god's announcement of a
sequel places it within a more authoritative frame; the action escapes the bounds of
reenactment, even as an authorial figure intervenes to assert control.

Only at a play's end does a prophecy have this effect. Prophecies earlier in the
play arouse suspense, anticipating events within the action rather than looking to a
sequel beyond the end. The single exception is very striking. *Trojan Women* begins
with a prologue scene in which Athena and Poseidon foretell the destruction of the
Greek fleet on its return from Troy, and in the first episode, Cassandra foretells the
murder of Agamemnon and the sufferings of Odysseus. These prophecies are
unusual in two respects: they describe—at the opening of the play—events that take
place at some time after its close, and they describe not the future of the play's protagonists but the futures of Greek men who never appear onstage.[9] Looking beyond
the end of the play reinforces the sense that the action is already finished: Troy is
fallen, the war is over, and a deus enters to comment upon the sequel. And describing the future of Greek men such as Agamemnon and Odysseus excludes the women
of Troy from the larger story that began before the war and will continue after the
city falls.[10]

Happy Ends

What kinds of sequel does Euripides provide? How does the prophecy of events to
come complete, or continue, or comment upon, the preceding action? The most
familiar use of the sequel is to tie up loose ends, allaying our curiosity about what
will happen next; hence the conventional assurances of marriage for the young and
happy retirement for the old. Such sequels tend to be straightforward, predictable—
and contradictory in their effects. On the one hand, they suggest that human events
have a life of their own, continuing beyond the end of the performance and still engaging our interest and curiosity. On the other hand, they show that the future offers
simply more of the same, promising no new departure from the pattern of earlier
events.[11] In a sense, the author has his cake and eats it too: he acknowledges that the

action continues beyond the end, while making it clear that nothing very new will follow. It's not really the end, but it might as well be. At the end of *Helen*, after Helen and Menelaus finally engineer their escape from Egypt and set sail for home, the Dioscuri offer the following prophecy:[12]

> Sail with your husband, with a favoring wind;
> and we, your twin savior brothers
> galloping across the sea, will send you home.
> And when you turn and end your life
> you will be called a god, and with the Dioscuri
> will share libations and have offerings with
> us from men. This is the wish of Zeus. . . .
> As for the wandering Menelaus, it is ordained
> by the gods that he dwell in the Blessed Isle.

> πλεῖ ξὺν πόσει σῷ· πνεῦμα δ᾽ ἕξετ᾽ οὔριον·
> σωτῆρε δ᾽ ἡμεῖς σὼ κασιγνήτω διπλῶ
> πόντον παριππεύοντε πέμψομεν πάτραν.
> ὅταν δὲ κάμψῃς καὶ τελευτήσῃς βίον,
> θεὸς κεκλήσῃ καὶ Διοσκόρων μέτα
> σπονδῶν μεθέξεις ξένιά τ᾽ ἀνθρώπων πάρα
> ἕξεις μεθ᾽ ἡμῶν· Ζεὺς γὰρ ὧδε βούλεται. . . .
> καὶ τῷ πλανήτῃ Μενέλεῳ θεῶν πάρα
> μακάρων κατοικεῖν νῆσόν ἐστι μόρσιμον.   1663–69, 1676–77

The happy outcome of the plot is confirmed and reinforced by a happy sequel. Nothing new is added; we are simply reassured that the couple's success is secure, guaranteed in this world by a promise of safe conduct, and in the next by divinely ordained honors. If the play has already reached its happy end, however, and if the sequel reinforces it, perhaps James's formulation should be reversed: rather than making continuous events seem circumscribed, the author makes a completed action seem part of a larger continuum.

The point, of course, is that the sequel negotiates in various ways between plot and continuum, and between the gestures of tying up and teasing out the action. The epilogue in *Helen* is unusual in reminding the viewer that unalloyed bliss shall be bestowed without an intervening struggle, without means that will justify the end. More commonly, the epilogue suggests a continuity between hardship and reward, trial and happy ending. Orestes, we are told, must spend a year in exile in the wilds of Arcadia, and then stand trial for his life in Athens on the charge of matricide, before eventually being acquitted and returning to rule in Argos with his wife Hermione. Unlike *Helen*, *Orestes* suggests that the difficulties of life continue beyond the end of the play, even if new complications are resolved in a predictable pattern of marriage and rightful rule. Complications beyond the end of the play are indicated more subtly in *Ion*. In her closing speech, Athena announces the happy return of Ion to Athens, where he will ascend the throne and become famous throughout Greece (1571–75), and his good fortune will be multiplied when all Ionia is named for him. But the sequel is not so simple. Athena concludes by advising Creusa to keep the truth from Xuthus:

But now keep silent that he was born your son,
so appearance may pleasantly hold Xuthus
and all go well for you and yours, my woman.
Farewell. After this respite from troubles
I foretell for you a blessed fate.

νῦν οὖν σιώπα παῖς ὅδ' ὡς πέφυκε σός,
ἵν' ἡ δόκησις Ξοῦθον ἡδέως ἔχῃ
σύ τ' αὖ τὰ σαυτῆς ἀγάθ' ἔχουσ' ἴῃς, γύναι.
καὶ χαίρετ'· ἐκ γὰρ τῆσδ' ἀναψυχῆς πόνων
εὐδαίμον' ὑμῖν πότμον ἐξαγγέλλομαι.   1601–5

The blessed fate of Ion and Creusa is contingent upon the successful deception of
Xuthus, and if the course of this play has shown anything, it is that plots of deception
will not necessarily succeed. In this case, the sequel repeats not the hardships of life
but its complications and duplicities, even as it promises a simple and happy outcome.

Partial Ends

As we shall see, the epilogue in later plays tends to recapitulate the plot as a whole,
with all its complications and difficulties. In earlier plays, the epilogue tends to
answer only to part of the action. At the end of *Andromache*, we may wonder what
will happen to Andromache, to her infant son, and to her husband Peleus; on this
score, at least, Thetis is reassuring, foretelling Andromache's marriage to Helenus,
the line of kings that will come from her son, and the deification of Peleus (1243–56).
For those who live, all loose ends are happily tied, but the play ends with the body of
Neoptolemus displayed onstage and with instructions for his burial and memorial at
Delphi. In a sense, the action has two endings. The death of Neoptolemus is an end
that is commemorated with the aition for his tomb, while the stories of Andromache
and her family continue on into the future. *Suppliant Women* also ends both with
commemoration of the Seven whose bodies have been recovered and with Athena's
prophecy of the sequel in which the Epigoni will complete the expedition that their
fathers left unfinished. The concluding prophecy again negotiates between plot and
continuum, but does so by means of a much more literal antithesis. The plot is finished, and the very completeness of the central action contrasts with the continuity
of secondary stories; the knot is a foil to the remaining loose threads.

Loose Ends

An unusual variation is the sequel in *Electra*. Rather than a contrast between aition
for the dead and happy sequel for the living, we have a lengthy prophecy that tries to
tie up loose ends and conspicuously fails to do so. After trying to justify the murders
of Aegisthus and Clytemnestra, Castor first announces the marriage of Pylades and
the exile of Orestes (1247–51), but the god proceeds to foretell Orestes' pursuit by
the Furies and his trial in Athens at such length that instead of tying up loose ends,
he embarks on a whole new story (1250–75). Castor then tries to dispose of the two
dead bodies, but cannot do so without beginning another story:

So much for you. As for this corpse of Aegisthus,
the citizens of Argos will cover it with a tomb.
And your mother: Menelaus, arriving just now
at Nauplion, after he seized the land of Troy—
he and Helen will bury her. For Helen has arrived
from the house of Proteus, from Egypt: she never went
to Troy, but Zeus sent Helen's image to Ilion
to bring about the strife and slaughter of mankind.

σοὶ μὲν τάδ᾽ εἶπον. τόνδε δ᾽ Αἰγίσθου νέκυν
Ἄργους πολῖται γῆς καλύψουσιν τάφῳ.
μητέρα δὲ τὴν σὴν ἄρτι Ναυπλίαν παρὼν
Μενέλαος, ἐξ οὗ Τρωϊκὴν εἷλε χθόνα,
Ἑλένη τε θάψει· Πρωτέως γὰρ ἐκ δόμων
ἥκει λιποῦσ᾽ Αἴγυπτον οὐδ᾽ ἦλθεν Φρύγας·
Ζεὺς δ᾽, ὡς ἔρις γένοιτο καὶ φόνος βροτῶν,
εἴδωλον Ἑλένης ἐξέπεμψ᾽ ἐς Ἴλιον.   1276–83

Mention of Menelaus introduces a tantalizing hint of another tale to be told about Helen in Egypt, a hint that some scholars have taken as a promotion of the playwright's forthcoming *Helen*.[13] But there are sequels in every direction. The last concerns Pylades and the farmer, who must both start new lives:

Let Pylades take the young woman as his wife
and travel home to the land of Achaia,
and let him settle your so-called brother-in-law
in Phocian land and load him down with wealth.

Πυλάδης μὲν οὖν κόρην τε καὶ δάμαρτ᾽ ἔχων
Ἀχαιίδος γῆς οἴκαδ᾽ ἐσπορευέτω,
καὶ τὸν λόγῳ σὸν πενθερὸν κομιζέτω
Φωκέων ἐς αἶαν καὶ δότω πλούτου βάθος.   1284–87

The god's prophecy continues the action into the future, but instead of tying up loose ends and confirming the outcome of the plot, it reveals instead a series of sequels that promise new directions for the plot. The failed epilogue is thus an effective counterpart to the failed explanation. Just as Castor's attempt to explain the wisdom of Apollo's oracle collapses in contradictions (1244–46),[14] the attempt to tie up loose ends scatters into a variety of new beginnings.

Different Angles

The concluding prophecy tends to expose the continuity of events, revealing that the plot, or a part of it, continues beyond the performance to a happy end, or to new beginnings. The speaker of the epilogue may also foretell a sequel that functions more as a foil to the preceding action than as a continuation of it. At the end of *Hippolytus*, for example, after a lengthy explanation of Phaedra's duplicity and her stepson's innocence, Artemis announces a whole new plot:

Enough. Not even beneath the gloom
of earth shall Aphrodite's willful anger
hurtle against you unavenged,
thanks to your good and pious heart.
With my own hand and these relentless
arrows I will be avenged on one of hers,
whatever mortal is most dear to her.

ἔασον· οὐ γὰρ οὐδὲ γῆς ὑπὸ ζόφον
θεᾶς ἄτιμοι Κύπριδος ἐκ προθυμίας
ὀργαὶ κατασκήψουσιν ἐς τὸ σὸν δέμας,
σῆς εὐσεβείας κἀγαθῆς φρενὸς χάριν·
ἐγὼ γὰρ αὐτῆς ἄλλον ἐξ ἐμῆς χερὸς
ὃς ἂν μάλιστα φίλτατος κυρῇ βροτῶν
τόξοις ἀφύκτοις τοῖσδε τιμωρήσομαι.   1416–22

The action of the play is finished: Hippolytus is dead, Phaedra has been exposed, and Theseus is both chastened and enlightened. Now that this human drama is over, the sequel shifts attention to the divine plot that frames it, the rivalry of Aphrodite and Artemis and their spiteful acts of revenge against one another. This type of sequel is both more open and more closed than the others we have looked at. On the one hand, the happy end and its variants close the story by removing questions and revealing a predictable sequel, while the prophecy in *Hippolytus* begins a new story and raises new questions (Whom will Artemis choose—Adonis perhaps?[15] How will this next phase proceed?). On the other hand, the happy end makes it clear that human events are continuous and do not end with the end of the play, while the sequel in *Hippolytus* circumscribes the action as a finite episode within the larger divine frame. The effect, in this play at least, is unsettling. The privileged perspective of Artemis not only renders events intelligible as a self-contained episode, but seems to rob them of meaning: the tortuous plot with all its misdirections and confusions becomes a simple act of spite, soon to be repeated. Yet Artemis' appropriation of the plot does not entirely succeed; after the goddess withdraws, the play continues with a minisequel onstage, in which father and son try on their own terms to grapple with what has happened.

There is a different shift of perspective at the end of *Children of Heracles*. This patriotic suppliant drama is apparently complete with the defeat and capture of Eurystheus—when Alcmene calls for the prisoner's execution and Eurystheus accedes to this lawless act:

Kill me. I won't plead with you. But since
this city released me and was ashamed to kill me,
I offer it the gift of Apollo's ancient oracle
which in time will be more useful than it seems.
For it's fated that when I die you'll bury me
next to the holy maiden of Pallene,
and I shall always lie below foreign ground,
friendly to you, a savior to the city, and

to these children's children the greatest enemy—
when they come here with many arms,
betraying this kindness.

κτεῖν᾽, οὐ παραιτοῦμαί σε· τήνδε δὲ πτόλιν,
ἐπεί μ᾽ ἀφῆκε καὶ κατηδέσθη κτανεῖν,
χρησμῷ παλαιῷ Λοξίου δωρήσομαι,
ὃς ὠφελήσει μεῖζον᾽ ἢ δοκεῖ χρόνῳ.
θανόντα γάρ με θάψεθ᾽ οὗ τὸ μόρσιμον,
δίας πάροιθε παρθένου Παλληνίδος·
καὶ σοὶ μὲν εὔνους καὶ πόλει σωτήριος
μέτοικος αἰεὶ κείσομαι κατὰ χθονός,
τοῖς τῶνδε δ᾽ ἐκγόνοισι πολεμιώτατος,
ὅταν μόλωσι δεῦρο σὺν πολλῇ χερὶ
χάριν προδόντες τήνδε.   1026–36

Eurystheus foretells a sequel that alters things entirely: sons of the suppliants will march against the city which has protected them, and the villain who attacked Athens to capture the suppliants will instead protect the city from their children. Rather than a larger divine perspective, we have a longer historical perspective that complicates the moral lesson of the drama. The sequel offers comforting proof that Athenian virtue shall be rewarded, but only by reversing the expected means to this end: the friends of Athens will become enemies and her enemies will become friends. In this historical and political frame, the action is both more intelligible and more uncertain.

The preceding sample of techniques in the concluding prophecy begins with the familiar and conventional description of a happy end that follows the plot, and then adds examples in which the relation between plot and sequel seems progressively more complex. In the development of Euripidean drama, however, we find the opposite: from prophecies that offer various foils to the close of the plot, Euripides came to favor sequels that emphasize the continuity of the plot as a whole. The details of this development are worth describing in some detail.

Promises and Warnings

In Euripides' later plays, the concluding prophecies, like the aetiologies, tend to become longer and more complex. In *Hippolytus*, Artemis briefly announces her plan of revenge (quoted previously), and the departing Medea taunts Jason with an incomplete description of his death: "struck on the head by a piece of the Argo" (*Medea* 1387). The prophecies in *Suppliant Women* and *Children of Heracles* are slightly longer, describing future expeditions against Thebes and Athens, and in *Andromache*, the prophecy foretells Andromache's exile and marriage, as well as the deification of Peleus. But prophecies in the later plays are especially long and complex. In *Electra*, as we have seen, the Dioscuri foretell a lengthy series of sequels relating to the exile and trial of Orestes, the burials of Agamemnon and Clytemnestra, and the marriages of Hermione and Electra. And in *Orestes*, Apollo provides detailed forecasts concerning not just Orestes, Electra, and Pylades but Menelaus and Neoptolemus as well (1643–60). This general trend toward greater length and complexity is closely related to a change in the plots themselves. Earlier plays more often end with a death or deaths, thus providing limited scope for a prophecy. At the end of *Hippolytus*, both Phaedra and Hippolytus are dead, and when a sequel continues with the revenge of Artemis, it will involve a new cast of characters. In later plays, the protagonists survive, provoking greater interest in what will happen to Helen or Orestes and their companions in the future.

We also find a change in emphasis from negative to positive forecasts. Only among the earlier plays are the sequels as negative as the death of Jason in *Medea*, the vengeance upon Aphrodite's favorite in *Hippolytus*, and the catalogue of atrocities foretold by Polymestor in *Hecuba*: Hecuba will first be turned into a dog, then fall from the ship's mast and drown, while her daughter Cassandra and Agamemnon himself will both be murdered by Clytemnestra on their return to Argos. Among the later plays a negative forecast may lead to a happy outcome, as when Orestes must suffer exile before being acquitted, and Cadmus must endure metamorphosis and exile before reaching the Land of the Blessed. Or the happy sequel may be largely undiluted: Ion will rule in Athens and will become the eponymous founder of the Ionian race, and not only will Helen and Menelaus return safely to Sparta, but one will become a god and the other will reach the Blessed Isle. This change in emphasis reflects Euripides' general shift from more "tragic" to more "melodramatic" plays, and from endings involving death and burial to those involving return and reintegration.

A more specific and perhaps more revealing change involves the relation among the ending's various forecasts of the future, in both aitia and concluding prophecies. *Medea*, for example, gives a short, ten-line speech which announces that she will bury the children, says that she will establish rites in their honor, reveals that she will join Aegeus in Athens, and foretells the death of Jason (1378–88). The aition looks back, memorializing the children and their death and promising that this terrible end will somehow be redeemed by the rites in Corinth. The prophecy gives a forward glimpse at the future careers of Medea and Jason, confirming Jason's misfortune and his helplessness before Medea. Together, these forecasts provide contrasting perspectives on the action: the children's murder will have its recompense, but Jason will continue to suffer; the positive close contrasts with a negative sequel. The sequel is essential to the lack of equilibrium in the ending. The horrifying act of infanticide is domesticated by the gesture of burial and ritual, even as the prophecy magnifies Medea's awful unaccountability.

In other early endings, there is a similar contrast among allusions to the future. In *Hippolytus*, the rites in Trozen offer a positive recompense for the death of Hippolytus, while the vengeance of Artemis promises a negative sequel to be visited upon a nameless mortal. As in *Medea*, the aition almost succeeds in converting the violence of the plot into the safer and more manageable crises of marriage ritual, but as in *Medea*, violence will return in the future to be visited upon others. In *Children of Heracles*, the antithesis is more complex. Eurystheus acquiesces in his death and reveals that according to an oracle his body buried near Athens will one day save the city; his death and burial restore to the action a positive outcome after Alcmene's surprising demand for revenge. But the future holds yet another reversal in the sequel of a Dorian attack upon Athens—a reversal that will somehow be neutralized by the tomb of Eurystheus. The concluding prophecy anticipates a new story that will repeat the threat against the city and the containment of this threat, postponing closure into the indefinite future.

In other early plays, the prophecy contributes to an antithetical close by contrasting the end of the main plot with the continuation of subplots. In *Andromache*, as we have seen, there is a sharp antithesis between the death and commemoration of Neoptolemus on the one hand and the happy sequels involving Peleus and Andromache on the other. In a more negative vein, *Hecuba* concludes first with Polymestor's announcement of the transformation and death that will be an appropriate end to Hecuba's suffering, and then with his prophecy of new troubles awaiting Agamemnon and Cassandra on their return to Argos. Athena's closing prophecy in *Suppliant Women* is part of a more complex double ending. Following recovery of the bodies of the Seven against Thebes, the goddess ordains elaborate oaths between Athens and Argos to secure and commemorate the conclusion to the action. Athena then describes a sequel involving the sons of the Seven, who are now children:

> When you are men you'll sack the city of Ismenus,
> avenging the murder of your dead fathers. . . .
> No sooner shall the shadow touch your chins
> than you must launch a bronze-clad army of Danaans
> against the seven-mouthed citadel of Thebes.
> Bitter for them shall be your coming, cubs
> raised from lions, sackers of cities.

> πορθήσεθ᾽ ἡβήσαντες Ἰσμηνοῦ πόλιν
> πατέρων θανόντων ἐκδικάζοντες φόνον. . . .
> ἀλλ᾽ οὐ φθάνειν χρὴ συσκιάζοντας γένυν
> καὶ χαλκοπληθῆ Δαναϊδῶν ὁρμᾶν στρατὸν
> ἑπτάστομον πύργωμα Καδμείων ἔπι.
> πικροὶ γὰρ αὐτοῖς ἥξετ᾽ ἐκτεθραμμένοι
> σκύμνοι λεόντων, πόλεος ἐκπορθήτορες.   1214–15, 1219–23

Although the plot is complete, the sequel locates it within the larger cycle involving Argos and Thebes: it was the first expedition that led to the present impasse concerning the bodies of the Seven, and the second expedition will avenge both the earlier defeat and the present maltreatment of the dead. Aition and prophecy offer contrasting reflections upon the plot and its completion. The entire play may in fact be viewed as a meditation on the process of completion and closure: now that the Seven are dead, how should they be treated and remembered? How can social and political institutions organize what has happened into a coherent and exemplary whole?[16] The recovery of the heroes' bodies, the affirmation of panhellenic values in the treatment of the dead, and the closing lamentations all serve to make complete lives that were otherwise simply finished. But the aition qualifies this sense of completeness with a dash of realpolitik: the solidarity between Argives and Athenians cannot last, and an oath inscribed on the Delphic tripod can only postpone a betrayal of their alliance.[17]

The prophecy qualifies the end by offering a longer view: the story of the Seven will be complete only when their sons return and finally take Thebes.

In Euripides' later plays, the concluding allusions to the future tend to be sequential rather than antithetical: Orestes will spend a year in Arcadia before his trial and acquittal in Athens, and Cadmus must endure a bitter exile before he may reach the Land of the Blessed. Instead of the contrast between an aition that looks back and a sequel that looks forward, we find the subordination of one future to another, as hardship continues before the protagonist finally wins success. The pattern is clear not only in *Orestes* and *Bacchant Women*, but also in *Electra* and *Iphigenia among the Taurians*. In *Electra*, we are told that Orestes will be hounded and driven mad by the Furies (1252–53) and will be saved from death by an even vote (1265–66) before he returns to Argos and marries Hermione. In *Iphigenia*, Athena announces that Orestes and his sister must return to Greece, travel to Athens, Halae and Brauron, and make their dedications to Artemis before finding deliverance in this life and ritual commemoration after death. The same pattern is sketched more briefly in *Heracles*, in which Theseus offers the hero refuge in Athens. Although Theseus does not dwell upon the hardships of exile, he reminds us that Heracles, like Orestes, is guilty of a murder that requires his banishment and will remain an outcast until purified in a foreign city (1322). In *Ion*, Athena varies this pattern: she announces that Ion will rule in Athens and will be famous for his descendants, with no mention of preceding hardships. But this promise of easy success is contingent upon the plot to keep Xuthus in the dark (1601–5), ignoring complications that will surely follow when Creusa's son is named heir to the throne. The Dioscuri in *Helen* will admit no such ambiguity, promising an unqualified happy ending that reflects, as we shall see, the unusual melodramatic movement of the plot.

As I have already noted, the fragmentary end of *Bacchant Women* also promises that future hardships will be followed by a happy end. After a substantial lacuna, the god Dionysus concludes his speech by telling Cadmus and Harmonia that they will be turned into snakes, will lead barbarians, sack many cities, plunder Apollo's oracles, and finally reach the Land of the Blessed (1330–39). But this is the bleakest of happy endings. Pentheus is dead. Agave discovers she has murdered her son. And as far as we can tell, the Thebans will be expelled from their city, and Agave and her sisters must go into exile.[18] If Cadmus alone has a happy future, he does not see it that way, concluding to Agave:

> I shall have no end
> of wretched evil; not even when I sail across
> deep-falling Acheron shall I have peace.

> οὐδὲ παύσομαι
> κακῶν ὁ τλήμων οὐδὲ τὸν καταιβάτην
> Ἀχέροντα πλεύσας ἥσυχος γενήσομαι. 1360–62

The sequential ordering of allusions to the future has an effect very different from that of the antithetical relation in earlier plays. In general, the prophecy extends the temporal dimension of the drama, playing out another action and postponing a sense of completeness. In earlier plays, the antithetical forecasts of prophecy and aition qualify or complicate the conclusion of the action. In later plays, the sequential forecasts instead play out the action and repeat the plot on a smaller scale, revisiting all its ups and downs, its complications and reversals.

Time and Continuum

An important effect of the concluding prophecy is therefore to place the action of the drama within a larger continuum. In *Hippolytus*, the sequel is enacted on a different plane, in a world peopled and directed by gods; more often the action and its sequel are parts of the same world, involving the same protagonists, but simply separated in time. *Medea* offers only a glimpse of this larger continuum, briefly suggesting what the future holds for Jason and Medea, while the epilogue to *Orestes* suggests that the events that follow are every bit as complex as the plot itself: Menelaus will remarry, Orestes will spend a year in exile in Arcadia and will then be tried and acquitted in Athens, Hermione and Orestes will marry while Neoptolemus will die at Delphi, Electra will marry Pylades, Orestes will rule in Argos, and Menelaus will rule in Sparta (1635–1661). Euripidean prologues likewise place the action within a continuum that stretches back into the past. Just as events do not end with the end of the play, so they do not begin at its beginning, and a god or mortal usually describes the plot's antecedents in some detail.[19] What brought Medea to Corinth, and why is she in such a rage? How does Ion happen to be in Delphi, and what are the circumstances of his birth? The point is not simply to facilitate our understanding of the plot, but to portray its dependence upon earlier events. The nurse in *Medea* goes all the way back to the Argo, and back even further to the pine tree on Pelion in order to explain the situation in Corinth:

> If only the ship Argo had never flown
> to the land of Colchis through the blue Symplegades;
> and the cut pine tree had never fallen
> in the glades of Pelion, nor given oars to the hands
> of valiant men who for Pelias pursued
> the Golden Fleece. Then my lady Medea
> would not have sailed for the towers of Iolcus,
> struck in her heart with love for Jason;
> nor would she have persuaded the daughters of Pelias
> to kill their father, and now be living here
> in Corinth with her husband and children . . .

> εἴθ᾽ ὤφελ᾽ Ἀργοῦς μὴ διαπτάσθαι σκάφος
> Κόλχων ἐς αἶαν κυανέας Συμπληγάδας,
> μηδ᾽ ἐν νάπαισι Πηλίου πεσεῖν ποτε
> τμηθεῖσα πεύκη, μηδ᾽ ἐρετμῶσαι χέρας
> ἀνδρῶν ἀριστέων οἳ τὸ πάγχρυσον δέρος
> Πελίᾳ μετῆλθον. οὐ γὰρ ἂν δέσποιν᾽ ἐμὴ
> Μήδεια πύργους γῆς ἔπλευσ᾽ Ἰωλκίας
> ἔρωτι θυμὸν ἐκπλαγεῖσ᾽ Ἰάσονος·

οὐδ᾽ ἂν κτανεῖν πείσασα Πελιάδας κόρας
πατέρα κατῴκει τήνδε γῆν Κορινθίαν
ξὺν ἀνδρὶ καὶ τέκνοισιν . . .   1–11

The action of the play may seem to be a single, self-contained crisis, but it is not. It is so dependent upon the past that if the tree had not fallen, if the ship had not flown, all now would be different. In this case, the necessity that apparently connects events within the play also connects them to events in the past and future outside the drama. *Electra* is situated within a more detailed continuum. The Dioscuri at the end describe at length the future exile and hardships of Orestes, and the farmer in the prologue describes the first mustering of ships before the Trojan War, the Greek victory at Troy, Agamemnon's return, and his murder by Clytemnestra and Aegisthus (1–10) before reaching the present situation. This detailed continuum, however, is not governed by a similar necessity. At various points, the farmer tells us, the course of events might have been different:

> As for the boy Orestes and the female child Electra,
> their father's old nurse carried the former off
> when he was about to die at Aegisthus' hand
> and gave him to Strophius to raise in Phocis.
> But Electra remained in her father's house . . .
> and when it happened that Aegisthus, afraid
> that she would secretly bear some nobleman a son,
> decided to kill her, then savage though she is
> her mother saved her from Aegisthus' hand.

> ἄρσενά τ᾽ Ὀρέστην θῆλύ τ᾽ Ἠλέκτρας θάλος,
> τὸν μὲν πατρὸς γεραιὸς ἐκκλέπτει τροφεὺς
> μέλλοντ᾽ Ὀρέστην χερὸς ὑπ᾽ Αἰγίσθου θανεῖν
> Στροφίῳ τ᾽ ἔδωκε Φωκέων ἐς γῆν τρέφειν·
> ἣ δ᾽ ἐν δόμοις ἔμεινεν Ἠλέκτρα πατρός . . .
> ἐπεὶ δὲ καὶ τοῦτ᾽ ἦν φόβου πολλοῦ πλέων,
> μή τῳ λαθραίως τέκνα γενναίῳ τέκοι,
> κτανεῖν σφε βουλεύσαντος ὠμόφρων ὅμως
> μήτηρ νιν ἐξέσωσεν Αἰγίσθου χερός.   15–19, 25–28

The action of the play will render less certain the inevitable murder of Aegisthus and Clytemnestra: Can this reluctant hero and his self-pitying sister find the resolve to do what legend says they will do? And the prologue places the action within an equally uncertain continuum in which Orestes and Electra might have been killed long before reaching this point where revenge is possible.

Together, prologue and epilogue describe a continuum, however certain or uncertain, within which the action takes place. This continuum as it extends into the future is typically described by a god, while the continuum extending into the past is more commonly described by a human character.[20] It is interesting that in a digression on the end of *Medea*, Aristotle allows for the narration of events outside the drama, before and after, and makes special provision for a god to do so, since mortals cannot know the past or future.[21] Such narration, however, by connecting the

plot to events that precede and follow, prevents the action from being complete
or whole in the manner Aristotle prescribes.[22] Whatever we make of this contradiction, Aristotle's notion of a single and self-sufficient action runs directly counter to
Euripides' interest in necessary connections between the plot and earlier and later
events. His impulse is the opposite of Henry James's. Whereas the novelist tries to
shape the continuity of things into the semblance of a single action, Euripides tries
to let a single enactment indicate the infinite continuity of experience. Prologues and
epilogues are both index and instrument of a realistic, antiorganic interest in the flow
of events and the web of relations in which we find ourselves.

As such, Euripides' novel use of narrative prologues and epilogues is part of a
new conception of narrative time. Traditionally, the Greeks conceived of time as a
circle—the cycle of the seasons, the rotation of heavenly bodies, and a regular pattern in events that distinguishes the order of the cosmos from the haphazard events
of everyday life.[23] Philosophers such as Pythagoras took for granted the cyclical nature of time and sought to rationalize it as a "surrounding sphere"—an endeavor parodied by the comic poet Hermippus:[24]

> [Time], you wretch, is round in appearance,
> it travels in a circle with everything inside it,
> and begets us running around the whole world.
> It's called the year, and since it turns, has no end
> and no beginning, and will never stop running,
> spinning its body day in and day out.

Poets and dramatists likewise tended to view events not as part of a linear continuum
unforeseeable in the future and unrecoverable in the past, but as instances of patterns and paradigms that regularly recur. In *Agamemnon*, the end of the Trojan War
is not so much an event that necessarily precedes the general's victorious return as
an archetypal transgression of the bounds between divinely sanctioned retribution
(for the crime of Paris) and the crime of excessive revenge (the sacking of temples
punished by the destruction of the returning fleet). It thus serves as a model for the
issue of just and unjust vengeance that recurs throughout the trilogy. In Euripides'
Andromache, however, past and future are important not as recurring models of the
present situation, but because of their absolute separation in time from the present.
Andromache begins her prologue speech by recalling her splendid marriage to Hector, only to lament that subsequent events betrayed the promise of that beginning.
The past is gone. Thetis in the epilogue consoles Peleus with the promise of immortality for himself and a happy future for Andromache and their descendants; if time
can make void the promises of the past, the future may redeem the sufferings of the
present. But the future is not yet. Time does not bring back a recurrent pattern or
order, but marks an unreversible advance from better to worse, or worse to better. In
short, Euripides' use of prologues and epilogues was not so much a rejection of
Aristotelian unity *avant la lettre* as part of a radical new interest in the temporal succession of events. The playwright (like some of his contemporaries), in a period of
radical change and upheaval, presented a novel portrait of human dependence upon

time, upon a linear continuum in which the fall of a pine tree or the contrition of Clytemnestra may unexpectedly alter all that will follow.

The Shape of the Future

The other surviving tragedians do not seem to have shared Euripides' interest in the temporal continuum. For Aeschylus and Sophocles the action of the drama is relatively self-contained, and there is nothing comparable to Euripides' narrative of subsequent events. The earlier playwrights do, however, glance beyond the end of the play in ways that partially anticipate the concluding prophecy. The *Oresteia*, for example, ends with Athena's prophecy of future happiness for the people of Athens:

> From these fearsome faces
> I see great profit for the people;
> for if these kindly women you always kindly
> hold in great honor, you will always excel
> in the just government
> of your land and your city.

> ἐκ τῶν φοβερῶν τῶνδε προσώπων
> μέγα κέρδος ὁρῶ τοῖσδε πολίταις·
> τάσδε γὰρ εὔφρονας εὔφρονες ἀεὶ
> μέγα τιμῶντες καὶ γῆν καὶ πόλιν
> ὀρθοδίκαιον
> πρέψετε πάντως διάγοντες. *Eumenides* 990–95

It is unusual that Athena's protagonist is a city rather than an individual, but instead of narrating the future growth and development of Athens, its empire and its legal institutions, she offers vague promises of peace and prosperity (903–12). Nor are these promises designed to explain what will follow once the play is over. In her negotiations with the Furies, Athena offers a deal: if the Furies give up their anger, the Athenians will honor them with a shrine and cult, and if the Athenians honor the Furies, they in turn will make the city prosper. This deal is worked out in the final scene of the play, is summarized in Athena's lines (990–95), and is ratified by the answer of the chorus: "farewell, amid the wealth you deserve, / farewell, people of the city . . . Under Athena's wings / the father reveres you" (χαίρετ' ἐν αἰσιμίαισι πλούτου, / χαίρετ', ἀστικὸς λεώς . . . Παλλάδος δ' ὑπὸ πτεροῖς / ὄντας ἄζεται πατήρ 996–1002). Just as the aetiology of the Areopagus is realized within the play by the trial and acquittal of Orestes, so Athena's promise of happiness for the city is fulfilled before the close by the benediction of the Furies. The process of closure is clearly a central problem for Aeschylus in *Eumenides*, but this is so because he wants to bring within the action of the trilogy any possible loose ends. Euripides, however, will draw attention to such loose ends lying outside the scope of the drama. A more specific sequel is described in Aeschylus' *Persians*, in which Darius foretells Xerxes' second defeat at Plataea. This ghost appears, however, not at the end but in the middle of the play and mentions the second battle only to reinforce his moral judgment against his son ("sand dunes of corpses will bear silent witness . . . that mortal thoughts must not aim too high," 818–20); his forecast of the future gives added authority to the condemnation of Xerxes.

The fullest and most extended prophecy of a sequel to the plot occurs in *Prometheus*—again in the middle of the play, and apparently in the first play of a connected trilogy.[25] In response to the entreaties of Io, Prometheus describes in detail her future trials (701–35, 788–815) and those of her descendants the Danaids (844–69), concluding with a brief allusion to his own eventual rescue by a more distant descendant, Heracles (870–74). This prophecy does at least two things: it establishes the privileged knowledge of Prometheus before he confronts Hermes with knowledge dangerous to Zeus,[26] and it anticipates his release by Heracles at some point in the following play of the trilogy. But it does not provide a sequel to the plot since Io has no real part in the action; her sufferings offer an important foil to those of Prometheus, but after we learn of them, she leaves and plays no further part in the play or the trilogy. There was apparently a similar prophetic forecast in the middle of *Prometheus Unbound*, in which Prometheus described at length Heracles' future travels and labors (frs. 195–96 and 198–99 *TrGF*). The two prophecies may have been complementary. Within each play, the sufferings and civilizing exploits of the immobile Prometheus have a thematic parallel in the travels of Io and of Heracles.[27] And outside each play, the prophecies fill out the expanse of time from beginning to end of the trilogy. Many generations passed between the wanderings of Io in *Prometheus Bound* and the arrival of Heracles in *Prometheus Unbound*, and many generations more may well have passed between the time of this play and that of the trilogy's conclusion.[28] We must assume that the trilogy did not literally reenact the thirty thousand years of Prometheus' punishment (fr. 208a *TrGF*), but it certainly embraced a remarkable stretch of time, and the prophecies concerning Io and Heracles allow the brief stage action to suggest something of the vast sweep of time from the chaining of the Titan to the present day. These prophetic narratives are therefore the closest thing to a concluding prophecy in Aeschylus. Yet they remind us not that the action will continue beyond the end of the drama, but that whole cycles of events take place between the episodes we see onstage. And they illustrate not the continual succession of events, but the recurrence of the drama's central themes in other figures such as Io and Heracles. Unfortunately, few plays and only one complete trilogy survive from Aeschylus' production of ninety plays or more. But if our remains are any indication, Aeschylus had no need for concluding prophecies such as those in Euripides, since the connected trilogy allows him to embrace great stretches of time within the action itself.[29]

Sophocles, however, tends to portray a single, self-sufficient action rather than the sweep of time suggested by an Aeschylean trilogy—a crisis that somehow stands outside the course of time. Sophocles thus has no more interest than Aeschylus in describing a sequel, but for different reasons. To Aeschylus there is no sequel since the movement of time is contained within the action. To Sophocles the sequel exists but is irrelevant to the crisis and its resolution, and is acknowledged, if at all, by the subtlest of hints. As the body of Ajax is carried off, for example, there is no indication of anything to follow, unless perhaps we remember the musings of Teucer four hundred lines earlier when he first found his brother's body: What will his father say when he learns the news? Will the peevish man blame Teucer for his brother's death, and perhaps even banish him from Salamis (*Ajax* 1017–20)? This earlier hint at events to follow, Telamon's unfair accusation against his son, reconciles the action of this play with the sequel that may have been dramatized in Sophocles' *Teucer*;[30] but there is no suggestion that the close of the play with burial honors for Ajax is not really the end of the story. The report of the hero's death at the end of *Oedipus at Colonus* likewise offers no suggestion of a sequel to follow. In Oedipus' earlier exchange with Polyneices, there are allusions to later events at Thebes familiar from Sophocles' *Antigone*, but these take the form of the old man's curse against his sons ("Never will you seize that city; sooner you will fall stained with blood, and your brother also," οὐ γὰρ ἔσθ' ὅπως πόλιν / κείνην ἐρείψεις, ἀλλὰ πρόσθεν αἵματι / πεσῇ μιανθεὶς χὠ ξύναιμος ἐξ ἴσου, 1372–74) and a brother's last farewell to his sisters:

> If father's curses are fulfilled,
> and if you make your way back home,
> then by the gods do not dishonor me
> but give me a tomb and rites of burial.
>
> μή τοί με πρὸς θεῶν σφώ γ', ἐὰν αἱ τοῦδ' ἀραὶ
> πατρὸς τελῶνται καί τις ὑμῖν ἐς δόμους
> νόστος γένηται, μή μ' ἀτιμάσητέ γε,
> ἀλλ' ἐν τάφοισι θέσθε κἂν κτερίσμασιν.   1407–10

This earlier gesture toward the plot of *Antigone*, however, does nothing to alter our impression that the end of this play is really the end.

In these plays and others, there are hints of the later legendary cycle,[31] but only in *Philoctetes* do we find a concluding prophecy of events that follow the end.[32] The play closes with the entrance of Heracles ex machina, commanding Philoctetes and Neoptolemus to return to Troy, and revealing that Philoctetes will be cured, will kill Paris, and together with Neoptolemus will sack Troy (1423–40). Heracles thus makes it clear that the goal of Odysseus, and the end anticipated by the audience, will finally be realized. The deus also alludes to a sequel of Greek impiety and divine retribution:

> For the city must be sacked a second time
> with my bow. But remember, when you
> destroy the land, to honor what is the gods'
> since Father Zeus considers everything else
> secondary.
>
> τὸ δεύτερον γὰρ τοῖς ἐμοῖς αὐτὴν χρεὼν
> τόξοις ἁλῶναι. τοῦτο δ' ἐννοεῖθ', ὅταν
> πορθῆτε γαῖαν, εὐσεβεῖν τὰ πρὸς θεούς·
> ὡς τἄλλα πάντα δεύτερ' ἡγεῖται πατὴρ
> Ζεύς.   1439–43

Heracles looks beyond Odysseus' immediate goal of sacking Troy to subsequent events such as the rape of Cassandra by the lesser Ajax and the murder of Priam by

Neoptolemus, as well as the divine punishment that will follow these deeds: the Greek fleet will be destroyed on its return and Neoptolemus will be murdered at Delphi. Sophocles thus borrows from Euripides a closing gesture that acknowledges the plot is part of a larger continuum, yet he does so in a way that draws the sequel into the plot. In Euripides, the prophecy inaugurates a new plot or plots: now that Hippolytus is dead, Artemis will find a way to take revenge; now that Orestes and Iphigenia have escaped from Thoas, they must find their way back to Greece, be purified of matricide, and establish shrines in Attica. In *Philoctetes*, the sequel completes the plot: the action has had a single goal, bringing Philoctetes and his bow to Troy, and thus ensuring that the city will be taken; Heracles' announcement of the future simply confirms that—with some delay—this end will be reached. And the allusion to impiety at Troy only hints at other stories that might be told (perhaps in Sophocles' own *Aias Lokros*), just as *Ajax* and *Oedipus at Colonus* hint at other stories.[33]

Neither Aeschylus nor Sophocles offers a clear precedent for Euripides' use of the prophetic sequel. The closest parallel in Aeschylus would seem to be the prophecies of Prometheus that fill out the time between plays of the trilogy, while Sophocles, even in *Philoctetes*, treats the action as essentially complete, offering only a hint of what may follow. A more distant precedent, noted in chapter 3, is Teiresias' prophecy of the future wanderings of Odysseus. I conclude with a sampling of critical models that may help to describe Euripides' peculiar postscripts.

The concluding prophecy creates problems for any interpretation that assumes the action is or should be complete. Those who regard the action of the drama as essentially complete tend to see the prophecy as an interesting but unnecessary appendage, one that gratifies the poet's own interest in the future, as A. S. Owen suggests,[34] or gratifies a comparable interest among the spectators. As Paul Decharme puts it, Euripides seeks "to satisfy his spectators' curiosity as fully and completely as possible by letting them follow the fortunes of the characters in whom they had been interested beyond the limits of the drama and into the most distant future."[35] At the price of minimizing the importance of the prophecy, this approach accounts for its distribution among the surviving plays: Euripides was often but not always interested in giving such tweaks of pleasure to his viewers, and he catered to them more fully in his later plays.

More common is the opposite view that the action as it stands is incomplete and that the epilogue reintegrates drama and myth, endowing the play with a fullness of meaning that it otherwise lacks. G. M. A. Grube argues that the epilogue "seems to raise the drama beyond the individual circumstances . . . it becomes a part of the universal experience of mankind,"[36] while H. D. F. Kitto takes a more aesthetic tack, finding a belated unity in the tying up of loose ends: "When the futures of Peleus, Andromache and Molossus are arranged for, when in fact the victims of this human accident are made comfortable, then the play can end."[37] Both attach a less trivial meaning to the concluding prophecy, but do so by implying that incompleteness in the drama must be corrected by invoking the mythic sequel. Wieland Schmidt offers a more sophisticated model in which the poet exploits and exposes the discrepancies between dramatic action and legendary background: it is *because* Euripides' plays are complete—on their own humane and realistic terms—that they are no longer comfortable within a traditional legendary framework, and the epilogue "is a direct result of the tension between dramatic and mythical reality, between the factual dictates of legend and his own free artistic arrangement."[38] The postscript, in other words, is a castoff, a shell of tradition that no longer fits our romantically original poet.

But as we have seen, the sequel is often a coda, repeating the dramatic action on a smaller scale; the point is not (it would seem) that events to follow are less real or authentic, but simply that some are dramatized and others are not. If the poet draws attention to the contrast between inside and out, the effect has less to do with the validity of myth than it does with drama's ability, or inability, to draw Henry James's circle in which relations appear to stop. Life is essentially continuous, and if in our hopes and in our fictions, we provide it with consoling or reassuring ends, we nevertheless know that these are not really the end. As Gerhart Hauptmann observes:

> True drama is by its nature endless. It is a continuous, internal struggle with no resolution, and the moment this struggle lapses, the drama ceases. But since we are forced to give every play a resolution, every drama performed has something fundamentally pedantic and conventional about it that life does not. Life knows only the continuous struggle—or it stops being life at all.[39]

We might conclude, in other words, that the Euripidean epilogue is anti-Aristotelian, showing that there is no ending followed by nothing else, showing that the infinite continuum of temporal experience cannot be contained in a single dramatic action. But this brings us back to another false contrast between the unordered or unshapeable events of "real" life and the apparent coherence imposed upon them by art. As Hauptmann reminds us, the sequel left over at the end is pedantic and conventional; this is not the raw stuff of real life, but a predictable story narrated by the author or the deus. One result may be to confuse the inside and the outside, implicating the viewer more deeply in the prison house of drama. But another is to multiply the drama's authoritative guises. At the end, the play is equally a public reenactment of legend, an original dramatic staging, and a privileged narration of the sequel. In juxtaposing these various forms of authority, and in questioning how and where the drama ends, Euripides invites us to reconsider both the nature of tragic performance and the authority vested in it.

II

The End Refigured

System and finality are pretty much one and the same.
KIERKEGAARD

6

Repetition: *Hippolytus*

If Henry James suggests that every novel should try to fashion a finite whole from
the seamless web of human relations, Gerhart Hauptmann argues instead that every
performance, despite its finite scope, should try to repeat the endless struggle of life.
Because this is impossible, because drama's subject knows no beginning or end, every
play has something conventional or pedantic about its conclusion. Obviously, this is
not quite true. First, not every ending is conventional or pedantic, and certain
authors, genres, and periods are more fond than others of such endings, and in particular of an overt display of conventionality. It is this that distinguishes Euripides
from Aeschylus and Sophocles, and to a lesser extent the later from the earlier plays
of Euripides. And second, these pedantic gestures need not reflect only a striving for
realism that is doomed by the limitations of dramatic art. In Euripides, at least, such
gestures betray a broader and more complex interest in problems of performance,
authority, historical truth, and temporal succession. To pursue these problems more
fully will take us from ways in which tragedy ends to the reinvention of drama—and
the end of tragedy.

I begin by turning from closing gestures to structural tropes, from what we might
call the vocabulary of Euripidean endings to revisions of the ending itself. In three
different plays, the familiar markers of the end have been radically altered or displaced by repetition, reversal, or erasure. The result is not just to deploy closing gestures in striking and unusual ways, but to reexamine the nature of dramatic coherence. If the ending is not at the end—if somehow we end where we began, or we
begin at the end, or the end fails to materialize—then in some fundamental way we
must reconsider how the play works and must entertain new notions of what drama
is and how it does (or does not) organize experience.

Beginning at the End

I begin with a play that would not seem to belong in this company. *Hippolytus* is
generally considered unusually well-constructed, leading to a very effective and tragic

conclusion. The hypothesis, for example, tells us that this play is one of the best (τὸ δὲ δρᾶμα τῶν πρώτων); G. M. A. Grube says that its structure "is quite unusually excellent; every part of it, prologos, choral odes and exodos, blend into an almost perfect unity";[1] and Ann Michelini describes the play as an aberration in which Euripides adopts the Sophoclean norm that he elsewhere strives to subvert.[2] The formal perfection of *Hippolytus* seems to be confirmed, if not guaranteed, by its symmetry. Prologue and epilogue balance one another, framing the action between two epiphanies, between the yin of Aphrodite and the yang of the virgin Artemis. As Bernard Knox points out, if these two goddesses are temperamental opposites, the language they use is similar and their effects upon human affairs are "exactly alike."[3] Margarete Bieber even suggests that the staging was balanced and symmetrical. In her reconstruction, there was a projection, or paraskenion, at either end of the skene-building, one on the left representing a shrine of Artemis and one on the right representing a shrine of Aphrodite, thus allowing the play to begin and end with mirror epiphanies in which the goddesses descend from the machine onto identical façades.[4] The resulting impression of organic unity and tragic closure is reinforced, as we have seen, by the particular form of the play's closing gestures: this is the only surviving play that ends with the death of its protagonist,[5] it is the only one that ends with an extended explanation of what has happened, and we might add that it ends with the clearest aetiological connection between the outcome of the plot and its later commemoration. But if we look more closely, we shall find that this impression is misleading. This play is not more complete than others; it is *overly* complete and *doubly* finished.

Hippolytus begins at the end. As the play gets under way, it seems that the action is already finished, and the hero of the drama is as good as dead. In her prologue speech, Aphrodite begins by reminding us that gods require mortals to honor them and by vowing that she will make an example of Hippolytus' arrogant neglect of her (1–20). She goes on to say that on this very day she will punish him for his crimes (ἃ δ᾽ εἰς ἔμ᾽ ἡμάρτηκε τιμωρήσομαι / Ἱππόλυτον ἐν τῇδ᾽ ἡμέρᾳ, 21–22) and proclaims that her vengeance is almost complete (οὐ πόνου πολλοῦ με δεῖ, 23). She foretells the manner of his death, struck down by his father's curses (43–46), and as she leaves the stage, she announces, with her very last words, that Hippolytus "doesn't know that the gates of Hades are open, and that this is the last light he will see" (οὐ γὰρ οἶδ᾽ ἀνεῳγμένας πύλας / Ἅιδου, φάος δὲ λοίσθιον βλέπων τόδε, 56–57). As the play begins, he is about to pay the penalty, poised on the threshold of death—and this is exactly where we find him at the end. The messenger who enters near the close of the play declares, "Hippolytus is no more, or virtually so; hanging in the balance he sees the light" (Ἱππόλυτος οὐκέτ᾽ ἔστιν, ὡς εἰπεῖν ἔπος·/ δέδορκε μέντοι φῶς ἐπὶ σμικρᾶς ῥοπῆς, 1162–63). And shortly before his death, the hero gives satisfaction to Aphrodite and proclaims, "I am finished, and now I see the gates of the dead" (ὄλωλα καὶ δὴ νερτέρων ὁρῶ πύλας, 1447).

This doubling, or repetition of the end, is reinforced by striking verbal echoes (φάος δὲ λοίσθιον βλέπων and δέδορκε . . . φῶς ἐπὶ σμικρᾶς ῥοπῆς; ἀνεῳγμένας πύλας Ἅιδου and νερτέρων ὁρῶ πύλας) and by a doubling of the gestures of closure. *Hippolytus*, alone among all the surviving plays of Euripides, begins and ends with an aetiology. In the prologue, Aphrodite leads up to the present situation—the pathological love of Phaedra for her stepson—by telling how Phaedra fell in love with Hippolytus when he came to Athens to celebrate the mysteries (24–28) and how she commemorated her love for him by establishing a shrine to Aphrodite:[6]

> Before coming here to the land of Trozen,
> beside the rock of Pallas, this land's
> lookout, she set up a shrine of Aphrodite
> in her foreign passion; and she named the goddess
> as established hereafter in honor of Hippolytus.

> καὶ πρὶν μὲν ἐλθεῖν τήνδε γῆν Τροζηνίαν,
> πέτραν παρ᾽ αὐτὴν Παλλάδος, κατόψιον
> γῆς τῆσδε, ναὸν Κύπριδος ἐγκαθείσατο,
> ἐρῶσ᾽ ἔρωτ᾽ ἔκδημον, Ἱππολύτῳ δ᾽ ἔπι
> τὸ λοιπὸν ὠνόμαζεν ἱδρῦσθαι θεάν.   29–33

The presence of an aetiology in the prologue is so anomalous that some editors have suspected interpolation.[7] But the anomaly is compounded. Not only do we have a closing device in the prologue, but we have one that promises future commemoration of the protagonist's death. On the Athenian acropolis, as at Trozen, a shrine of Aphrodite and a tomb, or *heroön*, of Hippolytus were closely associated with one another, and the epithet that Phaedra uses to record her love (Ἱππολύτῳ δ᾽ ἔπι, "in honor of Hippolytus" 32) alludes to the Athenian shrine of Ἀφροδίτη ἐφ᾽ Ἱππολύτῳ established "in honor of [the deceased] Hippolytus."[8] The play begins not only with a hero on the threshold of death, but with a shrine where in future ages Athenians will honor and remember this death.

This premature ending is administered by the premature entrance of a deus ex machina. The prologue is generally delivered by a human character who enters to describe the situation, review the past, and generate interest in the action that follows.[9] There are, of course, several gods and supernatural figures who deliver the prologue, but in two cases, a pair of gods engage in dialogue (Apollo and Death in *Alcestis*, Poseidon and Athena in *Trojan Women*); in two cases, a single god enters in the guise of a servant (Hermes as λάτρις in *Ion*) or a mortal (Dionysus as Stranger in *Bacchant Women*); and in one case, the prologue is spoken by a ghost (Polydorus in *Hecuba*). In *Hippolytus*, by contrast, Aphrodite enters as a deus, proclaiming at once her identity and divine authority (1–2), asserting her prerogative to reward and punish mortals (5–6), reminding the viewer of her active intervention in human affairs (21, 28, 42, 48), and delivering both an aetiology (29–33) and a detailed prophecy of events to come.[10] We have already noted that the prologue aetiology is unique, and so too is this prologue prophecy.

Typically, the prologue is spoken by a human character, whose fears or forebodings arouse suspense: what terrible vengeance will Medea take? the nurse asks herself (*Medea* 36–45), and how can Heracles possibly return to rescue his family? Megara asks Amphitryon (*Heracles* 73–81).[11] A god in the prologue can tease the viewer with partial hints of what is to come: Dionysus says he will make himself known at Thebes, but does not explain how (*Bacchant Women* 39–42),[12] Hermes says (correctly) that Ion will be presented as Xuthus' son, and (falsely) that Apollo's rape will remain hidden (*Ion* 69–73), and Apollo warns that Heracles will save Alcestis, while Death contradicts him (*Alcestis* 64–76).[13] *Trojan Women*, as we shall see, is unusual in that Athena and Poseidon arrange the destruction of the Greek fleet sometime *after* the conclusion of the drama (78–91). But nowhere else in Euripides' surviving plays does the prologue give a detailed forecast of events to come: Aphrodite reports that Hippolytus and Phaedra will both die, Phaedra in a relatively noble manner (εὐκλεής 47) and Hippolytus killed by the curse of his father Theseus (*Hippolytus* 43–48). This opening prophecy, like the opening aition, helps to mark the difference between this play and Euripides' first *Hippolytus*.[14] But it also reminds us that we are beginning at the end: Aphrodite has intervened and all that follows will simply play out the sequel she has foretold. Finally, where the deus is usually greeted with a gesture of acknowledgement and acceptance, the speech of Aphrodite is answered instead by the entrance of Hippolytus, singing the praises of Artemis (58–60), yet the scene ends with a belated speech of acknowledgement from the servant, whose protest against excessive punishment ("pretend not to hear him: gods should be wiser than men," μὴ δόκει τούτου κλύειν· / σοφωτέρους γὰρ χρὴ βροτῶν εἶναι θεούς 119–20) seems directed to a deus whose intervention is already complete. In *Ion*, one intermediary of Apollo (Hermes) is replaced at the end by another (Athena), and in *Bacchant Women*, the god's entrance in disguise is answered at the end by his terrifying epiphany. But when Aphrodite leaves the stage at the beginning of *Hippolytus*, she is making her final exit, having finished everything she came to do.[15]

This impression that the play begins at an end is reinforced by a series of close correspondences between prologue and epilogue. As we have seen, the play begins and ends with the death of Hippolytus, and with verbal echoes reinforcing this similarity. It also begins and ends with the gestures of deus ex machina, aition, and concluding prophecy, and each of these involves further similarities. We have already noted that both aetiologies refer to a tomb and hero shrine of Hippolytus, but the parallels involve Aphrodite as well. In the prologue, Phaedra's love for Hippolytus is commemorated with a shrine of Aphrodite that looks toward Trozen ("a lookout of this land," κατόψιον / γῆς τῆσδε, 30–31), while the epilogue alludes to a shrine of Aphrodite the Spy (Κατασκοπίας) where the love-smitten Phaedra used to watch Hippolytus at his exercises.[16] In her opening prophecy, Aphrodite promises to punish Artemis' favorite Hippolytus (ἃ δ' εἰς ἔμ' ἡμάρτηκε τιμωρήσομαι, 21) just as Artemis in the epilogue promises to punish the favorite of Aphrodite (τόξοις ἀφύκτοις τοῖσδε τιμωρήσομαι, 1422), repeating the vow of vengeance in the same line-end position. The god's presence in the prologue is ignored by Hippolytus and is only acknowledged belatedly by the servant (114–20), just as Artemis' entrance at the end is not formally acknowledged until the dying Hippolytus is brought onstage more than a hundred lines later (ἔα· / ὦ θεῖον ὀσμῆς πνεῦμα· καὶ γὰρ ἐν κακοῖς / ὢν ᾐσθόμην σου κἀνεκουφίσθην δέμας. / ἔστ' ἐν τόποισι τοισίδ' Ἄρτεμις θεά, 1391–93). And just as Aphrodite in the prologue withdraws at the approach of Hippolytus, who is about to die (56–57), and leaves events to play themselves out, Artemis in the ending makes an identical gesture, withdrawing from the scene as the hero is about to die (1437–39), and allowing Hippolytus and Theseus to play out their grief and sympathy. This early departure of the deus is unique in Greek tragedy and reinforces the many similarities between prologue and epilogue, which create the disconcerting impression that the play begins at the end.

This premature sense of finality is heightened throughout the first half of the play. Aphrodite concludes her opening speech with the cold pronouncement that Hippolytus stands at the gates of death (56–57), and the servant ends the scene with an ironic comment upon the finality of her decision, asking the goddess to show forgiveness since gods should be wiser than mortals (117–20). In the next episode, the nurse finally discovers the cause of Phaedra's distress and concludes, "Cypris is no god after all, but some creature greater than a god, who has destroyed Phaedra, and me, and the whole house," Κύπρις οὐκ ἄρ᾽ ἦν θεός, / ἀλλ᾽ εἴ τι μεῖζον ἄλλο γίγνεται θεοῦ, / ἢ τήνδε κἀμὲ καὶ δόμους ἀπώλεσεν (359–61). The servant ironically, and the nurse directly, both acknowledge that Aphrodite's destructive scheme is already complete. The next two episodes likewise end, first with an ode on the destructive power of Aphrodite and Eros, "who destroys mortals and hurls them through all misfortune when he comes," πέρθοντα καὶ διὰ πάσας ἱέντα συμφορᾶς / θνατοὺς ὅταν ἔλθῃ (542–44), and then with Phaedra's recognition that the goddess has had her way: "departing life today, I shall give pleasure to Cypris who destroys me," ἐγὼ δὲ Κύπριν, ἥπερ ἐξόλλυσί με, / ψυχῆς ἀπαλλαχθεῖσα τῇδ᾽ ἐν ἡμέρᾳ / τέρψω (725–27). As the action of the drama gets underway, we are constantly reminded that it is already finished.

Ending at a Beginning

The formal symmetry of *Hippolytus* works both ways. If the prologue takes on the qualities of an ending, the epilogue is in some ways a beginning. This is clearest in the premature departure of the goddess. As previously noted, Aphrodite departs at the approach of the dying Hippolytus, leaving events she has set in motion to play themselves out in the course of the play. And in the epilogue, Artemis avoids association with death by leaving before the young man dies. This premature exit of the *deus* is unparalleled in Greek tragedy, handing over the stage to Theseus, Hippolytus, and the chorus for a brief closing scene (1440–66) of purely human pathos and human forgiveness. As Hippolytus remarks, it is easy for the goddess to leave behind a long friendship (μακρὰν δὲ λείπεις ῥᾳδίως ὁμιλίαν, 1441), but as the chorus says, mortals must struggle on, somehow finding the courage to forgive and the strength to endure their sufferings (πολλῶν δακρύων ἔσται πίτυλος, 1464). With his last words Theseus remembers Aphrodite, the speaker of the prologue (ὡς πολλά, Κύπρι, σῶν κακῶν μεμνήσομαι, 1461), and now, as then, the goddess's departure from the scene marks a new beginning to the action.

This shift of focus to the mortal sequel is accompanied by a certain ambivalence in the play's closing gestures. In *Hippolytus*, these gestures are more emphatically closed than in any other Euripidean drama—yet succeed in somehow remaining open. If every tragedy ends with a death, then Hippolytus is surely Euripides' most tragic play since it is the only one that ends with the death of its protagonist. Medea's children are dead at the end, but Medea herself is most emphatically alive. Neoptolemus' body is brought onstage, but Andromache is alive and will take her son to Molossia.

And Hecuba will die, but in a future foretold by Polymestor, while most other protagonists look forward to future adventures.[17] The only parallel is Pentheus in *Bacchant Women*, who dies at least 400 lines before the end of the play, ceding the stage
to Cadmus and Agave. The action of *Hippolytus*, in other words, focuses in an
exceptional way upon the hero's tragic end. But here there is a more perplexing parallel between prologue and epilogue. When Aphrodite withdrew, she announced that
Hippolytus was virtually dead, standing before the gates of Hades and looking
his last upon the light (56–57). When Artemis departs, the situation is the same:
Hippolytus is almost dead and sees the gates of death before him (1447). So when
does he die? Where is the climactic stroke that will distinguish the end from the
beginning, that will make it clear that the hero does not linger on into yet another
story or another drama? Strangely enough, the end is not marked.

   Hippolytus is about to die when Artemis leaves in order to avoid being polluted
by his death: "Goodbye. It is not right for me to see or defile my eyes with mortal
death; I can see you are near this evil" (1437–39). Hippolytus bids her farewell and
asks his father to lay out his corpse for burial (λαβοῦ πάτερ μου καὶ κατόρθωσον
δέμας, 1445), and then Hippolytus announces that he is finished and can see death's
door (1447). After several lines of dialogue, he again bids farewell to his father (ὦ
χαῖρε καὶ σύ, χαῖρε πολλά μοι, πάτερ, 1453), and after another brief exchange, repeats that he is finished and asks Theseus to cover his body (ὄλωλα γάρ, πάτερ. /
κρύψον δέ μου πρόσωπον ὡς τάχος πέπλοις, 1457–58). Theseus then exclaims "O
famous bounds of Athens and Pallas, what a man you will have lost!" (1459–60),
and the chorus departs, remarking that this pain is shared by all the citizens (1462–
63) and looking forward to a sea of tears (πολλῶν δακρύων ἔσται πίτυλος, 1464).
There is no mention of Hippolytus' death. We may assume that his body is carried
out at the end, but we are never told this. And there is no mention of any preparations for the burial or funeral of the hero. Of course, in staging there must have been
a significant silence and a significant gesture: between lines 1458 and 1459 (we can
infer) the last words of Hippolytus are followed by silence, and slowly, without a
word, Theseus covers the dead man's face. Yet all the more surprising that neither
he nor the chorus acknowledge his death. Instead, Theseus speaks of a future loss:
"what a man you will have lost" (οἵου στερήσεσθ᾿ ἀνδρός, 1460), and the chorus
speaks of future grief: "many tears will fall like oars" (πολλῶν δακρύων ἔσται
πίτυλος, 1464); the chorus places in the past not the prince's death but an undefined
suffering: "for all the citizens in common this suffering came unexpectedly" (κοινὸν
τόδ᾿ ἄχος πᾶσι πολίταις / ἦλθεν ἀέλπτως, 1462–63).

   The problem of locating Hippolytus' death is not just a verbal quibble, nor a ten-
dentious illustration of the slipperiness of language. In his tour of the famous sanctuary of Hippolytus in Trozen, Pausanias mentions a statue of the hero, a priest of
Hippolytus, various sacrifices, and continues: "they [the Trozenians] won't have him
dragged to death by his horses and they do not show his grave, even though they
know it. Instead they believe that what is called the Charioteer in the sky is in fact
Hippolytus, who receives this honor from the gods" (2.32.1). Pausanias is skeptical
of this catasterism, but it had long been told that Hippolytus did not die—or rather
that he was brought back to life by Asclepius.[18] And when Pausanias stubbornly identifies the site of Hippolytus' burial, he also notes the (apparent) presence of Asclepius:

"[near the shrine of Aphrodite the Spy and the myrtle tree] is the grave of Phaedra, not far from the tomb of Hippolytus, and this [the tomb of Hippolytus] is a mound near the myrtle. The statue of Asclepius was made by Timotheus, but the Trozenians say it is not Asclepius but an image of Hippolytus" (2.32.4). Did Hippolytus die or not? Perhaps he died and was restored by Asclepius. If so, did death claim him again at a later date? Or did he never die, as the locals in Pausanias believe, made immortal as a constellation by the gods? So in one respect the uncertainty surrounding the hero's death is negative: the absence of a definitive end leaves him lingering—just as he did in the prologue—on the threshold of death. Yet in another respect this uncertainty is more constructive: it leaves room for the possibility that Hippolytus does not die, that he is in fact ready to make a new beginning as a mortal saved from death, or as a constellation, or as a god, or even with a new identity as Virbius.[19]

This elision of the hero's death is assisted by the honors recently promised by Artemis; she makes no mention of death or burial and makes no allusion to the famous tomb in Trozen:[20]

> You who have suffered so much, I will give you
> for your sufferings great honor in the city
> of Trozen: unmarried girls before they wed
> will cut their hair for you, harvesting
> throughout long time a great sorrow of tears.
> You will always be musically remembered
> by virgins, and Phaedra's love for you
> will never fall silent or nameless.

> σοὶ δ᾽, ὦ ταλαίπωρ᾽, ἀντὶ τῶνδε τῶν κακῶν
> τιμὰς μεγίστας ἐν πόλει Τροζηνίᾳ
> δώσω· κόραι γὰρ ἄζυγες γάμων πάρος
> κόμας κεροῦνταί σοι, δι᾽ αἰῶνος μακροῦ
> πένθη μέγιστα δακρύων καρπούμεναι·
> ἀεὶ δὲ μουσοποιὸς ἐς σὲ παρθένων
> ἔσται μέριμνα, κοὐκ ἀνώνυμος πεσὼν
> ἔρως ὁ Φαίδρας ἐς σὲ σιγηθήσεται.   1423–30

Artemis promises the living and suffering hero that his sufferings will not be forgotten, but neither here nor in the action that follows is the hero's death clearly acknowledged.

This brings us to another ambivalent gesture. In many respects, this aition is an exceptionally effective closing device: the hero dies at the end of the play, and a god proclaims that his tragic death will be commemorated in rituals performed at Trozen. We have already seen that only in *Hippolytus* does the protagonist die in the course of the play; and only here does the contemporary vestige directly commemorate the action. Later aitia tend to offer only a verbal relic: Orestes survives in the name of the town Oresteion, Helen in the name of the island Helene, adventures in the Crimea survive in the epithet Tauropolos, and so on. Many aitia, as we have noted, remember an event not in the action itself, but in its sequel: the exile of Orestes, the transformation of Hecuba, or the treaty between Argives and Athenians. And many are factitious to a greater or lesser degree: a new place of burial for Eurystheus, an unusual cenotaph for the Seven against Thebes, or an amalgam of fact, fantasy, and literary revision at Halae and Brauron. Only in *Hippolytus* does the aition describe a familiar contemporary institution that directly honors the events of the play.

Lest it seem that I exaggerate the exceptional nature of the aition in *Hippolytus*, I offer a brief digression on *Medea*, which also concludes with a promise of rites in honor of the dead, in this case the murdered children. The children are not protagonists, but at least there is a direct connection between a climactic event of the play and rites performed in Corinth. When Jason pleads with Medea to let him bury the children, she answers:

> No! I shall bury them with this hand,
> taking them to Hera Akraia's shrine
> lest one of their enemies dishonor them,
> tearing up their tombs; and in the land of Sisyphus
> I shall establish for the future a holy
> festival and rites for this impious murder.

> οὐ δῆτ', ἐπεί σφας τῇδ' ἐγὼ θάψω χερί,
> φέρουσ' ἐς Ἥρας τέμενος Ἀκραίας θεοῦ,
> ὡς μή τις αὐτοὺς πολεμίων καθυβρίσῃ
> τυμβοὺς ἀνασπῶν· γῇ δὲ τῇδε Σισύφου
> σεμνὴν ἑορτὴν καὶ τέλη προσάψομεν
> τὸ λοιπὸν ἀντὶ τοῦδε δυσσεβοῦς φόνου.   1378–83

The murder of the children in the course of the play will be commemorated in two ways: by their burial at the shrine of Hera Akraia and by rites performed in their honor in Corinth, the land of Sisyphus. Can we assume that this tomb and these rites were familiar to the audience, as the tomb and rites of Hippolytus at Trozen surely were? Yes and no. Although the close proximity of Trozen to Athens, and the close connection of Hippolytus with Athenian legend, would make the hero's commemoration more familiar, some account of the burial and honors for Medea's children in Corinth was well established. The problem is that there is no evidence for these as described by Euripides. Our sources for the story of the children's death are mostly late and often contradictory,[21] but the most prevalent account, and the one that most resembles Euripides' version, differs from him in important details. According to Parmeniscus, Creophylus, and other sources, Medea's children were killed not by their mother but by the people of Corinth, who wanted to hurt or punish Medea.[22] The children had sought refuge at the temple of Hera Akraia (in Perachora) and were murdered in her sanctuary. To atone for this sacrilege, Apollo ordered the Corinthians to establish rites in their honor. We cannot prove that Euripides knew this fuller and more widespread account, but his own aetiology suggests that he did. When Medea tells Jason she will bury the children herself, she gives as her reason, "lest one of their enemies dishonor them," ὡς μή τις αὐτοὺς πολεμίων καθυβρίσῃ (1380); this remark makes no sense in this play, in which their only enemy is Medea, but it makes complete sense in the story of their murder by the Corinthians. Again, Medea says she will establish rites "for this impious murder," ἀντὶ τοῦδε δυσσεβοῦς φόνου (1383)—a motive that does not ring true for Euripides' unrepentant Medea, but is entirely appropriate to Corinthians chastised and punished by the oracle. These inconsistencies could easily have been avoided, but they were not. Instead, the Medea who dramatically murdered her children promises to protect them from their enemies at the temple, and the Medea who performed the hideous act of matricide prescribes atonement for their impious murder. The inconsistencies draw attention to Euripides' rewriting of Corinthian practice in particular, and of Medea's story in general. The death of secondary characters is honored in a way that seems to clash with viewers' knowledge of contemporary institutions, thus underscoring the poet's innovations.[23]

Hippolytus is different: the epilogue refers to rites established in honor of the play's central figure, and it does so without contradicting common knowledge of those rites. Yet given the exceptional nature of this aition, it remains to acknowledge its failings.[24] After all, if the aition commemorates the hero's death, it does so only by implication. As we noted, the play itself makes no direct mention of the death of Hippolytus. The aetiology likewise makes no mention of the hero's tomb in Trozen, nor does it refer to his death or burial. Instead it describes a custom associated with wedding ritual; as Pausanias reports, "each virgin cuts off a lock for him [Hippolytus] before marriage and after cutting, takes it to the temple as an offering" (2.32.1). The ritual connections between marriage and death are widespread and important,[25] both marking an important point of transition and using similar ritual gestures to confirm a successful passage from one stage to the next. But at least as Artemis describes it, the ritual of the virgins is as incomplete as the death it commemorates. The young women of Trozen are frozen in lamentation, harvesting tears "throughout long time," preserving forever a musical memory of Hippolytus in their capacity as *parthenoi* (ἀεὶ δὲ μουσοποιὸς ἐς σὲ παρθένων / ἔσται μέριμνα, *Hippolytus* 1428–29)—that is, as women who have not made the transition to married status. The hero who seems to linger forever on the threshold of death is commemorated by an endless succession of lamenting women, lingering forever on the threshold of marriage.

Perhaps this absence of ritual closure would be less troubling if we knew what they were singing, if we could hear their "muse-making concern" (μουσοποιὸς . . . μέριμνα). Are they singing about Hippolytus' suffering and death in what some have taken as an aetiology for Euripides' play?[26] Apparently not. What the virgins keep alive is not memory of the hero's death, but the passion of Phaedra: "and Phaedra's love for you will never fall silent or nameless," (κοὐκ ἀνώνυμος πεσὼν / ἔρως ὁ Φαίδρας ἐς σὲ σιγηθήσεται, 1429–30). The aition that ostensibly commemorates the death of the protagonist is not concerned with him after all. What lives on from the drama, what survives and is given a name (κοὐκ ἀνώνυμος, in a variation of the familiar formula) is the story of his antagonist. The substitution of Phaedra's love for Hippolytus' death prevents the honors in Trozen from pointing to the play's ostensible end. But it also suggests more actively the open or unresolved nature of the drama and the issues it raises.

First, in the plot of *Hippolytus*, Phaedra's love is not an end but the means to an end. Her passion is the instrument Aphrodite will use to punish Hippolytus, and her death is less important than the goddess's demand for revenge and satisfaction (47–50). It is Phaedra's tragedy that however nobly she deals with her affliction (εὐκλεὴς μὲν ἀλλ' ὅμως, 47), she must die to further Aphrodite's goals. Yet the aition undermines this logic. What survives from the action, what lives on into the present day, is not the goal announced in the prologue and apparently fulfilled in the epilogue, but a prior means to that end. Incompleteness is immortalized; the in-between lasts forever.

Second, in the symbolic structure of *Hippolytus*, Phaedra's love bears the seeds of its own destruction. It is a curious reversal, as Froma Zeitlin reminds us, that punishes the abstinent Hippolytus by inspiring passion not in him but in someone else.[27] But the reversal has its own logic, a symmetrical logic in which the excessive desire of the temperate Phaedra and the excessive restraint of the hybristic Hippolytus feed on one another and destroy one another. From this point of view, the passion and death of Phaedra are necessary not in causal terms as means to the punishment of Hippolytus, but in symbolic terms as a counterpart to, and reflection of, her stepson's death. Yet after both mortals are dead, Phaedra's passion is neither spent nor destroyed. Her love for Hippolytus will return forever in the longing of Trozenian women, and a passion once hidden by her modesty and guarded by silence will finally have both a name and a voice: "Phaedra's love for you will not fall nameless and will not be silenced," κοὐκ ἀνώνυμος πεσὼν / ἔρως ὁ Φαίδρας ἐς σὲ σιγηθήσεται (1423–30). The problem of desire returns to its beginning.[28]

A final example of the play's ambivalent closing gestures is Artemis' explanation of events. We noted above that a full and coherent account of what has happened can allow the deus to close the action in a very effective manner; in the extant plays, however, such explanations tend to be universal ("all men must die," *Andromache* 1271–72), largely formal (the gullible Theoclymenus receives an explanation only after Helen and Menelaus have escaped), or irrelevant (Zeus' plan to reduce overpopulation, *Electra* 1278–83). Only in *Hippolytus* does the explanation of a deus ex machina play a major role in resolving the action: Artemis explains to Theseus (at considerable length, 1282–1341) Phaedra's love for Hippolytus, the role of the nurse, Phaedra's false accusation, the hasty curse of Theseus, and the responsibility of Aphrodite, and after Hippolytus enters she repeats her account of Aphrodite's role (1400–6). Yet as we saw in chapter 3, this exceptional explanation is too much: Artemis leaves us with so many conflicting justifications and contradictory motives that in the end we have no satisfactory account of events at all.

The formal similarities between prologue and epilogue, the premature departure of the deus from the stage, and the ambivalence of the otherwise emphatic closing gestures, all cast the play's conclusion as a new beginning. And for Artemis, at least, the end is literally a beginning, as she announces her intent to avenge the death of Hippolytus. A whole new drama is about to begin:

> Enough. Not even beneath the gloom
> of earth shall Aphrodite's willful anger
> hurtle against you unavenged,
> thanks to your good and pious heart.
> With my own hand and these relentless
> arrows I will be avenged on one of hers,
> whatever mortal is most dear to her.   1416–22

How will this next story proceed? The death of Hippolytus may offer a model, but we are left uncertain who the protagonist of this new plot will be and how he will meet his death.[29]

Yet in a sense it has already begun. The deus makes her premature exit, and as Theseus and Hippolytus share their grief, Artemis is presumably setting her revenge in motion. When Aphrodite in the prologue announced her plan to punish Hippolytus, the young man was already as good as dead, and as Artemis makes a similar pronouncement in the epilogue, we can be sure that the next drama of revenge is already under way. The goddess has given us a preview of this revenge in her treatment of Theseus. When she has finished with him, Artemis promises, he will wish he were dead, his body buried beneath the ground (1290–91). She insists that Theseus suffer by hearing the ghastly truth ("Hear, Theseus, how your evils stand, and if I gain no advantage, at least I will hurt you," ἄκουε, Θησεῦ, σῶν κακῶν κατάστασιν. / καίτοι προκόψω γ᾽ οὐδέν, ἀλγυνῶ δέ σε 1296–97). When he cries out in pain (οἴμοι, 1313), she says he has more crying to do ("Does the story sting you, Theseus? Then wait and listen further, so you can cry in pain some more," δάκνει σε, Θησεῦ, μῦθος; ἀλλ᾽ ἔχ᾽ ἥσυχος, / τοὐνθένδ᾽ ἀκούσας ὡς ἂν οἰμώξῃς πλέον, 1313–14). He responds by exclaiming δέσποιν᾽, ὀλοίμην ("Lady, I wish I were dead," 1325); and Artemis concludes with grim satisfaction that gods punish wicked mortals utterly, together with their children and their houses (τούς γε μὴν κακοὺς / αὐτοῖς τέκνοισι καὶ δόμοις ἐξόλλυμεν, 1340–41). In Theseus, the angry goddess can take her revenge upon a surrogate victim onstage, before resolving eighty lines later to kill the unnamed favorite of Aphrodite.

The action stands poised at a single ambivalent moment: in prologue and in epilogue it stands poised at the moment of Hippolytus' end, just as it stands poised at the beginning of a goddess's revenge. There is no familiar ring-composition, no arc that unites beginning to end in a grand cycle of recurrence, but a fearful symmetry that immobilizes the action in a single, unredeemable situation. Without a beginning, there can be no closure, and without an end there can be no new beginning. This unusual play owes its strange and fascinating power to the fact that it lacks a beginning or a middle or an end.

Repetition and Repression

At the beginning of the play, Hippolytus concludes his prayer to Artemis by saying "May I run the course of life to the end just as I began" (τέλος δὲ κάμψαιμ᾽ ὥσπερ ἠρξάμην βίου, 87). He wants his end to be just like his beginning, and because it is, because he cannot or does not change, he is destroyed. The play imitates Hippolytus' life, achieving an unlikely and impossible perfection by ending just as it began. One result of this mimicry is to produce a plot that is equally doomed. If the end repeats the beginning and the beginning anticipates the end, nothing can happen: there is no room for change, no space for progress or discovery. With horror and fascination we watch the hero being destroyed, just as Aphrodite promised he would. This is a rather perverse pleasure, one that does not carry us forward to a new understanding or a heightened awareness as does the destruction of Oedipus, but simply plays out its sordid and violent spectacle—and at the end promises more of the same.

This repetition inhibits or paralyzes the action by obliterating opposites, turning beginnings into endings and endings into beginnings, making Artemis into another Aphrodite, and vice versa. I want to look more closely at this dysfunctional repetition. After all, repetition can be fluid and therapeutic: Peter Brooks has shown that Freud's discussion of the instinctual process of repetition can serve as a useful model for the way in which narrative repeats its subject matter.[30] Narrative is always a retelling, and Freud's "masterplot" describes on a psychological level how repetition serves to bind the flood of threatening stimuli. The ultimate goal of repetition is sameness and death. But repetition with a difference, repetition through displacement or transference, postpones that end and allows memory to revisit experience and to rework what is past or repressed. Deviant or discursive repetition thus generates the interest and liveliness of a narrative middle. In *Hippolytus*, however, this process is cut short by the substitution of opposites. Artemis and Aphrodite become interchangeable: the second goddess replicates the first without introducing challenging differences; she simply takes us back to the initial situation without forcing us to work through the difference between beginning and end and revisit one in light of the other. Aphrodite's plot of revenge makes a similar exchange. When the goddess decides to punish Hippolytus, she does so through his opposite, substituting the unbridled desire of Phaedra, daughter of the monstrous Pasiphae, for the unnatural virginity of Hippolytus, son of the Amazon. In a sense, the punishment of Hippolytus is displaced onto another, but the result is not a pregnant shift or transference from Hippolytus onto another, but just a doubling: the excess of Aphrodite's revenge will destroy both the hero *and* his opposite. In the same way, Theseus in the epilogue does not become a meaningful scapegoat, a surrogate who takes the place of Artemis' intended victim and thus makes it possible to work through guilt or desire; his punishment simply repeats and multiplies the suffering of her victims. The pattern of repetition throughout the play signals a miscarriage in the process of transference, a deadly breakdown that has reached its end before it begins. Or, if metaphor is the ability of language to repeat with a difference, to transfer or shift meaning in a way that detains and delays us, *Hippolytus* stages the death of language, its inability to signify the other. (Or, shifting models again, we might say that the equivalence of opposites short-circuits the process of mimetic desire, which begins by collapsing the distinctions between opposites. By erasing the distinctions with which a community defines itself yet failing to reassert them, *Hippolytus* stages the end of culture.)[31]

Yet the most intriguing repetition is not *in* the play but *of* the play. The story of Phaedra and Hippolytus had already been told by Euripides, and the second *Hippolytus* that survives today seems to enact repetition with a difference. The story of Phaedra, her incestuous desire for Hippolytus, his angry rejection, and her false accusation leading to his death, were told again in the second version, with the scene perhaps displaced from Athens to Trozen and with a crucial change in the character of Phaedra. All that was unseemly and reprehensible in the first Phaedra (τὸ γὰρ ἀπρεπὲς καὶ κατηγορίας ἄξιον, Hypothesis) was apparently corrected by substituting her opposite.[32] Instead of the shameless woman who acknowledged her desire, who personally propositioned her stepson and then accused him to Theseus, we have a paradigm of restraint who denies and represses her desire, who makes no advances to Hippolytus, who conceals her accusation in the form of a letter, and who tries to hide and extinguish her passion by committing suicide. All that was shameful in the first enactment and was denounced by the critics is repressed in the second. Yet for all the poet's attempt to contain this desire by displacing it onto Phaedra's chaste opposite, the result is the same. The same illicit desire destroys the same human victims in a similar way.[33]

We might conclude that this restaging gives Euripides the last laugh. He can have his cake and eat it too, yielding to the critics and repressing his licentious drama, while using the new, chastened version to repeat the first. This reenactment will have a lesson or moral: just as (within the action) desire cannot be repressed—or rather, when repressed, it simply finds new and more destructive channels—in the same way, what the poet has to say (within the theater) about passion and denial cannot be repressed, and public censure of a play that "makes a whore out of Phaedra" (Aristophanes, *Frogs* 1043) will only result in a new and more effective staging. Unfortunately, since the earlier play does not survive, we cannot measure with any confidence the differences between the two versions. Yet there is good reason to believe that the formal repetition I have described, and the immobility that results from it, are peculiar to the second *Hippolytus*. As Froma Zeitlin reminds us,[34] the prologue speech of Aphrodite would have no place in the earlier play, in which Phaedra's illicit passion sets the drama in motion, but is required by the second, in which a chaste and unwilling Phaedra becomes a vehicle in the goddess's punishment of Hippolytus. And without a divine plan announced in the prologue, there is no place or need for a similar plan in the epilogue. If a deus appeared at the end of the first *Hippolytus*, he or she may have explained more or less of the preceding action (less if, as is likely, Phaedra's false accusation had already been exposed), but there would be no question of the deus announcing reciprocal revenge in particular, or future schemes in general.[35]

In the earlier play, the passion of Phaedra propelled the plot toward its destructive end, but the later play, in repressing this desire, in substituting a chaste Phaedra and a more seemly drama, blocks this movement and reduces the plot to a lifeless repetition. Yet in so doing it infects with shame and disgrace an even larger body of victims. The first Phaedra welcomes Desire as a teacher of daring and brazen courage, a god who makes the course easy for those who lack means or contrivance (ἔχω δὲ τόλμης καὶ θράσους διδάσκαλον / ἐν τοῖς ἀμηχάνοισιν εὐπορώτατον, / Ἔρωτα, πάντων δυσμαχώτατον θεόν, fr. 430 Nauck).[36] The second Phaedra, however, trapped and silenced by her desire, wants a contrivance that will turn shameful things into good (ἐκ τῶν γὰρ αἰσχρῶν ἐσθλὰ μηχανώμεθα, 331). But the attempt to repress this shame and hinder its course will only spread it more widely. Theseus, in his attempt to contain and punish the licentious behavior of Hippolytus, becomes an accomplice in his son's destruction, and in his shame he will want to die (πῶς οὐχ ὑπὸ γῆς τάρταρα κρύπτεις / δέμας αἰσχυνθείς; 1290–91). For her complicity in what has happened, Artemis is likewise tainted with disgrace:

> This is the custom of the gods:
> no one wants to oppose the zeal of
> another's will, but we always stand aside.
> Believe me, but for the fear of Zeus
> never would I have suffered the shame
> of allowing the mortal most dear to me
> to die.

θεοῖσι δ᾽ ὧδ᾽ ἔχει νόμος·
οὐδεὶς ἀπαντᾶν βούλεται προθυμίᾳ
τῇ τοῦ θέλοντος, ἀλλ᾽ ἀφιστάμεσθ᾽ ἀεί.
ἐπεί, σάφ᾽ ἴσθι, Ζῆνα μὴ φοβουμένη
οὐκ ἄν ποτ᾽ ἦλθον ἐς τόδ᾽ αἰσχύνης ἐγὼ
ὥστ᾽ ἄνδρα πάντων φίλτατων βροτῶν ἐμοὶ
θανεῖν ἐᾶσαι.   1328–34

And it may be that the spectator, in viewing this corrected (διώρθωται according to the Hypothesis) and immobilized plot, is also in some sense an accomplice. In rejecting the unseemly Phaedra and in endorsing a new, chastened, and formally perfect drama, the spectator plays an important part in the death of the plot. The lifeless and repetitive action replicates suffering without transforming it, enacting *pathos* without *mathos*. And if Phaedra herself is no longer disgraced, those who pass judgment upon the action—Theseus who demands death for her death, Artemis who demands retribution for retribution, and the spectator who requires a barren perfection—all are disgraced in her stead.

7

Reversal: *Trojan Women*

The most beautiful order is a heap of random sweepings.
HERACLITUS

In *Hippolytus*, the unusual symmetry of closing gestures in prologue and epilogue is more than a curious detail. The repetition that seems to enhance the play's formal perfection succeeds instead in paralyzing the plot; an exceptional play that is often judged Euripides' best makes drama impossible. So it is with a certain sense of critical symmetry that I turn to a play that has often been considered Euripides' worst and that deploys its closing gestures in a decidedly unbalanced and asymmetrical manner. "The *Troades*, produced in 415, is perhaps the least interesting of the extant tragedies. The plot consists merely of unconnected scenes, depicting the miserable fate of the Trojan captives; and the execution is not in the best style of Euripides."[1] A. E. Haigh's condemnation is not entirely typical. More recent scholars, rather than dismiss the play out of hand, try to defend or justify its disconnected and episodic plot. Gilbert Murray, for example, argues that emotional intensity upstages dramatic coherence: this is "a study of sorrow, a study too intense to admit the distraction of plot interest."[2] G. M. A. Grube insists that pathos rather than plot or characterization gives the play "its beauty and appeal."[3] Gennaro Perrotta suggests that if we look not to Aristotelian notions of plot but to the "invisible" realm of feeling and emotion, we will find that "the unity of *Trojan Women* is perfect and absolute."[4] And Shirley Barlow argues that the play's unity consists in a network of recurring themes and in the central role of Hecuba.[5] This ambivalence is summed up in Richmond Lattimore's conclusion that "in candor, one can hardly call *The Trojan Women* a good piece of work, but it seems nevertheless to be a great tragedy."[6] Rather than plead for the play's redeeming virtues (which certainly exist), I want to begin with its defects, which are acknowledged by the scruples of its defenders no less than by the criticisms of Haigh: the plot is not a single action but a sequence of episodes, it contains no major reversal of fortunes, and it lacks movement or direction. Troy has fallen, the war is over, the city has been sacked and the women taken into slavery; pathos may remain, but no events worth telling. Whatever this play's virtues, they are not those of *Hippolytus*.

The use of closing gestures is also irregular and disruptive. *Trojan Women* ends more abruptly than any other surviving play of Euripides, with none of the familiar closing gestures, while it begins with a double deus ex machina that displaces those gestures to the prologue. In *Hippolytus*, beginning and ending mirror one another, but *Trojan Women* begins at the end and remains stuck there. This inversion of the plot and this absence of direction give the play its remarkable emotional intensity; they also leave the drama itself violently dismembered.

An Unmarked End

The arsenal of closing gestures in Euripides (among other things) gives a clear signal that the performance is over. And despite many individual variations in the form of these gestures, they mark the end of almost every play. As we shall see in the following chapter, there are two plays (*Alcestis* and *Heracles*) in which the closing gestures are less pronounced, but only in *Phoenician Women* and *Trojan Women* are they absent altogether.[7] Yet even here there is a difference. As we shall see in more detail later, the epilogue of *Phoenician Women* is packed with allusions to the future, and in particular to the various ways in which the sequel could be, and had been, dramatized, and it ends with at least one (but perhaps two) versions of the choral exit that empties the stage and ends the performance. *Trojan Women*, however, ends with no such allusions to the future and breaks off suddenly at the close of a lyric exchange.

In every other extant play of Euripides, the chorus speaks the closing lines in a recitative meter (marching anapests in most cases, and trochaic tetrameters in *Ion*), clearly signaling the "curtain" that will empty the stage. *Trojan Women* is unique: it is the only play of Euripides that ends in a lyric meter.[8] The final scene is a lamentation sung by Hecuba and the chorus, which apparently breaks off after the first antistrophe,[9] and in which the last few lines are sung perhaps by Talthybius, perhaps by Hecuba and the chorus:[10]

> On to the day
> that spells a life of slavery.
> The city suffers; but all the same
> step onward to the ships of the Greeks.

> ἴτ᾽ ἐπὶ
> δούλειον ἁμέραν βίου.
> ἰὼ τάλαινα πόλις· ὅμως
> δὲ πρόφερε πόδα σὸν ἐπὶ πλάτας Ἀχαιῶν.   1329–32

There is nothing like this in Sophocles, who always ends with anapests or tetrameters, and in Aeschylus the only comparable ending is that of *Persians* (which Euripides seems to echo in Trojan Women).[11] The formal abruptness of these closing lyrics is reinforced by the absence of the usual closing themes. Here there is no moral, no generalizing reflection, and no summary of the action. The final lines neither draw attention to the end of the performance nor pray for victory in the dramatic contest; they move the actors offstage and nothing more.

There is nothing to signal an end to the performance, and no figure of authority to bring the action to an end. As we have seen, nine of Euripides' plays end with a divine epiphany, three more end with a demonic epiphany (Medea in *Medea*, Eurystheus in *Children of Heracles*, and Polymestor in *Hecuba*), and two more conclude with the entrance of a human savior (Heracles in *Alcestis* and Theseus in *Heracles*). Only two surviving tragedies, *Phoenician Women* and *Trojan Women*, lack a special figure in the epilogue who can help to conclude the plot. In a sense, *Phoenician Women* needs no such figure because the action does not end: the sufferings of the house of Cadmus will continue with the exile of Oedipus and the burial of Polyneices by Antigone. And in a sense, it already has such a figure: if the lines in *Phoenician Women* are genuine, Oedipus' allusion to his place of burial establishes his own special authority:[12]

OEDIPUS: Now, daughter, Apollo's oracle is fulfilled . . .
ANTIGONE: What is it? Will you tell of evil added to evil?
OEDIPUS: That I will die an exile in Athens.
ANTIGONE: Where? What rampart in Attica will welcome you?
OEDIPUS: Sacred Colonus, home of the horseman god.

Οι. νῦν χρησμός, ὦ παῖ, Λοξίου περαίνεται.
Αν. ὁ ποῖος; ἀλλ᾽ ἦ πρὸς κακοῖς ἐρεῖς κακά;
Οι. ἐν ταῖς Ἀθήναις κατθανεῖν μ᾽ ἀλώμενον.
Αν. ποῦ; τίς σε πύργος Ἀτθίδος προσδέξεται;
Οι. ἱερὸς Κολωνός, δώμαθ᾽ ἱππίου θεοῦ.   1703–7

In *Trojan Women*, however, the absence of such a figure is strongly felt. Hecuba means to call upon the gods for help, hoping perhaps for a god to appear upon the machine, but she knows this will be futile:

[Troy,] they are burning you and carrying us away
to slavery. Oh Gods! But why do I call on the gods?
They never listened when I called on them before.

πιμπρᾶσί σ᾽, ἡμᾶς δ᾽ ἐξάγουσ᾽ ἤδη χθονὸς
δούλας. ἰὼ θεοί· καὶ τί τοὺς θεοὺς καλῶ;
καὶ πρὶν γὰρ οὐκ ἤκουσαν ἀνακαλούμενοι.   1279–81

And when she calls on Zeus, the "Phrygian Lord" and father of Dardanus who should be a savior for the Trojans, asking if he sees their sufferings (1287–90),[13] the chorus answers, "He sees. But the great city is city no more. Troy is destroyed and ceases to exist" (δέδορκεν· ἁ δὲ μεγαλόπολις / ἄπολις ὄλωλεν οὐδ᾽ ἔτ᾽ ἔστι Τροία, 1291–92). This pointed absence of help from the machine is driven home by the chorus's exclamation:

Ah!
Who is this I see on the crest of Troy?
What hands are shaking flaming
torches? Some new disaster
is about to strike Troy.

ἔα ἔα·
τίνας Ἰλιάσιν τούσδ᾽ ἐν κορυφαῖς
λεύσσω φλογέας δαλοῖσι χέρας
διερέσσοντας; μέλλει Τροίᾳ
καινόν τι κακὸν προσέσεσθαι.　1256–59

In *Hippolytus* (ἔα· / ὦ θεῖον ὀσμῆς πνεῦμα . . . 1391) and *Ion* (ἔα· τίς . . . πρόσωπον ἐκφαίνει θεῶν; 1549–50) the same exclamation announces the epiphany of a deus ex machina, as it heralds also the entrance of a god in *Heracles* (815) and *Rhesus* (885). Here, however, the chorus looks up to see, not a divine intervention, not a god as savior on the palace roof or on the crane, but faceless soldiers among the parapets, lighting the flames that will destroy the city.[14]

The closing aetiology is also conspicuous in its absence. As we have seen, nearly every surviving play concludes with an explicit link between the past enacted onstage and the present world of the audience; in connecting stage action to contemporary institutions, the aition contributes to a sense of closure by marking the distance between them. This extra-dramatic reference is marginally present in *Heracles* (Theseus alludes to the Heracleia of Attica, 1326–33) and may or may not be present in *Phoenician Women* (the oracle reported by Oedipus, 1703–7, quoted previously). In *Trojan Women*, however, and here alone,[15] it is certainly absent, and its absence is brought to our attention. From the apocalypse that destroys the city of Troy, will any vestige remain? Immediately before the lines in which Hecuba concludes that no god will help her (1279–81), she likewise concludes that the city's name will *not* live on: "O Troy, that once stood tall among foreign peoples, now you will lose your famous name," ὦ μεγάλα δή ποτ᾽ ἀμπνέουσ᾽ ἐν βαρβάροις / Τροία, τὸ κλεινὸν ὄνομ᾽ ἀφαιρήσῃ τάχα (1277–78).[16] And however we assign the lines, the same point is repeated with greater emphasis in the closing antistrophe:[17]

> Oh temples of the gods and beloved city—
> Ah! Ah!—
> you take murderous flame and blade of the spear.
> Now you will fall nameless to the dear earth. . . .
> The name of the land will vanish; each thing
> is gone in its own way, and suffering Troy
> no longer exists.

> ἰὼ θεῶν μέλαθρα καὶ πόλις φίλα,
> ἒ ἔ,
> τὰν φόνιον ἔχετε φλόγα δορός τε λόγχαν.
> τάχ᾽ ἐς φίλαν γᾶν πεσεῖσθ᾽ ἀνώνυμοι. . . .
> ὄνομα δὲ γᾶς ἀφανὲς εἶσιν· ἄλλα δ᾽
> ἄλλο φροῦδον, οὐδ᾽ ἔτ᾽ ἔστιν
> ἁ τάλαινα Τροία.　1317–24

Finally, the epilogue fails to distinguish enacted events from those that follow. In most plays, as we have seen, a concluding prophecy describes a sequel to events of the play, drawing attention to the ending as a somewhat arbitrary but necessary boundary. Even those without an explicit prophecy conclude by alluding in one way or another to the future: Heracles says he will go to Diomedes to perform his next labor (*Alcestis* 1149–50), Theseus foretells the honors that Heracles will receive in Attica (*Heracles* 1331–33), and Oedipus speaks of his exile in Attica and death at Colonus (*Phoenician Women* 1705–9). *Trojan Women,* however, ends with no such reference or allusion to what follows; the women lament together in song, and with their closing words the stage is emptied. There are, of course, events to come: for the Trojan women, death or further suffering as slaves, and for the Greek men, destruction of the ships and the hardships of return. But the sequel, if it is told at all, is told at the beginning of *Trojan Women.* The final scene does not look forward. On the contrary, it reminds us that there is nothing to look forward to: the city is destroyed, its name is gone, and as Hecuba reminds us, there is nothing more to say:

> Oh, my suffering! This is truly the end,
> all that is left of all I have suffered;
> I shall leave my country, and the city burns.

> οἲ 'γὼ τάλαινα· τοῦτο δὴ τὸ λοίσθιον
> καὶ τέρμα πάντων τῶν ἐμῶν ἤδη κακῶν·
> ἔξειμι πατρίδος, πόλις ὑφάπτεται πυρί.   1272–74

A Premature Curtain

The gestures of closure that regularly signal the end of the play are conspicuously absent from the ending of *Trojan Women;* the chorus departs in lamentation, and the city will remain nameless. Yet those devices which are missing from the epilogue are just as conspicuously present in the prologue.

The entrance of a god is a commonplace in Euripidean endings, but a divine epiphany is less common in the prologue and is answered almost always by an epiphany in the epilogue. *Hippolytus* is framed by the epiphanies of Aphrodite and Artemis, and *Ion* is likewise framed by the entrances of Hermes and Athena. In a similar vein, *Bacchant Women* begins with the god in disguise and ends with Dionysus ex machina, while *Hecuba* begins with the ghost of Polydorus and ends with the prophetic Polymestor. A minor exception is the prosatyric *Alcestis,* which begins with the double epiphany of Apollo and Death and ends with the triumphant entrance of Heracles, who has defeated Death and brings Alcestis back to her husband. A major exception is *Trojan Women,* which begins with a double epiphany of Poseidon and Athena, yet has nothing to balance this in the ending.[18] The result is entirely different. Rather than framing the action with interventions from a divine or superhuman sphere, the opening scene combines prologue speech with deus ex machina, exhausting the devices of beginning and end before the play has begun. When the gods depart, their departure is final: they have made their plans and foretold the outcome, and have nothing left to do.

This transposition of the deus ex machina to the beginning of the play[19] is reinforced by a similar displacement of the gestures that accompany the deus. The play begins, for example, with a prophecy that belongs in the epilogue. In the prologue, the prophecies of a god or the forebodings of a mortal always anticipate events *within* the action: Hermes announces that Apollo will reunite Ion with Creusa, and the nurse fears that Medea will harm her children. As critics have noted, because these anticipations are not entirely complete or correct, the opening prophecy generates interest in how the plot will reach its goal.[20] A prophecy in the epilogue, however, announces events *later than* the action (the death of Jason, for example, or the descendants of Ion) and helps to bring the plot to an end by containing all that is left over, diverting into an authorial postscript whatever the plot did not include. The one exception is *Trojan Women*, which lacks a prophecy in the epilogue but begins with Athena and Poseidon foretelling how the Greek fleet will be destroyed *after* the play is finished:

> ATHENA: [They will suffer] when they set sail for home from Troy.
>   Zeus will send a storm and unspeakable
>   hail and dark blasts of heaven,
>   and says he will give me the fire of lightning
>   to blast the Greek ships and burn them in fire. . . .
> POSEIDON: So be it. My favor does not need long
>   words: I will shake the waters of the Aegean Sea,
>   and the cliffs of Mykonos and reefs of Delos
>   and Skyros and Lemnos and the cliffs of Kaphareus
>   will be filled with the bodies of many dead corpses.

> Αθ. ὅταν πρὸς οἴκους ναυστολῶσ᾽ ἀπ᾽ Ἰλίου.
>   καὶ Ζεὺς μὲν ὄμβρον καὶ χάλαζαν ἄσπετον
>   πέμψει δνοφώδη τ᾽ αἰθέρος φυσήματα·
>   ἐμοὶ δὲ δώσειν φησὶ πῦρ κεραύνιον,
>   βάλλειν Ἀχαιοὺς ναῦς τε πιμπράναι πυρί. . . .   77–81
> Πο. ἔσται τάδ᾽· ἡ χάρις γὰρ οὐ μακρῶν λόγων
>   δεῖται· ταράξω πέλαγος Αἰγαίας ἁλός.
>   ἀκταὶ δὲ Μυκόνου Δήλιοί τε χοιράδες
>   Σκῦρός τε Λῆμνός θ᾽ αἱ Καφήρειοί τ᾽ ἄκραι
>   πολλῶν θανόντων σώμαθ᾽ ἕξουσιν νεκρῶν.   87–91

Before the action really begins, an extra-dramatic prophecy turns our attention to events outside the drama; rather than generating interest in what is to come, it turns away from the plot to its sequel. This effect is heightened by the content of the prophecy, which concerns not the Trojan women but the Greek soldiers. These men will prove to be literally extra-dramatic: they never appear onstage, never play a direct role in the action, and make themselves felt only through an intermediary, the herald Talthybius.[21] This turn away from the action is repeated on a smaller scale in the first episode, in which Cassandra foretells the wanderings of Odysseus and the murder of Agamemnon (431–50)—sequels involving the absent villains rather than the women who occupy the stage. So the plot begins, not by generating interest in what is to come, but with a closing gesture that marks off the action from a sequel outside it.

This reversal of beginning and end is reinforced by the presence in the prologue of other features that typically accompany the deus. The first is an etymological derivation resembling an aition, in which Poseidon explains the name of the Wooden Horse:[22]

> The Parnassian,
> Epeius of Phocis, by the schemes of Athena
> fashioned a horse teeming with weapons
> and sent the destructive cargo inside the ramparts;
> hence later men will call it the Wooden Horse,
> since it held hidden spears of wood.

> ὁ γὰρ Παρνάσιος
> Φωκεὺς Ἐπειὸς μηχαναῖσι Παλλάδος
> ἐγκύμον᾽ ἵππον τευχέων συναρμόσας
> πύργων ἔπεμψεν ἐντός, ὀλέθριον βάρος·
> ὅθεν πρὸς ἀνδρῶν ὑστέρων κεκλήσεται
> Δούρειος Ἵππος, κρυπτὸν ἀμπίσχων δόρυ.   9–14

The explanation is not strictly an aition, since the "later men" who will call this contrivance a Wooden Horse are not clearly distinguished from men of the play: a contemporary viewer would use the term, but so too would characters in the action, as does Odysseus among the Phaeacians (δουράτεος ἵππος, *Odyssey* 8.492–93 and 8.512). Nevertheless, Poseidon's words do refer to a time outside the drama; they use an expression, κεκλήσεται, that is very common in aitia;[23] and it is possible that they allude more specifically to a statue of the horse recently dedicated on the Acropolis.[24] Excepting the equally unusual references in the prologue of *Hippolytus* and at the midpoint of *Iphigenia among the Taurians*, this is the only aetiological explanation in Euripides that occurs outside an epilogue. Thus the play begins with an etymological derivation that disturbs the dramatic illusion in a manner generally reserved for the conclusion of the drama.

Poseidon concludes his prologue speech with another closing gesture, his words of farewell to the city of Troy:

> So I bid you farewell, once fortunate city
> and polished ramparts. If Athena, daughter of Zeus,
> had not destroyed you, you'd rest on your foundations still.

> ἀλλ᾽, ὦ ποτ᾽ εὐτυχοῦσα, χαῖρέ μοι, πόλις
> ξεστόν τε πύργωμ᾽· εἴ σε μὴ διώλεσεν
> Παλλὰς Διὸς παῖς, ἦσθ᾽ ἂν ἐν βάθροις ἔτι.   45–47

As John Wilson has shown,[25] the audience has every reason to expect that Poseidon will now leave the stage, abandoning the walls he loves. His exit, postponed by the entrance of Athena, anticipates the ending of the play by establishing the recurrent theme of imminent departure from Troy. And it does so in a way that separates divine from human concerns. Poseidon has not arrived, like Hermes in *Ion*, to get the plot rolling and help it toward its goal; he has come only to pay his last respects, and now that Hera and Athena have destroyed his beloved city (23–24), he cannot remain:

I leave famous Troy and my altars;
for when evil desolation takes a city,
religion grows sick and gods do not want honors.

λείπω τὸ κλεινὸν Ἴλιον βωμούς τ᾿ ἐμούς·
ἐρημία γὰρ πόλιν ὅταν λάβῃ κακή,
νοσεῖ τὰ τῶν θεῶν οὐδὲ τιμᾶσθαι θέλει.   25–27

Just as Artemis leaves the stage and the mortal realm lest death defile her eyes
(*Hippolytus* 1437–38), Poseidon prepares to quit the stage and the scene of human
suffering lest his prerogatives should sicken. In *Hippolytus*, the god's departure shifts
attention to the father and dying son for the final twenty-six lines, while in *Trojan
Women* it shifts attention to human suffering for the entire play.

Poseidon's departure is interrupted by the entrance of Athena, the agent of the
city's destruction, who has unexpectedly shifted her loyalties. She now enlists the
help of Poseidon in a plot to destroy the Greek ships as they return from Troy, and
the scene concludes with the exit of both gods, Athena to Olympus and the arsenal
of thunderbolts (92–93), while Poseidon completes his interrupted departure. Like a
deus departing at the end of the play or the chorus filing out at the end of the performance, Poseidon concludes by delivering a moral:

Foolish is the mortal who sacks cities,
shrines and tombs, holy places of the dead;
he makes [them] desolate and then is destroyed himself.

μῶρος δὲ θνητῶν ὅστις ἐκπορθεῖ πόλεις
ναούς τε τύμβους θ᾿, ἱερὰ τῶν κεκμηκότων·
ἐρημίᾳ δοὺς ‹σφ᾿› αὐτὸς ὤλεθ᾿ ὕστερον.   95–97

The exact construction of this moral, both in syntax and in meaning, continues to be
debated,[26] but the important point for our purposes is the presence of a summarizing
gesture. A concluding moral is usually spoken in the epilogue by the deus ex machina
or the exiting chorus, although such reflection upon the action may also follow
major developments in the plot.[27] In this case, however, before the drama has even
begun, Poseidon draws a lesson from it and then departs. We begin at the end not
only with a deus ex machina and with a prophecy and aetiology that look outside the
action, but with a moralizing conclusion that reflects up on events of the drama.[28]

The epilogue of *Trojan Women* is unique in that it specifically lacks those features that usually mark the conclusion of the action, and the prologue is unique in
that it includes these same features to suggest an ending before the play begins.

Reversal and Catastrophe

Trojan Women, like *Hippolytus*, begins at the end, but does so in an entirely different manner. In *Hippolytus* the end is described in the prologue, played out in the action,
and will be repeated upon a favorite of Aphrodite; as we have seen, this repetition of
beginning and end contributes to the formal symmetry and perfection of the play. In

Trojan Women, however, the end promises nothing more. The action is already complete at the beginning of the play, and the ending is unmarked because nothing more has happened; there is no change or progress or repetition to record. This reversal of beginning and end contributes in several ways to the play's apparently defective asymmetry.[29]

It does so, first, by contributing to the disconnectedness of the action. The opening scene between Poseidon and Athena is largely independent of the play: the prophecy concerning the Greek fleet refers to times, people, and places far removed from the women of Troy; the exchange between Poseidon and Athena (rather than the appearance of a single πρόσωπον προτατικόν) makes the opening scene more dramatically self-contained, and after the gods make their exit, the action shifts to the mortal sphere with the lament of Hecuba. Furthermore, the closing scene, because it lacks the usual features of the epilogue, cannot give meaning or coherence to the preceding episodes; no summary or moral ties the action together, and no concluding prophecy shows where it will lead.

This reversal also disfigures the play by heightening its relentless pathos. The prologue, which suggests that the plot is finished rather than about to begin, leaves us with a tableau of human suffering that cannot and will not change. And the lack of finality in the epilogue robs this pathos of meaning: the suffering of the Trojan women is relieved by no divine intervention or redeeming prophecy; it is not even rationalized by aetiology or moral.[30] Finally, the reversal of prologue and epilogue produces a pervasive yet barren irony. From the moment Poseidon and Athena leave the stage, spectators are aware that the Greeks who now inflict suffering upon the Trojan women will suffer themselves in the course of their return; the women onstage, however, have no idea that the men, in time, will suffer also. In *Oedipus the King,* such irony gives direction and coherence to the play, as the blindness of Oedipus and the insight of the audience slowly but relentlessly converge. In *Trojan Women,* however, there is no convergence: the suffering women remain blind, and the spectators' knowledge fails to redeem their plight. We might conclude that the inversion of beginning and ending in *Trojan Women* serves a larger purpose: it is a further means of producing the disconnectedness of plot and emotional intensity that (for whatever reason) are the hallmarks of this peculiar play. But it is more useful to see disjointedness and pathos and barren irony as part of a larger strategy of reversal and disfigurement.

The inversion of beginning and ending accompanies a more general inversion in the action of the play. Rather than a sequence of events leading to some conclusion, *Trojan Women* portrays a situation in which movement is impossible: the play begins and ends with the destruction of Troy and the departure of all survivors. Rather than generating interest as to where individual desires will propel the action, it portrays characters whose desires achieve nothing, who suffer mightily but can never act. This inversion of the action allows Euripides to dramatize the hopeless situation of the women of Troy. As D. J. Conacher observes, the only movement in the play is a rhythm of hope and despair: "Again and again, this hope is stamped out and gives way to desolation, only to flicker forth in some new place until its final quenching at the end of the play."[31] Can the clairvoyant Cassandra see any future for Troy? The city's glory has already been decided by the way in which its soldiers met their death

(386–90). Is Polyxena still alive? Andromache reports that she has already been killed on the grave of Achilles (622–23). Will Astyanax survive to avenge the death of his father and the destruction of Troy? The Greeks have decided to throw the young boy to his death from the walls of the city (713–25). Can Hecuba take comfort in the condemnation of Helen? Menelaus does not kill her, but promises ineffectually to punish her when he returns to Sparta (1053–59). And what of Hecuba's argument that life, unlike death, still carries hope (οὐ ταὐτόν, ὦ παῖ, τῷ βλέπειν τὸ κατθανεῖν· / τὸ μὲν γὰρ οὐδέν, τῷ δ' ἔνεισιν ἐλπίδες, 632–33)? The best thing, she decides in the end, is to throw herself into the blaze and die with the city (1282–83)—but the Greeks will not allow this and keep her alive as a prize for Odysseus. All hopes and expectations lead nowhere. The play begins with the end: the end of Troy and of all that the women love. And there is no movement of the plot. The end, the destruction, simply becomes more complete.[32]

The reversal, in other words, dramatizes a situation that is profoundly *undramatic*. The catastrophe that destroyed the Trojans and annihilated their city has also destroyed the possibility of drama. Elsewhere, the prologue of the play sets the plot in motion by hinting at where it will lead, and arousing interest in how it will reach its goal. The prologue of *Trojan Women*, however, does not begin the story, but finishes it: the city, Poseidon tells us, is now burning, sacked and destroyed (8–9), Priam and his children are gone (φροῦδος δὲ Πρίαμος καὶ τέκν', 41), and the captive women have been taken as slaves (28–31). The few women not yet allotted will soon learn who their masters will be (240–77), and all that remains to be told, all that gives suspense to the drama, is how the women will react to their hopeless situation. In negative terms, the play lacks the excitement, the movement, the interest, and suspense of drama. But this reversal does not only take away. In "positive" terms this non-drama confronts us with a pageant of misery, a catalogue of suffering that serves no purpose. The play, disfigured by a premature end, presents an ugly spectacle of pain without meaning, and in so doing, it casts the viewer in an ugly and unpleasant situation. How can we watch the suffering of others, how can we profit from witnessing their pain, if it has no meaning and serves no end?[33] Normally, of course, we learn from others by watching and listening, even if we cannot share their experience directly; this is certainly the case with Hecuba, who is spectator to sailors and understands the meaning and purpose of their actions:

> I have never stepped in the hull of a ship myself,
> but I know by hearing and by seeing pictures.
> When sailors find the wind moderate and bearable,
> they are eager to keep out of trouble's way,
> one manning the rudder, one the sails,
> one keeping water from the hold.

> αὐτὴ μὲν οὔπω ναὸς εἰσέβην σκάφος,
> γραφῇ δ' ἰδοῦσα καὶ κλύουσ' ἐπίσταμαι.
> ναύταις γὰρ ἦν μὲν μέτριος ἦ χειμὼν φέρειν,
> προθυμίαν ἔχουσι σωθῆναι πόνων,
> ὁ μὲν παρ' οἴαχ', ὁ δ' ἐπὶ λαίφεσιν βεβώς,
> ὁ δ' ἄντλον εἴργων ναός·   686–91

But when the situation is hopeless, when those we are watching suffer to no purpose, then drama is destroyed and language is useless:

> But if the sea is stirred up,
> great and overwhelming, they yield to chance
> and surrender themselves to the running waves.
> So I too, in all my sufferings,
> am speechless and hold my tongue.
> This wave of misery from the gods conquers me.

> ἢν δ᾽ ὑπερβάλῃ
> πολὺς ταραχθεὶς πόντος, ἐνδόντες τύχῃ
> παρεῖσαν αὑτοὺς κυμάτων δραμήμασιν.
> οὕτω δὲ κἀγὼ πόλλ᾽ ἔχουσα πήματα
> ἄφθογγός εἰμι καὶ παρεῖσ᾽ ἔχω στόμα·
> νικᾷ γὰρ οὐκ θεῶν με δύστηνος κλύδων.   691–96

The Body Disfigured

Do we want to watch and listen to this unpleasant spectacle? In his prologue speech, Poseidon describes at length offstage events—the end of Troy, the desolation of its shrines, and the death of Priam—before turning to the only human figure we can see, the suffering Hecuba:

> And this wretched woman here, if anyone wants to look,
> this is Hecuba lying by the doorway
> shedding many tears for many reasons . . .

> τὴν δ᾽ ἀθλίαν τήνδ᾽ εἴ τις εἰσορᾶν θέλει,
> πάρεστιν Ἑκάβη κειμένη πυλῶν πάρος,
> δάκρυα χέουσα πολλὰ καὶ πολλῶν ὕπερ . . .   36–38

If we want to listen, Poseidon will list the reasons for her tears (38–44): the slaughter of Polyxena (which Hecuba does not yet know of), the deaths of her husband and her sons, and the sacrilegious abduction of Cassandra (which she also does not know of). The scholiast is right: this is a cold invitation to the audience indeed (ψυχρῶς τῷ θεάτρῳ), as the god makes it clear she has more sufferings yet to come. If we want to watch, we will see the queen rolling in the dirt and defiling her body:

> I am in misery, my limbs reclining
> ill-fated, lying like this with my
> back stretched on a hard bed.
> Oh my head, oh my temples
> and my ribs, how I long to roll
> and move around my back and spine
> to either side of my body
> with continuous tearful lament.

δύστηνος ἐγὼ τῆς βαρυδαίμονος
ἄρθρων κλίσεως, ὡς διάκειμαι,
νῶτ᾽ ἐν στερροῖς λέκτροισι ταθεῖσ᾽.
οἴμοι κεφαλῆς, οἴμοι κροτάφων
πλευρῶν θ᾽, ὥς μοι πόθος εἰλίξαι
καὶ διαδοῦναι νῶτον ἄκανθάν τ᾽
εἰς ἀμφοτέρους τοίχους μελέων,
ἐπιοῦσ᾽ αἰεὶ δακρύων ἐλέγους.   112–19

And if we watch Hecuba through all her sufferings, we will find her in the same position at the end of the play, "casting my aged limbs on the ground, and beating the earth with both my hands" (γεραιά γ᾽ ἐς πέδον τιθεῖσα μέλε᾽ ‹ἐμὰ› / καὶ χερσὶ γαῖαν κτυποῦσα δισσαῖς, 1305–6). The disfigurement of drama is represented through the disfigurement of a woman's body, the assortment of limbs, head, ribs, and spine that desires to grovel (ὥς μοι πόθος) on the ground before us. In a similar way, the chastened plot of the second *Hippolytus* was represented through the newly chaste body of Phaedra. And if in the earlier play the viewer is somehow complicit in this seemly repression of Phaedra's desire, in the later play we are guilty of answering Poseidon's summons (εἴ τις εἰσορᾶν θέλει), of wanting to look upon the ugly spectacle of gratuitous suffering.

We cannot finish discussing the end of *Trojan Women* without taking account of the end of its trilogy. The play was apparently produced after *Alexander* and *Palamedes*, and before the satyr-play *Sisyphus*, and it is hard to believe that the tragedies, at least, were not in some way connected. Yet how could a connected trilogy possibly end in this way, with a non-drama that renders action impossible? I think it is not too fanciful to speculate briefly on the radical reversals attempted by the production as a whole.

The "Trojan trilogy" is remarkable in two ways. As far as we can tell, this is the only Euripidean production in which three tragedies dramatize successive portions of the same legend.[34] And the legend chosen for this special treatment is the privileged story of the Trojan War. In Greek poetry and drama, the authority of Homer was so great that the *Iliad*'s narrative of the war was not repeated: the cyclic and tragic poets filled out a vast array of episodes that took place before, during, and after the war, but none covered the same ground as Homer.[35] This fact is usually taken to illustrate the derivative nature and inferior talent of the cyclic epics, but it should better be seen as evidence of a struggle against the authority of Homer waged both by the epic poets and by the tragedians, who found many ways to correct or complete the story of the *Iliad*.[36] The *Oresteia*, for example, which takes place between the *Iliad* and the *Odyssey*, struggles against both, tarnishing Agamemnon's victory at Troy, and complicating the story of Orestes' revenge told to Telemachus. The Trojan trilogy, however, instead of using a longer or shorter episode of the cycle to revise Homer, engages the legend in an epic and comprehensive manner that goes far beyond anything Homer attempted. The *Iliad* gave us only a short period in the tenth year of the war, but Euripides gives us the origins of the war in *Alexander*, the Greek camp besieging Troy in *Palamedes*, and the end of the war with the sack of Troy in

Trojan Women. Here, and only here, does one telling of the story take us from beginning to middle to end.

Euripides challenges the authority of Homer and the meaning of the war in an unprecedented manner. Let us start at the beginning, with the origins of the war and Euripides' *Alexander.* In Homer, the war begins with the abduction of Helen from Sparta, which leads to the gathering of the Greek expedition; the beginning gives meaning to the war, through which Zeus will punish the Trojans and Menelaus will recover his wife. This coherent causality is challenged by the *Cypria,* which gives two earlier beginnings to the war. First, the abduction of Helen is the result of an earlier story, the judgment of Paris; the Trojan War, in other words, is not a story of Greeks punishing a Trojan crime, but of Greeks and Trojans swept into war by the strife and jealousy of Athena, Hera, and Aphrodite.[37] And second, the judgment results from an earlier cause, Zeus' plan to reduce overpopulation by starting wars against Thebes and Troy; the Trojan War, in other words, is a side-effect of divine housecleaning.[38] Both revisionist beginnings were taken over by Euripides in other plays (e.g., *Electra* 1278–83 and *Orestes* 1639–42),[39] but here he takes a different tack. In *Alexander,* Euripides makes Paris once more the beginning of the story, but begins with his birth and with Cassandra's prophecy that he will cause the destruction of Troy. The form of this prophecy, a vision of a firebrand, ties this beginning very closely to the end of the city described in *Trojan Women.*[40] But the rest of this play, with its story of intrigue, mistaken identity, and belated recognition of Paris by his mother and brothers, takes us in the wrong direction. Instead of moving from this ominous beginning to fulfillment of the young man's catastrophic fate, the play leads to the false and premature happy end of family reunion.

The second play takes us to the Trojan War, to the Greek camp outside Troy, and to three Greek leaders instrumental in the ten-year siege of the city. Agamemnon, who will judge the dispute between the other two leaders, led the expedition to Troy. Odysseus, who charges Palamedes with treachery, will devise the ruse that eventually takes the city. And Palamedes apparently allowed the Greeks to survive the siege by discovering means of finding food, inventing dice to pass the time, and devising more effective battle formations.[41] Here, then, we come to the real "middle" of the war, not the anger of Achilles in the tenth year, but the resourcefulness that kept the siege in place for so long. But the plot that unfolds is a perverted middle; the scheme of Odysseus against Palamedes is not a means to the end of the war, but the jealousy of a fellow Greek that leads to an innocent man's death. Instead of a virtuous cunning and deceit that allows the Greeks to win the war, we have a gratuitous and treacherous cunning that serves no larger purpose.

The third play takes us to the very end of the war, to the moment at which the city is put to the torch. This moment of triumph and revenge, although not described in the *Iliad,* is the end that completes the whole, the goal that justifies the expedition, fulfills the prophecy of Cassandra, and makes the long siege worthwhile. Yet *Trojan Women* does not really show us that end. In the prologue we glimpse a part of it, the Greek sacrilege in sacking the city that does not end the story, but will lead to destruction of the returning ships. And in the course of the play, we see an extinction of hope among the women who remain, an annihilation of the future that is at best a perversion of the end. The ambitious scope of the trilogy follows the course of the war from beginning to middle to end in a manner that epic had not attempted. Yet each of these crucial moments that should give coherence to the war conspicuously fails to do so, and the trilogy dissolves into a set of three unrelated plays.[42]

Euripides' epic project is a deliberate disaster. Its ostentatious lack of unity is evident also in the fact that it skirts the war itself, nowhere enacting an episode of the conflict and leaving instead, in Ruth Scodel's words, "the empty space the poet has placed with such emphasis in the center of his work."[43] As a result, it is also emptied of ideological importance. The Trojan War became through Homer and others the central moment in Greek culture because the conflict between united Greeks and Trojan allies helped to define Greek values. Yet Euripides manages to construct a Trojan trilogy in which the two sides never meet. In the first play, Trojans conspire against one another in a comedy of errors. In the second play, Greeks conspire against one another in a travesty of justice. And in the third play, after the war is over, the only commerce between offstage Greeks and onstage Trojans is through the herald Talthybius. The Greeks will pay for their sacrilege, and the Trojan women will suffer because they have no choice, but the mighty conflict between them has disappeared.

Finally, the symbol of this war, and the symbol of the Greek cause, is Helen's body. Because she was taken from Menelaus, the Greeks have justice on their side, and until her body is returned, the war will not be finished. I do not need to rehearse the connections between the female body and the ideology of war and conquest. Yet it is worth noting that a few years later in *Helen*, Euripides would portray her body as a phantom that men fought over and died for to no purpose. In *Trojan Women*, however, her body is very real and is the object of a bitter debate involving Hecuba and Menelaus. Now that the war is over and the city has been sacked, her body is returned to Menelaus and justice will be realized. Yet here we have a final, surprising twist. Justice will consist not in punishing the Trojans in order to repossess Helen, but in punishing Helen. And the conflict is not between two male factions disputing ownership of the woman, but between Helen and a female antagonist. Finally, the outcome of the conflict is ambiguous: Menelaus says he will kill Helen, but only when he gets back to Sparta, and the audience knows he will never do this. Just as the shape and coherence of play and trilogy have been disfigured, the figure that should give meaning to the episodes does not do so. Beautiful Helen is irrelevant. Her transcendent form, and the transcendent justification she offered for years of suffering and destruction on both sides, have no place in this play. As she leaves, Menelaus says that he pays no attention to her (τῆσδε δ᾽ οὐκ ἐφρόντισα, 1046), he jokes about her weight (1050), and concludes with a blatant falsehood: her death will teach all women to be chaste (1055–57). And as she leaves, we realize she is not worth our attention either. It is not the empty promise of the beautiful Helen but the brutal reality of the suffering and disfigured Hecuba that claims our reluctant and offended attention.

8

Erasure: *Heracles*

> Man, life, destiny, have a beginning and an end, a birth and a death; but
> not consciousness, which is infinite by its very nature.
>
> BAKHTIN

My third trope—and the phenomenon it intends to describe—is more subtle. In *Hippolytus*, the gestures of closure are doubled, repeated both at the beginning and at the end of the work; in *Trojan Women*, they are moved, displaced from the end of the work to its beginning; and in *Heracles* these gestures are uncertain, seeming to appear—and seeming not to appear—where we expect them. The trope, like erasure itself, is a complex one: not a simple absence, but a presence that is somehow denied or effaced or rendered uncertain. At the end of *Trojan Women*, the lyric antistrophe precludes the use of Euripides' closing gestures. The end of *Heracles*, however, both gives and takes away; the familiar closing gestures seem to be present until we look more closely and find that they have been emptied of force. Yet as we shall see, these partial or incomplete gestures are multiplied, thus "erasing" the end in a more radical manner.

An Ending Effaced

Heracles ends, as a tragedy well might, with burials, farewells, and departure. After agreeing to go with Theseus to Athens, Heracles says goodbye to his father Amphitryon (1418). He bids his father bury the bodies of his children and promises to bury Amphitryon in turn (1419–22). And then Heracles leaves the stage. These familiar closing themes, however, are in various ways robbed of their proper force. After Heracles in half a line reminds his father to bury the children (θάφθ' ὥσπερ εἶπον παῖδας 1419), Amphitryon changes the subject to ask who will bury him (ἐμὲ δὲ τίς, τέκνον; 1419). Heracles answers that he will, and when his father asks how (since Amphitryon will presumably stay in Thebes to bury the children while Heracles goes to Athens with Theseus), Heracles says he will have him brought to Athens after the children are buried (1420–21). The focus has shifted from an imminent burial that will close the action of the play to a more distant and problematic event: does Heracles mean that after his father dies in Thebes, he will have the body brought to Athens for burial? Since tradition placed Amphitryon's grave in Thebes, does he mean instead that Amphitryon, while living, will join Heracles in Athens, and that after his death, Heracles will bury him in Thebes? Or are the place and circumstances of Amphitryon's death and burial deliberately left as vague as those of Heracles? The problem cannot easily be resolved by emendation or by deleting one or more lines,[1] and perhaps it should stand, since the theme of departure is equally problematic. After father and son say goodbye to one another (1418), Amphitryon will presumably remain in Thebes and Heracles will go to Athens (although this is never explicitly stated). Yet Heracles earlier implied that he would be present at the children's funeral at Thebes ("O land of Cadmus and all the Theban people, cut your hair, join in lament, come to the children's tomb, and all with one voice lament the corpses and myself" 1389–92).[2] And a few lines earlier, Heracles asks Theseus to help him take Cerberus to Argos (1386–88). So when the hero departs at the end of the play, his ultimate destination will be Athens, but somehow he will first take Cerberus to Argos (presumably presenting the dog to Eurystheus and concluding his period of servitude), and either will be present or imagines that he will be present at the children's funeral in Thebes.

The closing theme of burial for the children is complicated by questions about the burial of Amphitryon, and the theme of farewell is complicated by questions about the hero's destination. In a similar way, the gestures of closure are unusually unsettled. As Heracles leaves the stage, his final words reflect upon his present situation:

> I've destroyed my house with shameful deeds
> and utterly ruined, I'll follow Theseus like a dinghy.
> No one in his right mind would rather have
> wealth or strength than good friends.

> ἡμεῖς δ' ἀναλώσαντες αἰσχύναις δόμον
> Θησεῖ πανώλεις ἑψόμεσθ' ἐφολκίδες.
> ὅστις δὲ πλοῦτον ἢ σθένος μᾶλλον φίλων
> ἀγαθῶν πεπᾶσθαι βούλεται κακῶς φρονεῖ.   1423–26

And as the hero departs for exile, the chorus of old Thebans concludes the play with two more lines:

> Sadly we go with many tears,
>   having lost the greatest of friends.

> στείχομεν οἰκτροὶ καὶ πολύκλαυτοι,
>   τὰ μέγιστα φίλων ὀλέσαντες.   1427–28

Taken together, the two closing passages do all we might expect to end the play: they briefly summarize the disasters to Heracles and his house (1423–24), draw a general moral from this outcome (1425–26), and empty the stage with anapests that draw attention to the chorus's withdrawal (1427–28). Yet this is, in every way, a minimal choral exit. Formally, it is the shortest possible, with a single anapestic dimeter followed by the closing paroemiac; no other choral exit is pared so short. Thematically, it says no more than is necessary, announcing departure and alluding to the theme of friendship without developing either the extra-dramatic implications of the one or the moralizing potential of the other. And in its closing role it is emptied of force by the lines of Heracles, whose (brief) summary and moral upstage the few words left to the chorus. The gesture, in other words, is unambiguously present even as its force is largely effaced. The same is true in a more pronounced manner of the other closing gestures. Earlier in this scene, Theseus (an uncertain deus, as we shall see) tried to persuade Heracles to come with him to Athens, and sweetened his argument with very tangible inducements:

> There I will purify your hands of their crime
> and give you a house and a part of my wealth.
> The gifts I received from the people when I saved
> fourteen youths by killing the Cretan bull—
> these I shall give you.

> ἐκεῖ χέρας σὰς ἁγνίσας μιάσματος
> δόμους τε δώσω χρημάτων τ᾿ ἐμῶν μέρος.
> ἃ δ᾿ ἐκ πολιτῶν δῶρ᾿ ἔχω σώσας κόρους
> δὶς ἑπτά, ταῦρον Κνώσιον κατακτανών,
> σοὶ ταῦτα δώσω.   1324–28

When Theseus moves beyond these immediate offers to promise or foretell additional honors, he takes on the formal attributes of a deus, delivering a prophecy and apparently offering an aetiological explanation for sanctuaries named for Heracles:

>   And everywhere I was apportioned
> precincts of land. In the future these will be
> named after you by mortals while
> you live; but after you die and go to Hades
> the whole city of Athens will honor you
> with sacrifices and rocky mounds.

>   πανταχοῦ δέ μοι χθονὸς
> τεμένη δέδασται· ταῦτ᾿ ἐπωνομασμένα
> σέθεν τὸ λοιπὸν ἐκ βροτῶν κεκλήσεται
> ζῶντος· θανόντα δ᾿, εὖτ᾿ ἂν εἰς Ἅιδου μόλῃς
> θυσίαισι λαΐνοισί τ᾿ ἐξογκώμασιν
> τίμιον ἀνάξει πᾶσ᾿ Ἀθηναίων πόλις.   1328–33

The first lines (1328–31) apparently offer an aetiology for Attic Heracleia, shrines or sanctuaries dedicated to Heracles in various places throughout Attica,[3] and the presence of this aition is clearly marked by the array of formulaic language that regularly accompanies this gesture (ἐπωνομασμένα / σέθεν τὸ λοιπὸν ἐκ βροτῶν κεκλήσεται).[4] An aition characteristically bridges the gap between events of the play and the world of the audience by invoking the god's knowledge of what mortals will do in the future (τὸ λοιπὸν ἐκ βροτῶν), yet Theseus is a mortal, not a god, and the future to which he alludes is not clearly outside the dramatic action, and is certainly not the world of the spectators since he describes what will happen while Heracles is still alive (ζῶντος). Thus far, the formal language heralds an aition that does not materialize.

The final lines of this passage (1321–33) look further into the future to promise honors that will be made after Heracles' death. The allusion to festivals and monuments seems to make the aetiology more concrete, establishing a specific correspondence between the action of the play and the world of the audience. But what in particular will the city of the Athenians honor? Surely not the events of this play, the hero's murder of his wife and children. And surely not his earlier career, the famous exploits of the Dorian hero whose importance is overturned by Heracles' own words (χαιρόντων πόνοι, "To hell with my labors" 575) and by his madness. Will they honor some future deeds performed by Heracles during his exile in Athens, just as the future travels of Orestes will be commemorated with the name of the town Oresteion? If so, the sequel so honored is a puzzling cipher: we are told in detail of the wanderings of Orestes that form the basis of that aetiology (*Electra* 1250–75, *Orestes* 1643–52), but the story of Heracles in Athens is not mentioned here and is not attested in any other source. (In fact, the only story connecting Heracles with Attica was the account of his initiation at Eleusis before journeying to the underworld,[5] but there is nothing to suggest that Euripides has the mysteries in mind here.) The event to be honored is so elusive that it might be better to read this passage, as ancient readers seem to have done, not as an aetiology but as a further promise and inducement by Theseus: if Heracles will come to Athens, Theseus will give him gifts and land, and will see that his friend is also honored by the city as a whole.[6] And how will this elusive sequel be honored? Not with a name or institution familiar to the audience, but with sacrifices and monuments that cannot be placed securely. The mention of sacrifices could have been used to allude to particular rites performed in Attica in Euripides' day, but the vague plural fails to do so (θυσίαισι), and the mention of monuments could have been used to bring to mind particular Athenian shrines, but the words of Theseus specify nothing more than heaps of stone (λαΐνοισί τ' ἐξογκώμασιν). Upon closer inspection, the gesture toward the world of the audience evaporates and may in fact be entirely illusory: these honors will be offered when Heracles is dead (θανόντα δ') or, lest we miss the point, when he goes to Hades (εὖτ' ἂν εἰς Ἅιδου μόλῃς)—in other words, as an audience raised on stories of Heracles' apotheosis will realize, at a time that does not really exist.[7]

This effacement of closing gestures is evident also in the entrance of Theseus. In the final scene of the play, after murdering his wife and children in a fit of madness, Heracles prepares to do the only honorable thing, to take his own life. At this climactic moment, Theseus suddenly enters, persuades Heracles not to commit suicide, and promises him gifts and honors in Athens. Theseus plays the part of a surrogate deus ex machina: he appears for the first time in the final scene, he intervenes to resolve an impasse, he delivers a command, as well as some form of aetiology and prophecy, and his dispensations are accepted by the characters onstage. But in a manner unique to this play, the surrogate deus is emptied of force. Theseus, after all, is a mortal, not a god, nor is he a mortal somehow endowed with special powers (as in the "demonic epiphanies" of Medea, Eurystheus, and Polymestor) but a mortal who lacks even the power and authority of the person he has come to save: we are constantly reminded in the latter part of the play that Heracles had earlier rescued Theseus from Hades (619, 1222, 1235, 1336, 1415). This surrogate deus likewise has no divine power to rescue Heracles from death, and must rely upon argument and persuasion.

In this exchange the would-be savior is again shown up by the man he would help: Theseus begins his speech by invoking the example of gods who manage to live with their crimes and failings (1314–19), and Heracles counters with a withering rejection of the "wretched stories" of criminal gods (1341–46).[8] And Theseus as deus has little to offer: he cannot bring or promise divine salvation, only a place of refuge for the outcast exile. Like a deus, he issues a command ("So leave Thebes, as the law requires, and follow with me to Athens," 1322–23), but this, in context, is no more than the attempt of one friend to persuade another. Even his entrance is emptied of all authority. The surrogate deus is greeted not with the exclamation of surprise or awe that attends the entrance of Thetis, Artemis, Athena, or the Dioscuri,[9] but with annoyance and frustration: "But now to foil my deadly plans, here comes Theseus . . ." (ἀλλ᾽ ἐμποδών μοι θανασίμων βουλευμάτων / Θησεὺς ὅδ᾽ ἕρπει . . . 1153–54). And instead of choosing the right moment to arrive, he seems to have come at the worst possible time: Theseus explains that he was on his way to save Heracles' family from Lycus (1163–68), but as the pile of corpses makes clear, he is far too late for that.

If the powers of Theseus are dubious, so too is the respect they earn. Usually, the authority of a deus ex machina is explicitly confirmed by the human characters, who promise to do as the god commands. When Athena orders a treaty and ritual dedications at the end of *Suppliant Women*, for example, the king ratifies this arrangement by announcing: "My Lady Athena, I will obey your words; you set me straight so I will not err" (1227–28). As we have seen, the gesture is a regular one, even if in some cases (e.g., the endorsement of Apollo's surprising settlement in *Orestes*) it seems to involve a certain degree of irony.[10] But when Heracles finally decides to live, he makes a point of casting this decision not as an acceptance of Theseus' advice but as a rebuttal, dismissing Theseus' arguments as irrelevant (πάρεργα ‹γὰρ› τάδ᾽ ἔστ᾽ ἐμῶν κακῶν, 1340). Each time Theseus offers help, Heracles is reluctant: "Stand up. No more tears."—"I cannot, my limbs are frozen" (1394–95); "Enough. Give your hand to a friend."—"I won't wipe blood on your clothes" (1398–99). At last Heracles tacitly acknowledges his dependence on the king ("Put your hand round my neck and I'll lead you."—"A friendly pairing, with one in misfortune" 1402–3), but he immediately reneges and turns back to embrace his father and the bodies of his children (1406, 1408). And when Theseus tries to shame him into submission ("No one who sees you playing the woman will approve" 1412), Heracles turns the tables on his benefactor by asking who saved Theseus from Hades: "Am I so lowly [ταπεινός]? I don't think I was back then" (1413). By the time they leave the stage a few lines later, Theseus' magnanimous gesture has been emptied of all authority and reduced to the verbal sparring of friends.

Horror Vacui

What do we make of this dubious ending, one that inscribes all the familiar signals of closure, only to erase them in the same stroke? Why would the poet end with these empty gestures? This question and the problem it addresses are closely related to the more familiar problem of the play's unity. The play begins with a slow and ineffectual debate between Megara and Amphitryon on whether Heracles is likely ever to return from the underworld (where he has gone to bring back Cerberus as the last of his labors for Eurystheus), and it builds with increasing speed and excitement to a remarkable climax. First Lycus, who has seized power in Heracles' absence, tells the suppliants that they all must die. As they prepare for death, all dressed in black, Heracles suddenly returns from the underworld and plots revenge against the tyrant. Then in one of the shortest episodes in Greek tragedy (701–33), Lycus is lured inside the palace and killed by Heracles, but before the hero can celebrate his victory and the liberation of his family, Iris and Lyssa arrive, sent by Hera to drive Heracles mad and make him kill the wife and children he has just rescued from death. This stunning and catastrophic end, engineered with the help of the machine, apparently leaves room for little more than a brief coda in which the hero (like Agave in *Bacchant Women*) wakes up to realize what he has done and (like Sophocles' Ajax) decides to deal with the horror of his crime by taking his own life. But somehow the action stubbornly continues. Heracles' decision to commit suicide is interrupted by the entrance of Theseus ("foiling my deadly plans" 1153), who promises asylum to the infanticide, and eventually convinces Heracles to return with him to Athens. Why does the drama continue? What connects this lengthy epilogue to the climactic events that precede?

If we read Heracles' catastrophic madness as the end of the story, then the last part of the play—the final scene with its empty closing gestures—is irrelevant. For a long time, critics argued in this vein that the play reaches a premature end and is therefore defective. Algernon Swinburne called *Heracles* "a grotesque abortion," and Gilbert Murray said that it was "broken backed" and not a great work of art.[11] Critics today rally to the play's defense, and they do so by investing greater meaning in the final scene. Instead of viewing the epilogue as an awkward appendage, they discover in it a meaning that responds to, and balances, the entire first part of the play. The most eloquent statement of this view is William Arrowsmith's introduction to his translation. The first half, he says, portrays a Heracles who "is recognizably the familiar culture-hero of Dorian and Boeotian tradition: strong, courageous, noble, self-sufficient, carrying on his back all the aristocratic *aretê* of the moralized tradition of Pindar." The second half, however, shows him "reduced to tears, helpless, dependent, and in love, stripped of that outward strength which until now had exempted him from normal human necessity, and discovering both his common ground with men and a new internalized moral courage." The meaning of the play, according to Arrowsmith, somehow consists in the "conversion" or "dramatic mutation" of one figure into the other.[12] Most contemporary readings argue in various ways for a similar change or conversion. Arrowsmith's scheme is not unlike that of H. H. O. Chalk, who argues that the end of the play replaces old heroic values with a revised and more humanistic notion of *aretê*. According to Justina Gregory, the heroic Heracles, son of Zeus, is replaced at the end by a humble and mortal hero, the son of Amphitryon. Harvey Yunis argues that traditional relations between mortals and gods are replaced with a new humanistic creed. And according to Helene Foley, archaic values centered in the individual are replaced at the end of *Heracles* with newer values defined by the polis.[13] There is much of value in these readings, but they try to read too much into an inconclusive ending, attempting to construct a satisfying symmetry in which a new and coherent world is born from the ashes of the old.

The discussion that follows asks instead why the play ends with an ending erased, with an epilogue that lacks the compelling gestures and redeeming transformation that may give meaning and coherence to the whole. But this effacement of the ending does not simply leave an empty space. The trope of erasure includes both writing and un-writing, suggestion and denial. And the final scene of *Heracles* includes multiple gestures both present and absent, competing with one another and failing fully to assert themselves; as a result, the epilogue is overfull with conflicting traces of an end, yet lacks a sense of finality. To look more closely at this pregnant emptiness, I turn again to Theseus, and then to Heracles' weapons.[14]

An Ending Multiplied

In one respect, Theseus, as we have seen, is a deus manqué, a figure with many attributes of the god on the machine but with the none of the god's power and authority. Yet Theseus plays another completely different role, and again fails to do so convincingly. When he arrives with an army (1165), when he shows concern for the polluted and exiled Heracles, when he offers him a place of refuge and promises to settle him on Athenian soil, Theseus plays a familiar role as the statesman who embodies Athenian values by protecting suppliants. For example, when the children in *Children of Heracles* want to escape unlawful persecution by Eurystheus and the Argives, the sons of Theseus offer them protection in Athens. When the suppliants in *Suppliant Women* want to guard the bodies of the Seven from Theban sacrilege, it is Theseus in Athens who offers them protection and support. And when Oedipus at Colonus is threatened with violence by Creon and the Thebans, it is Theseus again who offers him refuge and military protection. Even Medea, contemplating exile from Corinth, turns to Aegeus, the father of Theseus, for a place of refuge in Athens. Medea looks forward to a reception that stands outside the action (and that she will betray by plotting against Theseus), but in the other plays, the act of receiving and defending suppliants is successfully performed onstage in an Athenian setting at Marathon, Eleusis, or Colonus. And the generous actions of Theseus and his sons, and the civic righteousness they represent, are commemorated in the resulting burials of Eurystheus, the Seven against Thebes, and Oedipus in Athenian soil.[15] When Theseus offers help to the outcast Heracles, he looks forward to a similar happy end of protection in Athens and commemoration after death (1331–33).

Yet if Theseus' role as deus is ambiguous, so too is his role as civic ambassador. Most telling is the fact that Theseus has no official, political authority. In other plays, he and his sons are invested with the authority of general or king,[16] an authority that derives from the sovereign powers of the city.[17] In this play, he comes to Heracles not as ambassador of the city, but simply as a kinsman and a friend (Θησεὺς ὅδ᾽ ἕρπει συγγενὴς φίλος τ᾽ ἐμός 1154). In other plays, Theseus or Demophon offers refuge because both divine law and the reputation of the city require it (*Children of Heracles* 236–46, *Suppliant Women* 301–31; compare *Oedipus at Colonus* 913–14, 921–23), and in *Suppliant Women*, this gesture is explicitly approved by the *dêmos* (355, 394) and defended in debate by invoking Athenian democratic values (399–455). In this play, when Theseus helps Heracles he is acting as a private citizen, and returning the private favor that Heracles performed by rescuing him from Hades. Even the concrete offers he makes to Heracles are private rather than public ones: houses, money, and gifts that Theseus will give to his friend (1325–28, quoted previously). In other plays, the Athenian setting is decisive. The suppliants arrive at Marathon, Eleusis or Colonus, where they are protected by the moral authority and the weapons of the Athenians, and where burial in Attic soil will bear witness to the city's virtuous deeds. In *Heracles*, however, Athens is an eventual destination—not a setting in which the crisis is resolved, but the venue for an unknown future. Nor is it a privileged site of burial; after death, the hero will be honored in Athens (1331–33), but there is no suggestion that he will be buried there.[18]

Theseus as ambassador of the city is no more effective than Theseus as deus ex machina. He has all the formal trappings of this familiar dramatic figure, but lacks the requisite civic power and authority. Rather than a mortal magnified, he is doubly deficient. Of course, this deficiency has its rewards. In the absence or erasure of Theseus' roles as deus and king, his role as friend becomes more evident: in the final scene, it is the φιλία or friendship between Theseus and Heracles that convinces the hero not to commit suicide.[19] Yet the "friend" is not a role that will compete with the deus or the king; he has no power or authority and is not defined by any formal trappings or attributes. All that defines the φίλος is a single action, an offer to repay the help Theseus received from Heracles in Hades. Because he lacks more formal roles, Theseus can make his gesture of reciprocity, but it does not follow that he becomes the ambassador of a new set of values. If Theseus is doubly deficient, then so too is the play: it lacks the presence of a deus ex machina who can resolve the action onstage before our eyes, and it lacks the presence of a civic ambassador who can guarantee a belated ending once the hero reaches Athens. The actual end and the promised end are both effaced, and all that remains is a modest and reciprocal exchange between friends.

Where does this leave Heracles? Is there something in the hero, a presence or greatness, that fills this void and compensates for the deficient Theseus? The action of the play would argue not: the great hero has been humbled, he renounces his labors (575) and his title as victor (καλλίνικος 582), he loses his wife and family, and in his madness and murder he becomes not an exemplary figure but an outcast and an exile. Having lost everything that once distinguished him, he is Theseus' perfect partner, the hero erased. This is dramatized in an interesting way in Heracles' final decision. His decision to accept the offer of asylum in Athens (1351–52) is never fully articulated, following rather abruptly upon his criticism of the wretched stories of poets.[20] But after lamenting the deaths of his wife and children and giving them a last embrace, Heracles pauses to make a more theatrical and symbolic decision, considering whether or not he should take his bow and arrows with him:

> How sad the pleasure
> of kisses, and sad the company of these weapons.
> I'm at a loss whether to keep or give them up
> since they will fall against my side and say:
> "With us you killed your children and your wife; we are
> your child-killers you are carrying." So shall I take
> them in my hands? Saying what? But stripped of the

weapons with which I did the greatest deeds in Greece,
shall I die in shame at the mercy of my enemies?
They cannot be left, but must be kept in misery.

ὦ λυγραὶ φιλημάτων
τέρψεις, λυγραὶ δὲ τῶνδ᾽ ὅπλων κοινωνίαι.
ἀμηχανῶ γὰρ πότερ᾽ ἔχω τάδ᾽ ἢ μεθῶ,
ἃ πλευρὰ τἀμὰ προσπίτνοντ᾽ ἐρεῖ τάδε·
Ἡμῖν τέκν᾽ εἷλες καὶ δάμαρθ᾽· ἡμᾶς ἔχεις
παιδοκτόνους σούς. εἶτ᾽ ἐγὼ τάδ᾽ ὠλέναις
οἴσω; τί φάσκων; ἀλλὰ γυμνωθεὶς ὅπλων
ξὺν οἷς τὰ κάλλιστ᾽ ἐξέπραξ᾽ ἐν Ἑλλάδι
ἐχθροῖς ἐμαυτὸν ὑποβαλὼν αἰσχρῶς θάνω;
οὐ λειπτέον τάδ᾽, ἀθλίως δὲ σωστέον.   1376–85

These are the weapons with which he performed the greatest exploits in Greece, so
how can he leave them behind? But they are also the weapons with which he killed
his wife and children, so how can he possibly take them with him? Clearly, the weapons define the man, and the decision Heracles makes will help to define what sort of
person he now is; as H. H. O. Chalk put it, "Herakles' decision here is crucial to the
tragedy."[21] But what sort of weapons does he put on? And what will he use them for?
"Stripped of my weapons," Heracles asks rhetorically, "shall I die shamefully at the
mercy of my enemies? These [weapons] cannot be left, but must be kept in misery."
He keeps them for a purely negative purpose, for self-defense. As we shall see, this
does little to define a hero and does not define in a positive or constructive manner
either old-fashioned, heroic virtues or new, humanistic ones.

In art and on stage, Heracles was identified with three props, three tokens of his
heroic stature: the club, the lion-skin, and the bow. In this play, however, only the
bow and arrows are important; they become a visual emblem of the hero, as well as
a token of the labors he performed with their help. As the great ode that celebrates
the Twelve Labors makes clear, it was with the bow and arrow that Heracles was
able to defeat the Centaurs ("The mountain-dwelling race of savage Centaurs he
scattered with deadly arrows, destroying them with his winged weapons" 364–67),
kill Kyknos ("And Kyknos who slaughtered strangers by Cape Malea and the springs
of Anauros he killed with his bow" 389–93) and kill Geryon ("after dipping his arrows
[in the blood of the hydra], with them he killed the triple-bodied cowherd of Erytheia"
422–24). If the weapons define the hero, then in this play it is the bow in particular
that represents the heroic exploits of Heracles.

But this symbol is not a simple one. Early in the play, as Amphitryon waits for his
son to return from the underworld, and as Lycus the tyrant prepares to put Heracles'
family to death, they have a debate on the virtues of the hero's weapons. Heracles,
according to Lycus:

is especially cowardly
because he never wore a shield on his left arm
or came near a spear, but holding his bow
(that worthless weapon) stood ready to flee.
A bow is no test of a man's courage!

... τἄλλα δ᾽ οὐδὲν ἄλκιμος,
ὃς οὔποτ᾽ ἀσπίδ᾽ ἔσχε πρὸς λαιᾷ χερὶ
οὐδ᾽ ἦλθε λόγχης ἐγγὺς ἀλλὰ τόξ᾽ ἔχων,
κάκιστον ὅπλον, τῇ φυγῇ πρόχειρος ἦν.
ἀνδρὸς δ᾽ ἔλεγχος οὐχὶ τόξ᾽ εὐψυχίας   158–62

In his reply, Heracles' father, instead of defending the honor of his son, simply praises the bow's expedience:

standing far off, he wounds his enemies
with bow-shot weapons they cannot see
and never shows them his body. This is
true wisdom in battle . . .

ἑκὰς δ᾽ ἀφεστὼς πολεμίους ἀμύνεται
τυφλοῖς ὁρῶντας οὐτάσας τοξεύμασιν
τὸ σῶμά τ᾽ οὐ δίδωσι τοῖς ἐναντίοις,
ἐν εὐφυλάκτῳ δ᾽ ἐστί. τοῦτο δ᾽ ἐν μάχῃ
σοφὸν μάλιστα . . .   198–202

This rhetorical exchange early in the play rehearses a widespread distrust of those who rely on bow and arrows. In Homer, for example, Odysseus with his bow is a foil to Achilles with his spear—Odysseus the antihero who practiced the art of cunning survival versus Achilles the archetype of heroic courage in battle. The infamous Paris also carried a bow—the effeminate Paris who seduced Helen from Sparta, and whom Diomedes denounces in the *Iliad*: "Archer, scoundrel glorying in your bow, philanderer, if you and your weapons were put to the test that bow would do you no good, nor a host of arrows" (11.385–87).[22] And in fifth-century Athens the bow conventionally distinguished cowardly Persians from Greek soldiers with their spears (e.g., Aeschylus, *Persians* 146–49) and Scythian slaves from Athenian citizens (e.g., Aristophanes, *Acharnians* 707). Herodotus embellished this view by telling how the barbaric Scythians made quivers for their arrows from human skin:

Whoever has the most scalps is judged the greatest man among these people. Many of them also make cloaks to wear from of the scalps, stitching them together like peasants' coats. And many also strip off the skin, nails and all, from the right hand and arm of their dead enemies, and use these to cover their quivers.   (4.64)

The archer, in other words, is an outsider, a devious and suspect figure who does not subscribe to the heroic values of the Homeric warrior, or to the civilized values of the fifth-century Greek.[23] So when Heracles at the end of the play, having lost and renounced his claim to greatness, nevertheless decides to put on the bow and arrows, how does he define himself? Can we agree with George Walsh, who says, "By choosing to live and to retain his weapons, Heracles accepts his public role as a hero"?[24] If the bow and arrows represent his public and heroic exploits against the Centaurs and three-bodied Geryon, they also cast him in the role of coward and outsider. Heracles lives on, but the weapons he carries cannot tell us what this new hero will be.

The bow is also significant in another way. In the course of the play, the weapon that performed the celebrated labors also performs a less glorious task. When Heracles, driven mad by Lyssa, murders his wife and children, he uses his bow to perform the hideous deed. A messenger describes what happened in grisly detail. First, he tells us, Heracles called out "Bring me my bow!" (942). Then, after raging against an imaginary Eurystheus, "he readied his quiver and bow against his own sons, thinking he was slaughtering Eurystheus' children" (969–70). The children ran away in terror but could not escape him. He took aim at the first son and hit him by the liver (977–79). The second son was so close he could not draw the bow, so he crushed him with his club (991–94). His wife picked up the third child and ran inside the house, but Heracles tore down the door and killed son and mother with a single arrow (999–1000). This hideous and pathetic scene is recalled at the end of the play when Heracles tries to decide if he should take the child-killing weapons with him. Because it recalls their murder, the gesture of putting on these wretched weapons seems to cast Heracles as a tragic hero: if tragic knowledge, knowledge through suffering, means that through his experience the hero has come to understand a horrendous or excessive suffering, then when Heracles puts on the murderous weapons, he seems prepared to show in this theatrical gesture that he understands the meaning of what he has done.

But nowhere does Heracles find such understanding. In the epilogue as a whole there is nothing to suggest that his experience has brought new insight; he endures the gratuitous punishment of Hera but does not and cannot find a redeeming lesson in it. And the weapons in particular will be constant reminders not of a tragic truth but of shame and disgrace:

> since they will fall against my side and say:
> "With us you killed your children and your wife; we are
> your child-killers you are carrying."   1379–81

Instead of symbolizing tragic insight, they replay with every step his children's pathetic gestures, "falling against their father's knee" for attention (ὡς πρὸς πατρῷον προσπεσούμενοι γόνυ 79) and for mercy (ὁ τλήμων γόνασι προσπεσὼν πατρός . . . 986); wherever he goes, he will hear their incessant, chattering complaint.[25]

At the end of the play, Heracles has lost his family and has been crushed by the revenge of Hera; with the blood of his wife and children on his hands, there is no way he can recover his former glory, or once again embody the ideals of *aretê*. When Heracles struggles to define himself anew, and finally decides to put on the bow and arrows, he puts on a symbol both of heroic achievement and of the cowardly outsider, a symbol both of tragic suffering and of unending disgrace. The sign of the hero fails to define him in a meaningful way. Yet, at the same time, the sign is packed with multiple, contradictory meanings; it is overloaded with the many different roles the hero might want to adopt. So Heracles remains poised at a remarkable moment: armed with a sign that might mean hero or coward, tragic lesson or constant shame, there is no way to know what or who he is.[26] There is no license here for trying to construct a story of new values born from the ashes of the old; only the unreadable future knows what or who our hero will be. Paradoxically, because he is destroyed so completely, Heracles at the end of the play enjoys a moment of unprecedented freedom: at the very lowest point in his life, he is completely free to find a new identity.

Freedom and Narrative

What does this freedom mean? Theseus, we found, was deus and not deus, statesman and less than statesman. Heracles is likewise hero and antihero, a tragic figure who transcends his sufferings and a pathetic figure who cannot escape his shame. Because the story of Heracles in Athens had never been told, he is free to play whatever part he wants: the possibilities seem endless. But for the very same reason, because the story had not been told, the possibilities are also limited: whatever may happen in Athens will not be among the hero's famous exploits. The play ends with a collapse of distinctions and a multiplication of possibilities in which almost anything—but nothing very remarkable—can happen. At this point, the relation of friendship becomes important. When Theseus enters, he is welcomed by Heracles as a kinsman and friend (1154). We are constantly reminded of Heracles' earlier favor to Theseus in rescuing him from Hades, and the play ends by replacing Heracles' bonds to his children (ἄξω λαβών γε τούσδ' ἐφολκίδας 631) with bonds of friendship that now tie him to Theseus:

> I've destroyed my house with shameful deeds
> and utterly ruined, I'll follow Theseus like a dinghy
> [Θησεῖ πανώλεις ἑψόμεσθ' ἐφολκίδες].
> No one in his right mind would rather have
> wealth or strength than good friends.   1423–26

This new, or newly important, relation binds individuals to one another in mutual obligations, yet it does not in any evident way characterize either figure. We do not really know who they are, except in the very ordinary and unremarkable sense that they are *philoi*.

To some extent, the emptiness and fullness of Heracles' situation extends and elaborates the unusual qualities of this mythical figure. Geoffrey Kirk has pointed out that the legendary Heracles embodies "to an unusual degree" the contradictions of the hero: humane and bestial, serious and burlesque, sane and mad, savior and destroyer, free and slave, human and divine.[27] Among this bundle of contradictions, Michael Silk has argued that one is especially pronounced: "Heracles is unique in his combination of human and divine properties," equally a god and a man, with his mortal father Amphitryon and his divine father Zeus, and worshipped both as a god and as a mortal hero.[28] Nicole Loraux adds to this list Heracles' contradictory attributes of virility and femininity, arguing that the hero's ambivalence allowed the popular imagination to explore the nature of this opposition.[29] The hero who embodies contradictions to an exceptional degree is full of possibility, available for ever new constructions and reinventions, and he is also empty, never a coherent or identifiable individual or character, but a constellation of images.[30] The ambivalent and liminal Heracles is therefore always in-between, standing outside familiar categories or devouring them all with his insatiable appetite. And as Silk reminds us, the figure who remains in-between is dangerous because he destroys the categories and distinctions that establish identity, confer status, and convey meaning. My concern, however, is not with the representations of Heracles in myth, but with the portrayal of the hero at the end of this play. In Euripides, his dangerous ambivalence threatens to destroy the very logic of drama. We have already seen that the structure of the play reduces the plot to a "grotesque abortion" or a "dramatic mutation." But the final scene, in which Heracles prepares to face an unknown future, is destructive in a different way.

I want to return to the freedom of Heracles, and in particular his freedom to fashion a new future and a new identity. In one respect, such freedom and indeterminacy seems antithetical to the designs of art. The point of writing a narrative is, after all, somehow to represent events as ordered and coherent—to suggest in Aristotle's formulation that events follow in a necessary or probable manner from one another, or to draw with Henry James a circle within which they appear to do so.[31] A moment in which a character is undefined and anything can happen is a moment at which there is no longer any story to tell. Yet in another respect, freedom and indeterminacy may be an artist's goal. In "Epic and Novel," Mikhail Bakhtin distinguishes two different impulses in narrative.[32] Those forms of narrative in which the end is known and in which events are organized so as to lead to that end, he calls "epic." In the *Aeneid*, for example, everything Aeneas does is directed toward the foundation of Rome and the establishment of the Roman Empire. Those forms of narrative in which the end is *not* known, in which characters have (or cunningly appear to have) the freedom to act in various ways, to drop in or out of the story, to follow tangents—these he calls "novel." The partition of literature into two types is rather sweeping and simplistic, but it has the virtue of focusing attention upon a particular impulse, a literary interest in reproducing or figuring the indeterminate nature of events as we live them. As we experience events, at the present moment, anything is possible.[33] Each moment of each day is pregnant with possibility: the chance encounter, the brilliant idea, the lucky Lotto ticket that has the power to transform everything that follows. On any particular day, however, nothing momentous is likely to happen and that moment of possibility will blend, in hindsight, into the featureless rhythm of everyday routine—unless, of course, that day turns out to be an especially lucky or significant or unfortunate one. In either case, a book of memoirs, ordering events in hindsight, will reduce the play of possibility in the present moment, either by reducing it to a predictable routine or by drawing attention to its decisive importance. A memoir that succeeds in preserving the real potential in every moment of a life would be formless, plotless, and unbearably long (just as a truly accurate map would be impossibly big, "on the scale of *a mile to the mile!*" in Lewis Carroll's words).[34] What Bakhtin describes is the attempt of novels, not to reproduce this play of possibilities, but to represent or imitate it. Both Tolstoy and Dickens, for example, used serial publication to give the impression of a continually unfolding story and to give their work a journalistic realism by seeming to report events as they unfolded from week to week, rather than presenting the reader with a story complete from beginning to end.[35]

Greek tragedy generally has an opposite impulse, imitating a single, complete action, reshaping already familiar legends, and regularly foreshadowing the end. *Oedipus the King*, for example, begins with an argument between Oedipus and Teiresias in which the seer hints darkly at the eventual blinding of Oedipus (412–19, 454–56). *Medea* begins with a speech in which the Nurse frets at Medea's anger and fears that she will hurt her children (36–39). And *Helen* begins, as we shall see, with the protagonist clinging in her misfortune to Hermes' promise that she will return safely to Sparta (56–59). Euripides' *Heracles* is unusual in several ways. It begins not by anticipating the end, but by entertaining different scenarios for the present situation as Amphitryon and Megara debate the likelihood that Heracles will ever return to Thebes. They are trapped in the uncertainties of the present moment, and in Megara's words, they are being eaten away by the time in-between (ὁ δ᾿ ἐν μέσῳ γε λυπρὸς ὢν δάκνει χρόνος 94). The plot is not a single and coherent action, but a sequence of episodes leading to a series of aborted ends: first death for the hero's wife and children at the hands of the upstart Lycus, then deliverance when Heracles suddenly returns from Hades to save his family and rescue the tyrant, then crushing reversal when Heracles in god-sent madness murders his wife and children, and finally the uncertain future that awaits the hero in Athens. The final scene of the play describes a situation whose outcome is unknown, and a protagonist whose identity remains undefined. Heracles is a perfect Bakhtinian hero. All known ends have been stripped away and his final decision not to commit suicide, instead of determining what will follow, leaves both his future and his identity profoundly unclear because it commits him to the total uncertainty and total freedom of living in the present. Yet *Heracles* does not have a Bakhtinian plot. For Bakhtin, the novel is characterized by what we might call systematic openness (or "aperture," to use Saul Morson's term):[36] at any moment in the narrative, characters are free to make choices and decisions just as we do in everyday life. The action of *Heracles* is largely the opposite. At each moment, the end is clear and decisive: from the inflexible resolve of Lycus to kill Heracles' family, to the triumphant return of Heracles from Hades, to the total catastrophe inflicted by Hera, the plot navigates a series of apparent endings.[37] Only at a single point in the action, only at the moment the play ends, do we have a sense of aperture as the hero lingers on the threshold between a catastrophic past and an unknown future.

Yet this single moment of narrative freedom is enough to undo the drama. Ann Michelini and others have drawn attention to Heracles' apparent repudiation of the dramatic fiction.[38] Theseus has told Heracles to abandon the grand gesture of suicide and learn to live with his crimes; after all, even the gods have committed adultery and harmed their parents (1313–19). Heracles answers by rejecting such stories and demanding higher standards of the gods:[39]

Ah! This has nothing to do with my troubles;
I don't believe the gods love forbidden
beds and fasten chains to their hands;
I never did and never will suppose
that one god is another's master.
God, if he is truly god, needs nothing;
these are poets' worthless stories.

οἴμοι· πάρεργα ‹γὰρ› τάδ᾽ ἔστ᾽ ἐμῶν κακῶν·
ἐγὼ δὲ τοὺς θεοὺς οὔτε λέκτρ᾽ ἃ μὴ θέμις
στέργειν νομίζω δεσμά τ᾽ ἐξάπτειν χεροῖν
οὔτ᾽ ἠξίωσα πώποτ᾽ οὔτε πείσομαι
οὐδ᾽ ἄλλον ἄλλου δεσπότην πεφυκέναι.
δεῖται γὰρ ὁ θεός, εἴπερ ἔστ᾽ ὀρθῶς θεός,
οὐδενός· ἀοιδῶν οἴδε δύστηνοι λόγοι.   1340–46

Heracles rejects the stories of divine infidelity as wretched lies, yet he is the product of Zeus' adulterous affair with Alcmene, an affair repeatedly brought to mind by mention of Heracles' two fathers, Zeus and Amphitryon (e.g., 1263–65). Therefore, with these words, Heracles erases or crosses out the legendary premise upon which the drama rests. With even greater effect, however, the episodic plot and the indeterminate final scene erase the familiar gestures of closure and reach at the end a remarkable moment of narrative uncertainty. If the shape of this play is strange or unusual, this is not least because it finally embodies a radical openness that is antithetical to the ends of tragedy.

III

The Ends of Tragedy

What were you thinking of, overweening Euripides, when you hoped to press myth, then in its last agony, into your service? It died under your violent hands; but you could easily put in its place an imitation that, like Heracles' monkey, would trick itself out in the master's robes.

NIETZSCHE, *Birth of Tragedy*

9

Helen and Romance

> The rest of the story need not be shewn in action, and indeed, would hardly
> need telling if our imaginations were not so enfeebled by their lazy depen-
> dence on the ready-mades and reach-me-downs of the ragshop in which
> Romance keeps its stock of "happy endings" to misfit all stories.
>
> SHAW, Pygmalion

In the epigraph to this chapter, Shaw registers annoyance at those who assume Eliza
will marry Higgins for two reasons. The first is the ending itself: if we consider Eliza's
self-interest and her instincts (Shaw assures us), and if we ask what she might do
when faced with the choice between a lifetime of fetching Higgins's slippers and a
lifetime of Freddy fetching hers, "there can be no doubt about the answer." Given a
woman like Eliza who knows what she wants, the sequel is clear and to remove any
possible doubts, Shaw spends fourteen pages describing Eliza's choices, her marriage, her later contacts with Higgins, and the flower stand she eventually opens in
Covent Garden. But there is more at stake than simply correcting the record. Shaw's
second reason has to do with what the ending implies: a hand-me-down ending can
only come from the ragshop of romance. *Pygmalion* advertises itself as "A Romance
in Five Acts," according to the subtitle, but does so with typically Shavian irony.
The mythical conceit of the title and the dramatic conceit of a play about phonetics
make it clear that this is no ordinary romance, and Shaw drives the point home in his
epilogue, contrasting the expectations of feeble imaginations with the calculus of
benefits in real life. "Complications ensued; but they were economic, not romantic.
. . . But when it comes to business, to the life that she really leads as distinguished
from the life of dreams and fancies, she likes Freddy and she likes the Colonel; and
she does not like Higgins and Mr Doolittle."[1] The stakes are high indeed. If Shaw
cannot convince us of his realistic sequel, he cannot convince us that his play, like
all great art (and unlike ordinary romance) is "intensely and deliberately didactic."[2]
The proof of the play is in the ending.

At first glance, the happy ending seems no more than an obvious target: Shaw
rails against the formulaic endings of romance just as critics today deride the predictable endings of Hollywood movies. But there is more to the question than this.
The ending fulfills certain expectations, and the kinds of expectations raised in the
course of a work, and the ways in which those expectations are (or are not) fulfilled,
tell us what sort of work it is. Works that generate familiar and predictable expecta-

tions (boy meets girl) and fulfill those expectations in familiar and predictable ways belong to the reassuring genre of romance that Shaw objects to. Those that generate different sorts of expectations (phonetic versus amatory conquest) that are realized in less familiar ways (the female object takes on a life of her own) attempt to subvert the reassuring genre and construct something new in its place. So in our reading of a play, attention to the end that is realized and the way in which that end is reached will have much to tell us about the generic intentions of the work as a whole. We have seen in part I that the closing gestures invented by Euripides draw attention to the process and the problems of closure, supplying a formal end that preempts expectations that the action will be complete. We also noticed a significant shift in the course of his career from plays that conclude with death and commemoration to those in which protagonists and their names live on, thus moving away from the catastrophic end familiar in tragedy. And we have seen in part II that distinctive variations in the use of these closing gestures are closely related to the anomalous shapes of individual plays; a plot that is especially shapely or dismembered or broken will lead to an equally unusual end. In part III, I will look more closely at plots and the expectations they generate. In three of Euripides' later plays, *Helen*, *Orestes*, and *Phoenician Women*, the unusual movement of the plot and the unusual end to which it leads mark a more radical attempt to reconstruct tragedy as what we, today, might call romance, tragicomedy, or narrative, respectively. My argument will not be served by starting from a definition of each genre and showing to what extent a play of Euripides approximates this model. I would like to show, through a careful reading of individual plays, that they generate expectations and organize the plot in novel ways, with the result that tragedy anticipates new and different generic patterns. Discussion of the ending itself will therefore lead, by means of a fuller reading of each play, to consideration of ways in which the tragic end is replaced by a new conception of the end and goal of drama.

The romantic qualities of *Helen* are unmistakeable. A man and a woman, separated by war, disaster and misunderstandings, are finally reunited, and after overcoming many more obstacles together, they at last reach home and live happily ever after. The perils of Helen include an evil king who threatens the woman's life and her honor, and an escape from this king that exploits his stupidity. They include unheroic protagonists: the otherwise cowardly and ineffectual Menelaus, and the proverbially fickle and adulterous Helen. And the play ends with the happiest of happy endings: not only does the couple escape from the king and defeat his minions, but they are wafted home by the Dioscuri to Sparta, where Menelaus can look forward to an afterlife in Elysium, and Helen to life among the immortals. Euripides did not invent the devices of romance; they are already evident in the *Odyssey*, and they begin to play a greater part in plays such as Sophocles' lost *Tyro* and Euripides' *Ion* and *Iphigenia among the Taurians*, but *Helen* presents them in their fullest and most exaggerated form.[3]

There is a curious and telling irony in the fact that whereas Shaw's didactic drama prides itself on avoiding the predictable ending, Euripidean drama is original because, among other things, it creates formulaic closing gestures; Shaw rails against stage-worn formulas, while Euripides invents a brand new wardrobe of hand-me-down endings. The nature of this strange invention has been explored at some length in part I. Now, in turning from gestures in general to particular plots, I begin with a play that brings us back to this paradox. The ending of *Helen* is distinctive not for any trope of reversal or repetition, but because it is so entirely conventional. It stretches the formulaic gestures to their limit, and in this experimental conformity provides the appropriate end to an equally experimental and puzzling plot, a "new Helen"[4] both disconcerting and melodramatic. This chapter will examine these achievements in detail, first exploring the unusually artificial or ready-made quality of the ending, and then following the plot in its gratuitous and unexpected movement toward its goal. As we shall see, the radical conventionality of Euripides' *Helen* directly challenges the possibility of finding order and meaning in experience and in drama.

An Artificial Ending

Preceding chapters have shown that formal variations in Euripidean endings are common and significant: in *Electra*, for example, the explanation of the deus is ineffective, and the characters proceed to question rather than accept what the gods have to say, while Thetis enters in double guise as god and as wife at the end of *Andromache*. The ending of *Helen* is also a variant by virtue of its conventionality, an unusual distinction reflected in every detail of the epilogue.

Helen ends with the most conventional of choral exits, the anapestic lines found at the end of five different tragedies (*Alcestis, Medea, Andromache, Helen,* and *Bacchant Women*):[5]

> Many are the shapes of divinity,
> and the gods fulfill many things surprisingly.
> What was expected has not been accomplished,
> and for the unexpected god found a way.
>   That is how this affair turned out.

> πολλαὶ μορφαὶ τῶν δαιμονίων,
> πολλὰ δ᾽ ἀέλπτως κραίνουσι θεοί·
> καὶ τὰ δοκηθέντ᾽ οὐκ ἐτελέσθη,
> τῶν δ᾽ ἀδοκήτων πόρον ηὗρε θεός.
>   τοιόνδ᾽ ἀπέβη τόδε πρᾶγμα.   1688–92

The repetition of these lines in several other endings, and the gnomic quality of the moral they contain, allow the parting words of the chorus to reflect upon the action only in a most general manner. In fact, of the five plays in which these ready-made lines are found, they have least relevance in *Andromache* and *Helen*. In *Bacchant Women*, for example, the moral—however vaguely phrased—has a very pointed relevance, since Dionysus changes his shape from god to man and apparently to a bull (hence the many shapes of divinity), and since the god in disguise clearly manipulates the outcome (thus finding a way or πόρος for the unexpected). The moral has a similar relevance in *Alcestis*, the earliest extant play in which it occurs: since a mortal is rescued from death just as Apollo promised, it is almost literally true that the god accomplishes things beyond hope. In *Medea*, the choral exit has been adapted to its context with a different first line (πολλῶν ταμίας Ζεὺς ἐν Ὀλύμπῳ, "Zeus in Olympus dispenses many things") that emphasizes the transgressive nature of Medea's epiphany: she has usurped the role of steward or dispenser of good and evil from Olympian Zeus.[6] In *Helen* and *Andromache*, the exit lines have no such relevance to the preceding action; in neither play can the surprising turns of the plot be directly attributed to a god, and the closing moral is no more than a vague and universal observation that god moves in mysterious ways. This irrelevance is emphasized by the abrupt change in meter. In *Medea* and in *Bacchant Women*, the choral exit is preceded by a longer passage also in anapests (twenty-six and twenty lines, respectively), while in *Helen*, *Alcestis*, and *Andromache* the preceding lines are trimeters. As a result, the latter plays end suddenly with formulaic lines that are not preceded by a metrical signal that the end is at hand. Thus not only does *Helen* end with this formulaic choral exit, but the lines come even more abruptly than in *Alcestis*, *Medea*, and *Bacchant Women*.

The same diminished relevance is found in the closing aetiology,[7] in which the Dioscuri announce that Helen will give her name to Helene, an island lying off the coast of Attica near Sounion:

> Where Maia's son first anchored you
> when he carried you off from Sparta through heaven
> and stole your body so Paris could not marry you—
> I mean the stretch of island guarding Acte—
> mortals in future will call this Helene
> since he took you stolen from the house.

> οὗ δ᾽ ὥρμισέν σε πρῶτα Μαιάδος τόκος
> Σπάρτης ἀπάρας τὸν κατ᾽ οὐρανὸν δρόμον,
> κλέψας δέμας σὸν μὴ Πάρις γήμειέ σε,
> φρουρὸν παρ᾽ Ἀκτὴν τεταμένην νῆσον λέγω,
> Ἑλένη τὸ λοιπὸν ἐν βροτοῖς κεκλήσεται,
> ἐπεὶ κλοπαίαν σ᾽ ἐκ δόμων ἐδέξατο.   1670–75

As a rule, the aition establishes a connection between the legendary plot and the world of the audience, but in this case the trace that remains is a minor curiosity whose relevance to the plot is altogether doubtful. The aition itself lacks the immediate relevance of the rites in *Medea* and *Hippolytus* that will commemorate the dead man or children displayed onstage, and it lacks the popular appeal of *Ion*'s celebration of the greatness of Ion's descendants; this is one of the few aitia that simply explain odd or curious place-names (the others being Kynossema in *Hecuba* and Oresteion in *Orestes*).[8] More important, this is the only aition in Euripides that commemorates neither the dramatic action nor its sequel, but an irrelevant episode in the distant past. The alleged layover near Athens, as Hermes carried Helen from Sparta to Egypt, took place seventeen years before the action begins and is mentioned nowhere else in the play.[9] This passage is clearly an aition, explicitly connecting the legendary plot to a place familiar to the fifth-century audience and employing the formulaic terms τὸ λοιπόν and κεκλήσεται. Yet it is irrelevant as it stands, and is made even more irrelevant by the final line, which derives the island's name from the verb ἑλεῖν, "to seize"—and not from Helen's name after all![10]

If the choral exit is literally ready-made, and the closing aetiology is irrelevant, the concluding prophecy describes a distant sequel to the plot. As Helen and Menelaus, offstage, set sail for Sparta, the Dioscuri foretell their happy future:[11]

> Sail with your husband, with a favoring wind;
> and we, your twin savior brothers
> galloping across the sea, will send you home.
> And when you turn and end your life
> you will be called a god, and with the Dioscuri
> will share libations and have offerings with
> us from men. This is the wish of Zeus. . . .
> As for the wandering Menelaus, it is ordained
> by the gods that he dwell in the Blessed Isle.

> πλεῖ ξὺν πόσει σῷ· πνεῦμα δ' ἕξετ' οὔριον·
> σωτῆρε δ' ἡμεῖς σὼ κασιγνήτω διπλῶ
> πόντον παριππεύοντε πέμψομεν πάτραν.
> ὅταν δὲ κάμψῃς καὶ τελευτήσῃς βίον,
> θεὸς κεκλήσῃ καὶ Διοσκόρων μέτα
> σπονδῶν μεθέξεις ξένιά τ' ἀνθρώπων πάρα
> ἕξεις μεθ' ἡμῶν· Ζεὺς γὰρ ὧδε βούλεται. . . .
> καὶ τῷ πλανήτῃ Μενέλεῳ θεῶν πάρα
> μακάρων κατοικεῖν νῆσόν ἐστι μόρσιμον.   1663–69, 1676–77

This is no prosaic sequel of Eliza and Freddy struggling to make ends meet in their little flower shop. The will of Zeus and the escort of the Dioscuri will guarantee not only a safe and swift voyage home, but immortality for Helen and retirement to Elysium for Menelaus. This is the happiest of Euripides' happy endings and also the most gratuitous. The hero usually has to earn his reward. Orestes must wander in exile, driven mad by the Furies, and must stand trial for his life in Athens before he is eventually acquitted and allowed to rule in Argos (*Orestes* 1643–52) or retire to Arcadia (*Electra* 1250–75); Orestes, with Iphigenia, must go back again to Athens and in Halae build a shrine and establish rites for Artemis before his troubles are over (*Iphigenia among the Taurians* 1446–61); Cadmus will be turned into a snake and must lead barbarians in war and sacrilege before he ever reaches the Land of the Blessed (*Bacchant Women* 1330–39); and Heracles must undergo exile and purification of his hideous murders before receiving honors in Athens (*Heracles* 1322–33). The happy end in which Ion discovers both his mother and his royal birthright is contingent only upon a scheme to deceive Xuthus (1601–2), but the failings of an earlier, almost identical scheme (69–73) does not suggest that the way will be smooth.[12] Only in *Helen* is the happy future so happy and so effortless, so devoid of deserving struggle. In fact, this easy and implausible gratification of desires is a common feature of the plot.

The deus ex machina is also artificial, abruptly intervening at the climax of a spectacular scene. A messenger has just announced that Helen and Menelaus have escaped, the furious king is about to rush inside and kill Theonoe for her part in the plot, an honorable servant blocks the door into the palace,[13] and Theoclymenus is about to murder both the servant and his sister, when suddenly two gods appear above the palace, commanding him to stop:

> Restrain the anger that wrongly sweeps you away,
> Theoclymenus, lord of this land. We the two
> Dioscuri call upon you, we whom Leda once
> bore—and Helen, who has escaped from your house.

> ἐπίσχες ὀργὰς αἷσιν οὐκ ὀρθῶς φέρῃ,
> Θεοκλύμενε, γαίας τῆσδ᾽ ἄναξ· δισσοὶ δέ σε
> Διόσκοροι καλοῦμεν, οὓς Λήδα ποτὲ
> ἔτικτεν Ἑλένην θ᾽, ἣ πέφευγε σοὺς δόμους.   1642–45

This is an unusually abrupt and forceful entrance. As the king and servant argue in tetrameters at a frantic pace, the Dioscuri enter unannounced and immediately call a halt. As we have seen, the god's command is usually no more than a call for attention (*Hippolytus* 1283–84, *Suppliant Women* 1183, *Electra* 1238, *Iphigenia among the Taurians* 1436) or a gesture of reassurance (μὴ φεύγετ᾽, *Ion* 1553, μηδέν τι λίαν δυσφορεῖν παρήνεσα, *Andromache* 1234). The god rarely intervenes directly in the action, and even then may first ask a question (*Iphigenia among the Taurians* 1437) or address the antagonist (Μενέλαε, παῦσαι λῆμ᾽ ἔχων τεθηγμένον, *Orestes* 1625); only in *Helen* does the deus intervene with the very first word.[14]

Of the gods who do intervene in the drama (Dioscuri in *Helen*, Athena in *Iphigenia among the Taurians*, and Apollo in *Orestes*), only Apollo substantially affects the outcome by arriving in time to prevent Orestes from murdering Hermione and burning the palace, and Menelaus from storming the palace and killing his niece and nephew. In the other two plays, the action is already complete when the god arrives: Helen has escaped with her husband and the couple is setting sail for Greece, and Iphigenia and Orestes are likewise sailing home on seas made calm by Poseidon. In each case, the call to arms by Thoas or the threats of Theoclymenus against his sister cannot affect the happy outcome of the play, and therefore seems a contrived pretext for bringing on a deus ex machina.[15] The intervention is especially artificial in *Helen*. In *Iphigenia*, the messenger has reported that the getaway ship is foundering, and Thoas has every reason to believe that he can still capture the protagonists. As the barbarian king calls all his people to the attack, the audience fears the worst until Athena arrives, announcing that Iphigenia and Orestes have already escaped. The suspense in *Helen* is every bit as great and is much more theatrical as we witness the angry Theoclymenus about to kill the servant. But there is never any doubt that Helen will escape; the happy ending has already been reported by the messenger, and the Dioscuri intervene to resolve a conflict that has nothing to do with Helen and Menelaus. In preventing the Egyptian king from killing his servant and his sister, the deus is sudden, effective, and entirely irrelevant.[16]

The irrelevance of the gods is reinforced by their uncertain status. The role of the deus requires a clear distinction between the human realm and that of the gods. This distinction is varied but not weakened in the demonic epiphanies of Medea, Eurystheus, and Polymestor, whose privileged power or knowledge gives each of them the stature of a deus ex machina. The distinction *is* weakened, however, when the deus is a god whose authority is not clearly superior to that of the characters. *Andromache*, for example, ends indecisively: Andromache and her son are safe but Neoptolemus has been foully murdered, and the noble Peleus has prevailed but so too have Menelaus and Orestes. The epiphany of Thetis, a humble sea divinity, is equally indecisive. She reassures Peleus and foretells a comforting future for Andromache and her child, but makes no mention of Hermione, Menelaus, and Orestes. She has kind words for her mortal husband and relatives, but does not have the divine authority to arrange their affairs or proclaim punishment for their enemies. The Dioscuri, like Thetis, occupy an ambiguous station between gods and men, but unlike Thetis, they try to play the role of Olympian deus—and fail. In *Electra*, their failure is bald and disconcerting; they try to explain why the matricide was necessary but simply cannot, provoking not understanding and acceptance but the awkward questions of Electra and Orestes. This failure is reinforced by Castor's wavering status: the demigod is a deus explaining the ways of gods to men, but also a brother moved by the death of his sister (1242–43) and a reluctant servant on an errand for Apollo (1245–46). In *Helen*, the Dioscuri fail because they are out of place: they make the grand entrance of a deus where the story does not require them. And rather than trying on too many roles, they never find a clear role at all. They announce their identity clearly enough, proclaiming at the outset both their mortal origins as sons of Leda (1644–45) and brothers of Helen (1645, 1658) and their present immortal stature (1659). Yet their role remains uncertain. It is literally unclear, since the two Dioscuri remain anonymous, never identified by name as they are in *Electra* ("I Castor and my brother Polydeuces here," Κάστωρ κασίγνητός τε Πολυδεύκης ὅδε, *Electra* 1240). And their purpose or mission is also unclear. Why did they arrive on the scene at this particular moment?

> We would have saved our sister long ago
> since Zeus has made us gods;
> but we are weaker than both fate
> and gods, to whom it seemed well this way.

> πάλαι δ᾽ ἀδελφὴν κἂν πρὶν ἐξεσώσαμεν,
> ἐπείπερ ἡμᾶς Ζεὺς ἐποίησεν θεούς·
> ἀλλ᾽ ἥσσον᾽ ἦμεν τοῦ πεπρωμένου θ᾽ ἅμα
> καὶ τῶν θεῶν, οἷς ταῦτ᾽ ἔδοξεν ὧδ᾽ ἔχειν.   1658–61

The answer is entirely negative. They might have come to help their sister at any time, but for a reason that is not explained they did not. Their forceful intervention does not affect the course of the plot, and does not advance an obvious purpose.

After making their sudden entrance and announcing themselves, the Dioscuri explain to Theoclymenus why Theonoe was right to help Helen escape. The divine explanation, as we have seen, tends to play a largely formal role, with notable exceptions in *Hippolytus* and *Electra*. In *Hippolytus*, a lengthy explanation is needed to reveal Phaedra's deception to Theseus and to reveal the role of Aphrodite to both father and son. In *Electra*, the aborted attempt to explain Apollo's purpose underlines the pointless nature of the matricide. Elsewhere the explanation has a real but largely formal effect: Athena confirms that Ion is the son of Creusa and Apollo (*Ion* 1560–62), Apollo explains the disappearance of Helen (*Orestes* 1629–34), and Athena tells Thoas of Orestes' mission to bring back the statue of Artemis (*Iphigenia among the Taurians* 1438–41). In *Helen*, however, the explanation is purely formal: no new knowledge is conveyed when the Dioscuri explain to Theoclymenus why Helen must be allowed to leave:[17]

> Always until the present day
> it was right for her to dwell in your house,
> but since Troy's foundations are overturned
> and offer its name to the gods—not any more:
> she should be joined in the same marriage,
> go to her home, and live with her husband.
> So take the black sword away from your sister
> and consider that what she did was proper.

> εἰς μὲν γὰρ αἰεὶ τὸν παρόντα νῦν χρόνον
> κείνην κατοικεῖν σοῖσιν ἐν δόμοις ἐχρῆν·
> ἐπεὶ δὲ Τροίας ἐξανεστάθη βάθρα
> καὶ τοῖς θεοῖς παρέσχε τοὔνομ', οὐκέτι·
> ἐν τοῖσι δ' αὐτοῖς δεῖ νιν ἐζεῦχθαι γάμοις
> ἐλθεῖν τ' ἐς οἴκους καὶ συνοικῆσαι πόσει.
> ἀλλ' ἴσχε μὲν σῆς συγγόνου μέλαν ξίφος,
> νόμιζε δ' αὐτὴν σωφρόνως πράσσειν τάδε.   1650–57

Theoclymenus knew from the very start that Helen had been left in Proteus' care until the war was over, and he knew that his pursuit of Helen directly contradicted his father's wishes; so the divine explanation is an entirely formal gesture, telling the king what he already knows.

If this account of past events is redundant, is the deus more effective in explaining divine affairs—that realm of action invisible to the mortal characters? In *Hippolytus*, for example, Artemis explains not only the past deeds of Phaedra that Theseus does not know, but also the schemes of Aphrodite that he cannot know, and in other plays, the deus does the same more briefly.[18] In *Helen*, the Dioscuri likewise explain Theonoe's actions by appealing to the realm of fate and the gods:

> You rage at a marriage that was never fated,
> and your sister Theonoe, daughter of a divine
> Nereid, did you no wrong but honored
> the gods and her father's just commands.

> οὐ γὰρ πεπρωμένοισιν ὀργίζῃ γάμοις,
> οὐδ' ἡ θεᾶς Νηρῇδος ἔκγονος κόρη
> ἀδικεῖ σ' ἀδελφὴ Θεονόη, τὰ τῶν θεῶν
> τιμῶσα πατρός τ' ἐνδίκους ἐπιστολάς.   1646–49

This vague assessment reveals no plan of Zeus, no divine purpose that belatedly makes sense of all that has happened.[19] If Theonoe has honored τὰ τῶν θεῶν, the affairs of the gods, the vagueness of this phrase suggests simply that she has conducted herself in a just and righteous manner. Whereas elsewhere the explanation tends to become formalized, in *Helen* it is entirely redundant, reminding Theoclymenus—as he all too well knows—that Helen is not rightfully his and that Theonoe has acted properly.

Perhaps even more irrelevant is the moral with which the twins conclude their speech:

> For gods do not hate the wellborn, and
> trouble falls instead upon the many.

> τοὺς εὐγενεῖς γὰρ οὐ στυγοῦσι δαίμονες,
> τῶν δ' ἀναριθμήτων μᾶλλόν εἰσιν οἱ πόνοι.   1678–79

It is no doubt true that the wellborn live happier lives than the many, and it turns out that our protagonists, one originally in rags and the other a helpless suppliant, are both Spartan aristocrats (Helen shares the noble blood of the Dioscuri, as Theoclymenus notes in his reply, 1684–85). But we are very hard pressed to find in this moral the lesson of the play, and editors often prefer to remove it.[20] A careful reading of the epilogue suggests instead that the closing moral is an essential part of the irrelevant and ready-made ending.

The epiphany concludes with a gesture of acceptance by which the human characters acknowledge the authority and testify to the effectiveness of the deus ex machina. This naturally involves an admission of error: Theseus now wishes he had never cursed his son (*Hippolytus* 1412), and Cadmus confesses his guilt to Dionysus (Διόνυσε, λισσόμεσθά σ᾿, ἠδικήκαμεν, *Bacchant Women* 1344; compare *Suppliant Women* 1228, *Ion* 1608 and 1609), while Orestes and Menelaus announce that they stand corrected by the god's commands (*Orestes* 1670–72, 1679–81; compare *Iphigenia among the Taurians* 1475–76, 1484–85). Since Thetis comes to comfort Peleus, not to rebuke him, there is no admission of error in *Andromache*, while the pattern is inverted in *Electra* as mortals question the conduct of the Dioscuri and Apollo (1298–1300, 1303–4). In *Helen*, however, Theoclymenus manages to proclaim that he will spare Theonoe and let Helen go without admitting that he stands corrected by the deus ex machina, without betraying a trace of humility:[21]

> Sons of Zeus and Leda, I renounce
> my earlier quarrel concerning Helen,
> and no longer would I kill my sister.
> Let Helen go home if the gods wish,
> and know that you were born from
> the same blood as the best and most
> temperate sister. Rejoice in Helen's most
> noble mind—something rare in women.

> ὦ παῖδε Λήδας καὶ Διός, τὰ μὲν πάρος
> νείκη μεθήσω σφῷν κασιγνήτης πέρι·
> ἐγὼ δ' ἀδελφὴν οὐκέτ' ἂν κτάνοιμ' ἐμήν.

κείνη δ᾽ ἴτω πρὸς οἶκον, εἰ θεοῖς δοκεῖ.
ἴστον δ᾽ ἀρίστης σωφρονεστάτης θ᾽ ἅμα
γεγῶτ᾽ ἀδελφῆς ὁμογενοῦς ἀφ᾽ αἵματος.
καὶ χαίρεθ᾽ Ἑλένης οὕνεκ᾽ εὐγενεστάτης
γνώμης, ὃ πολλαῖς ἐν γυναιξὶν οὐκ ἔνι.   1680–87

Rather than admitting his own error or acknowledging the authority of the gods, Theoclymenus congratulates the Dioscuri on the virtues of their sister, instructing them to respect the noble qualities of the woman he has treated so barbarously; where Thoas concludes by saying he will do as Athena wishes (*Iphigenia among the Taurians* 1484–85), Theoclymenus concludes by remarking that noble women are few. The king's reply does confirm that the divine intervention will have its desired effect, but his conversion is gratuitous, with no explanation for his change of heart.[22]

If the various elements of the ending seem somehow irrelevant or superficial to the action, each of these elements is clearly articulated in form, from the πολλαὶ μορφαί choral exit to the emphatic intervention by the Dioscuri. The same is true of the epilogue as a whole, which has a very clear and simple structure: (1) speech of the deus ex machina, (2) short speech of acquiescence, and (3) anapestic choral exit. Most endings involve some variation or complication of this simple pattern, excepting only *Andromache*, *Suppliant Women*, and *Helen*;[23] this clear articulation of form reinforces the artificiality of the ending in *Helen*.

The entire closing scene in all its details, from the misplaced deus to the ready-made exit of the chorus, seems to heighten or exaggerate the formal gestures of Euripidean endings. Yet what is most striking about this final scene of the play is not the conventional and ready-made details, but the overall effect of what might best be called avant-garde conventionality. This hand-me-down happy ending is the result not of a lazy author appeasing his audience with hackneyed devices, but of a playwright inventing new and unprecedented variations upon the usual form of the ending. In this play, he is not satisfied with the familiar gestures that neatly tie things up. Instead he uses these gestures to surprise us with an irrelevant epiphany, an illogical moral, and in general a gratuitous manner of reaching the happy end.

What does this tell us about the play as a whole? It turns out that the movement of the plot is equally striking, proceeding by surprising twists and illogical leaps to its gratuitous outcome.[24] *Helen*, in other words, is itself an experiment in avant-garde conventionality, pushing the limits of Greek tragedy in ways that we now associate with the predictable plots of romance and melodrama. In order to describe this experiment more fully, I turn now to the ways in which the plot moves toward its ending—the predictable, surprising, or gratuitous ways in which it realizes our expectations. In Greek tragedy, the course of events acquires direction or coherence in three ways. First, on the divine level, there is the will of Zeus, the oracle of Apollo, or some divine plan that often seems to direct the action. Second, on the mortal level, there is the logic of human motivations and interactions that makes the course of events believable. And third, on a literary level, there is the traditional legend and its framework of familiar characters and events within which the playwright places his story. We find that on each of these levels, the plot of *Helen* realizes our expectations in novel and gratuitous ways.

Accidental Gods

The Olympian gods play an important but ambiguous role in the action of *Helen*, setting the plot in motion but having little to do with its direction or outcome. The play begins with a prologue speech in which Helen describes the scene in Egypt and repeats the story of the judgment of Paris, which Aphrodite won by promising Helen to Paris (1–30). But how did this bring Helen to Egypt? Euripides introduces a new twist to the quarrel[25] at the point when Paris came to Sparta to claim his prize:

> Hera, annoyed that she did not defeat the others,
> turned into wind my marriage with Alexander
> and gave to King Priam's son not me,
> but a breathing image she took from heaven
> and made like me; in empty seeming, he seems
> to have me, but does not.

> Ἥρα δὲ μεμφθεῖσ᾽ οὕνεκ᾽ οὐ νικᾷ θεὰς
> ἐξηνέμωσε τἄμ᾽ Ἀλεξάνδρῳ λέχη,
> δίδωσι δ᾽ οὐκ ἔμ᾽ ἀλλ᾽ ὁμοιώσασ᾽ ἐμοὶ
> εἴδωλον ἔμπνουν οὐρανοῦ ξυνθεῖσ᾽ ἄπο
> Πριάμου τυράννου παιδί· καὶ δοκεῖ μ᾽ ἔχειν,
> κενὴν δόκησιν, οὐκ ἔχων.   31–36

Originally, Helen was Aphrodite's bribe to Paris (27–28), now her image sent to Troy is Hera's ploy for gaining revenge, and later we shall find that the real Helen's return to Sparta is a further scheme to discredit Aphrodite (880–83). The play's unusual plot, so it seems, is the figment of a jealous spat, while Helen, her double, and all those involved in the Trojan War are merely pawns in this divine quarrel. Helen reminds us of this background in the parodos (238–49) and in her explanation to Menelaus (585–86; 669–83)—but does this petty squabble serve a larger purpose? Zeus has his own project to relieve overpopulation and advertise Achilles by starting a war (38–41), and the scheme of Hera conveniently coincides with his own (τὰ δ᾽ αὖ Διὸς / βουλεύματ᾽ ἄλλα τοῖσδε συμβαίνει κακοῖς 36–37), but there is no evidence of a larger plan or moral purpose.[26] The only suggestion that Zeus takes an interest in Helen or Menelaus comes from Helen herself: after Hera sent the εἴδωλον to Troy, Hermes came and took Helen to Egypt "for Zeus did not overlook me," οὐ γὰρ ἠμέλησέ μου / Ζεύς (45–46). Is Zeus taking care of a detail the quarreling goddesses forgot? Is he simply looking after his daughter, or does he have some larger purpose? We are not told, and this vague hint is not repeated or explained. The Olympian gods are thus directly responsible for the action, but each seems to act from selfish motives without any coherent goal or purpose.[27]

This is not typical. In Euripides, the prologue, if it describes the role of the gods at all, usually presents some sort of plan: Artemis proclaims her intention to punish Hippolytus, Apollo announces that he will try to save Alcestis from death, and Hermes will help Apollo reunite Ion and Creusa. If a god does not appear in person, we may learn indirectly, through dreams and oracles, of Apollo's purpose in *Electra* or *Iphigenia among the Taurians*. In the prologue of *Helen*, however, no such plan is revealed, although we are teased by a single passing comment. After reciting all she has endured, Helen says that she has been comforted by the word of Hermes:

> So why do I still live? This word I heard from the god
> Hermes: that I would return to the famous plain
> of Sparta with my husband . . .

> τί οὖν ἔτι ζῶ; θεοῦ τόδ᾽ εἰσήκουσ᾽ ἔπος
> Ἑρμοῦ, τὸ κλεινὸν ἔτι κατοικήσειν πέδον
> Σπάρτης σὺν ἀνδρί . . .   56–58

It is tempting to reconstruct a divine purpose, announced by the messenger god in the prologue and fulfilled by the deus at the end.[28] Yet Hermes makes no mention of a divine plan. There is no relation between the promise here and the quarrel between Hera and Aphrodite that is so prominent elsewhere, and the Dioscuri in the epilogue make no allusion to Hermes' promise. The promise is dramatically significant because it serves as a foil to Helen's premature despair in the following scene with Teucer; more important, it reinforces our expectation of a happy outcome, but it does so gratuitously without revealing how or why we can expect to reach this end.

It may be that a divine plan is revealed only in the course of the play, just as halfway through *Heracles* we suddenly learn of the brutal designs of Hera. But later events in *Helen* only confirm the irrelevance of the gods. In a central and climactic episode, Helen and Menelaus realize that their lives are in the hands of Theonoe, the sister of Theoclymenus. With her prophetic powers she will know that Menelaus is in Egypt, and if she tells this to her brother, he will surely kill Menelaus and prevent Helen's escape. At this point, Theonoe suddenly enters, identifies Menelaus, and explains that his fate is in the hands of the gods:

> Today there will be a council of the gods,
> and before Zeus they will argue your case.
> Hera, who was your enemy before, is now
> your friend and wants to get you safely home with
> Helen, so Greece may learn that the wedding of
> Paris, the gift of Aphrodite, was a phony marriage.
> But Aphrodite wants to destroy your homecoming,
> so it will never be exposed that she bought her
> name for beauty with Helen's empty marriage.

> ἔρις γὰρ ἐν θεοῖς σύλλογός τε σοῦ πέρι
> ἔσται πάρεδρος Ζηνὶ τῷδ᾽ ἐν ἤματι.
> Ἥρα μέν, ἥ σοι δυσμενὴς πάροιθεν ἦν,
> νῦν ἐστιν εὔνους κἀς πάτραν σῶσαι θέλει
> ξὺν τῇδ᾽, ἵν᾽ Ἑλλὰς τοὺς Ἀλεξάνδρου γάμους
> δώρημα Κύπριδος ψευδονύμφευτον μάθῃ·
> Κύπρις δὲ νόστον σὸν διαφθεῖραι θέλει,
> ὡς μὴ ᾽ξελεγχθῇ μηδὲ πριαμένη φανῇ
> τὸ κάλλος Ἑλένης οὕνεκ᾽ ἀνονήτοις γάμοις.   878–86

No sooner has Theonoe described this strife, reminding us that mortal lives hang on the squabbles of immortals, than she announces that the outcome of the conflict between Hera and Aphrodite lies with herself:[29]

> The outcome rests with me, whether as Aphrodite wishes
> I will destroy you by telling my brother you are here,
> or standing instead with Hera I will save your life,
> deceiving my brother who instructed me
> to tell him when you happen to reach this land.

> τέλος δ᾽ ἐφ᾽ ἡμῖν εἴθ᾽, ἃ βούλεται Κύπρις,
> λέξασ᾽ ἀδελφῷ ‹σ᾽› ἐνθάδ᾽ ὄντα διολέσω
> εἴτ᾽ αὖ μεθ᾽ ῞Ηρας στᾶσα σὸν σώσω βίον,
> κρύψασ᾽ ὁμαίμον᾽, ὅς με προστάσσει τάδε
> εἰπεῖν, ὅταν γῆν τήνδε νοστήσας τύχης.   887–91

Theonoe, with her privileged knowledge of the Olympian gods, describes the conflict between Hera and Aphrodite only to ignore it: she will decide the issue herself and for her own reasons. Rather than weighing the claims of Hera and Aphrodite, she bases her decision upon her own ideas about justice and the mind:

> There is a great temple of justice in
> my nature, which I received from Nereus
> and which I shall try to preserve, Menelaus.

> ἔνεστι δ᾽ ἱερὸν τῆς δίκης ἐμοὶ μέγα
> ἐν τῇ φύσει· καὶ τοῦτο Νηρέως πάρα
> ἔχουσα σῴζειν, Μενέλεως, πειράσομαι.   1002–4

This innate sense of justice is reinforced, as she tells us, by her belief that the mind somehow survives death and therefore may still suffer punishment (1013–16). Theonoe's philosophy is no doubt humane and enlightened, but it is also unconventional and subjective, depending upon an abstract notion of retribution and a personal notion of justice.[30] Whereas Hera and Aphrodite act from personal motives, with no larger plan in mind and with no thought for the human consequences, Theonoe disregards the gods and acts upon lofty motives that are entirely idiosyncratic.[31]

Finally, if there is a divine plan, perhaps it is not revealed until the end, when a god on the machine can explain what has happened. But when the Dioscuri make their appearance, as we have seen, they invoke fate, Zeus, and the will of the gods only to explain why they are too late to help Helen escape:

> We would have saved our sister long ago
> since Zeus has made us gods;
> but we are weaker than both fate
> and gods, to whom it seemed well this way.   1658–61

It has often been observed that Euripides tends to present events as driven by human rather than divine motives, even as the plot retains a formal connection to the myths and the gods.[32] In *Helen*, this process is carried to an extreme and is perhaps best represented by Theonoe's trust in her own personal beliefs rather than in the arguments of Hera or Aphrodite. To see how far Euripides carries this process in *Helen*, it is useful to compare *Iphigenia among the Taurians*—a play very similar to Helen in theme and plot structure. Both plays begin with an unexpected reunion, continue with a scheme to escape from a foreign king, and end with a somewhat artificial deus ex machina; the action of both plays is propelled by chance and by human resourcefulness. But in *Iphigenia among the Taurians* the divine scheme is crucial to the outcome.

Iphigenia begins with two signs from the gods: first Iphigenia tells of her dream in which she touches Orestes with the sacrificial water (42–58), and then Orestes tells of Apollo's oracle that he must bring back the statue of Artemis (77–94). The two signs reveal a plan for the protagonists that is eventually fulfilled on both the divine and the human level: the holy statue is returned to Attica, and brother and sister escape together.[33] Although human misadventures constantly threaten fulfillment of the plan, Apollo's will provides a clear goal for the action. The contrast with *Helen* is clear: there the quarrel between Hera and Aphrodite and the promise of Hermes are not part of a coherent plan and involve the protagonists only accidentally. In *Helen*, the dramatic action is uncertain because the divine framework lacks a goal, whereas in *Iphigenia* the action is uncertain because the divine goal is misunderstood: Iphigenia misinterprets the dream to mean that her brother is already dead, while Orestes is not sure if the oracle is reliable. The melodramatic plot receives its impetus from the heightening of this misunderstanding: Iphigenia cannot believe Artemis would want her to administer such cruel rites (386–91), and Orestes doubts the validity of all oracles (570–75), especially Apollo's (711–15). The ups and downs of the plot, and the mistaken identities, lead Iphigenia to wonder if god or fate controls events (895–97; compare *Helen* 1137–43, quoted in the next section of this chapter), but these doubts are never as profound as in *Helen*, and Orestes can reassure Pylades that god will help those who help themselves:

> Well said; I think we share this task
> with Chance, and whoever exerts himself
> will likely find divinity more potent.

> καλῶς ἔλεξας· τῇ τύχῃ δ' οἶμαι μέλειν
> τοῦδε ξὺν ἡμῖν· ἢν δέ τις πρόθυμος ᾖ,
> σθένειν τὸ θεῖον μᾶλλον εἰκότως ἔχει.   909–11

Iphigenia is no morality play. The tone is too light and fulfillment of the oracles too circuitous to regard the drama as a demonstration of divine power,[34] but the divine frame does establish a goal and direction for the human action. This goal and this direction are at times foils to the confused and undirected human action, but by the end of the tragedy the human action has reached the goal anticipated by the god. In *Helen*, the human action is equally confused and undirected, but the divine frame fails to provide a foil: the quarrel between Hera and Aphrodite is indifferent to the situation of Helen and Menelaus and irrelevant to the decision of Theonoe, while no larger plan is apparent. The result is a drama that fully explores the confusions and delights of undirected human action.

Nevertheless, the outcome of *Helen* does not contradict the will of the gods; it coincides with the jealous schemes of Hera, with the cynical project of Zeus, and with the loyalties of Helen's brothers. But for all we know, it is only accident that things turned out this way. If there is a divine purpose, it has been realized—but realized in a novel and surprising way.

Comic Chance

The role of the gods in *Helen* is clearly articulated, with motivations announced in the prologue, a council of the gods in the central scene, and a deus ex machina in the finale, yet this divine frame is largely irrelevant to the human events and gives only the appearance of order or design to the action. On a human level, the action proceeds in a similar manner: the protagonists' desire for, and expectation of, the happy outcome of reunion, escape, and return home is eventually realized, but the outcome is largely fortuitous and accidentally related to their attempts to realize these goals.

We know from the start that Helen's goal is to escape from Egypt and to find her long-lost husband. But apart from the spectacular hoodwinking of Theoclymenus in the final scenes, nearly every means to this end relies upon chance, or τύχη. In fact, the entire play has an unlikely coincidence as its premise: after wandering for seven years, Menelaus is shipwrecked at the very place where Helen has been held in Egypt. He lands there just when the king's advances have driven her to seek protection at the tomb of Proteus, and he arrives just when Theoclymenus has gone off hunting. In addition, whole scenes are built upon similar coincidences: Menelaus arrives onstage at the precise moment when Helen exits to ask Theonoe if her husband is alive (386). Later, just when Helen has given up trying to convince her slow-witted husband that she is his wife, a servant interrupts to announce that the phantom of Helen has flown off into the sky, proving Helen's identity beyond any doubt (597). And no sooner have Helen and Menelaus completed their suicide pact in fear of Theonoe, than the seer enters (865).[35] It happens that in several of Euripides' later plays chance plays an important role. In *Heracles*, for example, the hero arrives just in time to save his wife and children from being killed by Lycus; in *Orestes*, Pylades enters just when the other characters have given up all hope; and in *Ion*, it is not until Ion is about to drag his mother from the altar and murder her that the priestess enters with the cradle that proves they are mother and son. But τύχη is mentioned more often in *Helen* than in any other play, and here it plays its fullest role.[36]

For Helen, the first twist of chance is the arrival of Teucer, who leads her to believe that her mother, brothers, and husband have all died. Helen bewails this evil τύχη (264, 267, 277, 293, 345), although the chorus advises her to find the truth from Theonoe, since chance can bring both joy and grief (ἐκμαθοῦσα δ᾽ εὖ / πρὸς τὰς τύχας τὸ χάρμα τοὺς γόους τ᾽ ἔχε 320–21). Further twists accompany the arrival of Menelaus, who survives the shipwreck by unexpected good fortune (ἀνελπίστῳ τύχῃ 412), but finds τύχη less charitable upon landing and approaching the palace (417,

463, 478). The reunion of Helen and Menelaus is good luck (645, 698, 738), although it prompts the messenger to reflect upon the fickleness of fortune (715) and Menelaus to hope for similar luck in escaping from Egypt (742). After the unfortunate coincidence of Theonoe's entrance (857) and the appeal to Theonoe to mitigate their misfortune (925), the chorus reflects upon the inscrutable gods and contradictory, unexpected fortune (ἀντιλόγοις. . . ἀνελπίστοις τύχαις 1142–43; compare 412). Finally, good luck hastens the escape of the couple (1374), although the issue of luck is now subjective and ironic, since Helen's and Menelaus' good fortune is Theoclymenus' misfortune (1409, 1424, 1445; compare 1195), and what chance gave, necessity can take away (1636).

Chance governs the language and the action of *Helen* to an exceptional degree, making progress toward the happy end uncommonly difficult, and leaving the play vulnerable to sudden and unexpected change. The absence of a divine plan and the pervasive role of chance together produce a radical uncertainty about the nature of human action. As a servant observes to Helen, god becomes invisible, and life loses all stability:[37]

> My daughter, how variable god is, and how
> hard to make out! With a curious skill, he moves
> everything here, there, upside down: one man suffers,
> and another who doesn't is cruelly destroyed,
> finding nothing secure in continuous chance.

> ὦ θύγατερ, ὁ θεὸς ὡς ἔφυ τι ποικίλον
> καὶ δυστέκμαρτον, εὖ δέ πως πάντα στρέφει
> ἐκεῖσε κἀκεῖσ᾽ ἀναφέρων· ὁ μὲν πονεῖ,
> ὁ δ᾽ οὐ πονήσας αὖθις ὄλλυται κακῶς,
> βέβαιον οὐδὲν τῆς ἀεὶ τύχης ἔχων.   711–15

The chorus goes further, suggesting that god is no more than our name for unpredictable chance:[38]

> What mortal claims he has discovered
> what god is, or not god, or in between?
> He has reached the furthest limit when he sees divinity
> skipping this way and that way again by contradictory,
> unexpected turns of chance.

> ὅ τι θεὸς ἢ μὴ θεὸς ἢ τὸ μέσον
> τίς φησ᾽ ἐρευνάσας βροτῶν;
> μακρότατον πέρας ηὗρεν ὃς τὰ θεῶν ἐσορᾷ
> δεῦρο καὶ αὖθις ἐκεῖσε καὶ πάλιν ἀντιλόγοις
> πηδῶντ᾽ ἀνελπίστοις τύχαις.   1137–43

Euripides portrays human action as devoid of absolute knowledge or a recognizable divine purpose, subject to chance in a profoundly disconcerting way.[39] But chance can give as well as take away, and if τύχη becomes pervasive in *Helen*, there is more opportunity for fortuitous success as well as for failure. In fact, the happy outcome of the plot reflects a τύχη that can best be described as comic and romantic.

We might say that in general terms the plot of *Helen* is governed by comic τύχη because the result is a happy one, just as we might say that a play with a happy ending is a comedy. But I am interested more specifically in the melodramatic quality of chance in *Helen*, a quality that depends upon the shared expectations of characters and audience. Euripides may or may not begin a play with a forecast of events to come, and when he does not, there is a latent or implied contrast between the characters' ignorance of the future and the audience's privileged knowledge of the legend being enacted. The playwright may heighten this contrast with an explicit statement of future events, delivered to the audience in the prologue. Such a prophecy is usually spoken by a god (Apollo in *Alcestis*, Aphrodite in *Hippolytus*, Poseidon in *Trojan Women*, Hermes in *Ion*, and the disguised Dionysus in *Bacchant Women*) or spirit (ghost of Polydorus in *Hecuba*), who thus shares privileged divine knowledge with the spectators. There are two exceptions, *Iphigenia among the Taurians* and *Helen*, in which such a prophecy is reported not directly by a god but by one of the characters.[40] The result in *Iphigenia* is again a contrast between characters and audience, but one that depends more on human folly than on mortal limitations. We begin with two divine forecasts, the oracle reported by Orestes and the dream of Iphigenia, which are both misunderstood; the result is a contrast between the correct understanding of the omens by the audience and the false conclusions drawn by Orestes and Iphigenia— a contrast not fully resolved until the epiphany of Athena. *Helen*, however, begins with a single forecast: the laconic promise of Hermes that Helen will return to Sparta with her husband (56–58). Although it is unclear on what authority Hermes makes this promise, character and audience are placed on the same footing in what they know or may suspect about the future. The similar expectations of protagonist and audience give *Helen* its distinctly suspenseful and melodramatic tone. If the spectators lack a privileged knowledge of the end, they too will be torn by the twists of τύχη, sharing the consternation and relief of the characters as events take fortuitous turns for better or worse. But this identification with the characters' immediate perils precludes a deeper, tragic sympathy. For example, when chance finally reunites Electra and Orestes, Electra's failure to recognize her brother is moving because of the contrast between character and audience: we can invest the scene with pathos because we know it is actually Orestes she is talking to. Yet a similar scene, in which Helen fails to recognize the long-lost Menelaus, is high comedy since there is no such contrast between character and audience. Theonoe has just told Helen that her husband is alive and has been shipwrecked nearby (538–39), and Helen nevertheless runs from him in horror (540–45). Because Helen knows everything that we do, we are ready and able to laugh at her mistakes.[41]

A second important feature of this comic τύχη is the romantic, almost fantastic, realization of desires. Of course, the entire plot is an exercise in wish fulfillment, as Helen's longings to find Menelaus and return home are unexpectedly realized. But more specifically, individual situations are transformed and obstacles are overcome in unlikely obedience to the characters' desires. The clearest example of such transformation is the change in Theoclymenus. The entire plot, from Helen's position as suppliant to the problem of escape from Egypt, is based upon the violent and barbarous nature of the king. Both Teucer (155) and Menelaus (439–40, 468) are warned that he will kill all Greeks, a violation of hospitality that recalls Polyphemus in the

Odyssey ("death will be your guest-gift," θάνατος ξένιά σοι γενήσεται 480; compare *Odyssey* 9.370). Theoclymenus is perceived as savage and barbaric in mind, as hybristic and tyrannical (βάρβαρος φρένας 501, ὠμόφρων 506, τύραννος 809, 817, ὕβριν γ᾽ ὑβρίζων 785), and both Helen (902, 921) and Theonoe (1021) take his wickedness for granted. This reported ogre is the chief obstacle to the happy outcome of the action. Yet when he appears, he piously addresses his father's tomb (1165–68). When he finds a Greek present, he rebukes himself, not others (1171), and his haste to catch Helen is quickly transformed into sympathy and concern for her (1186–92). In the two bamboozling scenes that follow, Theoclymenus is a naïve and love-struck young man rather than a violent despot; he expresses concern for Menelaus (1197), Priam (1220), and Helen (1392–98) and is swept away by a lover's generosity (1254, 1256, 1264, 1280, 1436–40). It is beside the point to try to reconcile these two portraits of Theoclymenus;[42] the lucky transformation of the ogre into a gullible stooge is fantastic, illogical, and pure romance.

There is a similar but more subtle transformation in Theonoe. Her entrance is the work of τύχη (857), another remarkable coincidence: Helen and Menelaus have given up all hope of escape and have sealed their despair with a dramatic suicide pact (835–54), when suddenly Theonoe enters without warning and for no intelligible reason (the only reason given is so that her attendants may render the gods some unspecified custom or νόμος, 871).[43] Yet the seer who might have been their destruction becomes by the end of the scene the savior of Helen and Menelaus. Before her entrance she is faceless, an oracle to judge from her name (822), and although Helen considers asking for her help (825), this is too dangerous since if she alerts her brother, all will be lost (833). Once onstage, Theonoe remains inscrutable. She enters in the manner of a deus ex machina—an imposing figure with divine knowledge (13–14, 878–86) and a divine name, who makes her way through the purified air (865–70)[44] and whose startling entrance is greeted with the panic (857–62, φεῦγ᾽ 860) that often attends a divine epiphany (*Andromache* 1226–30, *Electra* 1233–37, *Ion* 1549–52)— yet we do not know whether the dramatic entrance is for better or worse, whether this divine being comes to destroy or to save. The enigmatic Theonoe baffles our expectations; her sympathy borders on a cruel tease ("poor [Menelaus], you come here escaping such troubles, and now do not know if you'll return home or stay here," 876–77). She describes the council of the gods (878–86) only to announce that the decision is hers (887), and then abruptly orders that her brother be told of Menelaus' presence (892–93).[45] This dreaded outcome is postponed as Helen and Menelaus make lengthy pleas that she reconsider (894–943, 947–95), and what follows is a startling change. She is no longer enigmatic, but direct and unambiguous in her moral judgements (εὐσεβεῖν 998, μίαναιμ᾽ 1000, δυσκλεής 1001, δίκης 1002, etc.), announcing at once that she will keep the truth from her brother (999–1001, 1017–19). Her change of heart is all the more surprising because it follows not from the arguments of the suppliants, but from her own novel and idiosyncratic notions (1002–4, 1013–16). Just as the barbarian king became a gullible lover, the unpredictable and dangerous seer has fortuitously become a pious daughter and a noble friend—to such an extent that she will deceive Theoclymenus in order to do him good (1020–21).

The fantastic transformation of character is most closely tied to the movement of the plot when it involves blocking characters such as Theonoe and Theoclymenus.

But there are also striking changes in the protagonists. In the early part of the play and in the comic recognition scene, Menelaus seems pompous and simple-minded, while his wife is absorbed in vain self-pity. As the intrigue proceeds, Menelaus seems to regain some of his dignity, and Helen takes the lead in the clever and audacious bamboozling of the Egyptian king.[46] A further change is reported by the messenger, who describes at epic length (1526–1618) the heroic exploits of the couple. The ragged Menelaus has earlier been washed and dressed as a warrior (1375–84); the humbled king who lamented the loss of his army (453) now rallies his men in heroic fashion (Ἀτρέως σταθεὶς παῖς ἀνεβόησε συμμάχους·/ Τί μέλλετ', ὦ γῆς Ἑλλάδος λωτίσματα . . . ; 1592–93); the man who planned to kill himself and his wife (842) now takes up arms against the Egyptians (1606–10); and the woman who felt such sympathy for the needless destruction of Troy (109, 196–99, 362–69) calls for a similar destruction of these foreigners (Ποῦ τὸ Τρωϊκὸν κλέος; / δείξατε πρὸς ἄνδρας βαρβάρους 1603–4). If there is an element of parody in this sea battle (the resounding exhortation "Oh you who sacked the city of Ilion" 1560, is used to get a bull onboard, and the exploit that earns Menelaus the epithet "son of Atreus" is an animal sacrifice, 1591–92), the battle itself is fantastically easy: the Egyptians' logs are no match for Greek swords (1600–1), and the slaughter is over without mention of a struggle (1602, 1605–6). When Menelaus looks where to strike, all his enemies jump overboard, and the Greeks calmly sail for home (1609–13). If the ease of the battle undercuts its heroic achievement, it reinforces the miraculous nature of Menelaus' transformation from bumbling soldier into heroic warrior.[47]

The transformations of Theoclymenus, Theonoe, Helen, and Menelaus reinforce the fortuitous wish fulfillment that pervades the play: not only do chance events conspire to bring about the desired outcome (as when a servant enters to announce the disappearance of the phantom), but blocking characters are converted and the protagonists redeemed in surprising and gratifying ways. If τύχη makes the means to an end uncertain, suspenseful, and disturbing, it also provides ends that are happy, fantastic, and the stuff of romance.

The Novel Legend

The juxtaposition of happy end with uncertain means is perhaps clearest in Euripides' handling of the legend. The audience has no doubt that Helen and Menelaus will return safely to Sparta. From oral tradition, from various poems in the epic cycle, and especially from the fourth book of the *Odyssey*, they know that the couple will return home and will spend many years of uneventful middle age in the palace at Sparta. Yet even though the outcome is beyond any doubt, Euripides' version of the legend leaves us uncertain how it will be reached. The usual story was that after the fall of Troy Menelaus carried Helen off, and although his ships were blown off course, he eventually returned with her to Sparta. But Euripides tells us that only a phantom went to Troy and that Helen spent seventeen years in Egypt, first protected by Proteus and then pursued by his barbaric son. Although Stesichorus also describes a phantom, and Herodotus also mentions an episode in Egypt, the plot of *Helen* was entirely invented by Euripides, as were two of its leading characters, Theonoe and Theoclymenus.[48]

It follows that we have no idea how the plot will reach its happy end. To some extent this is true of any story, for the pleasure we take in narrative depends upon reliving the uncertainties of the plot; knowledge of the end in no way detracts from our desire to repeat the confusions of the middle, just as children enjoy hearing the same story over and over.[49] This is especially true of Greek tragedy, which as a rule reenacts an episode from traditional legend. The outline of the plot, and in particular its general outcome, is familiar to the audience, although the pleasure of the performance lies in living or experiencing the means to this end—a pleasure enhanced by the immediacy of the dramatic form and sharpened by unfamiliar details or novel obstacles. What makes *Helen* unusual is the degree to which the certainty of the end and the uncertainty of the means are heightened or exaggerated. Let us begin with the ending. In certain plays, the outcome is relatively unfamiliar simply because the legend presented was less well known; the stories of Alcestis and Ion, for example, were relatively obscure before Euripides brought them to the stage. Sometimes the playwright will continue on to a less familiar end. The recovery of the Argive dead, the madness of Heracles, and the death of Pentheus were all famous episodes in their respective stories, but *Suppliant Women, Heracles,* and *Bacchant Women* each concludes with a subsequent scene: the suicide of Evadne and lamentation for the Seven, Heracles' journey to Athens with Theseus, and Agave's slow return to her senses. Elsewhere, the author provides a less certain end by employing a novel or unconventional version of the legend. We thus find that Medea's children are killed not by the Corinthians but by Medea herself, the exile of Orestes takes him on apocryphal travels from Athens to the Crimea and back again to Attica, and the aftermath of the matricide leads in *Orestes* not immediately to exile but to a novel and startling showdown on the palace roof.[50] Only *Electra* has an outcome as familiar as that of *Helen*, namely the famous murders of Aegisthus and Clytemnestra.[51] Yet the familiar end of *Electra* concludes an equally familiar action: the entire plot and many of its individual episodes were well known to the audience, and had been given a canonical form onstage by Aeschylus' *Oresteia*.[52] In *Helen*, however, the end is familiar while the action is not.

In the plot of *Helen*, the means to the end are as unfamiliar as the end itself is familiar. In any drama, the excitement of the action and the involvement of the audience rely upon a necessary sense of uncertainty, and in Greek tragedy, where the legendary background is common knowledge, the outcome will often be of less interest than the manner in which it is reached. We have already noted some of the devices Euripides used to make his traditional subject matter fresh and engaging: leading to a climax later than the usual end of the story, adding novel details or episodes, and emphasizing apocryphal or less familiar aspects of the legend. Remarkably uncommon by modern standards, however, is the free invention that we take for granted in prose and dramatic fiction. Without going as far as Agathon's singular experiment in *Antheus*,[53] Euripides nevertheless introduced an unprecedented amount of free invention in several plays of this period, especially in *Helen*. In *Ion*, for example, the shadowy eponymous hero is brought to life by the invention of an orphaned childhood at Delphi and a circuitous reunion with his mother. In *Iphigenia among the Taurians*, the playwright connects the canonical story of Orestes' exile with a variant version of Iphigenia's sacrifice by spinning a fantastic tale of peril and reunion among the distant Taurians.[54] And in *Helen*, he combines the age-old story of the returns from Troy with the competing and apocryphal versions of Stesichorus and Herodotus by inventing the melodramatic sequence of refuge, reunion, and escape in exotic Egypt. If any play goes furthest in rendering the action unfamiliar, it is *Helen*. The novelty of the setting has a parallel only in *Iphigenia*, and the fictional characters have no equivalent. Ion, Creusa, and Xuthus may have been little more than names before *Ion*, but they were historical figures nevertheless.[55] Thoas may be an invented character, but his role is small compared to those of Orestes, Pylades, and Iphigenia. Theonoe and Theoclymenus, however, dominate the entire second half of *Helen*, and their fictional status is made clear from the start by the contrived nature of their names (9–10, 13–14).[56] The characters of the play are also made unfamiliar by confusing them with figures who should be their opposites. The story of an evil Egyptian king who kills all Greeks who land on his shores is a commonplace in satyr-plays such as Euripides' *Busiris*,[57] but is out of place in tragedy, so what do we make of the apparently satyric Theoclymenus? The story of a chaste and virtuous wife waiting many years for her husband to return from the Trojan War, and enduring arrogant advances in his absence, is familiar from the *Odyssey*. But what do we make of Menelaus, the well-known weak and self-centered cuckold, now redrawn as Homer's noble and long-suffering hero? And what do we make of Helen, the notoriously fickle and indifferent adulteress, now recast as a chaste and virtuous Penelope?[58] The plot of *Helen* is unpredictable both because the fictional subject matter is unfamiliar to the spectators and because its characters do not conform to their expectations.

This contrast between certain end and uncertain means is the source of the play's unprecedented suspense: although we know that the couple will eventually escape together, we are baffled as to how they can possibly reach this goal. Insofar as the novel treatment of the legend heightens this contrast, *Helen* might fairly be called our first suspense or adventure drama. The interest of the play centers not upon the knowledge or blindness of an Oedipus, nor upon the transforming passion of a Medea, but simply upon the turn of events from one moment to the next. This unheroic concern with surviving the buffets of chance, and contriving a means to the desired end, is established at the very beginning of the play. In her prologue speech, Helen describes her situation, bewails her sufferings, and concludes with a moment of crisis:

> For as long as Proteus saw the light of day,
> I was safe from marriage; but now that
> he's buried in the shady earth, the dead man's son
> is hunting to marry me. Honoring my past
> husband I fall before this tomb of Proteus as
> a suppliant, hoping he will preserve my marriage;
> if my name is infamous throughout Greece,
> let not my body be dishonored also.

> ἕως μὲν οὖν φῶς ἡλίου τόδ᾽ ἔβλεπεν
> Πρωτεύς, ἄσυλος ἦ γάμων· ἐπεὶ δὲ γῆς
> σκότῳ κέκρυπται, παῖς ὁ τοῦ τεθνηκότος
> θηρᾷ γαμεῖν με. τὸν πάλαι δ᾽ ἐγὼ πόσιν

τιμῶσα Πρωτέως μνῆμα προσπίτνω τόδε
ἱκέτις, ἵν' ἀνδρὶ τἀμὰ διασώσῃ λέχη,
ὡς, εἰ καθ' Ἑλλάδ' ὄνομα δυσκλεὲς φέρω,
μή μοι τὸ σῶμά γ' ἐνθάδ' αἰσχύνην ὄφλῃ.　60–67

This is only the first of many crises in this play; they multiply throughout the drama, reaching an almost ludicrous climax in the refusal of the sacrificial bull to go on board (1554–68). As the first of countless perils facing our protagonists, the suppliant scene at the beginning of the play sets the mood and the pattern for the suspenseful plot to follow. And in doing so, it introduces yet another innovation. When a play begins with a suppliant scene, it usually does so in order to present a moral or political crisis in clear, unambiguous terms: What are our obligations to oppressed refugees (*Children of Heracles*)? What lengths must we go in defending inalienable rights (*Suppliant Women*)? In each case, the remainder of the play meditates upon this crisis and tries to resolve it. In *Heracles*, the device becomes more formal; it establishes the moral high ground of the hero's family in fleeing the tyrant, and of Heracles in killing him, but it serves above all as a theatrical red herring—leading to a shocking outcome in which the suppliants accept their death, in order to heighten the surprise of Heracles' sudden return. In *Helen*, the suppliant scene loses its moral force altogether. The ethical crisis posed by the suppliant opening, one that pits pious Greek woman against hybristic, barbaric man, is never decided because it quickly dissolves into an amoral struggle to escape, pitting native guile against foreign stupidity.[59] The suppliant action provokes not a crisis of principles but a crisis of action: How can the couple escape? What must they do to avoid the clutches of the king? In this sense, the suppliant scene becomes a formal gesture not unlike the deus ex machina.[60] The moral force of supplication before the tomb of Proteus is secondary to the gesture of beginning—a gesture that serves to set the suspenseful plot in motion.

The beginning thus brings us back to the end, and back to the formal gestures that are so pronounced in the ending of *Helen*. But the conventionality of the ending—the exaggerated misfit between action and outcome—also describes the movement of the play as a whole. The role of the gods, the interventions of τύχη, and the novel version of the legend, all heighten the mismatch between uncertain events and their curiously predictable outcome.

The New Helen

If we require our tragedies to be serious and profound, as critics often do, there is more than enough to satisfy us in *Helen*.[61] This seriousness does not lie in the gratuitous and ready-made ending, however, but in the disconcerting means to this end: there is no apparent plan or purpose in the actions of the gods, human fortunes change from one moment to the next according to unpredictable τύχη, and unexpected obstacles interfere with the familiar happy ending of legend. The order that characters and audience expect to find in the action is exposed as illusory, and any congruence between expectation and experience turns out to be accidental. The radical skepticism of *Helen* is objective in the sense that the workings of τύχη demonstrate the absence of an order or logic in this chaotic world, and this skepticism is also subjective in that the drama focuses upon the frustrated desires of characters and audience to find an order in experience. In this respect, *Helen* goes further than other Euripidean plays. *Hippolytus* and *Bacchant Women*, for example, offer variations upon the tragic πάθει μάθος: they presume a larger, divine order that is accessible to the audience but not to the protagonist, and when Hippolytus or Pentheus belatedly recognizes this order, we may question its justice, but not its existence. In the "intrigue" plays, the emphasis is less upon ignorance of an (objective) order than upon the (subjective) difficulty of finding such order.[62] In *Ion*, for example, the burden of the drama falls not upon the fact of divine parentage (belatedly recognized by Ion), but upon the confusion that attends the attempt to sort out this parentage. This more subjective and more skeptical approach is taken furthest in *Helen*. Here there is no larger plan at all, and although audience and characters persist in their desire for and expectation of order, the reversals of τύχη and the gratuitous nature of the outcome show that these desires are realized—if at all—only by coincidence.

This play has often been described as philosophical in content, most often, perhaps, because of the way in which it plays with the distinction between appearance and reality; if we cannot distinguish between Helen and her image, or between the chaste and the adulterous Helen, then our capacity for apprehension and knowledge is severely limited.[63] Another philosophical argument has been extrapolated from the role of Theonoe: if she acts correctly by ignoring the squabbles of Olympian gods, then perhaps we need new concepts of justice and divinity.[64] These are certainly important themes, but the play's philosophical content is a broader concern with the lack of order—or rather the accidental order—in human affairs. Accustomed as we are to clichés about fickle fate and to the simplistic use of coincidence in later comedy and romance, it is hard to appreciate Euripides' originality and seriousness in presenting this issue so directly. The incomprehensibility of the phenomenal world and the limits of human understanding are fundamental questions that exercised the sophists throughout this period, and which were presented most forcefully by Gorgias in his lost work *On Not Being*, or *On Nature*. Here he asserted, "first that nothing exists, second that if it exists, man cannot apprehend it, and third that if it can be apprehended, it cannot be expressed or interpreted to another," πρῶτον ὅτι οὐδὲν ἔστιν, δεύτερον ὅτι εἰ καὶ ἔστιν, ἀκατάληπτον ἀνθρώπῳ, τρίτον ὅτι εἰ καὶ καταληπτόν, ἀλλὰ τοί γε ἀνέξοιστον καὶ ἀνερμήνευτον τῷ πέλας.[65] *Helen* dramatizes a similar profound skepticism, suggesting that the order we take for granted may not exist, that if there is an order in the world we cannot apprehend it—and that even if it can be apprehended, drama is somehow unable to express it.

Before elaborating upon this final literary concern, it is important to note that the play's interest in unpredictable change reflects major events of this period. As Thucydides makes clear, the prolonged Peloponnesian War with Sparta, the dislocation of the Athenian population, the plagues, and social unrest all contributed to a pervasive sense of doubt, uncertainty, and rootlessness that increased as the war continued.[66] The catastrophic and unexpected destruction of the huge Athenian force in Sicily brought home to the Athenians the profound unpredictability of experience, showing that even the surest hopes and most confident expectations could suddenly and inexplicably be reversed. Thucydides describes the situation in 413:

When the news reached Athens, for a long time people would not believe it . . . And when they did recognize the facts, they turned against the public speakers who had been in favour of the expedition, as though they themselves had not voted for it, and also became angry with the prophets and soothsayers and all who at the time had, by various methods of divination, encouraged them to believe that they would conquer Sicily.[67]

The first and most important reaction of the Athenians was anger at the betrayal of their expectations. In the following year, Euripides' *Helen* suggests that the reversals of fortune may just as inexplicably fulfill our hopes and expectations, bringing the fortuitous happy end of reunion and deliverance. If the play is an antidote to the calamity of the year before, it is not an escapist fantasy or a sugary diversion from the recent disaster.[68] The action of *Helen* is firmly rooted in the Athenians' new experience of profound uncertainty. What escape or fantasy there is in *Helen* depends entirely upon the chance, or τύχη, that is otherwise so disconcerting. By closely observing his chaotic world, by honestly reporting how it resists the search for order, Euripides shows that chance can lead to success, as well as to failure, that an uncertain world can be both exciting and terrifying, and that the desire for happy endings may be entirely irrelevant even as it is realized.

These serious philosophical and civic concerns, however, are only part of the story. *Helen* is also undeniably comic and romantic, melodramatic and suspenseful. If we are reluctant to read the play as serious tragedy, as many critics are, we can draw attention to any one of these qualities.[69] There is high comedy in several scenes: the farcical dressing down of the bedraggled Menelaus by an old gatekeeper, the ironic humor of his failed recognition scene with Helen, and Helen's comic success in bamboozling Theoclymenus. In the second half of the play, as we have seen, fortuitous wish fulfillment and the happy conversion of blocking characters make the drama romantic, almost fantastic, in its outcome. And throughout the play the capricious role of τύχη and the surprising novelty of the plot fill the action with melodrama and suspense. What do we decide? Is the play serious and philosophical, or comic and entertaining? We might search for a middle ground and decide that *Helen* is neither philosophy nor comedy, but some sort of combination—a comedy of ideas or a philosophical romance.[70] It seems to me, however, that the novelty of *Helen* lies not in a blending of different genres, but in the play's independence from familiar generic categories.[71]

Insofar as *Helen* does fall into an existing category, it belongs to the new class of melodramas that also includes *Ion*, *Iphigenia among the Taurians*, and Sophocles' lost *Tyro*. In plays such as these, the multiplication of incident and the sentimental theme of reunion with a long-lost child or sibling anticipate the formulaic plots of New Comedy.[72] As a member of this group, *Helen* tests the limits of its genre, making the twists and reversals of the plot even more fortuitous, and the happy ending especially formulaic. We might therefore conclude that the worn-out conventions of the British stage, the rags of romance that for Shaw were symptoms of lazy writing for a lazy audience, were for Euripides the stuff of an exciting new genre, a genre that he explored in other plays before making his most radical experiment with this conventional form in *Helen*.[73] Yet in testing the limits of this genre, Euripides also moves beyond it. In other plays of this group, the playwright searches for suitable material for his melodramas, digging up minor legends and apocryphal episodes that he can develop into romantic and suspenseful plots. In *Helen*, however, he does the opposite, beginning with the most famous and least suitable of legends and making it into a melodrama only by turning it inside out: the crime of Paris did not lead with divine sanction to the sack of Troy and recovery of the guilty Helen, but a divine quarrel led fortuitously to a happy reunion of Helen and Menelaus in Egypt. The poet likewise creates his romantic leads only by turning the cowardly Menelaus and the adulterous Helen into their opposites. Romance is purchased only by confounding epic, replacing the *Iliad*'s Helen with a phantom and casting Helen and Menelaus as Penelope and Odysseus. And suspense is purchased only by contradicting known events and removing the familiar logic of divine and human action.

Helen is less an example of a new genre than a subversion of old ones. This novelty may be due simply to the poet's own exuberance, but I suspect that it also reflects doubt about the viability of his medium. Euripides might not have agreed with Gorgias that what we apprehend cannot be expressed, but he probably would have agreed that what he saw and understood in the later years of his career could no longer be expressed by means of tragedy.[74]

10

Orestes and Tragicomedy

It all comes to the same thing anyway; comic and tragic are merely two
aspects of the same situation, and I have now reached the stage where I find
it hard to distinguish one from the other.

EUGENE IONESCO

The baffling *Helen* generates confusions about the nature of the drama just as it generates confusion about the identity of Helen; the radically uncertain course of events threatens to reduce the action to an unintelligible chaos, while the happy end provides the reassuring frame of romance. In the predictable plots that Shaw reviles, the two impulses reinforce one another: the damsel must first be threatened with demons and dangers in order to justify the happy end. But in *Helen*, as we have seen, the two impulses are severed: profound uncertainty and comforting conclusion are connected in a purely artificial manner; the end does not seem to warrant the means, and the viewer is unable to make sense of the whole. If the play, in the end, is neither a hand-me-down from the ragshop of romance nor an illustration of the unintelligibility of life, we are left wondering what sort of play it is.

Four years later, in *Orestes*, Euripides posed similar problems in a more spectacular way. Rather than sever means from ends, he constructed an action that leads relentlessly towards two contradictory endings, toward a comic and a tragic resolution. Ionesco discovered that tragedy and comedy are really the same thing, two different aspects of the same situation: domestic life in *The Bald Soprano*, for example, is so utterly banal that we can't decide whether to laugh or cry. *Orestes*, however, is at each moment both tragedy and comedy; it is not one situation with two different faces, but two competing actions in one. This violent contradiction, and the contrasting expectations it generates, leaves tragedy unable to give coherent shape to events— not because these events lead to ends that are gratuitous, but because they lead to ends that are completely at variance with one another. Whereas *Helen* realizes expectations in an artificial manner, *Orestes* generates and realizes contradictory expectations. A detailed reading both of the ending and of the ends that the plot anticipates will show that *Orestes* advertises the end of tragedy—and heralds something entirely new.

A Doubled Ending

If one feature distinguishes the ending of *Helen*, it is an exaggeration of the formal quality of the closing gestures; a familiar stylization is carried to an extreme. The opposite is true of *Orestes*. As we have seen, the deus of this play is exceptional insofar as he intervenes directly and effectively in the stage action: unlike other gods who intervene in a largely formal manner, Apollo arrives to prevent the real and very dangerous showdown between Orestes and Menelaus, and he succeeds in reconciling the antagonists and averting the crisis. But this ending is doubly exceptional. The effective intervention of Apollo is required only because a prior epiphany, by Orestes, has already proven successful; one unusually effective deus is cancelled out by the other.

The epilogue begins by replaying the spectacular and controversial ending of one of Euripides' earlier plays. A Phrygian slave has described at length (1369–1502) the commotion inside the palace, where Orestes and his accomplices have been putting into action their scheme for revenge and escape. Betrayed by the pusillanimous Menelaus, they will punish him by killing his wife and will then use his daughter Hermione either to secure escape from Argos (where Orestes has been sentenced to death), or at least to inflict more suffering on Menelaus. The situation replays the end of *Medea*, in which Medea, betrayed by Jason and banished from Corinth, plots to take revenge against him by killing his bride and murdering his children. After a messenger reports the ghastly death of Jason's bride when she put on the poisoned robe, Medea goes inside the palace to complete her revenge by killing the children and to plan some means of escape. In *Orestes*, the Phrygian reports that the plot against Helen did not proceed so smoothly: at the moment of death, she vanished from the palace "by drugs or wizardry or stolen by the gods" (1495–98). Orestes hauls the slave back inside the palace, promising that if Menelaus does not help him escape, he will find his daughter dead, as well as his wife (1533–36). The chorus sings a brief interlude, in which their fears are confirmed by the sight of smoke arising from the palace (1541–45), and then Menelaus arrives. He stands before the palace, calling upon servants to open the doors and vows he will rescue his daughter and kill in revenge those who murdered his wife (1561–66)—when suddenly Orestes appears on the palace roof, taunting Menelaus, boasting that he will kill his child, and promising that he will rule in Argos. The echoes of *Medea* are pervasive. After a brief choral interlude, in which the cries of children confirm the chorus's fears, Jason arrives and standing before the palace calls upon servants to open the doors so he can see the dead children and take revenge upon Medea—when Medea appears on the palace roof, taunting Jason, boasting that she killed the children and promising to make her escape to Athens. There are further similarities in detail between the two scenes,[1] as well as important differences: Medea can foretell the manner of Jason's death while Orestes can only offer threats, and Medea's unusual powers are visibly evident in her divine chariot while Orestes attempts to seize power with the threat of force against Menelaus (1569) and Hermione (1578). But the systematic parallels clearly portray the entrance of Orestes as a version of the demonic deus ex machina.

The epiphany of Orestes is underscored by several formal details. The first words of Orestes take the form of a command, a negative injunction addressed by name to the mortal below: "You there, do not touch the bolts with your hand—yes you, Menelaus, towering bold" (οὗτος σύ, κλῄθρων τῶνδε μὴ ψαύσῃς χερί· / Μενέλαον εἶπον, ὃς πεπύργωσαι θράσει, 1567–68). This surprising entrance above is greeted with the cry of amazement that often heralds the entrance of a god: ἔα, τί χρῆμα; (1573; compare *Hippolytus* 1391, *Ion* 1549, *Heracles* 815, *Rhesus* 885). And some details of the scene are rendered in burlesque form: instead of a deus who asserts his own divine power and invokes the higher authority of Zeus, Orestes on the rooftop promises to enforce his command with blocks of masonry (1569–70). And instead of a speech from the machine followed by the mortal's explicit acceptance of the god's dispensations, we have a lengthy sequence of stichomythia and antilabê, alternating lines and then half-lines, which concludes with two words from Menelaus: ἔχεις με, "You have me" (1617). Yet if Orestes is a new and somewhat farcical Medea, he also improves upon his model. Medea, for all her demonic power and divine stature,[2] exercises no control over the stage below; she can taunt Jason as Orestes taunts Menelaus, but the mark of her privileged stature is entirely negative: with the chariot of the Sun, she is able to escape from Corinth and flee from the consequences of her actions. Orestes, however, has immediate control over Menelaus: with his knife at Hermione's neck and torches ready to burn the palace, he orders Menelaus not only to capitulate, but also to help install Orestes as ruler of Argos (1600–1). This power, in fact, is his own undoing. After Menelaus capitulates (1617), Orestes nevertheless orders the palace be torched, provoking Menelaus to order an assault and triggering the entrance of Apollo.

At the very moment at which Orestes, playing deus, wields his power so effectively and recklessly, he is interrupted by Apollo's entrance upon the machine. In a theatrical tour de force, Menelaus and his soldiers at ground level are upstaged by Orestes, Electra, and Pylades brandishing torches on the palace roof, and they in turn are upstaged by a god suspended in heaven and accompanied by the soon-to-be deified Helen.[3] The god overturns Orestes' triumph, forbidding the murder of Hermione or the burning of the palace, explaining that the attempt to murder Helen had failed and commanding the bitter enemies to be friends. Orestes playing deus is upstaged by a real god, who first delivers an amended injunction to Menelaus ("Menelaus, end your sharpened temper; it is I, Phoebus son of Leto, who call upon you," Μενέλαε, παῦσαι λῆμ' ἔχων τεθηγμένον· / Φοῖβός σ' ὁ Λητοῦς παῖς ὅδ' ἐγγὺς ὢν καλῶ, 1625–26), before delivering a similar command to Orestes as well ("And you, Orestes, guarding the girl with sword in hand, learn what I have come to tell you" 1627–28). The real deus was sent by Zeus (1634). He is able to explain the past and foretell the future, and he intervenes directly in the action, forestalling a bloody and catastrophic showdown. Apollo's role is exceptional. As a rule, the god's command and intervention are largely formal, and even in *Helen* and *Iphigenia among the Taurians*, in which the deus does affect events onstage, these events are a sideshow: the protagonists have already escaped and the god steps in to end the futile anger of a duped barbarian king. The staging reinforces the point: the protagonists in those plays are offstage and already far from land, while onstage the deus and the king are left behind. In *Orestes*, however, the play's central crisis—whether Orestes should pay the penalty in Argos for his act of matricide—reaches an impasse with the showdown between Orestes and Menelaus; the god steps in to resolve this crisis and to reconcile the protagonist with his chief opponent. The staging reinforces this dramatic intervention, with Orestes holding a sword to Hermione's neck and his attendants wielding torches ready to burn down the palace, while Menelaus and his soldiers prepare to storm the building. Apollo not only makes an effective and spectacular intervention, but like Orestes seems to revel in his power. He tells the most bitter enemies to end their quarrel, adding that Orestes must marry the woman he is about to murder ("And the woman at whose throat you hold your sword, Orestes, it is fated that you marry her—Hermione,"ἐφ᾽ ἧς δ᾽ ἔχεις, Ὀρέστα, φάσγανον δέρῃ, / γῆμαι πέπρωταί σ᾽ Ἑρμιόνην 1653–54) and that Menelaus must let Orestes rule as king in the palace he has been trying to destroy (1660–61). The mortal Orestes, who outdoes Medea in his exercise of demonic power, is answered by Apollo, who surpasses all other gods in his demonstration of power from the machine.

As we shall see, this double epiphany, first on the palace roof and then from the machine, provides the plot with two different and contradictory conclusions. And because the play ends with this spectacular contradiction, the epiphany is doubled in another way: Apollo performs his role as deus ex machina twice. First, Apollo delivers a speech commanding Orestes and Menelaus to end their quarrel (1625–28), providing a series of explanations of the past and prophecies of the future, and concluding with a reminder of Apollo's responsibility (1664–65), to which Orestes and Menelaus respond by graciously accepting his dispensations (1666–1677). But this is not the end. Apollo again commands them to depart and resolve their quarrel (1678–79), Orestes and Menelaus again announce that they will obey (1679–81), and the god repeats his command and gives a fuller prophecy concerning the deified Helen (1682–90). The only other two-part epiphanies in Euripides are interrupted either by an entrance (Hippolytus in *Hippolytus*) or by challenges to the "deus" (from Jason in *Medea*, and from Electra and Orestes in *Electra*). In Orestes, there is no such interruption, and this doubling seems required instead by the impasse at the end of the play: after two contradictory epiphanies, the action remains unresolved, and Apollo's second intervention is needed if only to dismiss the characters and empty the stage ("each of you depart as I command," χωρεῖτέ νυν ἕκαστος οἳ προστάσσομεν, 1678; "now go on your way," ἴτε νυν καθ᾽ ὁδόν 1682). As if to reinforce this abrupt and unsatisfying conclusion, the actors are escorted offstage not with moralizing reflections from the chorus, but with Apollo's own anapests on the deified Helen (1682–90).[4]

Speech and Silence

Euripides' *Orestes* is well known, if not notorious, for its disconcerting variations and contradictions. William Arrowsmith made the point well, describing *Orestes* as "tragic in tone, melodramatic in incident and technique, by sudden wrenching turns savage, tender, grotesque, and even comic."[5] We need only think of Orestes' sudden alternations between sleep and mad outbursts early in the play, or the sudden shift later from a heroic vow to commit suicide together to an outrageous scheme to murder Helen and hold Hermione hostage. What is the reason for these bewildering shifts? What, if any, is the method to this madness? It is true enough that variety makes for an exciting spectacle, and it is true as well that the play's confusions reflect the upheavals in Athens around 408 B.C.E.[6] But there is also a fundamental contradiction in the plot of *Orestes*, a contradiction born in the tension between silence and speech, and elaborated in a radical confusion of the tragic with the comic. As events of the play follow a course of increasing license, from silence to unbridled speech and to the brink of criminal action, this escalating license moves relentlessly in incompatible directions, toward extreme visions of the comic and the tragic end. Because the play between speech and silence is so pervasive in *Orestes*, and because it articulates the conflict between comic and tragic outcomes, I shall trace the increasing license of speech in some detail.[7]

Central to the plot of *Orestes* is a tension between silence and speech that is figured or represented almost entirely by two extremes: on the one hand, an inability to speak that indicates helplessness and inhibition and, on the other hand, an unbridled or reckless speech that is the mark of power and freedom from inhibition. As Orestes and Electra move from one extreme to the other, from total silence to unbridled speech, they not only acquire power but also overcome inhibitions and violate tabu. As they do so, their words and actions will seem tragic or comic depending upon the outcome: license checked or punished represents the hybris leading to catastrophe so common in tragedy, while license unchecked and unpunished represents the audacity and the immunity from consequences typical of comedy. The action of *Orestes* is fairly simple: from silence and helplessness to unbridled speech and (almost) to reckless deeds, the three companions follow a course of ever-increasing license; the two extremes are the silence of Orestes for the first 210 lines of the play, and his arrogant threats to Menelaus in the finale. The consequences of this action, however, are ambiguous. In the first half of the play, Orestes speaks out with impunity but always in fear of the outcome, creating an uneasy mixture of comic and tragic tone. In the second half, the consequences are uncertain, as the license becomes so great that the audience is unable to foresee either success or failure for the conspirators and unable to separate the comic from the tragic.[8]

Before we follow the double course of this plot, it should be noted that the opposition between speech and silence has important implications. The first is dramatic: speech may take the place of actions that are tabu upon the stage. In portraying blasphemy, for example, the tragedian cannot depict violence to an altar or a priest, but he can show Oedipus verbally threatening and insulting Teiresias. *Orestes*, however, threatens to overstep these bounds. The plot to cut Hermione's neck and burn down the palace is almost enacted before our eyes; by portraying unbridled speech that almost overturns the prohibitions of the theater, Euripides suggests a degree of license that threatens to overturn the prohibitions of society. Other implications reflect the significance of speech in Athenian society. Religious ritual frequently enjoined holy silence with a command, εὐφημεῖτε, that forebade tabu or inauspicious speech; unbridled speech may therefore be not only rude but blasphemous (as in the case of Tantalus). The new field of rhetoric also drew attention to the persuasive power of speech and to the moral relativism of words. Logical and persuasive arguments could be used to support a reprehensible position, employing speech in a socially unacceptable manner (as Orestes does). Finally, freedom of speech, or παρρησία, was a prerogative of the democratic assembly in which Athenians took great pride,[9] but it also gave free rein to the violent upheaval of this period. *Orestes* is the first work to portray this freedom of speech as a negative and dangerous license (as in the ἀμαθὴς παρρησία of the demagogue, 905).[10] Silence is mentioned more often in *Orestes* than in any other surviving play of Euripides,[11] while uninhibited speech is a central theme. The movement from silence to unbridled speech represents ever-increasing license, with connotations of blasphemy, moral duplicity, and political turmoil. But such license also suggests the comic hero, whose verbal license includes both indecent language and ridicule of political figures and religious institutions, and whose license in action is exemplified by the outrageous scheme in Aristophanes' *Birds*, in which Peisetairos and the birds succeed in overthrowing the gods and usurping the place of Zeus.[12]

The play begins with a speech by Electra, recounting the past misfortunes of her family and describing the present situation. She begins with great uncertainty: "There is nothing terrible—so to speak . . ." (Οὐκ ἔστιν οὐδὲν δεινὸν ὧδ' εἰπεῖν ἔπος 1); "For Tantalus, son—so they say—of Zeus . . ." (Διὸς πεφυκώς, ὡς λέγουσι, Τάνταλος 5); "And this is the penalty he pays—so they say . . ." (καὶ τίνει ταύτην δίκην, / ὡς μὲν λέγουσιν 7–8); "Famous Agamemnon—if he was really famous—was born . . ." (ὁ κλεινός, εἰ δὴ κλεινός, Ἀγαμέμνων ἔφυ 17). As Electra proceeds to fill in the unpleasant details, she repeatedly hesitates between speech and silence. She is reluctant to speak of Atreus' rivalry with Thyestes ("Why should I measure out unspeakable deeds?" 14), yet briefly mentions the unspeakable act ("Atreus feasted him on the children he had killed," 15), while passing over other details: "And Atreus— but I keep silence about events in between" (16). She likewise alludes to her mother's adultery without actually mentioning it (as for the reason Clytemnestra killed Agamemnon, "a maiden cannot properly speak of it," ὧν δ' ἕκατι, παρθένῳ λέγειν / οὐ καλόν 26–27), and she hesitates before criticizing Apollo: "And what is the point in charging Phoebus with injustice? But he persuaded Orestes to kill the mother who gave him birth" (28–30). Finally, her fear of naming her brother's tormentors is not enough to prevent her from doing so: "his mother's blood drives him on with bouts of madness—for I am afraid to name the goddesses, Eumenides, who drive him wild with fear" (37–38). The first half of Electra's prologue speech, in which she describes her family history (1–38), is thus marked by her uncertain reluctance to speak of this past.[13] The second half of her speech (39–70) describes the situation at the beginning of the play, in which the characters are trapped in silence. Brother and sister are barred from speaking to anyone in Argos:

Argos here decided that we are welcome
neither in homes nor at hearth, and being matricides
may talk to no one:

ἔδοξε δ' Ἄργει τῷδε μήθ' ἡμᾶς στέγαις,
μὴ πυρὶ δέχεσθαι, μήτε προσφωνεῖν τινα
μητροκτονοῦντας·   46–48 (compare 428, 430)

This legal restraint has a counterpart in the silence that madness imposes upon Orestes: for six days now, he has neither eaten nor washed, but sleeps wrapped in a cloak and wakes only to run or weep (42–45).

The verbal impasse that Electra describes is dramatized by the opening scene as a whole. The hero lies in a prominent position onstage and remains there in silence for 210 lines: the prologue speaker was reluctant to speak, and the protagonist cannot speak at all.[14] After an intervening scene with Helen, what follows is even more surprising. The chorus enters and prepares to sing its parodos or entrance song, but before its members can utter a word, they are silenced by Electra: "Dear women, walk gently, hush, let there be no noise" (ὦ φίλταται γυναῖκες, ἡσύχῳ ποδὶ / χωρεῖτε, μὴ ψοφεῖτε, μηδ' ἔστω κτύπος 136–37).[15] What follows instead is a lyric exchange conducted partly in stage whispers as the chorus members try to comply with Electra's request ("Silence, silence, walk onstage gently, make no noise" 140–41), while Electra tries to silence not only their voices but also the music and dancing that usually accompany their entrance: "Ah! Ah! Sound only the breath of a gentle reed pipe, my friend" (145–46), "Down, down, approach without shaking, without shaking" (149). The verbal impasse with which the play begins is almost made complete with the silencing of the chorus, but now Orestes awakes (211) and a new stage of the drama begins. At first it is only noise: mad speech that reflects Orestes' lack of control over himself and his situation, but later he will begin to speak and to act more effectively.

Thus far, silence represents the political powerlessness of the two matricides, as well as the emotional weakness of Electra and the physical weakness of her brother, and their situation is dramatized by the verbal impasse that almost brings the drama to a halt. In the middle of this scene, the outrageously tactless Helen provides an amusing foil to the silence of Electra and Orestes. She cheerfully asks how the old maid and the murderer are doing ("Child of Clytemnestra and Agamemnon, and virgin for a very long span of time—Electra, how are you, poor woman, and how is your poor brother, Orestes here, his mother's murderer?" 71–74), and then asks Electra to make offerings to Clytemnestra in her place (94–96). For now, Electra suggests that Helen send Hermione instead and only vents her anger once Helen has gone (126–131).[16] Helen has no reservations about speaking, and her freedom of speech is amusing because she gets away with it: she remains blissfully and selfishly oblivious while Electra seethes in silence.

The darker side of free speech is suggested by the story of Tantalus. At the beginning of the play, Electra laments human suffering (1–3) and gives the example of her ancestor Tantalus, who was punished because, when he was given the honor of dining in the company of the gods, "he kept an unbridled tongue, that most shameful affliction" (10). This example should be a warning to Electra and Orestes, who are trapped in silence and will soon attempt to speak out. The warning is especially relevant because the crime of unbridled speech is placed at the beginning of the sequence of crimes that destroyed the house of Atreus. Electra and Orestes are therefore at an impasse: trapped in silence, they face almost certain death, yet if they speak out they risk repeating the ancestral crime that has destroyed their family.

Euripides modifies the legendary material in two ways, both of which introduce the theme of free speech. He is the first author to describe Tantalus' crime as free speaking (7–10),[17] and twice states that Tantalus (rather than Pelops) is the source of the family curse (7–10, 984–987); he reinforces this new version of the myth by naming Tantalus more often in *Orestes* than in any other play.[18] His second innovation is to associate fear of the Eumenides not with their hideous appearance but with their unmentionable name (37–38 and 408–10; contrast δεινὰ δ' ὀφθαλμοῖς δρακεῖν, "terrible to behold with the eyes," Aeschylus, *Eumenides* 34). Paradoxically, *Orestes* introduces this tabu only to break it repeatedly (38, 321, 836, 1650)—a license especially striking since the name otherwise appears only twice in Greek tragedy.[19] Euripides' introduction of criminal and tabu speech into the legend of Orestes is reinforced by mention of Tantalus and the Eumenides throughout the play (as in the ode that follows this scene, which begins with a long description of the running, winged, black-robed Eumenides who drive Orestes mad and ends with a reflection on the past glories of the house of Tantalus).

The prologue portrays the helplessness and speechlessness of Orestes and Electra, and introduces the theme of criminal free speech; the following episode portrays Orestes' attempt to escape from this situation. To do so, he must enlist the support of Menelaus and counter the opposition of Tyndareus, the angry and unsympathetic father of Clytemnestra. Although frustrated by the ambivalent Menelaus and reduced to silence by the authority of Tyndareus, he eventually succeeds in speaking freely— perhaps too freely.

Menelaus enters first, and although Electra and Orestes have placed their hopes in him (241–46, 382–84), he shows little interest in their case; when Orestes persists, he puts him off with an endless series of questions (419–45) until rescued by the arrival of Tyndareus. Clytemnestra's father almost reduces Orestes to silence. The young man explains that he is ashamed to be seen by Tyndareus (459–61), and after his grandfather's long and bitter speech (491–541), Orestes wrestles with his inability to speak: "Old man, I am afraid to speak to you" (544). "I want your old age to keep far from the discussion, since it scares the words out of me" (ἀπελθέτω δὴ τοῖς λόγοισιν ἐκποδὼν / τὸ γῆρας ἡμῖν τὸ σόν, ὅ μ' ἐκπλήσσει λόγου 548–49), "and if I speak badly of [Clytemnestra], I will be speaking of myself as well; but speak I must" (559–60). When Orestes finally finds the courage to speak, he seems to lose all shame. He begins with parody of Aeschylus, mimicking Apollo's argument that only the father is a true parent, since he provides the seed while the mother offers only nourishment (551–56), and lampooning the scene in which Clytemnestra appeals for pity by baring her breast to Orestes (566–70).[20] He then turns against Tyndareus, blaming his grandfather for the deaths of Agamemnon and Clytemnestra and for his own misfortune (585–87). Finally, he attacks Apollo, reminding Tyndareus that he obeyed the god in everything he did: "I killed my mother trusting in him. Hold *him* unholy and kill *him*. He sinned, I did not" (594–96). Orestes knows no half measures; at once he goes from helpless silence to completely unbridled speech. Tyndareus responds by trying to reimpose silence; he rebukes Orestes for his boldness of speech (607) and blames Electra for being an accomplice with her words (616–18). With remarkable prescience the old man associates the free speech of Electra with the unbridled actions that will follow: she filled her brother's ears with hostile rumors, dreams, and stories of adultery, "until she set the house ablaze with flames not of fire," ἕως ὑφῆψε δῶμ' ἀνηφαίστῳ πυρί (621). Tyndareus then exits abruptly without allowing Orestes to speak in response.

If Tyndareus tries to silence Orestes, Menelaus is more ambivalent.[21] With Tyndareus gone, Orestes turns to his uncle instead, but Menelaus dodges with a rhetorical comment on speech and silence: "Sometimes silence is better than speech, and sometimes speech is better" (ἔστι δ᾽ οὗ σιγὴ λόγου / κρείσσων γένοιτ᾽ ἄν, ἔστι δ᾽ οὗ σιγῆς λόγος 638–39). Orestes takes this as license to speak at length, τὰ μακρά (640–79), but his license consists even more in the liberties he takes with the conventions of friendship. Rather than an exchange of favors, he demands an exchange of crimes:[22]

> I have done wrong, and in exchange for that wrong
> I deserve some evil deed from you. Agamemnon
> my father wrongly gathered Greece at Troy,
> doing no wrong himself, but correcting
> the crime and injustice of your wife.
> So you must repay me crime for crime.

> ἀδικῶ· λαβεῖν χρή μ᾽ ἀντὶ τοῦδε τοῦ κακοῦ
> ἄδικόν τι παρὰ σοῦ· καὶ γὰρ Ἀγαμέμνων πατὴρ
> ἀδίκως ἀθροίσας Ἑλλάδ᾽ ἦλθ᾽ ὑπ᾽ Ἴλιον,
> οὐκ ἐξαμαρτὼν αὐτός ἀλλ᾽ ἁμαρτίαν
> τῆς σῆς γυναικὸς ἀδικίαν τ᾽ ἰώμενος·
> ἐν μὲν τόδ᾽ ἡμῖν ἀνθ᾽ ἑνὸς δοῦναί σε χρή.   646–51

He sweetens the deal by offering ten years of Agamemnon's crimes at Troy for one day of Menelaus helping Orestes escape (655–57), and then throws in a final incentive: Menelaus can have Iphigenia for free. Agamemnon sacrificed his own daughter in Menelaus' cause, but Orestes will not require Menelaus to return the favor by killing Hermione (658–59). Menelaus seems oblivious to the insults; he responds by pleading powerlessness (688–90) and by delivering platitudes comparing the people's anger to a fire or storm that must run its course (696–703, 706–9). The newfound license of Orestes has both comic and tragic overtones. His attack against Tyndareus has a bitter humor, but his grandfather's stern response forebodes tragic consequences. His speech to Menelaus, however, is comic because it seems he can insult his spineless uncle with impunity. Yet comic license will not save Orestes' life or improve his situation in Argos, and he therefore still has reason to fear a tragic outcome: "Ah, I have been betrayed, and there are no more hopes I can turn to, to avoid death from the Argives" (722–23).

At this very moment, Pylades enters and learns of the desperate situation. His entrance is startling; he arrives on the run (726) and immediately escalates the pace of the dialogue to frantic tetrameters ("What's up? How are you? What are you doing, dearest friends?" τί τάδε; πῶς ἔχεις; τί πράσσεις, φίλταθ᾽ ἡλίκων ἐμοί; . . . 732).[23] This reversal of the traditionally silent role of Pylades accompanies Orestes' own change from silence to speech. After describing his "betrayal" by Menelaus, Orestes tells Pylades that he faces almost certain death at the hands of the Argive people, and learns that his friend is also in trouble, banished by his father from Phocis. The situation seems hopeless, until Orestes suddenly finds new hope:

ORESTES: The mob is terrible when it has scoundrels as leaders.
PYLADES: But when they have good ones, they always decide well.
ORESTES: That's it! It's time to speak openly.   PYLADES: On what issue?
ORESTES: What if I go and speak before the people? . . .

Ορ. δεινὸν οἱ πολλοί, κακούργους ὅταν ἔχωσι προστάτας.
Πυ. ἀλλ' ὅταν χρηστοὺς λάβωσι, χρηστὰ βουλεύουσ' ἀεί.
Ορ. εἶέν· ἐς κοινὸν λέγειν χρή.   Πυ. τίνος ἀναγκαίου πέρι;
Ορ. εἰ λέγοιμ' ἀστοῖσιν ἐλθών; ... 772–75

The seemingly irrelevant arguments against and for democracy prompt Orestes to consider the persuasive power of speech in the democratic assembly. His new hope accelerates the dialogue from single to half lines, the friends agree to choose speech rather than silence (777), and they leave for the assembly extolling friendship. The two halves of this episode are parallel, in that Orestes twice decides that the only escape from his helpless situation is to speak out; the scene with Tyndareus and Menelaus has a less than favorable outcome, and the plan to address the assembly is no more promising. The chief difference is that Orestes now has an ally and will feel confident enough to speak even more freely than before.

Following a second stasimon on the calamities of the royal house—beginning with the stain upon Tantalus' descendants (813) and ending with the punishment exacted by the Eumenides (836)—a messenger reports on those who spoke before the assembly: the two-faced Talthybius followed by the moderate Diomedes, and the violent demagogue followed by the honest farmer. The symmetry is calculated: the violent bluster of the demagogue ("a man with reckless tongue . . . relying on the mob and his ignorant outspokenness, ἀνήρ τις ἀθυρόγλωσσος . . . θορύβῳ τε πίσυνος κἀμαθεῖ παρρησίᾳ 903–5) is answered by the generosity of the farmer; unbridled speech is answered by words of praise, and the fate of Orestes hangs in the balance. A weighty silence follows in anticipation of the vote (931), but Orestes unexpectedly breaks this silence to speak in his own defense.[24] To the people of Argos, Orestes speaks even more recklessly than he did to his uncle and his grandfather; he says that he killed his mother as much for the Argives' sake as for his father's (934–35), and he tells his audience that if they are going to let a woman murder her husband with impunity, they might as well drop dead themselves—or become their wives' slaves (935–37). The farmer's praise is now undone, and the reckless speech of Orestes, as before, fails to deliver him from his helpless situation and threatens to make it worse.[25] This time there is no humor in Orestes' license, at most an uneasy amusement at his audacity that soon gives way to Electra's sad lament (960–1011). Following his unbridled speech, Orestes is on the verge of death (1018–21), and at this low point, the lifeless appearance of Orestes recalls the prologue and the fear of the chorus that he was dead (208–10).

In the next scene the situation is reversed. Orestes is resolved to take his life, but his despair has a comic outcome. His lugubrious determination ("This is our appointed day. We must either tie a hanging noose or sharpen the sword" 1035–36) is first interrupted by Electra, who insists on dying with him (1037–55). Now accompanied by his sister, he again bids farewell to life ("Come let us die nobly, in a manner worthy of Agamemnon; I shall show the city my good breeding by striking to the liver with my sword, and you must follow the example of my daring" 1060–64), only to be interrupted by Pylades, who also demands to die with Orestes and makes a resounding plea for a triple suicide (1086–91). Finally, this new resolve is interrupted by Pylades: "but since we shall die, let's consider together how Menelaus can suffer also" (1098–99). The conspiracy to die is an amusing failure and is at once replaced by a grand comic scheme: Pylades imagines the trio bamboozling Helen with "an inward smile" (1121–22) and being made national heroes for the murder of a woman (1132–52), while Orestes goes further, wishing they might not only punish their enemies but also live themselves (1173–74). When Orestes checks his idle words that "delight the mind at little cost, with words flitting from the mouth" (1175–76), Electra bursts in with her plan to hold Hermione hostage, if need be cutting her throat, and words are idle no more ("the speech has been spoken," εἴρηται λόγος 1203). Extravagant praise is lavished on Electra, and her bold words prepare the way for action in a conspiratorial scene which culminates with an invocation of Agamemnon.[26] From the dark despair following the assembly is born a fantastic scheme that, if carried out, will be as reckless in action as Orestes was earlier in speech.

In the final episode of the play, speech and action lose all inhibition, and the stage is overwhelmed by a degree of noise and commotion that borders on the farcical. In the first half of the play, the license of Orestes veers between comic success and tragic failure, now promising a bold and outrageous escape from a hopeless situation, now threatening to hasten the hero's destruction. In the second half, the action becomes so uninhibited that distinctions between comic and tragic are no longer meaningful. The hybris of the characters produces neither laughter nor tears but simply shock, and the plot seems to violate the traditional legend, which provides precedent neither for a comic victory (the triumph of Orestes over Menelaus, and his rule in Argos) nor for a tragic defeat (the death of the conspirators and burning of the palace). The tone is often comic, but the overall effect is neither comic nor tragic as we wonder where this license will lead.

The commotion begins at once as Orestes and Pylades go inside the palace to murder Helen, while Electra and the two half-choruses station themselves outside, alternately crying out (1271, 1281–84) and urging calm (1273, 1291–92), fearing in their excited state that all is lost. Then the long-awaited screams of Helen (1296, 1301) are magnified by the bloodthirsty cries of Electra ("Murder, kill, destroy, hurl from your hands twofold, double-edged swords at the woman who left her father, abandoned her marriage . . ." 1302–5), only to be silenced by the approach of Hermione. The young girl, of course, is walking straight into a trap; Electra tells Hermione that she and Orestes are sentenced to death, and asks her cousin to help them by enlisting the aid of her mother Helen. When she agrees and enters the house, the noise builds to a crescendo as Electra shouts to those inside ("Friends in the house, take your swords and seize your prey!" 1345–46), Hermione screams in fear (1347), and both are drowned out by the chorus:[27]

Oh! Oh!
Raise a noise, friends, raise a noise and shout
before the palace, so the murder performed
will not cast fear upon the Argives . . .

ἰὼ ἰὼ φίλαι,
κτύπον ἐγείρετε, κτύπον καὶ βοὰν

πρὸ μελάθρων, ὅπως ὁ πραχθεὶς φόνος
μὴ δεινὸν Ἀργείοισιν ἐμβάλῃ φόβον . . . 1353–55

A welcome calm at the entrance of a messenger ("Silence! A Phrygian is coming out, who will tell us how things are in the house" 1367–68) is followed not by a speech explaining what has happened inside, but by an agitated, high-pitched, and partly incoherent aria that only heightens the confusion (1369–1502).[28] No sooner does the Phrygian describe the chaos within the palace than the commotion spills onto the stage, as Orestes charges out in tetrameters to silence the servant (1510) and send him back inside, and the agitated chorus debates whether to raise the alarm or keep silent (1539–40).

At this point, the action takes another important step. From silence to unbridled speech, to unbridled action first plotted then reported, we come now (it appears) to unbridled action upon the stage:

> Look, in front of the house! Look, that smoke
> rushing skyward is bringing news!
> They are lighting torches, to burn down the house
> of Tantalus, and they won't shrink from murder.
> A god holds the end for mortals,
> whatever ends he wants.

> ἴδε πρὸ δωμάτων ἴδε προκηρύσσει
> θοάζων ὅδ᾽ αἰθέρος ἄνω καπνός.
> ἅπτουσι πεύκας ὡς πυρώσοντες δόμους
> τοὺς Τανταλείους οὐδ᾽ ἀφίστανται φόνου.
> τέλος ἔχει δαίμων βροτοῖς,
> τέλος ὅπᾳ θέλῃ. 1541–46

This will be no ordinary end, if the violence breaks the bounds of the drama to destroy the skene-building, as it seems it will. Suddenly Menelaus appears onstage, and the apocalypse is postponed by the ensuing battle of words between Orestes on the roof and Menelaus below. Threats and insults fly back and forth in rapid stichomythia, until Orestes calls Menelaus' bluff (MENELAUS: "Go ahead and kill her [Hermione]; if you do, you'll pay for it." ORESTES: "Here goes." MENELAUS: "Ah, ah, don't do it!" 1597–98) and demands he yield in silence (1599). But Menelaus will not be silent, and the verbal abuse escalates to faster half-lines and finally to violent action, as Orestes shouts for fire to destroy the palace (1618) and Menelaus calls upon the Argive army to begin the assault (1621–22). The violent showdown is unavoidable because all other options have disappeared. The conflict between Orestes and Menelaus seems to issue in success as Menelaus capitulates ("Ah, ah, don't do it!" 1598) and Orestes claims the victory ("Be silent, and accept your just misfortune!" 1599). Yet they immediately resume bickering for another seventeen lines until Menelaus again capitulates ("You have me!" 1617) and Orestes again exults ("You trapped yourself with your own evil" 1617)—only to call on Electra and Pylades to torch the palace (1618–20) and provoke Menelaus to bring on his soldiers (1621–24), leading to another and more violent confrontation. Only now that the apocalypse is complete does Apollo arrive to resolve the impasse.

No Way Out

Apollo has no easy task; as the showdown at the end makes clear, the play has reached an impasse from which it can find no way out. And this blockage, this dramatic aporia, has several aspects. The first and most important involves the plot itself. As the action veers between hope and despair, it veers between two increasingly polarized possibilities. If Orestes succeeds, he will not just achieve the negative result of escaping the sentence of death, but expects to achieve remarkable positive achievements. Orestes has already, he tells Tyndareus, put an end to the custom or practice (νόμος) of wives killing their husbands (570–71), and for this reason, the farmer at the assembly says that Orestes should be awarded a crown in recognition of his service to the city (923–25). When the plot for escape turns from words before the assembly to deeds within the palace, Orestes' success will mean not only the death of Helen, Pylades assures us, but public celebrations in his honor (1137–39), and instead of being called "matricide," he will be called "killer of Helen who killed many men" (1140–42). Electra improves the plan by suggesting they take Hermione hostage, and when the plan is set into action, Orestes will not only murder the evil Helen but use his hostage to make himself king of Pelasgian Argos (1600–1). Yet just as the implications of success are progressively magnified, so too are those of failure. Orestes and Electra, we learn at the outset, have been condemned by the Argives, but the decision between a sentence of life (i.e., exile) or death has not yet been voted (46–51). The outcome of the assembly is a vote that both must die, and the good friend Pylades nobly announces that he will die with them (1069–74). Not only will all three protagonists die, but as Orestes argues, respect for husbands will vanish and the men of Argos are as good as dead (935–42), and as Pylades points out, the man who regained his bride with the help of Agamemnon will take possession of the palace belonging to Agamemnon and Orestes (1146–47). Where earlier Menelaus at least professed sympathy for his nephew, at the end he is determined to kill those who murdered his wife (1565–66), and even while his daughter is held hostage, he promises that Pylades (1593) and Orestes (1597) will die. No middle ground remains between the two extreme scenarios of success and defeat; it will be total victory or total disaster. Yet neither is possible. Both scenarios contradict the established legend in which Orestes will suffer for his deed, pursued and harassed by the Furies, but will eventually be acquitted in Athens. It is impossible that Orestes, Electra, and Pylades should die immediately after killing Clytemnestra, and it is equally impossible that they should kill Helen and Hermione, and that Orestes should rule in Argos without being driven into exile by the Furies. The playwright could alter any number of details, but as we have seen in the endings of Euripides' *Electra* and *Iphigenia among the Taurians*, he could not alter the canonical sequel described in Aeschylus' *Eumenides* any more than he could after the happy sequel to the *Iliad* in which Helen and Menelaus live to a ripe old age in Sparta.

Apollo does not and cannot mediate this impasse; instead he imposes the traditional outcome that the play will no longer tolerate. Helen was not murdered in the palace, but was snatched away by Apollo, and he displays her beside him on the machine (1631–32, 1683–90), as aloof from mortal troubles (whether at Troy or in Argos) in her lonely beauty as Apollo is in his divine power. Orestes will not murder

Hermione, he tells us, but will marry her. Menelaus will not storm the palace to kill Orestes, but will let Orestes rule there. Orestes will not burn down the palace, but will eventually rule there. Pylades and Electra will not die in the inferno, but will marry one another and live happily ever after (1658–59). This may be the proper and familiar outcome, but it has nothing to do with the play that has just been enacted. Only a god has the power and authority to impose a "resolution" that resolves nothing, to prescribe a conclusion that is totally oblivious of all that has gone before.

The impasse in the plot remains unresolved, and so too does the conflict between tragic and comic outcome. The increasingly licentious and outrageous Orestes, veering with each twist of the action between comic triumph and tragic defeat, finally accomplishes both—or neither. When he appears on the palace roof, wielding power and commanding silence like a god, he plays the part of a triumphant comic hero: a Dikaiopolis or Peisetairos who has somehow succeeded in overcoming all odds and turning the tables on his enemies, and a Strepsiades free to vent his anger by burning down Socrates' Thinkery. This triumph, however, is suddenly overturned by a second epiphany, as Orestes on the roof is upstaged by Apollo on the machine. The god checks the demonic Orestes, preventing him from killing Hermione, preventing the conspirators from destroying the palace, and apparently replacing comic triumph with tragic defeat. If before we were uncertain how the action would end, now we have two endings and a deeper uncertainty: Is the final outcome success or failure? On the one hand, the scheme of Orestes is halted in its tracks: the god aborts his desperate plot to take revenge upon Menelaus and shows that the attempted murder of Helen was also a failure. His command and explanation restore the plot to its traditional course and impose upon the human agents a larger, divine order. On the other hand, the scheme of Orestes has succeeded: he will not be executed by the Argives, he will be purified of his crimes, and will eventually be allowed to rule in Argos. His licentious speech and action achieve their desired result through the intervention of a god who comes to restrain him. The two tendencies of the action—toward comic success and tragic failure—are both realized in the double epiphany, and the appearance of the deus does not resolve, but confirms, this impasse.[29]

And the impasse remains unresolvable because the play has embarked on a course of unprecedented license. As Orestes has moved from silence to unbridled speech to the brink of unbridled action, he has displayed qualities of both the tragic and the comic hero, but the monstrous figure on the palace roof at the end, poised between total success and total disaster, no longer fits either category. The Orestes who lay silent for 210 lines now gives his name to Parrhasion, the Land of Free Speech (1643–47),[30] but what name can we give to the hero himself?

If *Orestes* maintains, in the end, the competing demands of success and failure, and of comedy and tragedy, we might ask how it bears the strain. In some sense the answer is that it cannot. Paradoxically, the plot that hurtles so impulsively in contradictory directions remains at an impasse, with nowhere to go. And the drama that embodies with such brio the opposing expectations of comedy and tragedy in a sense breaks down, unable to function as drama at all. This is true, as we have seen, at the beginning. The prologue speaker is hesitant and reluctant to speak; where we expect her to describe the past and the antecedents to the action, she cannot bring herself to mention them. The protagonist is unable to play his part; where we expect him to respond to the crisis confronting him, he lies on the ground sleeping in a heap of dirty clothes, while Electra delivers her halting prologue, while Helen breezes in, arranges offerings for Clytemnestra's tomb and breezes out again, and while the chorus makes its labored entrance. The chorus is virtually unable to enter; where we expect members of the chorus to sing and dance their entrance song, Electra insists that they march in quietly without stamping their boots (136–37), without the music of the flute to accompany them (145–46), and without expressive movements (149). The paralyzed drama is unable to begin. But the play, like its protagonists, gradually loses inhibitions. When the mad and squalid Orestes finally awakes and belatedly responds to his dangerous situation, nothing can restrain his impetuous and self-destructive course of action, and when the drama eventually grinds into action, nothing will be able to stop it from careening out of control. The story that the actor Hegelochus brought down the house by mispronouncing the line ἐκ κυμάτων γὰρ αὖθις αὖ γαλήν' ὁρῶ, "from the waves I once again see calm" (279), as αὖθις αὖ γαλῆν ὁρῶ, "I once again see a weasel," indicates, perhaps, that the audience realized how closely the play was skirting the verge of nonsense.[31] Late in the play, Euripides treats us to a bizarre and unparalleled messenger speech that reports events offstage not in a spoken exposition but in a high-pitched aria, one that employs for this purpose not the relatively featureless messenger or servant but a terrified, babbling Phrygian eunuch, and that instead of explaining what has happened, leaves us uncertain whether Helen has actually been killed or has somehow, miraculously been rescued. Shortly after this spectacular, farcical tour de force, Menelaus comes onstage to avenge the murder of Helen and remarks in an aside that the notion that she did not die but disappeared "is an elaborate contrivance by the matricide, it's all a big joke" (ἀλλὰ τοῦ μητροκτόνου / τεχνάσματ' ἐστὶ ταῦτα καὶ πολὺς γέλως 1559–60).[32]

He might as well be commenting on the play itself, which proceeds to unravel at the seams. As smoke rises ominously from the skene-building, the antagonists begin to dismantle it: Menelaus below sends soldiers to break down the doors, and they are presumably battering away when Orestes warns that the doors are securely bolted (1571–72); meanwhile Orestes above threatens Menelaus with a piece of masonry that he obtained by breaking apart the ancient cornice (1570). After their long and futile exchange, they redouble their destructive efforts, as Electra and Pylades set fire to the building and Menelaus sends in his storm troopers (1618–22). The literal dismemberment of the stage building is accompanied by a dismemberment of legend, as Hermione or Orestes or both will die. And when Apollo enters to restore order, to make Orestes and Menelaus friends, to marry Hermione to Orestes, and to make Helen a goddess, he confirms that the plot that careened out of control was indeed a joke and a contrivance. After this apotheosis of madness, what lesson could the chorus possibly draw from all that has happened? Telling the characters one more time to depart (1682), Apollo strikes up the anapests. Characters and chorus leave the stage not singing and marching their recessional, but walking in silence as the god chants an irrelevant exit song from space:

> Go now on your journey, honoring
> Peace, the most beautiful god. I shall
> bring Helen to the palace of Zeus

reaching the pole of bright stars
where she will sit next to Hera and
Hebe the wife of Heracles, a god herself
always honored in men's libations,
and with the Dioscuri, sons of Zeus,
  will rule the salt sea for sailors.

ἴτε νυν καθ᾽ ὁδόν, τὴν καλλίστην
θεῶν Εἰρήνην τιμῶντες· ἐγὼ δ᾽
Ἑλένην Ζηνὸς μελάθροις πελάσω,
λαμπρῶν ἄστρων πόλον ἐξανύσας,
ἔνθα παρ᾽ Ἥρᾳ τῇ θ᾽ Ἡρακλέους
Ἥβῃ πάρεδρος θεὸς ἀνθρώποις
ἔσται σπονδαῖς ἔντιμος ἀεί,
σὺν Τυνδαρίδαις τοῖς Διὸς ὑγρᾶς
  ναύταις μεδέουσα θαλάσσης.   1682–90

All that remains for the chorus is a three-line prayer to Victory.

A Carnival of Forms

Yet the play's contradictions are more complex than this. The licentiousness that
enacts an extravagant comedy and an extravagant tragedy at one and the same time
is both an aborted drama and something much more than the ordinary drama; its
competing impulses cannot break out of the impasse, yet together they suggest a chaos
teeming with potential. I want to begin by using the double nature of *Orestes*—its
conflicting embodiment of tragic failure and comic success—to revise familiar readings of the play as negative and pessimistic. And from a better understanding of the
comic and tragic *Orestes*, I shall show how this ambivalent doubling makes room
for new and unexpected forms.

  Orestes is usually viewed as a "tragic" and pessimistic reflection of moral depravity
in man and society. According to Hugh Parry, *Orestes* is "the dark night of the Greek
soul,"[33] and according to Seth Schein, it is "the most negative, the most pessimistic,
the most nihilistic of Euripides' extant plays."[34] Some critics emphasize the demor-
alization, even dehumanization, that takes place within the conspirators in general
and within Orestes in particular; others emphasize the moral vacuum that pervades
the play's characters and institutions as a whole.[35] This consensus, insofar as it draws
attention to the play's repeated and outrageous failures, is certainly correct. But the
play's outrageous failures are also outrageous successes, and the depravity of its
characters has a comic side in their exuberant lack of scruples. According to Ludwig
Jekels, "the feeling of guilt which, in tragedy, rests upon the son, appears in comedy
displaced on the father"; in the latter "we find the ego, which has liberated itself from
the tyrant, uninhibitedly venting its humour, wit, and every sort of comic manifesta-
tion in a very ecstasy of freedom."[36] In *Orestes*, this freedom from inhibition, the
most extreme form of license, is reflected not only in Orestes' complete lack of shame,
but also in his youthful rebellion against the authority of Menelaus and Tyndareus,
and even in the licentious parody of Aeschylus in which the action is cast. In the end,

Orestes remains caught between tragedy and comedy by the double epiphany: he triumphs over the ineffectual father figure Menelaus, but is compelled to acknowledge the authority of Apollo. Yet he also transcends the impasse, displaying an outrageous license without suffering harmful consequences.

If the licentious moral depravity of Orestes has its comic side, can the same be said of social decay? It has often been noted that the drama's moral vacuum and lawless atmosphere reflect the upheavals that in 408 B.C.E. threatened to destroy Athenian society, upheavals such as a questioning of values, conflict between the generations, and lawless violence and assassinations.[37] Critics often compare Thucydides' description of civic upheaval in the late fifth century, a description occasioned by the narrative of events in Corcyra in 427, but which clearly reflects similar upheavals in Athens in 411 and 410:

> So revolutions broke out in city after city, and in places where the revolutions occurred late the knowledge of what had happened previously in other places caused still new extravagances of revolutionary zeal, expressed by an elaboration in the methods of seizing power and by unheard-of atrocities in revenge. To fit in with the change of events, words, too, had to change their usual meanings. What used to be described as a thoughtless act of aggression was now regarded as the courage one would expect to find in a party member. . . . Fanatical enthusiasm was the mark of a real man, and to plot against an enemy behind his back was perfectly legitimate self-defense.[38]

The outrageous violence of *Orestes* surely reflects in some way the violence and upheaval in Athenian society, but does it follow that Euripides views these in an entirely negative or pessimistic light? License and insubordination may have their positive or creative side. Jan Kott compares the license of tragicomedy to Carnival in Rome, where social upheaval and violence were given free rein.[39] Here the people carried candles and shouted, "Sia ammazzato chi non porta moccolo" ("Death to anyone who is not carrying a candle"); Goethe describes the license of the scene: "A boy blows out his father's candle, shouting: 'Sia ammazzato il Signore Padre!' In vain the old man scolds him for this outrageous behavior; the boy claims the freedom of the evening and curses his father all the more vehemently."[40] The ritual license of Carnival reenacts the lawlessness of eighteenth-century Rome without its deadly consequences; similarly the license of *Orestes*, performed at the City Dionysia in 408, reenacts the upheaval in Athenian society and the violence of the oligarchic clubs without their dire and familiar consequences. In Euripides' tragicomedy, a gradual crescendo of noise, spectacle, and action propels us toward a dénouement that is finally neither tragic nor comic, while the frantic pace and uncertain goal of the final scenes reenact the terrifying and exhilarating experience of those chaotic times. Drama was always a public concern in ancient Athens, and *Orestes*, a spectacular play produced in one of Athens' most difficult years, stages Athenian anxieties with extravagant license and an exuberant sense of humor.

The fact that *Orestes* is organized around contradictory and unreconcilable impulses, and progressively heightens the conflict between them, produces an impasse, a sense of blockage or futility, that contributes to the play's distinctive pessimistic tone. Yet in doing so, it also unleashes a riotous excess and exuberance. This is evident not only in the comic license that at every turn accompanies the play's depravity, but also in the form of the drama, which simultaneously breaks down and embraces a multitude of new forms. If the play does not succeed as tragedy, it nevertheless manages to impersonate tragedy, comedy, parody, and other non-tragic genres.

The drama begins by adopting two different guises. The first situates this tragedy very specifically and self-consciously. The action begins, Electra tells us, shortly after Orestes killed his mother in obedience to Apollo:[41]

Since then he wastes away with savage
sickness, Orestes here, lying collapsed in
his bed, while his mother's blood drives him on
with madness—I am afraid to name the goddesses,
Eumenides, who wrestle him down with fear.

ἐντεῦθεν ἀγρίᾳ συντακεὶς νόσῳ νοσεῖ
τλήμων Ὀρέστης ὅδε πεσὼν ἐν δεμνίοις
κεῖται, τὸ μητρὸς δ' αἷμά νιν τροχηλατεῖ
μανίαισιν· ὀνομάζειν γὰρ αἰδοῦμαι θεὰς
Εὐμενίδας, αἳ τόνδ' ἐξαμιλλῶνται φόβῳ.   34–38

The play begins, in other words, at the very point where Aeschylus' *Libation Bearers* left off. That play ended as Orestes' mind began to wander (1021–25), seeing a ghastly vision of Furies invisible to others (1058, 1061), and driven prematurely from the stage (1062). Whereas Aeschylus began the third play of the trilogy in a different place (Delphi, not Argos), at a different time (days if not weeks later), and in different circumstances (Orestes is entirely sane, while the Furies are present and visible to all), Euripides returns to the earlier situation and prepares to write the immediate sequel that Aeschylus did not. Every tragedy in one way or another revises or corrects earlier versions of a myth; the story of Agamemnon and Orestes told in the *Odyssey*, for example, was retold in the *Nostoi* and in Stesichorus' *Oresteia* before being revised again by Aeschylus, Sophocles, and Euripides. *Orestes* is unusual, however, in adopting the gesture of completion ("tessera" in Harold Bloom's terms,[42] filling out or completing a prior version) by literally picking up the story where a dramatic precursor left off. The gesture is both complementary and complimentary. The poems of the epic cycle, for example, complete the stories left unfinished by Homer, and although they may revise the Homeric account (as the *Cypria* does, presenting Zeus' plan at Troy not as punishment of Paris, but as a scheme to reduce overpopulation), they do so by stepping into the epic poet's shoes. In venturing to finish out the story at Argos, Euripides pays homage to the monumental *Oresteia* just as the cyclic poets paid homage to Homer.[43] Yet he also adopts a very different gesture of infiltration and competition. Rather than adding a postscript to the authoritative trilogy, telling, for example, what happened to Orestes after the end of *Eumenides*, he promises instead to fill in the gap between the second and third plays; elaborating what the master left out is less deferential than picking up the story again when the master has had his say. But there is more: as the plot of *Orestes* progresses, it presents a radical alternative to *Eumenides*, an entirely different way of playing out the issue of Orestes' crime that competes with Aeschylus by assigning jurisdiction not to Apollo and Athens but to the people of Argos; if we accept one version, we cannot (without Apollo's help) accept the other.

These opposing gestures, which cast *Orestes* (programmatically) both as follower and as rival, are more fully elaborated in what follows. Electra's opening words promise to fill out the story with an emphasis on human suffering and endurance: "There is nothing terrible to speak of, no suffering, no heaven-sent disaster, that human nature cannot bear its weight" (Οὐκ ἔστιν οὐδὲν δεινὸν ὧδ᾽ εἰπεῖν ἔπος / οὐδὲ πάθος οὐδὲ ξυμφορὰ θεήλατος, / ἧς οὐκ ἂν ἄραιτ᾽ ἄχθος ἀνθρώπων φύσις 1–3). And the action will bear this out by portraying in a detailed and sympathetic manner the frenzied suffering of Orestes (a suffering Aeschylus did not present):

> It is now six days since the body was burned
> of our mother who died in slaughter,
> in which time he took no food
> nor washed his skin, but hides in his
> blankets and when his body's illness lightens
> he is sane and weeps, or leaps and rushes from
> his bed like a foal beneath the yoke.

> ἔκτον δὲ δὴ τόδ᾽ ἦμαρ ἐξ ὅτου σφαγαῖς
> θανοῦσα μήτηρ πυρὶ καθήγνισται δέμας,
> ὧν οὔτε σῖτα διὰ δέρης ἐδέξατο,
> οὐ λούτρ᾽ ἔδωκε χρωτί· χλανιδίων δ᾽ ἔσω
> κρυφθείς, ὅταν μὲν σῶμα κουφισθῇ νόσου
> ἔμφρων δακρύει, ποτὲ δὲ δεμνίων ἄπο
> πηδᾷ δρομαῖος, πῶλος ὡς ὑπὸ ζυγοῦ.　39–45

But the project of deepening the story's humanity and tragic pathos is followed by a very different one. As Electra hopes for some way out of her desperate situation, Helen enters, bringing libations and an offering of hair. The absent villain of *Agamemnon* ("destroyer of ships, destroyer of man, destroyer of cities" 689–90) becomes a vain and selfish beauty who parodies Electra to her face, bringing to her sister's tomb the very same offerings Electra brought to her father's tomb in *Libation Bearers*, and likewise reluctant to perform the duty herself. When Helen adds insult to injury by asking Electra to make the offering for her (now playing Clytemnestra to the real Electra), her niece returns the insult by telling her to ask Hermione (and thus play Clytemnestra to her own daughter's Electra); Helen does so at once, and Electra must watch as a mute and more docile version of herself is sent offstage to make the offerings at Clytemnestra's tomb. The sustained parody, here as throughout the play, rejects the model of Aeschylus, defacing rather than deepening the tragic predecessor.

By embracing two conflicting strategies from the very beginning, *Orestes* resists definition, and in the space created between these opposing guises of humane (neo-Aeschylean) tragedy and critical (anti-Aeschylean) parody, further possibilities proliferate. One of the most interesting invokes another predecessor. Soon after Orestes awakes, he is struck with a fit of madness, imagines he sees the Furies pursuing him (255–61), and calls for a bow, "the gift of Loxias, with which Apollo told me to ward off the goddesses if they should panic me with frenzied madness" (δὸς τόξα μοι κερουλκά, δῶρα Λοξίου, / οἷς μ᾽ εἶπ᾽ Ἀπόλλων ἐξαμύνασθαι θεάς, / εἴ μ᾽ ἐκφοβοῖεν μανιάσιν λυσσήμασιν 268–70). He then tries to shoo away the Furies until he collapses and comes to his senses with the notorious line of Hegelochus (mentioned previously). As the scholiast observes, Euripides is following the version of Stesichorus, in which Apollo promised Orestes a bow to defend himself.[44] I suspect that the scene was intended, at least in part, as a parody of Stesichorus, but since we have only a few words of his early, lyric *Oresteia*, it is dangerous to speculate about Euripides' relation to this predecessor. It is worth noting, however, another double program in this scene. Euripides' Orestes, in his (literal) madness, seeks relief by pitting Stesichorus against Aeschylus, pitting the bow of the lyric poet against the Furies of the tragedian. It was Stesichorus who invented the bow as a physical token of Apollo's support for Orestes, and Aeschylus who first brought onstage the Furies as physical tokens of his terrible crime. These two authors have created Orestes' unbearable situation, and the hero would let their symbolic instantiations of divinely sent suffering and divine release from suffering vie with one another. He does so by revising both authors and both symbols, recasting the tangible embodiments of Revenge and Absolution as imaginary equivalents of fly and fly swatter:

> Can't you hear me? Don't you see winged
> notches rushing from the far-striking bow?
> Ah, ah!
> What are you waiting for? Skim over the air
> with your wings, and blame Apollo's oracles.

> οὐκ εἰσακούετ᾽; οὐχ ὁρᾶθ᾽ ἑκηβόλων
> τόξων πτερωτὰς γλυφίδας ἐξορμωμένας;
> ἇ ἇ·
> τί δῆτα μέλλετ᾽; ἐξακρίζετ᾽ αἰθέρα
> πτεροῖς, τὰ Φοίβου δ᾽ αἰτιᾶσθε θέσφατα.   273–76

As invisible creatures buzz around his head, Orestes tries to shoo them away with an invisible bow in what must have been a very striking mime.[45]

Programmatically, the double invocation of Aeschylus and Stesichorus, the great lyric poet and the great tragedian, instead of helping to define this play, again succeeds in clearing space: those familiar versions are pitted against one another, while this one remains undefined. Theatrically, the double allusion does more, upstaging the lyric poet and the dramatist with mime—a technique more at home in the subliterary charades later adapted into literary mime, and in the contemporary dithyramb.[46]

Early in the action, programmatic ambivalence (humane tragedy versus parody, lyric versus drama) allows the play to adopt a number of different guises. This generic license is more fully exploited later in the action, when the Phrygian performs a remarkable mimetic dithyramb. Helen's oriental slave enters on the run, apparently miming for the audience the acrobatic manner of his escape from the dangers inside the palace:

The Argive sword I escaped
from death in foreign slip-
    pers, over the cedared
    private chambers
and Doric entablature,
gone, gone, oh Earth! Earth!
with foreign scampering.

Ἀργέιον ξίφος ἐκ θανάτου
πέφευγα βαρβάροις ἐν εὐ-
μάρισιν κεδρωτὰ πα-
στάδων ὑπὲρ τέραμνα
Δωρικάς τε τριγλύφους,
φροῦδα φροῦδα, Γᾶ Γᾶ,
βαρβάροισι δρασμοῖς.   1369–74

The colorful and expressive aria that follows is full of cues for miming: the entrance of Orestes and Pylades, swaggering like lions or like Agamemnon and Odysseus (1400–1406), their melodramatic gesture, weeping and sitting on this side of Helen and on that (1408–15), the terrified reaction of the Phrygian servants, running in every direction (1416–20), while the speaker continues "fanning, fanning, in Phrygian manner, manner" (1426–27), the sudden attack of the Greeks like mountain boars (1460), Helen screaming and beating her breast (1465–67), Orestes holding her by the hair and forcing her head back to cut her neck (1469–72), and the final commotion that includes the entrance of Pylades, the seizure of Hermione, and the apparent disappearance of Helen. This physical impersonation is accompanied by vocal impersonations of Orestes and Pylades (1438–43, 1447, 1461–64), Helen (1465), and the lamenting Phrygians (1395–99). It is delivered in a high-pitched Phrygian mode (compare 1384 with scholiast), and it displays both poetic and metrical virtuosity (using iambo-trochaic and enoplian dochmiacs). All these are features of the new and controversial dithyrambs of Timotheus,[47] and shortly before the production of *Orestes*, Timotheus acted his *Persians* with a similar exotic and extravagant impersonation of Phrygian speech, music, and action, as the Persians defeated at Salamis shriek, drown, and babble on the verge of death.[48] For more than a hundred and thirty lines, with no one onstage but the Phrygian and the chorus, the Theater of Dionysus becomes the Odeion and the drama turns into a dithyramb. If there is any truth to the anecdote that Euripides helped Timotheus compose his *Persians*, the audience would have witnessed a remarkable blurring of generic boundaries: the tragedy transforms itself into a version of the lyric genre which had recently found greater favor with the help of the tragedian.[49]

The aria ends with an ironic twist as the slave, whose countrymen fought so long to keep Helen at Troy, sings of Menelaus' tragic loss, who fought so long to recapture Helen, only to lose her in the melee inside the palace (1500–1502). Another twist follows immediately, as Orestes emerges running from the palace (1505) and looking for the Phrygian slave. At once we shift from dithyramb to comedy or farce. Orestes is audibly huffing and puffing his first line (ποῦ 'στιν οὗτος ὃς πέφευγεν ἐκ δόμων τοὐμὸν ξίφος; 1506), as he changes meter into the fast-paced trochaic tetrameters of comedy and upstages the exotic aria with low slapstick. The slave begs for his life, kissing the ground in oriental manner (1507), and after he justifies this groveling by claiming that all wise men would rather live than die (1508), Orestes begins an outrageous game:

ORESTES: So was it right for Helen to be destroyed?
PHRYGIAN: Very right, even if she had three throats to cut.
ORESTES: The words of a slave, but that's not how you think.
PHRYGIAN: It is, since she ruined Greece and Phrygians alike.
ORESTES: Swear you mean that or I'll kill you.
PHRYGIAN: I swear by my life, which means everything to me.
ORESTES: Did iron cause such panic in Troy as well?
PHRYGIAN: Take the sword away; it mirrors ghastly murder.
ORESTES: Are you afraid of turning to stone, as if you saw a Gorgon?
PHRYGIAN: Turning into a corpse; the Gorgon's head is something else.

Ορ.   ἐνδίκως ἡ Τυνδάρειος ἆρα παῖς διώλλυτο;
Φρ.   ἐνδικώτατ', εἴ γε λαιμοὺς εἶχε τριπτύχους θενεῖν.
Ορ.   δειλίᾳ γλώσσῃ χαρίζῃ, τἄνδον οὐχ οὕτω φρονῶν.
Φρ.   οὐ γάρ, ἥτις Ἑλλάδ' αὐτοῖς Φρυξὶ διελυμήνατο;
Ορ.   ὄμοσον (εἰ δὲ μή, κτενῶ σε) μὴ λέγειν ἐμὴν χάριν.
Φρ.   τὴν ἐμὴν ψυχὴν κατώμοσ', ἣν ἂν εὐορκοῖμ' ἐγώ.
Ορ.   ὧδε κἀν Τροίᾳ σίδηρος πᾶσι Φρυξὶν ἦν φόβος;
Φρ.   ἄπεχε φάσγανον· πέλας γὰρ δεινὸν ἀνταυγεῖ φόνον.
Ορ.   μὴ πέτρος γένῃ δέδοικας ὥστε Γοργόν' εἰσιδών;
Φρ.   μὴ μὲν οὖν νεκρός· τὸ Γοργοῦς δ' οὐ κάτοιδ' ἐγὼ κάρα.   1512–21

The scholiast remarked that the scene is "comic," "prosaic," and "unworthy of tragedy," and some modern critics have registered their agreement by excising the lines.[50] But the scene is effective precisely because it is unseemly. The long dithyrambic flourish is followed not by a reassertion of tragic decorum, but by a scene of low humor that alters the tone completely while remaining just as far removed from tragedy. Bernd Seidensticker, in searching both passages for traces of comedy in *Orestes*, concludes that there is dark and bitter humor here, but nothing comic.[51] The point should rather be that both passages are un-tragic in distinctly different ways. After deliberately losing its bearings in the early scenes, the play now alternates wildly between dithyramb and farce, preparing for the wild contradictions of the final epiphanies, while displaying all that drama is capable of. The end of tragedy, in this case, is less a destruction or negation of the traditional genre than an extravagant medley or *satura* of new ones, an exuberant and fertile chaos that stages a mad expansion of dramatic horizons.[52]

11

Phoenician Women and Narrative

In the case of these *knots* then, and of the several obstructions, which, may it please your reverences, such knots cast in our way in getting through life—every hasty man can whip out his penknife and cut through them.—'Tis wrong. Believe me, Sirs, the most virtuous way, and which both reason and conscience dictate—is to take our teeth or our fingers to them.

Sterne, *Tristram Shandy*

Around the time of the production of *Orestes*,[1] Euripides produced another play that was just as experimental and would become just as popular: *Phoenician Women* and *Orestes* were the most commonly read and quoted classical works apart from Homer throughout antiquity, and together with *Hecuba* came to form the "Byzantine triad" of select plays.[2] It is an interesting item in the history of reception that ancient audiences and readers showed much greater interest in these innovative plays than do their modern counterparts, although there are signs that this is beginning to change. But my interest here is not in the play's reception, but in its highly original narrative structure. *Phoenician Women* is a remarkable pastiche of legends about Oedipus and his family; the cast list, as Elizabeth Craik observes, "reads like a guest list for a macabre house party of the Theban royal family,"[3] and these legends and characters are woven together in a way that explores the possibilities, uncertainties, and prosaic pleasures of a narrative text. Where *Helen* offers a happily fortuitous and romantic end, and *Orestes* is torn between the opposing ends of tragedy and comedy, *Phoenician Women* becomes immersed in the difficulties of seeing or choosing an end, in the mundane pleasures and problems of grappling with knots. I will therefore let this play with its unprecedented narrative impulse serve as a final example of the ways in which Euripides' experimentation with closing gestures and closural patterns transformed tragedy into something entirely different.

I am aware that in closing with a reading of *Phoenician Women*, I am cheating my own readers of a certain sense of closure. Rather than develop a narrative or a drama of the last days of tragedy, showing how the genre gradually exhausted itself, and rather than arguing with Nietzsche that Euripides progressively squeezed the life from it, I choose to give a different account of the end of tragedy. The end of tragedy is not a coherent action, and it has no recognizable signs of closure. It is, in large measure, a coincidence: on the one hand, as I try to show, Euripides in successive plays redefines what tragedy is and is capable of, and on the other hand, tragedy in succeeding generations is gradually upstaged by other literary genres. Tragedy continues to flourish through much of the following century,[4] although its eventual decline in prominence may have been abetted by Euripides' experiments redefining the scope and the nature of drama. The new ends and new expectations explored in *Helen, Orestes,* and *Phoenician Women* open up imaginative horizons that will eventually be occupied by New Comedy and the novel. It is therefore not essential that my argument consider the last two surviving plays of Euripides, *Iphigenia at Aulis* and *Bacchant Women,* since I am interested not in constructing a drama of the poet's death and the death of tragedy, but in showing how the end and the expectations of various late plays explore and create new possibilities. Furthermore, since the ending of *Iphigenia* is spurious,[5] and since much of the ending of *Bacchant Women* is missing, I would not be able to discuss closing gestures and closural strategies in these plays as I have in others. Yet brief remarks on these posthumous plays will further illustrate the range of Euripidean innovation.

Iphigenia at Aulis in a sense unravels the tragic plot by demystifying the tragic end. As I observed in chapter 1, a human life can properly be evaluated only once it has reached its end, while a protagonist can make such an evaluation only if he somehow survives the end. Typically, this reflection focuses upon what has been called "tragic error"—namely the recognition, in hindsight, of excessive or inappropriate actions: Xerxes in *Persians* can acknowledge in hindsight that invading Greece was a deed of hybris, and Creon in *Antigone* can see, in looking back, that his edict against Polyneices was wrong. Herodotus in his story of Croesus has a double strategy. The moral tale of the foreign king and his infatuation with wealth has a didactic (and non-tragic) purpose in contrasting Greek with barbarian values; we do not expect that the Lydian king will come to recognize that Greek simplicity is better than barbarian ostentation. But the story of the ambiguous oracle and of Croesus' mistaken belief that he would destroy his enemy's empire by attacking Cyrus is a tragic plot in which hindsight makes Croesus acutely aware of his error; no sooner is he saved from the pyre than he interrogates the oracle and learns that his own presumption led to his downfall. I dwell on this point because the sacrifice of Iphigenia at Aulis is a decisive moment in Agamemnon's career, one that the fearful chorus in Aeschylus' *Agamemnon* looks back upon as a possible occasion of tragic error. It is in hindsight that this action, like the crossing of the Hellespont or the treatment of Polyneices' corpse, acquires its full significance.[6] Euripides' *Iphigenia at Aulis,* however, turns this process on its head. Instead of coming to see (by looking back upon the past) how important and decisive that event truly was, this play shows (by enacting the event in the present) that Agamemnon's deed was in many ways quite ordinary and accidental. Instead of coming to appreciate the king's error, we are required to acknowledge his good intentions and his humanity.[7] Hence the strange and controversial prologue that opens the play not with a narrative situating the action within a larger continuum and describing the present crisis as a consequence of prior events, but with an anxious exchange in broken anapests that dramatizes the king's abject uncertainty.[8] Hence Iphigenia's notorious change of heart that implicitly acknowledges her father's helplessness and exonerates him of guilt for the deed.[9] And hence, we might speculate, the state of the ending, added or altered at a later date, which Euripides may have left incomplete, still struggling to find an end that would read neither tragedy nor triumph into the king's vacillations.

The case of *Bacchant Women* is very different. Archaic features of its form and diction,[10] together with the taut logic of its plot, might suggest that the author has reverted to a more traditional conception of tragedy. To some extent, this is borne out by the end of Pentheus: in this play, as seldom in Euripides, the protagonist dies in the course of the action and events that follow involve an attempt to understand what has happened. Yet the tragedy of Pentheus is upstaged, in the end, by the mystery of Dionysus. Pentheus, after all, is torn apart offstage and unlike Hippolytus, who is then brought onstage to be enlightened by Artemis and reconciled with Theseus before he belatedly expires, Pentheus dies far away on Mount Cithaeron, with no wisdom born from his suffering apart from the brief and futile plea reported by the messenger: "I am yours, mother, your son Pentheus whom you bore in the house of Echion. Pity me, mother, and do not kill your son for my mistakes" (1118–21). When the body of Pentheus is brought onstage it is not so that he or others can make sense of his death, but to heighten the contrast between human suffering and divine jealousy. Before the young man's death might become, in hindsight, a tragic end, it is upstaged by the epiphany of Dionysus that is the real subject and the true end of this play. From the prologue in which the human "stranger" reveals to the audience his divine identity, to the ironic exchange in which the stranger mocks Pentheus' ignorance of the god behind the curls of his mask (451–518), to the shocking epiphany in which Dionysus reveals the full extent of his power and vindictiveness, the drama plays less with blindness and insight in human nature than with disguise and revelation in the theater and in worship.[11] The layers of disguise and impersonation that constitute the dramatic performance are progressively stripped away to provide immediate and unbearable access to the god of the theater. In the process, theatrical performance is dismembered as violently as Pentheus. Drama exists only insofar as it represents through impersonation, yet *Bacchant Women* undoes this theatrical metaphor to lay bare a single inexplicable meaning behind it. Whereas other late plays create new possibilities for tragic drama, *Bacchant Women* returns to a more traditional form only to destroy it; if the groveling Hecuba embodies onstage the grotesque poetics of *Trojan Women*, the annihilation of drama is embodied onstage by the severed head and limbs of Pentheus.[12]

Bacchant Women is a remarkably powerful and effective play. But this stripping away of theatrical metaphor cannot be repeated, and in terms of dramatic innovation, it leads to a dead end.[13] It is in other late plays that Euripides opens up new possibilities for drama, and I therefore conclude with a reading of *Phoenician Women* and the pleasures of narrative.

The Ending and the Text

We shall begin, once again, with the ending. But this is not an easy place to begin. Among modern scholars it has commonly been agreed that the epilogue of *Phoenician Women* is riddled with later interpolations, some based upon other plays on the Theban cycle, that are inconsistent with one another and with other parts of the play. Yet the play as a whole is a dense pastiche of Theban legend, and the process of discovering interpolations can be quite subjective: Eduard Fraenkel may be correct in identifying inconsistencies, for example, but incorrect in assuming that the text is therefore deficient.[14] Elizabeth Craik has recently argued for the "fundamental integrity" of the text of the play, marking as spurious only two lines in the entire final scene and noting that in general "subjective considerations of literary taste are inconclusive."[15] I shall argue more specifically that incorporation of many different and conflicting details of the Theban cycle is part of a larger narrative strategy that gathers together many available stories while refusing to reduce them to a single plot or action. In the textual and intertextual incoherence of the ending, and in the narrative incoherence of the play as a whole, I believe we shall find one of Euripides' most remarkable achievements.

Phoenician Women is unique (among the complete and extant plays of Euripides) in lacking almost entirely the familiar gestures of closure. Where deus, prophecy, and so on are lacking, we may find instead a mortal savior (*Alcestis*) or a demonic epiphany (*Medea, Children of Heracles, Hecuba*), or we may find these gestures displaced to the prologue (*Trojan Women*) or present yet erased at the end (*Heracles*). In *Phoenician Women*, however, there is no deus and no comparable figure to take its place; the play (as we have it) ends entirely absorbed in the human relations among Creon, Antigone, and Oedipus, and fleeting allusions to familiar closing devices serve only to underscore the open and inconclusive nature of the epilogue. The final scene, which began with the entrance of Oedipus (1539), concludes with a lengthy stichomythia between Creon and Antigone and between Antigone and Oedipus (1646–1707), and is followed by a lyric exchange in which Oedipus and Antigone say goodbye to one another (1710–57). Yet the astrophic song of father and daughter, which lacks any form of metrical closure,[17] apparently ends with a question ("Do you mean I should dance to Dionysus?" Antigone asks, 1754–57) and is followed at last by two different exit passages.

The first passage is chanted in tetrameters by Oedipus, who apparently quotes the exit lines of the chorus in *Oedipus the King*:[18]

Citizens of this famous land, look: this is Oedipus
who knew the famous riddle, a great man who
alone checked the power of the murderous Sphinx—
now dishonored and pitied I am driven from the land.
But why do I sing these sorrows and lament in vain?
One who is mortal must endure the gods' necessity.

ὦ πάτρας κλεινῆς πολῖται, λεύσσετ'· Οἰδίπους ὅδε,
ὃς τὰ κλείν' αἰνίγματ' ἔγνων καὶ μέγιστος ἦν ἀνήρ,
ὃς μόνος Σφιγγὸς κατέσχον τῆς μιαιφόνου κράτη,
νῦν ἄτιμος αὐτὸς οἰκτρὸς ἐξελαύνομαι χθονός.
ἀλλὰ γὰρ τί ταῦτα θρηνῶ καὶ μάτην ὀδύρομαι;
τὰς γὰρ ἐκ θεῶν ἀνάγκας θνητὸν ὄντα δεῖ φέρειν.   1758–63

The last three lines are chanted in anapests by the chorus, as they quote from previous plays in appealing for victory in the dramatic contest:[19]

O most holy Victory,
embrace my life
and do not cease crowning me.

ὦ μέγα σεμνὴ Νίκη, τὸν ἐμὸν
βίοτον κατέχοις
καὶ μὴ λήγοις στεφανοῦσα.   1764–66

A scene notably lacking any trace of a deus ends with two curious versions of the choral exit. The first has the recitative meter and the moralizing content that usually signal the emptying of the stage, but is spoken by Oedipus in what can only be a self-conscious quotation of the ending of Sophocles' play. The second is in the more common anapests and is spoken by the chorus, but consists of the formulaic and extra-dramatic gesture alone. In *Iphigenia among the Taurians*, the prayer for victory follows a seven-line anapestic choral exit in which the chorus says goodbye and proclaims its acceptance of Athena's dispensations (1490–96). In *Orestes*, the prayer for victory follows more abruptly upon Apollo's command to depart and the nine lines of anapests with which Apollo departs upon the machine (1682–90). In either case, the prayer comes on the heels of a sequence of anapests that accompany the departure of the deus ex machina. In *Phoenician Women*, however, the extra-dramatic appeal to Nike comes on the heels of an extra-dramatic quotation, which follows an inconclusive musical exchange.

There is another hint of familiar closing signals in the final lines of dialogue between Oedipus and Antigone, just before they begin to sing their lyric duet:[20]

OEDIPUS: Now, daughter, Apollo's oracle is fulfilled.
ANTIGONE: What is it? Will you tell of evil on top of evil?
OEDIPUS: That I will die an exile in Athens.
ANTIGONE: Where? What Athenian bastion will receive you?
OEDIPUS: Sacred Colonus, home of the horseman god.

Οι.   νῦν χρησμός, ὦ παῖ, Λοξίου περαίνεται.
Αν.   ὁ ποῖος; ἀλλ᾽ ἦ πρὸς κακοῖς ἐρεῖς κακά;
Οι.   ἐν ταῖς Ἀθήναις κατθανεῖν μ᾽ ἀλώμενον.
Αν.   ποῦ; τίς σε πύργος Ἀτθίδος προσδέξεται;
Οι.   ἱερὸς Κολωνός, δώμαθ᾽ ἱππίου θεοῦ.   1703–7

Oedipus, as he prepares to leave Thebes, remembers an oracle that he will die an exile in Athens, and in recalling this oracle, he alludes to what later sources describe as a hero cult near Athens.[21] In the timely recollection of an oracle, there is a hint of the mantic power of Polydorus in *Hecuba* ("You will become a dog with fiery eyes ... Prophetic Dionysus told the Thracians this" 1265–67), and in the mention of Colonus, there is a hint of the elaborate yet evasive aetiology for Oedipus' burial place that will be staged in Sophocles' *Oedipus at Colonus*. Yet in *Phoenician Women*, these are no more than hints. They do not look beyond the play, and they do not signal an end to the action. They leave us with hints of the future that conflict with one another (the evil of dying in exile versus reception in sacred Colonus) and, as we shall see, with other hints of other futures.

The drama concludes without a privileged voice that will lend authority to the end, nor does it play with the presence of such a voice as *Trojan Women* and *Heracles* do. Instead we have fleeting and contradictory hints toward the future and outside the text. These hints, however, are part of a larger series of brief and conflicting allusions both to the future and to other texts throughout the final scene. The scene begins, after Oedipus and Antigone welcome one another in song, with Creon claiming a very mortal authority and using this to arrange the mortal ends of burial and marriage:[22]

> Stop weeping; it is time to make the grave's
> memorial. And hear what I have to say,
> Oedipus: your son Eteocles gave me
> command of this land, and gave a dowry to
> Haemon and marriage to your daughter Antigone.
>
> οἴκτων μὲν ἤδη λήγεθ', ὡς ὥρα τάφου
> μνήμην τίθεσθαι· τῶνδε δ', Οἰδίπου, λόγων
> ἄκουσον· ἀρχὰς τῆσδε γῆς ἔδωκέ μοι
> Ἐτεοκλέης παῖς σός, γάμων φερνὰς διδοὺς
> Αἵμονι κόρης τε λέκτρον Ἀντιγόνης σέθεν.   1584–88

The new ruler at once begins by banishing Oedipus, opening up an uncertain future:

> I allow you to live in this land no longer;
> Teiresias said clearly that while you live
> in this land the city will never prosper.
> So leave.
>
> οὔκουν σ' ἐάσω τήνδε γῆν οἰκεῖν ἔτι·
> σαφῶς γὰρ εἶπε Τειρεσίας οὐ μή ποτε
> σοῦ τήνδε γῆν οἰκοῦντος εὖ πράξειν πόλιν.
> ἀλλ' ἐκκομίζου.   1589–92

The literary tradition offers at least two very different versions of Oedipus' future. Homer and Hesiod imply that he remained king in Thebes and received an honorable burial there, while at least by the fifth century it was told that he went into exile instead.[23] This play, in which Creon orders Oedipus into exile and Oedipus protests (1620–21), reverses Sophocles' version of the scene, in which Creon orders that Oedipus be taken inside while the old man pleads to be sent into exile (*Oedipus the King* 1430, 1436).[24] In the exchange that follows, Creon prevails, only to add another command that plunges us into the world of a different play: he announces that Polyneices' corpse must lie unburied outside the city and that any attempt at burial will be punished with death (1629–36). Rather than an uncertain future and a reversal of *Oedipus*, we now find a stark conflict that promises to repeat the action of *Antigone*:[25]

> CREON: I tell you, this man will be unburied.
> ANTIGONE: I will bury him even if the city forbids it.

CREON: Then you'll bury yourself next to the corpse.
ANTIGONE: And a fine thing that two kin should lie together.

Κρ. ἄταφος ὅδ᾽ ἀνήρ, ὡς μάθῃς, γενήσεται.
Αν. ἐγώ σφε θάψω, κἂν ἀπεννέπῃ πόλις.
Κρ. σαυτὴν ἄρ᾽ ἐγγὺς τῷδε συνθάψεις νεκρῷ.
Αν. ἀλλ᾽ εὐκλεές τοι δύο φίλω κεῖσθαι πέλας. 1656–59

Uncertain exile, or crisis and confrontation; the undoing of one performance or the repetition of another—in which direction will the ending take us? The conflict remains at an impasse, with Creon vainly vowing to seize Antigone (1660), and Antigone vainly vowing to bury him (1657, 1661), and then with Antigone asking leave to wash the body or bind its wounds, while Creon again refuses. When Antigone leans over to kiss her brother, Creon suddenly launches us on yet another course:[26]

ANTIGONE: My love, at least I shall cling to your lips.
CREON: I won't let you ruin your marriage with these sobs.
ANTIGONE: Do you think I'll marry your son as long as I live?
CREON: You must. Where can you escape this union?
ANTIGONE: That night will make me one of the Danaids.
CREON: Do you see her brazen taunts?
ANTIGONE: The steel sword bears witness to my oath.

Αν. ὦ φίλτατ᾽, ἀλλὰ στόμα γε σὸν προσπτύξομαι.
Κρ. οὐκ ἐς γάμους σοὺς συμφορὰν κτήσῃ γόοις.
Αν. ἦ γὰρ γαμοῦμαι ζῶσα παιδὶ σῷ ποτε;
Κρ. πολλή σ᾽ ἀνάγκη· ποῖ γὰρ ἐκφεύξῃ λέχος;
Αν. νὺξ ἄρ᾽ ἐκείνη Δαναΐδων μ᾽ ἕξει μίαν.
Κρ. εἶδες τὸ τόλμημ᾽ οἷον ἐξωνείδισεν;
Αν. ἴστω σίδηρος ὅρκιόν τέ μοι ξίφος. 1671–77

Antigone's threat that, like a daughter of Danaus, she will murder her husband on their wedding night introduces a new confrontation, a new crisis that instead of replaying Sophocles' *Antigone* will undo the *Antigone* of Euripides. In Euripides' version, now lost, Antigone and Haemon plotted together to bury Polyneices, risking discovery and death because of their mutual love.[27] Euripides' earlier Antigone, driven to bury her brother by the strength of her love for Haemon, is totally reversed in *Phoenician Women*, in which the strength of her love for Polyneices will drive Antigone to murder Haemon. And Antigone figures this reversal by promising to play the part of a character from Aeschylus' *Danaids*.

The showdown is again deflected in another direction as Antigone promises to avoid marriage to Haemon by going into exile with her father (1679), painting a picture of the loyal and suffering daughter (1686, 1690–92) that reflects an account of Oedipus' exile that is presupposed in Sophocles' *Oedipus the King*, and that survives most memorably for us in *Oedipus at Colonus*.[28] Creon makes his exit and the ensuing dialogue between father and daughter concludes as Oedipus accepts her decision to share his uncertain future:

ANTIGONE: Where? What Athenian bastion will receive you?
OEDIPUS: Sacred Colonus, home of the horseman god.
But come, attend to your blind father here,
since you desire to share this exile.

Αν. ποῦ; τίς σε πύργος Ἀτθίδος προσδέξεται;
Οι. ἱερὸς Κολωνός, δώμαθ᾽ ἱππίου θεοῦ.
ἀλλ᾽ εἶα τυφλῷ τῷδ᾽ ὑπηρέτει πατρί,
ἐπεὶ προθυμῇ τῆσδε κοινοῦσθαι φυγῆς. 1706–9

Clearly, there is no single, correct end. Antigone cannot die attempting to bury her brother at Thebes (1659) and also die accompanying her father in exile (1681). The final scene surveys the different possible sequels, samples the different ways in which the end might be written and has been written, and leaves us with no way of choosing among them—like a blind exile confronting the uncharted void. The lyrics that follow offer a reprise of these and other endings: Antigone will accompany her father into exile, taking his hand and guiding him "like the wind that guides a ship" (1710–12), Antigone laments the outrage against her brother and says she "will bury the unburied corpse in shadowy earth" even if she must die (1741–46), and/or Antigone will join women from Thebes and become a maenad dancing on the mountains and worshipping Dionysus (1747–57).[29] Antigone says her resourceful mind will make her famous (1741–42), but famous for what? And what of Oedipus? When Antigone asks "And where is Oedipus and his famous riddle?" (1688), he answers "Destroyed; one day made me happy and one day destroyed me" (1689). Will he be received at Colonus or will he die "just anywhere" (1736)? Will he wander into exile "with the strength of a dream" (ὥστ᾽ ὄνειρον ἰσχύν 1722) or will he leave us at least with an impressive echo of *Oedipus the King* (1758–63)? The epilogue that lacks an authoritative voice and presence is filled instead with competing voices and impersonations.

We might look at the ending of *Phoenician Women* in a different way. It might be that the action reaches such a resounding and tragic conclusion that gestures of closure are unnecessary, and the uncertain future is of little moment. The scholiast, for example, comments on the catastrophic outcome of the plot: "*Phoenician Women* is very calamitous; Creon's son died for his country by falling from the wall, the two brothers died at each others' hands, their mother Jocasta killed herself upon her children, the Argives who marched against Thebes were destroyed, Polyneices lies unburied, Oedipus is thrown out of his native land, and so too is his daughter Antigone with him."[30] But a stage full of dead bodies does not necessarily guarantee an effective end. It is worth looking back to see how the various deaths in the latter part of the play are portrayed and to see if individual calamities somehow build toward an effective and tragic conclusion.

The first of these is striking and notorious: the self-immolation of Menoeceus, who took his own life to put an end to the dragon's curse and thus save Thebes. The exodos proper (1307–1766) begins with the entrance of Creon, who reports and laments the death of his son (1310–21). It is three hundred lines since Menoeceus left the stage (1018) in order to kill himself and save the city in accordance with

Teiresias' prophecies. As we return to this subplot, we expect to dwell upon the double aftermath: a father's grief at the loss of this young and noble son, and the city's deliverance from the curse of the dragon. Instead, a messenger enters to report at great length (1356–1479) the duel between Polyneices and Eteocles, the deaths of both brothers, and the suicide of Jocasta. The subplot of Menoeceus is discarded and its double aftermath is never picked up again. Critics have long remarked upon the puzzling way in which the promise that the city will be delivered from its curse drops out of the play, and they ask, for example, if we are meant to doubt the effectiveness of Menoeceus' sacrifice: there is no sign that Thebes has been saved, and the city's troubles seem to continue.[31] Just as puzzling is the manner in which Creon's grief and the burial of his son are abruptly forgotten. It will not do to imagine a dumb play of silent tribute to the young man's corpse;[32] the duties of burial no less than the city's safety are abruptly upstaged by the messenger. By this device, the playwright chooses not to gather threads together and combine the deaths of Menoeceus and Jocasta into a tragic crescendo; instead one thread and its doubly climactic potential (as personal loss and as civic redemption) are simply dropped, and another thread is picked up.

The messenger speech returns us to the main thread of the story, and with the report of Jocasta's death added to those of Polyneices and Eteocles, we reach a climax in the fortunes of the royal house that might seem to excuse neglecting the death of Menoeceus: the death of both captains puts an end to the war, and Jocasta's suicide crowns the family's loss. But as the messenger reports, this is not the end:

> . . . and she lay dead, holding both in her arms.
> At once the people rose in fighting words, as we
> claimed that our chief won, and they claimed that
> theirs did. Then there was fighting among the soldiers . . .

> . . . θανοῦσα κεῖται περιβαλοῦσ᾿ ἀμφοῖν χέρας.
> ἀνῇξε δ᾿ ὀρθὸς λαὸς εἰς ἔριν λόγων,
> ἡμεῖς μὲν ὡς νικῶντα δεσπότην ἐμόν,
> οἱ δ᾿ ὡς ἐκεῖνον· ἦν δ᾿ ἔρις στρατηλάταις . . .   1459–62

The battle now begins all over again, the soldiers rush again to arms, and blood flows from countless corpses (1471) until the Thebans score a decisive victory over the Argives that they commemorate with a trophy to Zeus (1473). This end, like that of Menoeceus, is double-edged: the city triumphs, while Antigone and others bring back the dead to be mourned (1476–77). Reflecting upon this latest end, the messenger concludes:

> Some struggles turned out most fortunate for
> the city today, and others most unfortunate.

> πόλει δ᾿ ἀγῶνες οἱ μὲν εὐτυχέστατοι
> τῇδ᾿ ἐξέβησαν, οἱ δὲ δυστυχέστατοι.   1478–79

How do we respond to this double outcome? At this point Antigone enters, accompanied by the bodies of the dead, and in her lament, like Creon before her, she acknowledges only loss and grief. Also like Creon, the grieving Antigone is suddenly upstaged as a new thread in the story demands our attention. In a fine aria grieving at "the twin breasts of my mother" and "the outrage of brothers' bodies" (1526–29),[33] Antigone suddenly calls upon her father Oedipus and, in one of the more startling scenes in Greek tragedy, the blind shade of a man just as suddenly enters. Briefly, Antigone reports that his wife and sons are dead, but the entrance of Oedipus serves not to tie together the threads of family misfortune, but to introduce new strands. Antigone laments a tragic end for the house, but the chorus looks to the future, and Creon sets a new plot in motion:[34]

> ANTIGONE: All these sorrows in one day, father, were
> brought together for our house by
> the god who accomplishes this.
> CHORUS: This day began many troubles for the house
> of Oedipus; may life be more fortunate.
> CREON: Stop weeping; it is time to make the grave's
> memorial. And hear what I have to say,
> Oedipus. . .

> Αν. πάντα δ᾽ ἐν ἄματι τῷδε συνάγαγεν,
> ὦ πάτερ, ἀμετέροισιν ἄχη
> μελάθροις θεὸς ὃς τάδ᾽ ἐκτελευτᾷ.
> Χο. πολλῶν κακῶν κατῆρξεν Οἰδίπου δόμοις
> τόδ᾽ ἦμαρ· εἴη δ᾽ εὐτυχέστερος βίος.
> Κρ. οἴκτων μὲν ἤδη λήγεθ᾽, ὡς ὥρα τάφου
> μνήμην τίθεσθαι· τῶνδε δ᾽, Οἰδίπου, λόγων
> ἄκουσον . . . 1579–86

The city's success and the family's grief are now upstaged by Creon's edicts banishing Oedipus and forbidding burial of Polyneices. Whereas earlier the messenger's entrance preempted Creon by returning to the conflict between the rival brothers, here the entrance of Oedipus preempts Antigone's lament with a new beginning and with what could easily be mistaken for a prologue speech:[35]

> Fate, from the beginning you conceived me—
> of all men born—for suffering and misery,
> and even before my mother bore me to the light
> Apollo gave an oracle to Laius that I, unborn,
> would be my father's murderer—wretched me!

> ὦ μοῖρ᾽, ἀπ᾽ ἀρχῆς ὥς μ᾽ ἔφυσας ἄθλιον
> καὶ τλήμον᾽, εἴ τις ἄλλος ἀνθρώπων ἔφυ·
> ὃν καὶ πρὶν ἐς φῶς μητρὸς ἐκ γονῆς μολεῖν
> ἄγονον Ἀπόλλων Λαΐῳ μ᾽ ἐθέσπισεν
> φονέα γενέσθαι πατρός· ὦ τάλας ἐγώ. 1595–99

Like any prologue speaker, Oedipus offers a narrative summary of the past (1597–1614) before turning to describe the present crisis, Creon's order of exile (1616–24). Yet the present situation turns out to contain several different crises: the proclamation of exile that Oedipus protests, the ban against burying Polyneices that

Antigone vows to defy, and the betrothal to Haemon that Antigone threatens to consummate with murder. As noted above, this new beginning is poised to take us in several different, and contradictory, directions.

The exodos of *Phoenician Women* thus marks a radical departure from Euripides' usual technique. In most of his plays, the gestures of closure cater to the expectation of a clear and emphatic ending, and Euripidean novelty consists in the various ways in which he complicates or frustrates this expectation. *Phoenician Women*, however, marks an entirely new departure by offering a confusion of endings and beginnings. Rather than (negatively or critically) playing against the manner in which tragedy resolves and unravels the end, this play offers a (positive and therefore less coherent) model of tangled threads and contradictory possibilities that remain unresolved.

Narrative Multiplied

These multiple possibilities are explored not only at the end but throughout the action of the play—or rather, throughout the many narrative threads it generates. An ancient preface remarks that *Phoenician Women* is "stuffed full" (παραπληρωματικόν), and this is true both of its large and unwieldy cast and of the historical sweep of episodes enacted, reported, and remembered. This narrative plenitude might be organized in any number of ways, and I shall argue here that Euripides deliberately stuffed the play full of discrete and independent plots. Rather than weaving these together into a single narrative thread, he lavishly adds them one upon one another.[36]

We might distinguish, first, a multitude of plots, a proliferation of characters and their stories. Whereas the cast of Aeschylus' *Seven against Thebes* includes three named roles (Eteocles, Ismene, and Antigone) plus two extra speaking parts (Messenger and Herald), *Phoenician Women* not only includes Eteocles, Antigone, and two messengers, but adds to these Jocasta, Oedipus, Creon, Polyneices, Teiresias, Menoeceus, and the tutor. And where the plot in Aeschylus focuses almost exclusively upon Eteocles, Euripides divides his attention much more evenly among the various characters, giving equal prominence to the two siblings Eteocles and Polyneices who are vying to rule Thebes and to the two siblings Jocasta and Creon who are trying to use their authority as regent or parent to maintain order. He even gives equal prominence to the youthful figures Antigone and Menoeceus who try selflessly to help save the family and the city. Yet the focus of the plot is not so much divided as multiplied; each of these characters seems to pursue goals and interests that are of little concern to the others. Eteocles lusts for power, Polyneices nurses an exile's resentment, Jocasta wants only to see her sons alive, Creon's ends are purely pragmatic and his son's are purely idealistic, Oedipus lingers on long after his story is finished, Antigone is poised as her story is about to begin, and the chorus waits until its own story, interrupted by the war, can begin again. There is, in other words, a certain solipsism in these characters, who pursue their own ends while claiming to speak for others. "There is no escaping it: all men love their country," (358–59) says Polyneices as he prepares to attack Thebes. "No man can live without loving children," (965) says Creon, ignoring the welfare of the city and the wishes of his son. Yet if each character is absorbed in his or her own little plot, most are also out of place in the larger story; in some sense they do not belong. The women of the chorus are literally out of place, journeying from Phoenicia to Apollo's temple at Delphi and accidentally trapped at Thebes by the state of war. Oedipus wastes away in limbo shuttered within the house and enters the stage at the end only to be sent into exile. Antigone is cloistered in the women's quarters (193–95) and reemerges only to join her father in exile. Teiresias is simply passing from one city at war to another (852–55). Polyneices is described with great sympathy as an exile (387–407), and he enters the city as a fearful stranger (269–71), no less out of place than the Phoenician women (278–79, 286–87). The chorus repeatedly invokes, as ancestor of the Thebans, Io the proverbial exile who wandered the length of the world in the form of a cow (248, 677, 828). Despite their many invocations of Earth and fatherland (e.g., 5, 51, 73–76, 154, 280, 359, 388, 406),[37] these characters are homeless and transient, pursuing their own ends but lacking the comfort of a larger story to which they truly belong. They must share the same stage, of course, and they are brought within the same city walls by the press of war, but without the god of war, their separate stories would have little in common:

> But now Ares has come
> rushing before the walls
> inflaming hostile blood for
> this city (may it not happen!).
> The suffering of friends is shared
> and if this seven-towered land
> suffers, it will be shared
> with Phoenicia. Ah ah!
> Common blood, common children
> born of horned Io;
> I share these troubles.

> νῦν δέ μοι πρὸ τειχέων
> θούριος μολὼν Ἄρης
> αἷμα δάιον φλέγει
> τᾷδ', ὃ μὴ τύχοι, πόλει·
> κοινὰ γὰρ φίλων ἄχη,
> κοινὰ δ', εἴ τι πείσεται
> ἑπτάπυργος ἅδε γᾶ,
> Φοίνισσα χώρᾳ. φεῦ φεῦ.
> κοινὸν αἷμα, κοινὰ τέκεα
> τᾶς κερασφόρου πέφυκεν Ἰοῦς·
> ὧν μέτεστί μοι πόνων.   239–49

To this intersection of multiple plots we should add the intersection of texts. Suzanne Saïd has well described the antagonistic relation between *Phoenician Women* and *Seven against Thebes*, showing how Euripides' various doublings, confusions, and delays undermine his Aeschylean model;[38] one of the clearest marks of this agonistic relation is the brusque manner in which Eteocles dispenses with a roll call of Theban heroes in the manner of Aeschylus: "To tell each man's name is a waste of time, with the enemy stationed at the very walls" (751–52).[39] But at least as important as this direct challenge to the authority of *Seven against Thebes* is the indirect challenge staged by appending so many other stories to it. The central plot is exactly the same as in Aeschylus, and it is a simple one: the city prepares for the final assault of the Seven, battle is joined, the invaders are defeated, and Eteocles and Polyneices kill one another. Into this simple plot Euripides weaves a multitude of episodes from the rich and varied literary accounts of Theban legend. Jocasta in her prologue speech weaves together the plot of Sophocles' *Oedipus the King* (13–62) with the curse of Oedipus against his sons which governs the action of *Seven against Thebes* (63–80). As the chorus takes the stage, it imitates the entrance of the chorus in Phrynichus' *Phoenician Women*,[40] while its first stasimon repeats the story of the founding of Thebes and the Sown Men which had earlier been told in Stesichorus' *Europa*.[41] The issue of burial for Polyneices, tangential or absent in Aeschylus,[42] is carefully woven into the action as if to prepare for Sophocles' *Antigone* (774–78, 1447–50, 1627–73). Jocasta's attempt to mediate the dispute between her sons brings into the play a belated version of the story earlier told by Stesichorus.[43] And the many details that clearly echo Aeschylus (disposition of the seven leaders at each of the seven gates, description of the shields of the Argive chiefs), are accompanied by many others (on the monstrous Sphinx 806–11, on the wedding of Harmonia 822–29, and so on) that may echo details from other accounts of Theban legend now lost, such as the epic cycle comprising *Oedipodeia*, *Thebaid*, and *Epigoni*.[44] As well as weaving together these various sources, Euripides manages to insert two scenes from the *Iliad*. The play begins with a scene in which Antigone and an old servant survey the warriors gathered below, giving a lyric version of the famous teichoskopia in which Helen and Priam survey the Greek captains. And the play ends with the bloody and evenly matched duel between Eteocles and Polyneices, echoing and bringing to completion the evenly matched duel between Hector and Ajax that was more fortunately interrupted by nightfall (*Iliad* 7. 219–82).[45] Furthermore, at the center of the play is the invented story of Menoeceus and his noble but apparently inconsequential sacrifice. Just as this novel episode is not fully integrated into the eclectic Theban tapestry, the young man appeals in vain for a shared vision of the city's good:[46]

> If each person took and pursued what good
> he can, and offered this for the common use
> of his country, cities would experience fewer
> troubles, and in future would prosper.

> εἰ γὰρ λαβὼν ἕκαστος ὅτι δύναιτό τις
> χρηστὸν διέλθοι τοῦτο κεἰς κοινὸν φέροι
> πατρίδι, κακῶν ἂν αἱ πόλεις ἐλασσόνων
> πειρώμενοι τὸ λοιπὸν εὐτυχοῖεν ἄν.   1015–18

The ending, as we have seen, makes no attempt to unravel these various strands, but allows them to suggest the complex and contradictory courses that events may follow in the future.

Briefly stated, characters in the play are piled one upon the other, as are the various texts that report their stories. In a similar way, the larger forces that might have given coherence to the action are multiplied in a bewildering fashion. We noted previously that in *Helen* the designs of Zeus and Hera are realized, but in an accidental or fortuitous manner. *Phoenician Women*, however, presents the radical spectacle of a world in which the divine order plays no part; if not absent entirely, it is fragmented beyond recognition. Onstage, the cast of this play is unique, with no god speaking the prologue or epilogue (as we find in eleven of Euripides' plays), no intervention of Iris and Lyssa, and no demonic epiphany at the end—only Teiresias the oracle-monger who speaks on his own behalf, wearing a crown that he won on his own (856–57), and contrasting his private oracles with those of Apollo at Delphi (Φοῖβον ἀνθρώποις μόνον / χρῆν θεσπιῳδεῖν ὃς δέδοικεν οὐδένα 958–59). Nor is there any divine plan or will of the gods that affects the course of events from offstage. This is not to say there are no divine agents lurking in the wings, but in *Phoenician Women*, these are not Zeus or Apollo or Hera with their conspicuous if conflicting purposes; the divine agents here are Earth, War, Furies, curses, and other nameless daimons who inhabit the play and its background in an unparalleled manner.[47] The actors in this drama feel the supernatural world pressing around them: they feel the vitality of Earth that supports them and the many dark forces that are working their ruin, but never do they glimpse an Olympian hand or purpose in what they endure. If Zeus is invoked, it is only as a being that, like Helios or the Sun (1–3), dwells in the gleaming folds of ether (ὦ φαεννὰς οὐρανοῦ ναίων πτυχὰς/Ζεῦ 84–85) and as one who fails to apportion unhappiness wisely (86–87). Apollo delivered an oracle warning Laius not to have children lest his son kill him (17–20, 1598–99), but the god has no evident plan or purpose in doing this, and is chiefly a figure for the beauty of Delphi (205–38) where the chorus might have performed their timeless duties instead of being trapped in a city at war.

If any force directs the action, it is the curse of Oedipus against his sons, but whereas the curse in Aeschylus is part of an overriding divine scheme, in Euripides it is simply one of several supernatural forces. In Aeschylus' *Seven against Thebes*, Eteocles responds to the messenger's report of impending war by praying:

> Zeus and Earth and gods that guard the city,
> and Curse and mighty Fury of my father,
> do not root out my city from Greece, destroyed
> entirely, captured by its enemies.

> ὦ Ζεῦ τε καὶ Γῆ καὶ πολισσοῦχοι θεοί,
> Ἀρά τ' Ἐρινὺς πατρὸς ἡ μεγασθενής,
> μή μοι πόλιν γε πρυμνόθεν πανώλεθρον
> ἐκθαμνίσητε δηάλωτον Ἑλλάδος.   69–72

The implication that all these gods belong to a single, coherent realm is reinforced by the parodos that follows, in which the chorus prays to Ares, to the city's gods, and to other Olympians in turn, including Zeus and Apollo (104–80). And the curse of Oedipus, which becomes so prominent in the second half of the play (655, 695, 709, 723, 833, 885–86), is associated in particular with the will of a nameless god (689), with Apollo's hatred for the race of Laius (691, compare 801–2), and with Fate (975). In Euripides, the curse of Oedipus is just as prominent (66–74, 334, 474–75, 874–77, 1051–54, 1354–55, 1426, 1556–58), but it remains independent from, and is sometimes opposed to, other divine agents. The fates of the city and of the two brothers, for example, depend upon two entirely different curses: the brothers have been cursed by their father for locking him up within the house (63–68, 874–77), while the city as a whole has been cursed by Ares because Cadmus, when founding Thebes, killed the god's dragon (931–36; compare 657–75). Apollo's oracle to Laius is linked or associated with neither of these curses. The Furies are likewise associated with two entirely independent motives, the curse of Oedipus against his sons (255, 624, 1306) and the anger of the Sphinx against Oedipus and Thebes (1029, 1503). And Ares, whose role is so pervasive (134, 240, 253, 658, 784, 934, 936, 1006, 1081, 1124, 1128, 1402, 1576), is little more than a personification of war—a figure who embodies the fearful spectre of war without explaining its cause or purpose. More tangible than the presence of Olympians are gods such as Ambition (532), Precaution (782), Strife (798), and Tyranny (506). When Jocasta tries to avert the inevitable conflict, she does so by asking Eteocles to stop following Ambition, "the worst of gods" (531), and honor another god in her place:

> This is better, my child:
> to honor Equity, who always binds together
> friends with friends, cities with cities, allies
> with allies; for equality gives men justice,
> while the lesser is always at war with
> the greater and begins the day of hatred.
> Among mankind Equity established measures
> and units of weight, and she defined numbers.

> κεῖνο κάλλιον, τέκνον,
> Ἰσότητα τιμᾶν, ἣ φίλους ἀεὶ φίλοις
> πόλεις τε πόλεσι συμμάχους τε συμμάχοις
> συνδεῖ· τὸ γὰρ ἴσον νόμιμον ἀνθρώποις ἔφυ,
> τῷ πλέονι δ᾽ αἰεὶ πολέμιον καθίσταται
> τοὔλασσον ἐχθρᾶς θ᾽ ἡμέρας κατάρχεται.
> καὶ γὰρ μέτρ᾽ ἀνθρώποισι καὶ μέρη σταθμῶν
> Ἰσότης ἔταξε κἀριθμὸν διώρισεν.   535–42

A multitude of superhuman agents are woven into this tapestry, but they nowhere comprise a common thread.

We might add the multiplication of episodes, which the hypothesis complains have been loosely stitched together: "The play is excellent in its theatrical effects, but it is stuffed full: Antigone looking from the walls is not a part of the action, Polyneices arrives under truce to no avail, and Oedipus going into exile with a chatty aria is stitched on in vain."[48] Why make elaborate arrangements to bring Polyneices onstage, when Jocasta's attempt at mediation is an immediate and complete failure? Why have Antigone and the tutor survey the enemy forces when the messenger will soon give a fuller and clearer account? Why have the messenger lavish such care on his narrative of the battle (1090–1199) when this will be upstaged by the duel and a second battle to follow? And why bring the senile Oedipus out of the palace only to send him off into exile? The action is filled with episodes that are as apparently inconsequential as the suicide of Menoeceus; they belong together not because one leads to the other in a logical or necessary sequence, but simply because all occur here, at Thebes, and now, as the Argives attack the city. I would like to tease out the method in this madness, in this careful and deliberate confusion, by looking more closely at some connections among three unrelated scenes at the beginning, middle, and end of the play.

Jocasta's prologue speech is followed by the singing entrance not of the chorus but of the tutor and Antigone, who emerge on the palace roof to look at the Argive army. The old man will search out the path for her (ἐπίσχες, ὡς ἂν προυξερευνήσω στίβον 92) and because he knows everything, will make it known to her (πάντα δ᾽ ἐξειδὼς φράσω 95). Slowly and laboriously, they step up to the roof together:[49]

ANTIGONE: Now reach, reach from the ladder
           old hand to young
           raising the tread of my foot.
   TUTOR: Take my hand, maiden . . .

      Αν. ὄρεγέ νυν ὄρεγε γεραιὰν νέᾳ
           χεῖρ᾽ ἀπὸ κλιμάκων
           ποδὸς ἴχνος ἐπαντέλλων.
      Πα. ἰδοὺ ξύναψον, παρθέν᾽ . . .   103–6

Our narrative begins in a halting manner, step by uncertain step, although the old man promises to read the way. We have a similar scene in the middle of the play, where Teiresias tells all he knows to Creon (866–67, 911) and explains the path of his oracles (ἄκουε δή νυν θεσφάτων ἐμῶν ὁδόν 911). Again the old man is accompanied by a young maiden (106, 838), this time his daughter, and again the two of them walk slowly, step by step:

Lead on daughter, since you are the eye
for my blind foot, like a star for sailors;
set my tread on level ground and lead the
way so I won't stumble; your father is weak.

ἡγοῦ πάροιθε, θύγατερ· ὡς τυφλῷ ποδὶ
ὀφθαλμὸς εἶ σύ, ναυβάταισιν ἄστρον ὥς.
δεῦρ᾽ ἐς τὸ λευρὸν πέδον ἴχνος τιθεῖσ᾽ ἐμόν
πρόβαινε, μὴ σφαλῶμεν· ἀσθενὴς πατήρ·   834–37

The path is not easy, and needs the knowledge of someone who can read the stars. The play ends with the aged Oedipus and his daughter Antigone, who will guide his steps now that his wife can no longer attend his blind foot (ἃ πόδα σὸν τυφλόπουν θεραπεύμασιν αἰὲν ἐμόχθει 1549). Slowly his unseeing foot reaches the light (βακτρεύμασι τυφλοῦ / ποδὸς ἐξάγαγες ἐς φῶς 1539–40), slowly the blind man is able to understand and explain the oracle about his death (1703–7), and slowly the two of them measure out together the steps of their journey:

ANTIGONE: Go to sad exile; reach your dear hand
           old father, and take me as your
           escort, like the wind that guides ships. . . .

OEDIPUS: Where do I place my aging step?
          Where shall I bring my staff, child?
ANTIGONE: Here, here, come with me,
          here, here, set your foot,
          with the strength of a dream.

Αν.   ἴθ᾽ ἐς φυγὰν τάλαιναν· ὄρεγε χέρα φίλαν,
          πάτερ γεραιέ, πομπίμαν
          ἔχων ἔμ᾽ ὥστε ναυσίπομπον αὔραν. . . .
Οι.   πόθι γεραιὸν ἴχνος τίθημι;
          βάκτρα πόθι φέρω, τέκνον;
Αν.   τᾷδε τᾷδε βᾶθί μοι,
          τᾷδε τᾷδε πόδα τίθει,
          ὥστ᾽ ὄνειρον ἰσχύν.   1710–12, 1718–22

The parallels among the three scenes are striking, and help to knit together the beginning, middle and end of the play. Yet the similarities are striking precisely because they are so extraneous: there is no logical connection among the young girl gazing at the mighty warriors, the seer presenting the king with an impossible choice between child and city, and the exile of Oedipus. Just as the accident of war has caused Phoenician women to share the sufferings of Thebes, accidental similarities unite independent scenes in the overfull drama.

There is of course a common theme of ineffectual knowledge. The tutor in passing back and forth, conveying terms of the truce to Polyneices, has learned about the Argives and the signs on their shields (95–98, 142–44), but his description leaves an unclear impression (ὁρῶ δῆτ᾽ οὐ σαφῶς, ὁρῶ δέ πως / μορφῆς τύπωμα στέρνα τ᾽ ἐξεικασμένα 161–62), and it will be left to the messenger, who also carries a sign or agreement back and forth (ξύνθημα παραφέροντι ποιμέσιν λόχων 1140) to describe the shields and the battle more clearly. Teiresias sees clearly what must be done to save the city, but his advice fails to prevent the deaths of Eteocles, Polyneices, and Jocasta, the deaths of countless soldiers (1471), the unhappy exile of Oedipus and Antigone, and (in the future) the eventual sack of Thebes by the sons of the Seven. Oedipus knows the place he will die, but in solving one more riddle does not seem to gain in wisdom or understanding; he does not see at the end how his story fits together. The powerful irony that connects the blind Teiresias at the beginning of *Oedipus the King* with the blind, yet "seeing," Oedipus at the end is here dissolved into separate scenes, each with its separate characters, and each with its own form of blindness. As they mirror one another and provide an ostensible frame for the play, these scenes also thematize uncertainty and inconsequentiality.[50] Yet there is another thread that connects them and provides what we might call a programmatic statement.

Jocasta begins the play and begins her story of Theban suffering by describing how Laius, after begetting a son, pierced the infant's ankles, from which Greece calls him Oedipus or "swollenfoot" (25–27). The etymology in Sophocles is a potent sign and a final confirmation of Oedipus' true and unspeakable identity (*Oedipus the King* 1034–36). In *Phoenician Women*, it introduces instead the theme of difficult and painful travel, which is soon picked up again in Jocasta's narrative: Laius and Oedipus were both journeying to Phocis when "they joined foot at the same part of the road" (37–38); when Oedipus would not make way for Laius and his carriage, the king's horses "bloodied the tendons of his feet" (42). The riddle of the Sphinx becomes a literal and repetitive enactment of the painful journey through life, as the feet once skewered in childhood are bloodied again by hooves in manhood and at the end of the play, in old age, will slowly totter into exile. The hobbled feet of Oedipus are not a badge of the hero's strange and enormous crimes but a symptom of the difficult roads that all people must travel: Antigone and the tutor making their slow and laborious entrance, Teiresias feebly trying not to stumble, Oedipus and Antigone taking halting steps into exile. Even Jocasta, when the chorus summons her from the palace, can only step forward with great difficulty: "Young women, I hear your Phoenician cry and drag my trembling step with aged foot" (Φοίνισσαν βοὰν κλύουσα / ὦ νεάνιδες γηραιῷ ποδὶ τρομερὰν / ἕλκω ποδὸς βάσιν 301–3). And the brothers who provoked the war eventually stumble in combat. Eteocles is the first to receive a wound when "brushing away with his foot a rock obstructing his tread, he placed his leg outside the shield" (Ἐτεοκλέης δὲ ποδὶ μεταψαίρων πέτρον / ἴχνους ὑπόδρομον, κῶλον ἐκτὸς ἀσπίδος / τίθησι 1390–92), while Polyneices is fatally wounded when his brother's footwork catches him off balance (1407–13). The recurrent motif of searching out a path for the foot's difficult and dangerous advance describes a process that is continuous and never ending, one that will measure out halting steps into years of exile for Oedipus and Antigone.

In Greek πεζῇ, "by foot," also means "in prose." The difficult journeys of the characters in *Phoenician Women* are themselves a part of the difficult and uncertain course of the narrative. Like Antigone or Oedipus, the plot must follow a path that has no recognizable measure, no comforting shape and structure, and no evident end; the plot dares to set out with blind foot upon a truly prosaic course.[51]

Prosaic Pleasures

This journey into uncertainty is a laborious one and would seem to have few charms. A narrative, after all, is directed to an end, and the pleasure of narrative consists, as we have seen, in the delays and detours that postpone the desired end. On the long path toward home, the wanderings of Odysseus and the wanderings of the narrative of the *Odyssey* give the epic its distinctly narrative charm. In *Phoenician Women*, however, instead of a single meandering journey,[52] we have a multitude of paths leading in different directions. Some lead to dramatic ends in death, whether noble (Menoeceus) or otherwise (Eteocles and Polyneices); some leave a character still trying to choose among various courses (Oedipus and Antigone); and some lead a character right out of this story (Teiresias and the Phoenician women). Jocasta's course is doubly surprising, first unexpectedly surviving the discovery of incest (which in Sophocles leads at once to her suicide), and then just as unexpectedly killing herself on the battlefield over the bodies of her sons. There is no question here of the *absence* of an end—no ironic or negative subversion of an expected end, no conceit of anticlosure that robs the work of completeness and unsettles the reader. But just as clearly there is no end—no outcome, however labored, however qualified—to the course of the narrative. This play offers something altogether different: neither an end nor the absence of an end, neither closure nor anticlosure, but a proliferation of paths and possibilities.

Without the pleasure of progress toward an end and without the more sinister joys of denying such pleasure, what do we gain from the play? Prevailing interpretations are negative and pessimistic, emphasizing the horrors of the war, the solipsism of the characters, and the inconsequence of the episodes, while placing different constructions upon them. For Jacqueline de Romilly, the incoherent drama reflects and criticizes the political situation in Athens, offering the playwright's "horrified clairvoyant reaction before the ravages caused by *philotimia*" and self-interest.[53] For Marylin Arthur, the play's descent into chaos reflects the violence inherent in human culture and offers "a highly pessimistic evaluation of the conditions for civilized life."[54] For Suzanne Saïd and Barbara Goff, the play's incoherence reflects the deliberate subversion of an Aeschylean model, or the unreadability of language in general.[55] These are four excellent readings of the play, but it is time to reassess their view of the play as an essentially negative project; both in the action as a whole and in its unusual narrative design, confusion breeds both uncertainty and possibility.[56] It is worth remembering, for example, that the action itself is not an unqualified disaster. Of the many deaths the scholiast remarked upon, those of Eteocles and Polyneices are well deserved. However hideous the spectacle of brother killing brother, it is no more hideous than the shameless ambition and stubborn pride they display in their argument before Jocasta; there is a cynical realism in the portraits of the brothers, but no bleak suggestion of senseless loss in their deaths. The duel is framed by the suicides of Menoeceus and Jocasta. Jocasta's suicide is familiar from *Oedipus the King* and is surprising chiefly because it is delayed so long. But her death invests her in this play with greater realism. Instead of immediately hanging herself in horror at the act of incest she has committed, the mother in Euripides devotes her considerable energy to saving her sons from themselves, and dies nobly by the sword when her efforts fail.[57] The death of Menoeceus is undeserved, briefly acknowledged, and not entirely effective. Yet it somehow succeeds in securing a Theban victory over the Argives, and the young man turns the occasion to his advantage with a grand display of self-sacrifice. Oedipus and Antigone apparently set out upon a long and difficult exile, but Oedipus can at least look forward to a welcome in Colonus, and Antigone is confident that her noble service to her father will make her famous (1692, 1741–42). And what of the chorus? In this play, they do not sing one of Euripides' "escape odes," longing to flee from the horrors of events onstage.[58] Instead, even though they do not belong here and are only distantly related to the people of Thebes, they share all the city's troubles (243), they sing of its past and present misfortunes, as well as its past glories (the beautiful and fertile spot chosen by Cadmus 638–56, the wedding of Harmonia, and the walls built by Amphion 822–25) and present deliverance (1054–59). In the sympathies they express and in the stories they tell, they weave themselves into the Theban narrative—and do this so effectively that by the end of the play their role as outsiders has been eclipsed, and no hint remains of their journey to Delphi.

The journey to Delphi was lyrical rather than prosaic. The women are offerings to Apollo, firstfruits (ἀκροθίνια 203) and things of beauty (καλλιστεύματα 215) whose service to the god frees them from time:

Like a statue crafted from gold,
  I am servant to Apollo,
and the water of Castalia
waits to moisten the virgin
charm of my hair
  in service to Apollo.

ἴσα δ᾽ ἀγάλμασι χρυσοτεύ-
  κτοις Φοίβῳ λάτρις ἐγενόμαν·
ἔτι δὲ Κασταλίας ὕδωρ
περιμένει με κόμας ἐμᾶς
δεῦσαι παρθένιον χλιδὰν
  Φοιβείαισι λατρείαις.   220–25

In service to the immortal god, they shall become themselves unaging memorials of transcendent beauty. At Delphi, at the center of the world, time stops; there they will find no relentless press of troubles, no uncertain path leading onwards through crisis and hope and uncertainty but a "circling dance free from fear" (εἰ- / λίσσων ἀθανάτας θεοῦ / χορὸς γενοίμαν ἄφοβος 234–36), and in place of the fears and delights of growing into womanhood, the clear water of Castalia awaits their "virgin charm." This timeless role as things of beauty is forgotten entirely as the women from Phoenicia share the troubles of Thebes, sharing the anxiety and sorrow as well as the courage and determination with which the people of Thebes follow their slow and uncertain path. And when Menoeceus announces his sacrifice to deliver Thebes from the dragon's curse, they want to be mothers and bear fine children (γενοίμεθ᾽ ὧδε ματέρες / γενοίμεθ᾽ εὔτεκνοι 1060–1). At the end of the play, Antigone faces a similar choice between a temporal and pedestrian course and a timeless, lyrical one. As she prepares to leave the stage, her father seems to make one more effort to dissuade her from sharing his exile (compare 1685, 1691) by telling her to join Dionysus and the maenads in the mountains (1749–52). It was in dancing to Dionysus on the mountain near Delphi that the chorus might free themselves from fear (226–36), and Antigone contemplates the same mystic, atemporal escape. As we have seen, she leaves us with a question, not an answer ("Do you mean I should dance to Dionysus?" 1754–57), but Antigone is most likely, we suspect, to choose instead the slow and pedestrian path with her father.

This path has the real but modest pleasure of remaining faithful to the process of life, sharing at every moment the radical uncertainty and liberating freedom that Heracles discovers only for an instant at the end of his play. *Phoenician Women,* in other words, has a novel's openness or "aperture," alive at every moment to the many different courses the plot may follow.[59] The pleasure of this openness consists not in deferring an end but in feeling the pulse of the present, feeling what Bakhtin calls the most important feature of the novel: "a living contact with unfinished, still-evolving contemporary reality (the openended present)."[60] Whereas a narrator tends to foreclose possibilities by suggesting—within the logic of narrative—that events had to turn out in a certain way, this contact with an inconclusive "world-in-the-making" tries to recover both the uncertain course of events and the ethical responsibility of human agents; the novel imitates a moment before hindsight has intervened to convince us that a certain course of events is necessary or probable, and in so doing it emphasizes the individual's ability and freedom to choose among various alternatives.[61] But *Phoenician Women* gives us something different and perhaps more prosaic. Rather than blessing a protagonist with the freedom and the power to choose one path among many, and thus to shape or create the future, Euripides forces a constellation of protagonists to share the stage and the narrative together. Some readers have concluded that the result is the opposite of aperture: the grand narrative of Theban history writes the story of the individuals who are swept up in its flow, denied their freedom by the destructive and unstoppable march of events.[62] But as I have shown, the actors in this story walk with a foot that is blind within a tapestry that is equally ignorant of its goal. The course of events does not deprive the actors of their freedom by imposing an end or a goal upon them; it simply makes clear that their prosaic journeys are interwoven and interconnected. Menoeceus and Antigone are equally free to choose their own ends, but they do so in a world where no one is independent, where personal ties, supernatural forces and invading armies construct a bewildering web within which they must try to find a path. In awareness of their place within this web, Menoeceus chooses a solitary suicide on behalf of the common good, Polyneices and Eteocles choose a duel that will fulfill the curse and will gratify a shared desire (ἔρως 622) to kill one another, while Antigone chooses (or seems to choose) to share the blind path of her father.

If the narrative pleasure of the *Odyssey* lies both in the wanderings of Odysseus and in those of the narrative, the prosaic pleasure of *Phoenician Women* lies both in the tapestry of lives and in the tapestry of their telling. Just as characters drop in and out of the action, or linger on when they are no longer effective, or intersect in inconsequential ways, the drama is full of extended descriptions that break off, digress, linger, and return in a manner that plays with the pleasures of narrative texture. The play is packed full of narrative. It begins with Jocasta's detailed survey of Theban legend in the longest prologue speech in Greek tragedy,[63] and it ends with two messengers, each of whom requires two speeches to narrate developments outside the city walls (1090–1199 and 1217–63; 1356–1424 and 1427–79). Jocasta not only spins out her story at unusual length, but plays with the different directions in which it may lead. In telling of Laius' murder by Oedipus, for example, she makes a rhetorical point of omitting all extraneous details from her narrative, only to introduce an entirely new thread: "The horses bloodied the tendons of [Oedipus'] feet with their hooves, and then—why should I tell of things outside the disaster?—he killed his father and taking the carriage gave it to his foster father Polybus" (41–45). Sophocles brought Oedipus directly from the murder scene to Thebes, but in Euripides an inconsequential detail (What happened to Laius' horses and carriage afterwards?) opens up an entirely new chapter, returning Oedipus to Corinth, introducing a gift to Polybus, entertaining new questions (Would Polybus not ask how he came by the carriage?), and weaving the foster father back into the story of Oedipus.[64] The two messengers play with narrative in different ways. The first begins with a description of the shields of the seven Argive leaders (at last supplying the description that the tutor had left out, 142–44) that is part of an extravagant report on the successful resistance of the Thebans and the rout of the Argives (1090–1199), but this speech, with all its epic pretensions (e.g., 1161–62), is cancelled out by the questions of Jocasta. When she insists on hearing more, the messenger must play a new role as bearer of sad tidings (1217–18) and deliver a second speech on the brothers' decision to meet in single combat (1217–63), which makes both the earlier battle and the narrative about it irrelevant. The second messenger plays a different game, narrating in the duel a grisly end to the confrontation that was earlier staged as a rhetorical debate (357–637), but when the chorus tries to wrap things up ("Oedipus, how I grieve at your troubles. Some god seems to have fulfilled your curse" 1425–26), the messenger insists on telling more: the last gasps and final words of the two brothers, Jocasta's suicide in the embrace of her dead sons—and then a new battle between Thebans and Argives that plays out the conflict one more time (1466–72). The drama plays with narrative in other ways, turning epic narration into lyric and vice versa. The exchange between Antigone and the tutor turns the narrative of Homer's teichoskopia into amoibaion, alternating snatches of dialogue from the old servant with emotional reactions sung by the girl, and offering both factual discrimination ("The Argive army is on the move, and they are separating divisions from one another" 107–8) and vague impressions ("I don't see clearly, but see something like an impression of shape and a semblance of torso" 161–62).[65] The choral odes, as Marylin Arthur has noted, are unusually narrative in content, complementing Jocasta's prologue by singing of the founding of Thebes, the curse of Ares' dragon, and the horrors of the Sphinx.[66] And the speech of the first messenger, giving his intriguing but unnecessary description of the shields of the Argive captains, suggests that the craft of the narrator, like that of the metalworker, has its own ingenious delights: "as a device upon [Polyneices'] shield were Potnian horses running and leaping in panic, circling somehow on pivots inside below the handle, so they seemed to go wild" (1124–27).[67]

Such delights are hard to resist. When the first messenger reports that the city is safe, Jocasta still needs to know more, and not even the safety of her children is more important than the desire to hear what happens next:

JOCASTA:	But recite for me
	what my two sons did after that.
MESSENGER:	The rest does not matter; now they are safe.
JOCASTA:	You arouse suspicion. It does matter.
MESSENGER:	Do you want anything more than your sons' safety?
JOCASTA:	Yes, to hear if my good fortune will continue.

Ιο.	ἀλλ᾿ ἄνελθέ μοι πάλιν,
	τί τἀπὶ τούτοις παῖδ᾿ ἐμὼ δρασείετον.
Αγ.	ἔα τὰ λοιπά· δεῦρ᾿ ἀεὶ γὰρ εὐτυχεῖς.
Ιο.	τοῦτ᾿ εἰς ὕποπτον εἶπας· οὐκ ἐατέον.
Αγ.	μεῖζόν τι χρῄζεις παῖδας ἢ σεσωμένους;
Ιο.	καὶ τἀπίλοιπά γ᾿ εἰ καλῶς πράσσω κλύειν. 1207–12

The following narrative (1217–63), which satisfies her desire to hear, reports that her sons are preparing for a duel to the death. When Creon presses Teiresias to tell him how the city might be saved, the seer asks, "Do you wish to hear, then? Are you eager?" and the king replies, "I could desire nothing more" (901–2). When Teiresias suggests that he send Menoeceus away, Creon adds that his son "would find pleasure in hearing of the [city's] salvation" (910). In the dialogue and narrative that follow (911–59), Teiresias tells him that he must sacrifice his son for the city. These are not the pleasures of poetry and song, which the chorus remind us no longer have a place in war-torn Thebes: "You do not sing the Muse blowing upon the flute, spreading your hair at the beautiful dances of garlanded girls as the graces set the dance, but with armed men, in blood, you [Ares] breathe the Argive army against Thebes, dancing a revel entirely without flutes" (786–91).[68] Jocasta and Creon have more prosaic pleasures, the need to know and the desire to hear as much of the story as possible, as fully as possible, however inconsequential and however difficult.

After Antigone reacts with horror at the spectacle of Capaneus and his impious threats against Thebes, the tutor says that she has indulged herself enough in such pleasures:

> Child, go in the house and stay inside
> in your maidens' quarters, since you have
> reached the pleasure of what you longed to see.

> ὦ τέκνον, ἔσβα δῶμα καὶ κατὰ στέγας
> ἐν παρθενῶσι μίμνε σοῖς, ἐπεὶ πόθου
> ἐς τέρψιν ἦλθες ὧν ἔχρηζες εἰσιδεῖν.   193–95

But he is wrong. Antigone, like her father, will emerge again from the palace to follow the uncertain path of exile. It is a path without end, and a longing to see more that can never truly "reach its pleasure." But once launched on this path there is no going back. Antigone is glad to embrace the endless uncertainty of her own situation. And generations of spectators, in a world increasingly dominated by prose discourse, would embrace not the intriguing paradox of the tragic end but the more prosaic pleasures that Euripides raveled and unraveled in *Phoenician Women*.

Notes

References in the notes employ the following standard abbreviations:

DK   H. Diels and W. Kranz, ed., *Fragmente der Vorsokratiker,*6th ed. (1954).
FGrH   *Fragmente der griechischen Historiker*, ed. F. Jacoby (1923–1958).
IG   *Inscriptiones Graecae*, ed. A. Kirchhoff et al. (1873–).
LIMC   *Lexicon Iconographicum Mythologiae Classicae* (1981–).
Nauck   A. Nauck, ed., *Tragicorum Graecorum Fragmenta*, 2nd ed. (1964).
PCG   *Poetae Comici Graeci*, ed. R. Kassel and C. Austin (1983–91).
PMGF   *Poetarum Melicorum Graecorum Fragmenta*, ed. M. Davies (1991).
POxy   *Oxyrhyncus Papyri*, ed. B. P. Grenfell, A. S. Hunt et al. (1898–).
RE   *Paulys Real-Encyclopädie der classischen Altertumswissenschaft*, ed. G. Wissowa et al. (1894–1959).
SEG   *Supplementum Epigraphicum Graecum*, ed. P. Roussel et al. (1923–).
TrGF   *Tragicorum Graecorum Fragmenta*, ed. B. Snell et al. (1977–).

Scholia to Euripides are cited from E. Schwartz, ed., *Scholia in Euripidem,* 2 vols. (Berlin, 1887).

Chapter 1

1. σκοπέειν δὲ χρὴ παντὸς χρήματος τὴν τελευτὴν κῇ ἀποβήσεται· πολλοῖσι γὰρ δὴ ὑποδέξας ὄλβον ὁ θεὸς προρρίζους ἀνέτρεψε, Herodotus 1.32.9.

2. Herodotus 1.86.6.

3. For another unifying pattern, the repetition at the end of themes from the beginning, see Herington, "Closure"; on closure in the *Histories,* see also Dewald, "Wanton Kings."

4. Aristotle, *Nicomachean Ethics* 1.10.

5. Aeschylus, *Agamemnon* 928–29; Sophocles, *Women of Trachis* 1–5 (quoted later), *Oedipus the King* 1528–30, *Tyndareus* (F 646 *TrGF*), and *Tyro* (F 662 *TrGF*); Euripides, *Children of Heracles* 865–66, *Electra* 954–56, and *Trojan Women* 509–10.

6. On the suicide of Ajax and the debate this provokes among Teucer, Agamemnon, and Odysseus, see, for example, Murnaghan, "Trials of the Hero." In some sense, Oedipus has already reached a final understanding that remains hidden from peers and audience by veils of mystery; see, for example, Dunn, "Beginning at Colonus."

7. On the legend of Heracles' apotheosis, see chapter 8, note 7. On the emphatically mortal end of Heracles in *Trachinian Women*, compare Stinton, "Scope and Limits" 84–91.

8. But the contrivance is still there and is worth bearing in mind when considering possible ironies in the ending of the history as a whole. See Dewald, "Wanton Kings."

9. I borrow the term *sapheneia* from Ludwig, "Sapheneia," who used it to describe the "canonization" of formal features elsewhere in the plays; yet those features he discusses were standard components of tragic structure further formalized in Euripides, while these closing gestures were substantially new inventions, as we shall see.

10. I refer here to the portraits of the Sophoclean hero in Knox, *Heroic Temper* and of the Aristophanic hero in Whitman, *Aristophanes.*

11. Michelini, *Euripides,* and Conacher, *Euripidean Drama.*

12. There are a number of "intrigue plays" or "Tyche-dramas" that seem to form a class of their own, but this is a small and unusual subgroup within the corpus of Euripides and Sophocles. For discussion, see chapter 9, on *Helen,* and notes 36 and 62.

13. The deus is studied at length, from radically different points of view, by Spira, *Untersuchungen* and W. Schmidt, "Deus ex Machina"; Schmidt includes a useful survey of earlier studies. The aition has not been studied at length, but is read in very different ways by Murray, *Euripides and his Age* 41 and Kitto, *Greek Tragedy* 286–87. The exit lines of the chorus are considered mostly spurious by Barrett, *Hippolytos* 417–18, but have recently been defended by Roberts, "Parting Words." See the full discussion in following chapters.

14. Brooks, *Reading for the Plot* and Bakhtin, *Dialogic Imagination.*

15. Barbara H. Smith, *Poetic Closure*; Richter, *Fable's End*; Kermode, *Sense of an Ending.*

16. Torgovnick, *Closure in the Novel*; Krieger, *Reopening of Closure*; Adams, *Strains of Discord*; Quint, *Epic and Empire*; DuPlessis, *Writing beyond the Ending.*

17. Compare Fowler, "Second Thoughts."

18. For a survey of questions associated with closure and of previous work on closure in classical literature, see Fowler, "First Thoughts." Recent work on closure in drama includes Willson, *Shakespeare's Reflexive Endings*; Hodgdon, *The End Crowns All*; and Henry J. Schmidt, *How Dramas End.* On closure in classical literature, see Heath, *Unity in Greek Poetics*, and Roberts, Dunn, and Fowler, *Classical Closure.*

19. On Euripides' anticipation of the novel, see also Dunn, "Euripidean Endings," chapter 6; on various features that align Euripidean drama with romance, see Fusillo, "Was ist eine romanhafte Tragödie?

Chapter 2

1. Compare Aeschylus, *Eumenides* 231; Sophocles, *Ajax* 814; Euripides, *Alcestis* 746.

2. See Herington, "Old Comedy" 119–20.

3. All quotations from Shakespeare follow the edition of W. J. Craig.

4. *Trojan Women* may be an exception; see note 7 of this chapter.

5. On the anapest and its use in drawing attention to staging, see S. G. Brown, "Contextual Analysis." On the possible accompaniment of anapests, see Pickard-Cambridge, *Dramatic Festivals* 160–62.

6. Drew-Bear, "Trochaic Tetrameter" notes the presence of trochees at the ends of *Agamemnon* and *Oedipus the King* and near the end of *Philoctetes.*

7. The manuscripts attribute the last three and a half lines to the herald (Hecuba 1325–29, Talthybius 1329–32). Seidler's attributions (Hecuba 1327–30, chorus 1331–32) have been accepted by all modern editors.

8. Compare the discussion of the final couplet in Shakespeare's sonnets in Barbara H. Smith, *Poetic Closure* 50–54. David Sansone reminded me that Euripides occasionally concludes a scene with a rhyming couplet (*Medea* 408–9, *Phoenician Women* 1478–79).

9. Gay, *Beggar's Opera* 112.

10. On the authenticity of these lines, see note 29 of this chapter.

11. The authenticity of these lines is discussed later in this chapter; see notes 35 and 36. In *Medea,* the first line is different: πολλῶν ταμίας Ζεὺς ἐν Ὀλύμπῳ, "Zeus in Olympus dispenses many things."

12. Beckett, *Waiting for Godot* 61.

13. στείχωμεν *Suppliant Women* 1232, στείχομεν *Heracles* 1427, στείχετ᾽ *Children of*

Heracles 1053; ἴτε *Hecuba* 1293, ἴτ' *Iphigenia among the Taurians* 1490; compare πρόφερε πόδα σόν *Trojan Women* 1332; χαίρετε *Electra* 1357, χαῖρ' *Ion* 1619, ἴτ' ἐπ' εὐτυχίᾳ *Iphigenia among the Taurians* 1490.

14. Contrast the spurious endings of *Iphigenia at Aulis* and *Rhesus*, in which words of departure (χαίρων . . . χαίρων *Iphigenia at Aulis* 1627–28 and στείχωμεν *Rhesus* 993) are incorporated into explicitly metaphorical appeals for victory (κάλλιστά μοι σκῦλ' ἀπὸ Τροίας ἑλών *Iphigenia at Aulis* 1629 and τάχα δ' ἂν νίκην / δοίη δαίμων ὁ μεθ' ἡμῶν *Rhesus* 995–96).

15. Aristophanes, *Acharnians* 1233 τήνελλα καλλίνικος, *Birds* 1764 τήνελλα καλλίνικος, *Lysistrata* 1293 ὡς ἐπὶ νίκῃ, *Ecclesiazusae* 1182 ὡς ἐπὶ νίκῃ, and every surviving ending in Menander, Plautus, and Terence. Compare Katsouris, "Formulaic End."

16. Jonson, *Volpone* 304.

17. Diggle deletes the prayer to Victory, lines 1497–99, but see discussion with notes 35–37 of this chapter.

18. Diggle deletes the prayer to Victory, lines 1691–93, but see discussion with notes 35–37 of this chapter.

19. The Cyclops goes into his cave, and the chorus concludes with two trimeters: "And we, Odysseus' sailor companions, will serve Bacchus in the future," ἡμεῖς δὲ συνναῦταί γε τοῦδ' Ὀδυσσέως / ὄντες τὸ λοιπὸν Βακχίῳ δουλεύσομεν.

20. The incomplete preface to *Phoenician Women* seems to record the first and second tragedies in the production: καὶ γὰρ ταῦτα ὁ Οἰνόμαος καὶ Χρύσιππος καὶ ‹. . .› σώζεται. But the text is too problematic to rely upon. I am not persuaded by arguments that *Antiope*, *Hypsipyle*, and *Phoenician Women* were produced together, followed by a "pro-satyric" *Orestes*; see chapter 11, note 1. For *Iphigenia among the Taurians*, we have no evidence at all.

21. Webster argues, however, that in some periods one poet's tragedies may have been produced on different days; see Webster, "Order of Tragedies." His argument takes no account of satyr-plays.

22. It should be remembered that we have a much smaller sample of Aeschylus' and Sophocles' output than we do of Euripides' and that the surviving plays of Euripides represent less than a fifth of his total production. For the sake of comparison, I shall include *Prometheus Bound* among the plays of Aeschylus, but see chapter 4, note 28.

23. In *Agamemnon*, the final words are those of Clytemnestra, and in *Prometheus Bound*, they are spoken by Prometheus. Although the manuscripts assign the final lines of *Eumenides* (1033–47) to the chorus, scholars generally follow the scholiast in assigning them to a second chorus of attendants. In *Suppliant Women*, the final choral ode is assigned to the chorus by the manuscripts, but to the chorus alternating with a second chorus of servants by Kirchhoff and others.

24. The finales of *Seven against Thebes*, *Libation Bearers*, and *Prometheus Bound* are in anapests; *Agamemnon* ends in tetrameters; the other three end in lyric meters. The authenticity of the ending of *Seven against Thebes* has been challenged; for arguments for and against, see Mellon, "Ending of Aeschylus' Seven" and Thalmann, *Dramatic Art* 137–41, respectively.

25. The long finale of *Seven against Thebes* concludes with a brief summary of the outcome (1074–78), while the shorter finale of *Libation Bearers* is devoted primarily to summary (1065–73).

26. *Persians* (1077), *Seven against Thebes* (1068–69), *Suppliant Women* (1018), and *Eumenides* (1032).

27. There are lengthy songs of celebration and invocation in *Suppliant Women* (1018–72) and *Eumenides* (1032–47), and shorter songs of lament in *Persians* (1077) and *Seven against Thebes* (1054–65).

28. *Seven* comes last in its trilogy, and *Persians* is not related to the other plays produced with it (*Phineus* and *Glaukos*). This leaves *Suppliant Women* and *Prometheus Bound*. In the former, the fears of the chorus (1031–33, 1043–46, 1052–53) anticipate their abduction in the following play, but the situation itself is closed, as the women withdraw in safety to the city. *Prometheus*, however, ends with the protagonist describing the imminent cataclysm (1080–93), just as Orestes describes the approaching Furies. But although this conclusion looks forward, there is no continuity such as that between *Libation Bearers* and *Eumenides*, for *Prometheus Unbound* could not open with the start of a cataclysm; the prolonged punishment of Prometheus (μακρὸν δὲ μῆκος ἐκτελευτήσας χρόνου 1020) marks a clear divide between the plays.

29. The possible exceptions are *Oedipus the King*, where the scholiast assigns the final lines to Oedipus, and *Women of Trachis*, where some manuscripts give the last lines to Hyllus. Some scholars delete the final lines of *Oedipus the King* altogether; see Dawe, *Studies*, vol. 1, 266–73. For a defense of their authenticity, see Arkins, "Final Lines" and Lloyd-Jones and Wilson, *Sophoclea* 113–14.

30. A possible exception is *Women of Trachis*, where some manuscripts give the last fifteen lines to Hyllus; thus Davies, *Trachiniae* while Easterling, *Trachiniae* gives them to the chorus.

31. *Ajax* concludes with a simple moral; *Oedipus the King*, *Antigone*, and *Women of Trachis* include both summary and moral; *Electra* combines congratulations with a summary; and *Oedipus at Colonus* ends with a command to cease lamenting and a brief moral.

32. Only two plays, *Electra* and *Antigone*, end with a metrically distinct choral exit; in the other plays, the lines of the chorus are preceded by up to twenty-six lines (*Oedipus at Colonus*) in the same meter. *Philoctetes* alone concludes with simple words of departure (quoted later), and there is no farewell such as we find in Euripides.

33. If Sophocles gives hints of other stories to follow, this is quite different from Euripides' suggestion that the story has not yet ended; see Roberts, "Sophoclean Endings."

34. "Ein Dichter wie Euripides würde doch wohl etwas Besonderes und Eigenthümliches dem Chor in den Mund zu legen gewusst haben," Hartung, *Alcestis* 189.

35. Barrett, *Hippolytos* 417–18. Barrett is answered in full by Katsouris, "Formulaic End" 253–54; see also Kannicht, *Helena*, vol. 2, 438–40, and Kovacs, "Treading the Circle" 268–70.

36. Diggle prints the final lines of *Alcestis* (attested in papyrus) and *Andromache*, but deletes those of *Medea*, *Iphigenia among the Taurians*, *Helen*, *Phoenician Women*, *Orestes*, and *Bacchant Women*, and reports doubts about those of *Children of Heracles*, *Hippolytus*, and *Electra*.

37. The only textual uncertainty is at the end of *Hippolytus*, where the scholiast reports that sometimes the prayer to Nike is added, and where Barrett reports that in one manuscript the prayer to Nike was added and erased. If this shows that such an error could occur, it also shows it did not.

38. "Scilicet, ut fit in theatris, ubi actorum partes ad finem deductae essent, tantus erat surgentium atque abeuntium strepitus, ut quae chorus in exitu fabulae recitare solebat, vix audire possent. Eo factum, ut illis chori versibus parum curae impenderetur," Hermann, *Bacchae* 163, followed by Dodds, *Bacchae* 242.

39. Compare the discussion in Rees, "Euripides, *Medea*" 177–78.

40. "Der Dichter setzt mit diesen Worten seines Chores ein persönliches, urkundliches Siegel unter sein Werk. Sein Bekenntnis hat sich in den letzten drei Jahrzehnten seines Lebens nicht geändert, hat also immer gegolten. Jeder Mythos, den er gestaltete, war für ihn eine neue Bestätigung seiner Gesamtansicht über Gott, Welt und Menschen," Mewaldt, "Heroische Weltanschauung" 13.

41. Rees, "Euripides, *Medea*" 178–81.
42. Mayerhoefer, "Über die Schlüsse" 38.
43. Roberts, "Parting Words" 56.

Chapter 3

1. Gay, *Beggar's Opera* 111.
2. Compare Samuel Johnson's criticism of Shakespeare's endings: "When he found himself near the end of his work, and, in view of his reward, he shortened the labour to snatch the profit. He therefore remits his efforts where he should most vigorously exert them, and his catastrophe is improbably produced or imperfectly represented" (*Johnson on Shakespeare* 21).
3. The phrase is applied to mortals as well as gods (Aristotle, *Poetics* 1454 a.37–b.2; scholiast on Lucian, *Philopseudes* 29), is used more loosely to mean savior (scholiast on Plato, *Clitophon* 407A), and is used figuratively to mean "unexpectedly" or "irrationally" (Suda s.v. ἀπὸ μηχανῆς). Duncan's broad use of the term includes the drinking of poisoned wine by a dove in Euripides' *Ion*; Duncan, "Deus ex Machina" 127–28.
4. It is often assumed that use of the μηχανή is a Euripidean innovation, but it was probably used for the entrance of Okeanos in *Prometheus* and may have been used in Aeschylus' lost *Psychostasia*; see Dunn, "Euripidean Endings" 132–39. Use of the crane for Athena's entrance in *Eumenides* cannot be excluded.
5. We might also compare the "savior figures" at the end of *Alcestis* and *Heracles*. The latter (Theseus' arrival to help Heracles) is discussed in chapter 8.
6. For a recent discussion of the latter, see Hubbard, *Mask of Comedy*.
7. Bain, *Actors and Audience* is looking only for unambiguous breaks in dramatic illusion; he is therefore uninterested in Euripides' very fruitful technique of testing this illusion without breaking it.
8. Compare Rosenmeyer, *Art of Aeschylus* 348, who observes that "we cannot after all think of Athena [in *Eumenides*] as a deus ex machina, for the good reason that the principal agents of *Eumenides* are themselves gods. For a machine god to be effective, he has to be shown breaking in upon a snarl of human confusion." On *Psychostasia*, see Plutarch, *Moralia* 16f *de audiendis poetis* = p. 375 *TrGF*.
9. The exception that proves the rule is *Heracles*, in which Iris and Lyssa appear *ex machina* in the middle of the play, producing a decisive break in the action; see discussion in chapter 8.
10. This is true even in *Bacchant Women*, which begins with Dionysus in his mortal guise as the "Stranger" and ends with his entrance as a god.
11. For an excellent discussion, see Mastronarde, "Actors on High." For a good review of earlier scholarship, see W. Schmidt, "Deus ex machina" 36–64.
12. *Electra* 1233–37, *Ion* 1570, *Orestes* 1682–85, *Medea* 1321–22.
13. "The gods appearing in divine epilogues, by almost universal agreement, distinguish themselves from the mortals they confront by standing on a different level," Mastronarde, "Actors on High" 278. Pollux also mentions a διστεγία (4.129) and θεολογεῖον (4.130), and this has been taken as evidence for a structure or platform above the palace roof by Pickard-Cambridge, *Theatre of Dionysus* 54–55, and Hourmouziades, *Production and Imagination* 33–34. In the fifth century, however, the skene roof was probably flat; see Mastronarde, "Actors on High" 254–58.
14. See chapter 10 for full discussion.
15. On the problematic nature of the epiphany as the visible staging of an invisible god, see Pucci, "Gods' Intervention" 22.
16. In lines 1233–34, I give Diggle's punctuation, retaining the manuscripts' φαίνουσι.

Diggle emends to βαίνουσί (following Hartung), while Murray breaks into a question: φαίνουσι τίνες–δαίμονες ἢ θεῶν / τῶν οὐρανίων;

17. The argument of P. Arnott, *Greek Scenic Conventions* 74–76, that the machine was only used when an exclamation could "cover" its deployment has not found favor; see for example Hourmouziades, *Production and Imagination* 166–68.

18. Compare *Andromache* 1231–32, *Suppliant Women* 1183–84, *Electra* 1238–40, *Iphigenia among the Taurians* 1435–37.

19. *Andromache* 1234, *Suppliant Women* 1183, *Electra* 1238, *Iphigenia among the Taurians* 1436, *Ion* 1553, *Helen* 1642, *Orestes* 1625; compare *Medea* 1319.

20. Compare *Andromache* 1266–67, *Iphigenia among the Taurians* 1446, *Helen* 1662–63, *Orestes* 1638.

21. Knox, "*Hippolytus* of Euripides," 228.

22. Thus also *Electra* 1354–56, *Helen* 1678–79; compare *Heracles* 1425–26. Of course, morals and *sententiae* are a common feature of tragedy, frequently occurring in messenger speeches and choral odes, as well as in the speech of the deus and the exit lines of the chorus; see C. W. Friedrich, *Dramatische Funktion*.

23. Athena also reports on concurrent events offstage (1442–45), but although this information is helpful to the audience, it does not explain anything that has happened onstage.

24. One might compare the irrelevant aition in *Iphigenia among the Taurians* (1469–72 on the Areopagus) and the irrelevant prophecy in *Orestes* (1654–57 on the death of Neoptolemus).

25. "The authoritative voice appears after all to be only provisional, unable to pass the judgement that will make sense out of the story and thereby complete it," Goff, *Noose of Words* 108.

26. According to the manuscripts, Electra and Orestes both question the Dioscuri in the course of this exchange (1292–1307); Murray and Diggle assign their questions to the chorus and Electra instead, leaving Orestes silent.

27. This is the general meaning of the lines, although editors cannot agree on how to emend the text of line 1301 (μοίρας ἀνάγκης ἡγεῖτο χρεών).

28. The only other figure in Aeschylus who resembles a deus is the ghost of Darius in *Persians*. This is a supernatural figure with knowledge of the future (foretelling defeat at Plataea, 816–17) who unlike Athena makes his epiphany among purely human characters. Yet he appears only in the middle of the play; he does not intervene but is summoned so the chorus may tell him of Xerxes' defeat, and rather than resolving the action, the old man's shade offers moral reflections on the hybris of Xerxes (805–12, 818–22, 827–31). As for other plays of Aeschylus, it is always possible that he used the deus in a work now lost, but the fragments offer no convincing examples, and Aeschylus' readiness to involve gods in the drama greatly limits the space available for an effective deus ex machina. Athenaeus reports that Aphrodite appeared onstage in *Danaids* (13.600b = F 44 *TrGF*), but it does not follow that she played the role of dea ex machina, as claimed, for example, by Murray, "Excursus" 347. Compare discussion with note 8 of this chapter.

29. For discussion, see chapter 4.

30. No deus can be reconstructed with certainty, but the most likely candidates are the entrance of Thetis in *Syndeipnoi* (F 562 *TrGF*) and the prophecy of Demeter in *Triptolemos* (F 598 *TrGF*). The intervention of Thetis reported by Dictys (*Cret.* 6.9) may derive from a *Peleus* by Sophocles (p. 391 *TrGF*), but the prominence of Acastus suggests Euripides' version (scholiast on *Trojan Women* 1128; p. 390 *TrGF*). The departure of Oedipus at the end of *Oedipus at Colonus* has some interesting similarities to the "demonic epiphanies" discussed later.

31. Euripides' contemporary Xenocles "δωδεκαμήχανος" ("equipped with twelve cranes,"

Suda s.v. Καρκίνος) was notorious for his use of the machine; it is pointless to speculate on Xenocles' debt to Euripides.

32. On the aborted ending of *Philoctetes*, and the cues, metrical and otherwise, that signal this ending, see Hoppin, "Metrical Effects." On the overturned ending of *Orestes*, see Dunn, "Comic and Tragic License" and chapter 10.

33. On the story of Heracles as a model for Philoctetes, see Hamilton, "Neoptolemos' Story." On the play's stories more generally, see Roberts, "Different Stories."

34. See, e.g., Hoppin, "Metrical Effects" 142, 151, 160.

35. On the narrative sophistication of the *Odyssey*, see esp. Peradotto, *Man in the Middle Voice*.

36. See Cunningham, "Medea" 158–60 and Knox, "*Medea* of Euripides" 304–5.

37. The *locus classicus* is Aristotle: "It is obvious that the resolution of a story should arise from the plot itself and not, as in *Medea*, from the machine," *Poetics* 1454 a.37–b.2.

38. Verrall, *Euripides the Rationalist* 166.

39. Verrall, *Euripides the Rationalist* sees the deus as a direct, rationalistic challenge to the traditional, anthropomorphic gods; Terzaghi, "Finali e prologhi" 309 sees the mannered intervention as an easy and convenient way to *avoid* spelling out the contradictions between his plot and the fragile religious edifice in which myth resides (compare Pohlenz, *Griechische Tragödie* vol. 1, 436); and von Fritz, *Antike und moderne* 316 and 312 finds in Euripidean realism a direct challenge not to religious belief but to the optimistic and romantic assumptions of myth.

40. Spira, *Untersuchungen zum Deus* 76: "Die Erscheinung Athenes öffnet Ion und Kreusa unmittelbar die Augen für die Hintergründe ihres Schicksals, zeigt ihnen, daß, was ihnen als Leid, Unrecht und Verwirrung erschienen war, in Wirklichkeit sorgender Plan von Apollo gewesen ist. Es ging uns daher darum, zu zeigen, daß der Dichter diesen Schluß des Dramas wortwörtlich verstanden wissen will, ohne Nebensinn und Ironie." Burnett, *Catastrophe Survived* 128–29; Kovacs, *Heroic Muse* 71–77.

41. W. Schmidt, "Deus ex machina" 217: "Die Verhinderung der Katastrophe durch den Machinengott sowie die Aufhebung des Pathos und der Schuld durch den Epilog sind gleichermaßen aus der Absicht des Dichters zu erklären, die emotionelle Katharsis beim Zuschauer zu vermeiden und ihn statt dessen zur Reflexion über die ungelöste innere Problematik zu veranlassen."

42. *Antiope* in Page, *Greek Literary Papyri* (pp. 68–70, fr. 10.64–97), *Hypsipyle* in Bond (p. 48, fr. 64.152), and *Erechtheus* in Austin (pp. 33–41, lines 55–117). If the hypothesis to *Phaethon* has correctly been restored (εθ]εσπισ[εν 16), this play apparently ended with a prophecy delivered by a deus. Countless other examples are proposed, on slender grounds, by Webster, *Tragedies of Euripides*.

43. For a survey of criticism on the deus ex machina, see W. Schmidt, "Deus ex Machina" 23–28, and Dunn, *Euripidean Endings* 162–67.

44. Kitto, *Greek Tragedy* 285.

45. *Amphitryo* apparently parodies a tragedy produced the previous year ("etiam, histriones anno quom in proscaenio hic / Iovem invocarunt, venit, auxilio is fuit," 91–92), perhaps an *Alcmene* by Ennius or Pacuvius. On the daring treatment of adultery, see E. Segal, *Roman Laughter* 171–91.

46. See Jagendorf, *Happy End* 93–100, who concludes that "because of its specific public theme, *Tartuffe* is ultimately not an independent structure as a comedy" (100).

47. On political satire and musical burlesque, see, for example, Lewis in Gay, *Beggar's Comedy* 1–23; Swift's letter to Pope, proposing that Gay write "a Newgate pastoral, among the whores and thieves there," is cited on page 1.

48. Gay, *Beggar's Opera* 109.
49. Brecht, *Threepenny Opera* 225 and 331.
50. Giraudoux, *Plays* 91.

Chapter 4

1. Aristotle mentions Agathon's fictional *Antheus* as an exception that proves the rule, *Poetics* 1451 b.21. Compare Vernant, "Historical Moment."

2. On tension between the private and public spheres in Greek tragedy, compare C. Segal, "Theatre, Ritual."

3. *Chester Mystery Cycle*, vol. 1, 55–56.

4. *Chester Mystery Cycle*, vol. 1, 123–24.

5. The term *aition* (or αἴτιον) may be used more generally to denote any aetiological explanation; I adopt a restricted usage as I did with the term *deus ex machina*.

6. At *Phoenician Women* 1703, 1705, and 1707, the departing Oedipus announces that the oracle is fulfilled that said he would die at Colonus near Athens. There may be an allusion to a tomb of Oedipus, but given its mysterious location in *Oedipus at Colonus*, we cannot regard this as a reference to the contemporary world; compare discussion with note 34 of this chapter. The authenticity of *Phoenician Women* 1703–7 has been contested; see chapter 11, note 20.

7. On *Iphigenia at Aulis*, see West, "Tragica V" 73–76.

8. Such punning derivations, or ἔτυμα, are quite common in the tragedians, especially in Aeschylus and Euripides; see Fuochi, "Etimologie," Looy, "Παρετυμολογεῖ ὁ Εὐριπίδης," and a briefer survey in Kannicht, *Helena*, vol. 1, 13–15. For a broader discussion of aetiological tendencies in Greek literature, see Codrignani, "L'aition."

9. Diggle follows Paley in deleting line 1647.

10. On the authenticity of these lines, see chapter 6, note 7.

11. Tournier and others have deleted 958–60.

12. See Hamilton, *Choes and Anthesteria* 24–25 and 118–19.

13. On the details of this connection between Hecuba and a light tower at Kynossema, see Burnett, "Hekabe."

14. Parmentier suggests that there may be a more topical allusion to a recently dedicated statue of the horse: Parmentier, "Notes sur *Troyennes*" 46–49.

15. She may be celebrated "in Sparta, when the Carneian month comes around," or "in shining, wealthy Athens," and since we know of no specific commemoration for Alcestis in either city, this seems to be a polar expression (in Sparta and in Athens) indicating the extent of her fame. On textual problems, see Dale on *Alcestis* 448–51.

16. τὸ λοιπόν, *Medea* 1383; δι᾽ αἰῶνος μακροῦ . . . κοὐκ ἀνώνυμος, *Hippolytus* 1426–29; ὄνομα . . . κεκλήσεται, *Hecuba* 1271; τοῖσι λοιποῖς . . . τεθήσεται, ἐπώνυμος . . . κεκλήσεται, *Electra* 1268, 1275; ἐπωνομασμένα . . . τὸ λοιπὸν ἐκ βροτῶν κεκλήσεται, *Heracles* 1329–30; ὀνομάζει, ἐπώνυμον, τὸ λοιπὸν ὑμνήσουσι, *Iphigenia among the Taurians* 1452, 1454, 1457. Compare *Ion* 1577, 1587–88, 1590, 1594; *Helen* 1667, 1674; *Orestes* 1646–47; *Erechtheus* fr. 65, lines 92–93 (Austin).

17. The traditional version is given by Pindar, *Paean* 6.109–20, Pausanias 1.4.4 and 4.17.4, Strabo 9.3.9, and others, and is alluded to earlier in the play at *Andromache* 50–55. The rehabilitation of Neoptolemus begins with Pindar, *Nemean* 7.42–48, although Euripides goes much further.

18. Craig prints the variant "As rich shall Romeo by his lady lie."

19. In 1427, Diggle follows Valckenaer in emending to καρπουμένῳ.

20. On the honors promised to Heracles after his death, see discussion in chapter 8.

21. These two most common types do not exhaust all examples. See later on *Suppliant Women*, in which (apparently fictional) relics commemorate the impending treaty between

Argives and Athenians, and *Iphigenia among the Taurians*, in which a ritual at Halae (we are told) commemorates the sacrifice of Orestes that did *not* take place.

22. See Schmid, *Klassische Periode*, vol. 3, 336–37, who cites many metrical and stylistic studies.

23. Dodds, *Bacchae* 235, claims that "the ox-wagon of 1333 must have been brought into the story to account for the name of the town Βουθόη, mod. Budua, on the coast of Montenegro, which Cadmus was said to have founded," but there is no aition in the portion of the epilogue that survives.

24. The extent of Aeschylus' innovation is contested. He certainly departed from tradition by placing the origin of the Areopagus in the trial of Orestes for the murder of Clytemnestra, rather than in the trial of Ares for the murder of Halirrothius (Euripides, *Electra* 1258–63, scholiast on Euripides, *Orestes* 1648 [= Hellanicus *FGrH* 4 F169], Demosthenes 23.66). He may have invented Orestes' trial on the Areopagus altogether (thus Jacoby, *FGrH* 323a F1 and F22), or he may have altered a story of his trial by twelve gods (Demosthenes 23.66, scholiast on Aristides 108.7 [p. 67 Dindorf], Euripides, *Orestes* 1650–52) to a jury trial by Athenian citizens; thus Lesky, *RE* s.v. Orestes, and Stephanopoulos, *Umgestaltung des Mythos* 148–52; compare Radermacher, *Das Jenseits* 133–40.

25. For burial by Sciron's Rocks, see Pausanias 1.44.6 and 10, and Apollodorus 2.8.1, a version alluded to earlier in the play at *Children of Heracles* 849–53; for burial at Thebes, see Pindar, *Pythian* 9.81–83 with scholiast; and for burial of Eurystheus' head at Tricorynthus in Marathon and his body at Gargettus, see Strabo 8.6.19 and Stephanus s.v. Γαργηττός. Gargettus and Pallene both lie on the road from Athens to Marathon, but they are not the same, and no other source mentions Pallene or Athena Pallenis in connection with Eurystheus.

26. On possible allusion to the treaty with Argos signed in 420 or to the negotiations that preceded it, see Collard, *Supplices*, vol. 1, 10–11 and his note 35. For burial of the Seven at Eleusis, see Herodotus 9.27.3, Lysias 2.7–10, Plutarch *Theseus* 29.4–5, Pausanias 1.39.2. For burial at Thebes, see Pindar, *Olympian* 6.15–17 and *Nemean* 9.22–24, Apollodorus 3.7.1, Diodorus 4.65.9.

27. On *Medea*, see discussion in chapter 6 with notes 21–23. On *Iphigenia among the Taurians*, see discussion at the end of this chapter.

28. The authenticity of *Prometheus* is still contested. The fullest arguments for and against are those of Herington, *Author of Prometheus* and Griffith, *Authenticity of Prometheus*, respectively. Hammond, "More on Conditions" 13–16 adds that a spurious *Prometheus* could not easily have replaced the well-attested Aeschylean drama. My comparisons with Prometheus serve to clarify Euripidean technique, and therefore need not presume that our play was written by Aeschylus.

29. On audience address here, see Wilamowitz-Moellendorff, *Aischylos Interpretationen* 185. On audience participation, see Herington, "Old Comedy."

30. On the Danaid trilogy, for example, see Robertson, "End of Supplices Trilogy" and on the Prometheus trilogy, see Thomson, *Prometheus Bound* 34–35.

31. Compare Zeichner, *De deo ex machina* 6: "At tamen ratio, qua Aeschylus αἴτιον introduxit atque probavit, multum differt a ratione Euripidis, apud quem aetium saepe extra actionem adhibetur."

32. Mentioned by Strabo 13.1.30, Diodorus 17.17.3, Pausanias 1.35.4–5.

33. Compare Aeschylus F 25e.13–14 *TrGF*: Εὐβοῖδα καμπὴν ἀμφὶ Κηναίου Διὸς / ἀκτήν, κατ᾽ αὐτὸν τύμβον ἀθλίου Λίχα.

34. We have no sure evidence for a surviving tomb of Oedipus at Colonus. Euripides mentions an oracle that Oedipus would die at Colonus (*Phoenician Women* 1705–7), Androtion is reported to have said (scholiast to *Odyssey* 11.271 = *FGrH* 324 F62) that Oedipus died at Colonus and that his tomb remained a secret, and Pausanias mentions a shrine for four heroes including Oedipus (1.30.4). The traditional account was that Oedipus was buried at Thebes (*Iliad*

23.679–80 with scholiast, *Odyssey* 11.275 with scholiast, Hesiod frr. 192–93 [M-W], Aeschylus *Seven against Thebes* 914 and 1004, Sophocles *Antigone* 899–902) or at Eteonos near Thebes (scholiast to *Oedipus at Colonus* 91 = Lysimachus *FGrH* 382 F2; compare allusions to this version at *Oedipus at Colonus* 399–400, 404–6, 784–86). The only other alleged tomb site was by the Athenian acropolis (Pausanias 1.28.7, Valerius Maximus 5.3.3). See Edmunds, "Cults and Legend" and the cautious conclusions of Kearns, *Heroes of Attica* 50–52 and 208–9.

35. There is evidence for a number of aitia among the fragmentary plays. At the end of *Erechtheus*, Athena describes at length the establishment of the Hyacinthia in honor of Erechtheus' children (65.75–89 Austin), as well as a temple to commemorate Erechtheus (90–94) and a priestship to honor his wife Praxithea (95–97). At the end of *Antiope*, Hermes announces that the river of Thebes will be named for Dirce (74–79 Page, *Greek Literary Papyri*), and the hypothesis to *Rhadamanthys* reports that Artemis ex machina instructed Helen to institute rites for the Dioscuri (hyp. 14.4–7 C. Austin, *Nova Fragmenta*). The summary in Apollodorus suggests that *Alkmaion in Corinth* ended with an aition for Amphilochian Argos delivered by Apollo (3.7.7 = Nauck p. 380), but the aetiology for the Nemean Games in *Hypsipyle* was spoken by Amphiaraus at some point before the exodos (60.98–108 Bond = 274–85 Page, *Greek Literary Papyri*). Many other proposed aitia are little more than plausible conjectures; see Schmid, *Klassische Periode*, vol. 3, 705, note 7; Schlesinger, *Gods in Greek Tragedy* 28–29; and Webster, *Tragedies of Euripides* 100.

36. Dieterich, "Entstehung der Tragödie" 190. Burkert likewise argues that the aition in *Medea* confirms the origin of tragedy as sacrificial ritual: Burkert, "Greek Tragedy" 118–19.

37. Murray, *Euripides and His Age* 41.

38. Foley, *Ritual Irony* 59; see also 21.

39. Pucci, *Violence of Pity* 133–34; compare Goff, *Noose of Words* 122–29 on the aition in *Hippolytus*.

40. Spira, *Untersuchungen zum Deus* 161, my translation. Compare Grube, *Drama of Euripides* 79, and Barrett, *Hippolytos* 412.

41. Lesky, *Greek Tragedy* 178. Compare Pohlenz, *Griechische Tragödie*, vol. 1, 436.

42. Kitto, *Greek Tragedy* 286.

43. In 1462, Diggle follows Pierson in emending to λείμακας.

44. Phanodemus *FGrH* 325 F14, Istros *FGrH* 334 F18, Apollodorus *FGrH* 244 F111.

45. Pausanias 1.23.7, 1.33.1, and 3.16.7.

46. Pausanias 3.16.8.

47. Burkert claims that human blood was spilt at Halae with no more evidence than the text of Euripides: Burkert, *Greek Religion* 59 and 152.

48. Acropolis: *IG* ii² 1514–31, with discussion in Linders, *Studies*, who speculates (70–73) that these inscriptions may actually refer to dedications in Brauron. Brauron: still unpublished, but Amandry, "Chronique" 527 reports dedications of gold, silver, and clothing to Artemis; for a survey of recent scholarship, see Brulé, "Retour à Brauron."

49. For reconstructions of ritual associated with Iphigenia, see for example Lloyd-Jones, "Artemis and Iphigenia" and Kearns, *Heroes of Attica* 27–35. For an attempt to close the gap between drama and ritual, see Wolff, "Euripides' *Iphigenia*."

50. Euripides is our first source for Thoas, and for Orestes and Pylades escorting Iphigenia back to Greece. It is possible that Euripides was anticipated by Sophocles' *Chryses*, but the contents of that play are uncertain; see Platnauer, *Iphigenia* xii–xiii.

Chapter 5

1. Aristotle, *Poetics* 1450 b.22–34.

2. James, "Preface" 5.

3. Brecht, *Good Woman of Setzuan* 141. On the later addition of the epilogue, see Bentley's note on the same page.

4. Eliot, *Middlemarch* 818.

5. Dickens, *Posthumous Papers of the Pickwick Club* 875.

6. But note that Hamlet's shrewd guess at the end is cast as a prophecy: "I die, Horatio; / The potent poison quite o'ercrows my spirit: / I cannot live to hear the news from England, / But I do prophesy the election lights / On Fortinbras."

7. The particular connection of the end of the play to its sequel should thus be distinguished from more general connections between the plot as a whole and the larger mythic cycle; on the latter, compare Lanza, "Redondances" 142–43.

8. See discussion in Stuart, "Foreshadowing," Kamerbeek, "Prophecy and Tragedy," and Hamilton, "Prologue Prophecy," and compare note 19 of this chapter.

9. For discussion, see O'Neill, "Prologue of *Troades*." Wilson, "Interpolation" argues that the unusual qualities of the prologue prophecy support its excision.

10. See discussion in chapter 7.

11. Compare Torgovnick's discussion of the epilogue to *Middlemarch*, in Torgovnick, *Closure in the Novel* 21.

12. Diggle follows F. W. Schmidt in deleting part of lines 1667–68.

13. This theory has fallen out of favor since the criticisms of Zuntz, *Political Plays* 64–65, who showed that *Electra* was more than a decade earlier than *Helen*.

14. See discussion in chapter 3.

15. On the identity of Aphrodite's favorite, see Barrett, *Hippolytos* 412.

16. Compare Murnaghan's comments on the closing scenes of *Ajax* in Murnaghan, "Trials of the Hero."

17. It is therefore likely that the exodos alludes to an actual or contemplated treaty between Athens and Argos, perhaps to the negotiations preceding the Peace of Nicias in 421; for a discussion of the contemporary situation, see Zuntz, *Political Plays* 91–92.

18. Hypothesis I, *Christus Patiens* 1668–69, 1674–77 with discussion in Dodds on *Bacchae* 1329.

19. For recent discussions of Euripidean prologues, see Erbse, *Studien zum Prolog* and C. Segal, "Tragic Beginnings."

20. Thus, the nurse in *Medea*, Iolaus in *Children of Heracles*, Andromache in *Andromache*, Aethra in *Suppliant Women*, the farmer in *Electra*, Amphitryon in *Heracles*, Iphigenia in *Iphigenia among the Taurians*, Helen in *Helen*, Jocasta in *Phoenician Women*, Electra in *Orestes* and (apparently after an opening dialogue) Agamemnon in *Iphigenia at Aulis*. The past is narrated by a god in *Alcestis, Hippolytus,* and *Ion* and by a ghost in *Hecuba*. An interesting exception is *Trojan Women*, in which the divine prologue speaker (Poseidon) describes not the past but the present and the future.

21. *Poetics* 1454 b.2–6. Compare Roberts, "Outside the Drama."

22. *Poetics* 1450 b.26–30.

23. Compare the important distinction between sacred and profane time in Eliade, *Myth of Eternal Return*.

24. Pythagoras in Aëtius I.21.1 (=Pythagorean school DK 58B33), Hermippus in fr. 73 *PCG*.

25. It is virtually certain that *Prometheus Bound* was followed by *Prometheus Unbound* in a connected trilogy (scholiast to *Prometheus* 513), and very likely that the third and final play of the trilogy was *Prometheus Fire-Carrier* (p. 329 and F 208a *TrGF*). For discussion, see Herington, "Study in *Promethia*" 182–83; for dissenting views, see Griffith, *Prometheus Bound* 281–83 and A. L. Brown, "Prometheus."

26. Just as Prometheus adduces his privileged knowledge of Io's past sufferings (823–43)

to confirm his knowledge of her future, so this privileged knowledge imparted by Themis (873–74) gives authority to his following claim to know of a marriage that will destroy Zeus (907–14).

27. Compare Conacher, *Aeschylus' Prometheus* 61, and Griffith, *Prometheus Bound* 190.

28. It is often argued that the trilogy ends with the institution of the torch-race at the Promethia; see Thomson, *Prometheus* 32–38, and Herington, "Study in *Promethia*."

29. Schlesinger, *Gods in Greek Tragedy* 33–34 mentions possible prophecies in the fragmentary plays, but many are simply etymologies or vague allusions to the future, and no prophecy can securely be placed at the end of a play or trilogy. The most interesting is a fragment from *Psychagogoi* (F 275 *TrGF*), in which Teiresias apparently foretells the manner of Odysseus' death; unfortunately, we know little about this play (probably first in its trilogy), and nothing about the context of this prophecy.

30. Thus Pearson, *Fragments*, vol. 2, 214 suggests that the allusion may date *Teucer* before *Ajax*, a suggestion described as "interesting but scarcely conclusive" by Sutton, *Lost Sophocles* 139.

31. On subtler hints in other plays, see Roberts, "Sophoclean Endings."

32. A search for concluding prophecies among the fragments of Sophocles yields little. There is no evidence, for example, that *Polyxena* ended with a prophecy by the ghost of Achilles (compare Pearson, *Fragments*, vol. 2, 162), and while *Syndeipnoi* may have ended with Thetis ex machina (F 562 *TrGF*), we do not know whether or not she delivered a prophecy. On the different sequels in *Philoctetes*, see Roberts, "Different Stories."

33. Compare Roberts, "Sophoclean Endings" 192 who concludes that for Sophocles "there *are* natural endings to tragic actions and to tragedies" whereas "Euripides (especially in his later plays) suggests the arbitrariness or artificiality" of the end.

34. "The goddess appears not so much to extricate the tangles of the plot . . . as to give occasion for a prophecy about the future," Owen on *Ion* 1549.

35. Decharme, *Euripides* 272.

36. Grube, *Drama of Euripides* 77.

37. Kitto, *Greek Tragedy* 285.

38. W. Schmidt, "Deus ex Machina" 202, my translation.

39. Translated from Chapiro, *Gespräche* 162.

Chapter 6

1. Grube, *Drama of Euripides* 177.

2. Michelini, *Euripides and Tragic Tradition*, chapter 9.

3. Knox, "*Hippolytus* of Euripides" 227.

4. Bieber, "Entrances and Exits" 280.

5. *Bacchant Women* has a dramatic climax in the death of Pentheus, but the first report of his death (1028 or 1030) is followed by more than 360 lines of text, plus a lacuna of at least fifty lines.

6. In line 33, Diggle emends to ὀνομάσουσιν, following Jortin. On the infinitive with ὠνόμαζεν, see Barrett, *Hippolytos* 161. On textual questions, see also the following note.

7. The lines have been suspected by Jahn (del. 29–33), Blomfield (del. 32–22), and others, and more recently by Wilson, "Etymology in *Troades*" 69 note 7; by Lewin, *Study of Prologoi* 87–90; and by Looy, "Observations sur l'*Hippolyte*." They are defended by Barrett, *Hippolytos* 161–62 and Erbse, *Studien zum Prolog* 36–37; see also Dunn, "Fearful Symmetry" 110–11.

8. On the shrine of Aphrodite, see *IG* i³ 369.66 = *SEG* x 227.66 (αφροδιτες εν hιπ̄πολυ[) and *IG* i³ 383.233–34; compare *SEG* x 225 (Αφροδ]ιτες ε|[πι Ιπ]πολυτο). On the Hippolyteion,

see scholiast to *Hippolytus* 30 and Pausanias 1.22.1. For identification of their remains on the slope of the Acropolis, see Beschi, "Contributi" 514–15, and Walker, "Sanctuary of Isis" 248. For ἐπί with a proper name in the dative meaning "in honor of [the deceased]," compare *Iliad* 23.776, *Odyssey* 24.91, Lysias 2.80, Bion 1.81, *IG* vii 1880, and many examples in Schwyzer, *Dialectorum graecarum* §§ 348, 452.1–11, 456.99–100. On parallels between the opening and closing aetiologies, see Dunn, "Fearful Symmetry."

9. Thus the nurse in *Medea*, Iolaus in *Children of Heracles*, Andromache in *Andromache*, Polydorus (or rather, his shade) in *Hecuba*, Aethra in *Suppliant Women*, the farmer in *Electra*, Amphitryon in *Heracles*, Iphigenia in *Iphigenia among the Taurians*, Helen in *Helen*, Jocasta in *Phoenician Women*, and Electra in *Orestes*. The opening dialogue of *Iphigenia at Aulis* is often emended to give a prologue speech to Agamemnon. For recent discussions, see Erbse, *Studien zum Prolog* and C. Segal, "Tragic Beginnings."

10. In *Bacchant Women*, Dionysus as Stranger plays a similar role, although his attributes as deus are less pronounced, thus affording a clear contrast between the disguised epiphany of the prologue and the full epiphany to be staged at the end.

11. See Stuart, "Foreshadowing" and Hamilton, "Prologue Prophecy." Some of the nurse's lines in *Medea* probably have been interpolated (see Page on 37–44), but even if genuine, they constitute false foreshadowing, since Medea will not enter the palace and stab Jason with a sword (*Medea* 40–41).

12. The mention of armies coming together in battle (*Bacchant Women* 51–52) is thus a false lead.

13. On *Ion* and *Alcestis*, see especially Hamilton, "Prologue Prophecy" 279–83 and 293–301.

14. It is generally assumed that Euripides' first *Hippolytus* was set in Athens, and if so, it is quite possible that it ended with an αἴτιον for the hero's tomb by the Acropolis (see Barrett, *Hippolytos* 32–34). When he came to write the second *Hippolytus*, which he would set in Trozen and which he would end with an αἴτιον for the famous sanctuary there, the playwright needed somehow to set aside memories of the earlier version. By alluding in the prologue to the first aetiology and by consigning it to a minor episode in the past (when Hippolytus went to Athens to celebrate the mysteries), Euripides closes off his earlier treatment of the legend and allows a new plot to begin. A forecast referring to the noble Phaedra (47) just as clearly distances the second version from the shameless deeds of the first.

15. In *Trojan Women*, Athena and Poseidon also quit the stage forever at the end of the prologue scene; the difference is that they have not intervened in events onstage. See chapter 7.

16. Pausanias 2.32.3–4. Both sites also have some association with Asclepius (Pausanias 1.22.1 and 2.32.4).

17. *Suppliant Women* is an interesting case. Death and commemoration are central to the plot, and one could argue that the Seven are the play's main character, yet the Seven are dead before the drama even begins.

18. Philodemus περὶ εὐσεβείας 52 and Apollodorus 3.10.3 both cite an epic *Naupactia*; compare scholiast to Pindar *Pythian* 3.96, and scholiast to Euripides *Alcestis* 1.

19. See Callimachus fr. 190 Pfeiffer; Virgil *Aeneid* 7.761–82, and Servius *ad loc.*; compare Pausanias 2.27.4.

20. In 1427, Diggle emends to καρπουμένῳ, following Valckenaer, but it is just as plausible that future women will harvest these tears as that the dead Hippolytus will do so.

21. Sources are listed in the following note. See also Eumelus in Pausanias 2.3.11, scholiast to Pindar *Olympian* 13.74g, Eusebius *Contra Marc.* 3.1.

22. See Parmeniscus in scholiast to *Medea* 264, Pausanias 2.3.6–7; compare Creophylus in scholiast to *Medea* 264, Apollodorus 1.9.28, Diodorus 4.54–55, Philostratus *Heroicus* 53.4.

23. For a fuller discussion, see Dunn, "Euripides and Rites."

24. "Indeed the connection between the future rite and the present stage action is obscure," Craik, "Euripides' First *Hippolytos*" 139. For discussion of the ambiguity of the closing aetiology, see Goff, *Noose of Words* 113–29, and Pucci, "Euripides: Monument" 184–86.

25. Compare Brelich, *Paides e Parthenoi* 33 and note 79 to that page, and Rehm, *Marriage* 11–29.

26. Thus Pucci, "Euripides: Monument" 185, and Goff, *Noose of Words* 111.

27. Zeitlin, "Power of Aphrodite" 107.

28. C. Segal, *Euripides and Poetics* 120–26 refers to the ambivalence of this aition in an interesting discussion of gender and space in *Hippolytus*. Rabinowitz, *Anxiety Veiled* 187 implies that the out-of-place aition underlines the irrelevance of women and marriage in a men's world represented by Theseus and Hippolytus.

29. If Aphrodite's favorite is Adonis, Euripides has promised a novel plot in which he is killed by Artemis' arrows; if we take these arrows literally, we must wonder if some favorite less well known will be Artemis' victim. Compare Barrett, *Hippolytus* 412.

30. Brooks, *Reading for Plot*, chapter 4.

31. In Girardian terms, *Hippolytus* enacts a mimetic crisis without enabling a rebirth of order. Mitchell, however, insists on finding a scapegoat that will rescue the play for Girard. The notion that Hippolytus is a scapegoat who displaces human violence and guilt onto the gods cannot be supported: Hippolytus, Phaedra, Theseus, "Adonis," and even Artemis (1338–39) are all victims, and as Artemis reminds us, Theseus, Aphrodite, the nurse, and Phaedra are all to blame. See Girard, *Violence and the Sacred* and Mitchell, "Miasma, Mimesis."

32. On the new Phaedra, see Zeitlin, "Power of Aphrodite" 52–54 and Reckford, "Phaedra and Pasiphae."

33. On shame as a thematic concern of the play, see C. Segal, "Shame and Purity." For a good discussion of the second Phaedra as a failed attempt to reenact the first, see Reckford, "Phaedra and Pasiphae."

34. Zeitlin, "Power of Aphrodite" 107–8.

35. On the first *Hippolytus*, see Barrett, *Hippolytos* especially 34–35 (on the prologue) and 44–45 (on the last scene).

36. Our source for these lines (Stobaeus 4.20.25) does not identify the speaker, but Phaedra is the only plausible one.

Chapter 7

1. Haigh, *Tragic Drama* 300.

2. Murray, "*Trojan Women*" 38.

3. Grube, *Drama of Euripides* 282.

4. "Intesa in questo senso, l'unità delle *Troiane* è assoluta e perfetta," Perrotta, "Le *Troiane*" 237.

5. Barlow, *Trojan Women* 32.

6. Lattimore, Introduction 124.

7. See the discussion of *Trojan Women* 1256–59, with note 14 of this chapter, on the verbal, and perhaps theatrical, gesture that fails to herald the entrance of a deus.

8. The satyr-play *Cyclops* ends in trimeters, with the last two parting lines spoken by the chorus.

9. The opening exchange (1287–1301) is followed by strophe (1302–16) and antistrophe (1317–32). As Lee, *Troades* 277 notes, "there is no justification for B[iehl]'s attempt to make 1287–1301 strophic by a process of wholesale rewriting."

10. The manuscripts assign 1325–29 to Hecuba and 1329–32 to Talthybius. All modern editors follow Seidler in giving the last two lines to the chorus, but his changes rest upon

assumptions that need to be reexamined, namely that there should be exact responsion in change of speakers and that the closing lines should be spoken by the chorus. (Seidler assigns 1315–16 at the end of the strophe to the chorus, although the manuscripts assign them to Hecuba, and then assigns 1331–32 at the end of the antistrophe to the chorus, to produce responsion.)

11. Two other plays of Aeschylus end with lyrics, but *Suppliant Women* closes with a brief, gnomic antistrophe (1068–72) in which the chorus reflects upon the justice of Zeus, and *Eumenides* ends with a brief antistrophe (1044–47) in which the secondary chorus reflects on the power of Zeus and appeals to the audience. Given the similar content of *Persians* and *Trojan Women*, Euripides' finale seems designed to recall that of Aeschylus: another *kommos* between chorus and shattered protagonist, the same cries of woe (ὀτοτοτοτοῖ, *Persians* 1043, 1051, *Trojan Women* 1287, 1293), concluding with a similar brief escort offstage (πέμψω τοί σε δυσθρόοις γόοις, *Persians* 1077, ὅμως / δὲ πρόφερε πόδα σὸν ἐπὶ πλάτας Ἀχαιῶν, *Trojan Women* 1331–32).

12. On the authenticity of these lines (marked spurious by Diggle), see chapter 11, note 20.

13. The text is corrupt; hence my paraphrase.

14. What the chorus sees is not necessarily staged. The original production might have employed extras on the palace roof and might have left everything to the imagination. But the exclamation of the chorus suggests that something at least was visible to the audience. Wisps of smoke? A flaming torch?

15. Unfortunately, the mutilated epilogue of *Bacchant Women* and the spurious ending of *Iphigenia at Aulis* must be left out of account. *Alcestis* also concludes with no aition, Admetus commands that sacrifices and choral celebrations be established (1154–56).

16. Survival of the ὄνομα is central to the aition: ἐπώνυμος δὲ σοῦ πόλις κεκλήσεται *Electra* 1275; τύμβῳ δ' ὄνομα σῷ κεκλήσεται *Hecuba* 1271; *Hippolytus* 1429; *Iphigenia among the Taurians* 1452, 1454; *Heracles* 1329–30; *Ion* 1577, 1587–88, 1594; *Orestes* 1646; and compare *Erechtheus* fr. 65, line 93 (Austin).

17. Diggle follows Seidler in assigning alternating lines to Hecuba and to the chorus.

18. Sartre's adaptation *Les Troyennes* restores this type of balanced frame by adding a final epiphany of Poseidon; the film version of Cacoyannis, *Trojan Women* adds a more subtle frame by repeating the opening words of Hecuba's monody in her parting lines.

19. Compare Pohlenz, *Griechische Tragödie*, vol. 1, 435. I do not agree that the transposition is a make-shift expedient: "Das gewaltige Finale, das Bild des brennenden Troia, vertrug am Schluß keinen Deus ex machina."

20. See, for example, Stuart, "Foreshadowing"; Gollwitzer, *Prolog- und Expositionstechnik*, esp. 82–91; and Hamilton, "Prologue Prophecy". Wilson regards this unique prophecy as further evidence of interpolation (Wilson, "Interpolation" 205). O'Neill, "Prologue of *Troades*" 289 observes that "So wide a departure from his usual practice is significant," but nevertheless maintains that the prophecy in *Trojan Women* establishes a "Known End" to the action in the same manner as Aphrodite's prophecy in *Hippolytus* (293).

21. Helen and Menelaus, of course, belong neither among the Trojan women nor among the victorious Greeks and are immune to the suffering of the former and the punishment of the latter.

22. Lines 13–14 are deleted by Diggle, following Burges, but as Wilson points out, their "awkwardness" or "frigidity" does not warrant excision (Wilson, "Etymology in *Troades*" 67). Wilson gives very different grounds for suspecting interpolation: in its reference "to the future beyond the limits of the play" and its "almost formulaic use of κεκλήσεται" (71), the etymology resembles those usually found in the epilogue. Yet this finding suggests not interpolation but inversion of beginning and ending, and the only remaining anomaly, "the fact

that it does not refer to a character in the play" (71), is an exact parallel to the prophecy of Poseidon, which concerns the Greeks rather than the Trojans.

23. *Hecuba* 1271, *Electra* 1275, *Heracles* 1330, *Ion* 1594 (κεκλῆσθαι), *Helen* 1674, and *Orestes* 1646. Compare *Erechtheus* frag. 65, line 92 (Austin), and *Suppliant Women* 1225 (κληθέντες). At *Trojan Women* 13, the manuscripts vary between κεκλήσεται (V) and κληθήσεται (PQ). For a discussion of Euripides' use of the word, see pages 383–94 in Ruijgh, "Observations sur κεκλῆσθαι."

24. On the statue created by Strongylion and dedicated by Chaeredemus, see Parmentier, "Notes sur les *Troyennes*" 46–49.

25. Wilson, "Interpolation" 205–12. It does not follow, however, that Athena's entrance has been interpolated.

26. See Kovacs, "Euripides, *Troades* 95–97" and more recently Manuwald, "μῶρος δὲ θνητῶν."

27. Especially in the prologue and in messenger speeches, but also in other parts of the play; see C. Friedrich, "Dramatische Funktion."

28. Mason, "Kassandra" 88, proposes correcting this reversal by transposing the *effect* of the moral to the end of the play: "the lesson of [lines 95–97] remains in our ears until the end of the play, so that no *deus ex machina* is required to establish justice or impose peace."

29. Wilson, "Etymology in *Troades*" recommends cosmetic surgery to eliminate this defect; see note 22 of this chapter.

30. As Poole, "Total disaster" 259 concludes, "never does a Chorus leave an emptier space at the end."

31. Conacher, *Euripidean Drama* 139.

32. Compare Poole, "Total Disaster" 259: "The play is concerned with analyzing, more coldly and clinically than most readers seem prepared to admit, the way in which people actually behave, values behave, words behave, in such a frontier situation."

33. It is now hard to maintain, as Delebecque (*Euripide et la guerre* 245–46) and Goossens (*Euripide et Athènes* 520–27) once did, that *Trojan Women* has the end or goal of attacking war in general and the Athenian expedition against Melos in particular. There is a great difference between a work depicting "the cultural and ideological crisis brought on by war" (Croally, *Euripidean Polemic* 231) and one designed to convey a particular lesson or message. As Erp Taalman Kip points out ("Euripides and Melos"), there was probably not time to compose and submit a play in response to the destruction of Melos, and the bleakness of Euripides' play consists in part in the absence of such a message. Contrast the reassuringly clear conclusion Sartre adds to his version, bringing in Poseidon to announce, "Faites la guerre, mortels imbéciles, ravagez les champs et les villes, violez les temples, les tombes, et torturez les vaincus. Vous en crèverez. Tous" (*Les Troyennes* 130).

34. See the excellent discussion in Scodel, *Trojan Trilogy*.

35. *Rhesus* is a special problem; it covers events described in book 10 of the *Iliad*, but its date and authorship are uncertain.

36. On the struggle against the poetic father or precursor, see Bloom, *Anxiety of Influence*.

37. Summary in Proclus (Allen 102–105). Homer nowhere refers directly to the story of the judgment, but a passing allusion (*Iliad* 24.28–30) may indicate that he knew the story: thus Reinhardt, "Parisurteil" and Stinton, *Euripides and Judgement* 1–4. The *Cypria*'s revision would then consist in describing at length what Homer preferred to pass over.

38. *Cypria* I (Allen 117–18) = scholiast to *Iliad* 1.5.

39. See Stinton, *Euripides and Judgement*.

40. For a reconstruction of *Alexander*, see Scodel, *Trojan Trilogy*.

41. See Sutton, *Two Lost Plays* 117–121. We cannot be sure exactly which inventions other than writing (fr. 578 Nauck) figured in Euripides' version of the legend.

42. For a much simpler view of their disconnectedness, see Koniaris, *"Alexander, Palamedes."*

43. Scodel, *Trojan Trilogy* 72. Compare the remarks of Croally, *Euripidean Polemic* 204 on the unmarked and temporary space the action inhabits.

Chapter 8

1. Diggle obelizes the end of 1420 and deletes 1421, while Conradt went further, deleting 1419–21. For other proposed emendations, with discussion, see Bond, *Heracles* 414–15.

2. This implication is sometimes softened by emending the text of 1391; for the manuscript reading παίδων, ἅπαντες δ' ἑνὶ λόγῳ πενθήσατε, Diggle, for example, prints παίδων. ἅπαντας δ' ἑνὶ λόγῳ πενθήσετε.

3. On altars and sanctuaries to Heracles in Attica, see Woodford, "Cults of Heracles." Herodotus (6.108 and 116) refers to a shrine of the god Heracles that existed at Marathon in the year 490.

4. See chapter 4.

5. Earlier in this play, Heracles alludes to an initiation: "I was lucky enough to see the rites of the *mystai*" (τὰ μυστῶν δ' ὄργι' εὐτύχησ' ἰδών 613), and a story of his initiation at Eleusis before descending to the underworld seems to lie behind Aristophanes' *Frogs*; possible earlier sources in poetry and art are discussed by Lloyd-Jones, "Heracles at Eleusis" and Boardman, "Herakles, Peisistratos." Isolated reports that Heracles was initiated at the instigation of Theseus (Plutarch, *Theseus* 30) or that the Lesser Mysteries in Athens were established in his honor (Diodorus 4.14.3) seem to be late attempts to improve upon this tradition by forging the close connection between Heracles and Athens that is lacking in Euripides.

6. Later tradition regards both τεμένη (Philochorus 328 F18.3 = Plutarch *Theseus* 35) and a βωμός (Aelian *VH* 4.5) as gifts from Theseus himself to Heracles. As Jacoby points out, Philochorus seems to follow and correct the account of Euripides (*FGrH* IIIB, supp. I, 307–8).

7. On the prevalence of stories of Heracles' apotheosis, see March, *Creative Poet* 72–75 and Holt, "End of *Trachiniai*" 70–74. If the words of Theseus are ironic (he does not know, as the audience does, what the future holds) and partially true (Heracles will be honored after his "death" even if he does not really die), they still betray the ignorance of a speaker who otherwise seemed to have privileged knowledge.

8. On this notorious exchange, see Halleran, "Rhetoric, Irony"; Heracles' reply is quoted at the end of this chapter.

9. *Andromache* 1226–30, *Hippolytus* 1391–93, *Ion* 1549–52, *Electra* 1233–37; compare discussion in chapter 3.

10. *Orestes* 1678–81; compare *Hippolytus* 1442–43, *Andromache* 1276–77, *Iphigenia among the Taurians* 1475–76, *Ion* 1606–7, *Helen* 1680–81.

11. Swinburne quoted by Verrall, *Essays* 136; Murray, "Heracles" 112, endorsed by Norwood, *Essays* 47.

12. Arrowsmith, Introduction to *Heracles* 49–50.

13. Chalk, "ἀρετή and βία"; Gregory, "Euripides' *Heracles*"; Yunis, *New Creed*; Foley, *Ritual Irony*.

14. See further Dunn, "Ends and Means." The trope of erasure is used in a different way at the end of Michelini's useful chapter on *Heracles*.

15. On problems with these apparent burials, see discussion in chapter 4.

16. ἄναξ *Children of Heracles* 114; *Suppliant Women* 113, 164, 367; προστάτης *Children of Heracles* 206; ἀλκιμώτατον κάρα *Suppliant Women* 163; compare *Oedipus at Colonus* 67, 549.

17. ἐλευθέρα *Children of Heracles* 62, 113, 198, *Suppliant Women* 405, 477; self-government *Children of Heracles* 423–24, *Suppliant Women* 403–8; compare *Oedipus at Colonus* 557–58. On the contrast between *Heracles* and *Oedipus at Colonus*, and Euripides' emphasis upon friendship, compare Kroeker, *Herakles* 99.

18. Compare *Medea*, in which Aegeus enters not as a king but as a friend, and Athens remains a future destination. An important difference is that the story of Medea's exile in Athens, unlike that of Heracles, was apparently known to the audience; see for example Gantz, *Early Greek Myth* 255–56.

19. On φιλία in *Heracles*, see Conacher, *Euripidean Drama* 83–88.

20. The digression on the gods (1340–46) is followed with mention of his fear of seeming a coward (1347–48) and with a proverb on endurance (1349–50) that introduce his decision to go to Athens. Compare Bond, *Heracles* 401: "Heracles' change of mind is rapidly indicated and given one single motivation, fear of the charge of cowardice."

21. Chalk, "ἀρετή and βία" 14.

22. Aeneas likewise taunts Pandarus the bowman, who curses his bow, *Iliad* 5.171–78, 204–16; compare Hera taunting Artemis the archer, *Iliad* 21.483, 491.

23. On the portrayal of archers as barbarians in Attic vase-painting, see Vos, *Scythian Archers*. If Lycus endorses the civic solidarity of hoplites, it does not follow that Heracles endorses an opposing set of values. Foley, for example, wants Heracles' bow to represent an older, individualistic heroism, while Michelini wants it to represent a newer, sophistic heroism: Foley, *Ritual Irony* 167–75; Michelini, *Euripides and Tragic Tradition* 242–46. Neither is correct. Odysseus' personal and domestic vendetta against the suitors is hardly an archetype of heroic warfare, while the sophistic tone of Amphitryon's debate with Lycus does not necessarily characterize Heracles. Otherwise, both have good observations on the bow and its connotations, as does Hamilton, "Slings and Arrows."

24. Walsh, "Public and Private" 308. George, "Euripides' *Heracles*" likewise sees the bow as endorsing civic values.

25. It is possible that the strange conceit of talking weapons alludes to the chattering Kerkopes who stole Heracles' weapons and, as he carried them off, remarked upon his hairy backside; for their story, see Nonnus in Westermann, Μυθογράφοι 375; *Suda* s.v. Κέρκωπες and s.v. Μελαμπύγου τύχοις; Brommer, *Herakles II* 28–32; *LIMC* s.v. Kerkopes; and Gantz, *Early Greek Myth* 441–42.

26. Michelini, *Euripides and Tragic Tradition* 272 draws attention in a more general way to "the kaleidoscopic fragmentation of Herakles' image, as we are continually presented with different and contradictory versions of the hero."

27. Kirk, "Methodological Reflections" 286.

28. Silk, "Heracles and Tragedy" 120.

29. Loraux, "Herakles."

30. It is worth noting that Prodicus elaborated a moral conflict between virtue and vice in the figure of Heracles; see, e.g., Kuntz, "Prodikean Choice." I would suggest that the failure of this story (as reported by Xenophon) to tell which choice Heracles made is more significant than Kuntz allows, and although Arete has the last word, Heracles' career was equally renowned for noble and for self-indulgent deeds.

31. Chapter 5, notes 1 and 2.

32. Bakhtin, *Dialogic Imagination* 3–40.

33. Compare the discussion of Morson, "For the Time Being."

34. Carroll, *Sylvie and Bruno* 169.

35. Compare Davis, "Social History."

36. On "aperture" see Morson, "For the Time Being"; on ethical freedom, compare Rubino, "Opening up the Classical Past."

37. See Dunn, "Ends and Means."

38. Michelini, *Euripides and Tragic Tradition* 275; Lesky, *Greek Tragic Poetry* 281; Conacher, *Euripidean Drama* 89–90; see also Halleran, "Rhetoric, Irony."

39. In line 1340, I give Barnes' supplement; for a brief discussion, see Bond, *Heracles* 398.

Chapter 9

1. Shaw, *Pygmalion* 115 and 124.

2. Shaw, *Pygmalion* 9, from his preface.

3. The genre has been dubbed "tragi-comedy" by Kitto, *Greek Tragedy* 311–29, and "romantic tragedy" by Conacher, *Euripidean Drama* 265, while its affinities with the novel have been pointed out by Winkler, "Aristotle's Theory." On the larger class of "intrigue plays," see note 62 of this chapter.

4. τὴν καινὴν Ἑλένην, as Aristophanes describes Euripides' protagonist, *Thesmophoriazusae* 850.

5. With a variation in the first line in *Medea*; on these lines and their authenticity, see chapter 2.

6. Compare Rees, "Euripides, *Medea*" 180–81.

7. In the preceding lines (1666–69, quoted later in this chapter), the Dioscuri prophesize that Helen will be called a god and will share the worship of her brothers. The passing allusion to offerings made to the Dioscuri (1668) is too vague to class as an aition, but as Foley, "*Anodos* Dramas" 145–48 points out, there are hints of Spartan cult elsewhere in the play, while at Therapne there was a cult of Helen that might have been introduced as a closing aetiology—but was not.

8. There is an allusion to the aetiology of Oresteion at *Electra* 1273–75, following the more explicit judicial aetiology in 1265–69.

9. Euripides apparently conflates his novel account of the phantom with prior attempts to place this island on Helen's route to (Homer, *Iliad* 3.443–46 with Strabo 9.1.22) or from Troy (Hecataeus *FGrH* 1 F128); compare Kannicht on 1670–75.

10. Compare Dale, *Helen* on 1673: the cult aetiology "has shrunk here to a mere perfunctory insertion, and the philology, if indeed ἑλ- is to be connected with κλέψας, κλοπὰς, 'taking' by stealth, is more than usually far-fetched." Austin, *Helen of Troy* 186 is a bit far-fetched in stating that Helena means "The Stolen."

11. Diggle follows F. W. Schmidt in deleting parts of lines 1667–68.

12. Ring-composition emphasizes the difficulties: the play begins with Hermes' announcement of Apollo's scheme to restore Ion in Athens by deceiving Xuthus (69–73), and it ends with Athena's announcement of an almost identical scheme (1601–2).

13. For my purposes, the identity of the servant is not important. The manuscripts assign this part to the (female) chorus leader, while Clark attributed them to a male servant (δοῦλος ὢν 1630). Clark's attribution is followed by Stanley–Porter, "Who opposes Theoclymenus?" and by Diggle; for a defense of the manuscripts, see Dale, *Helen* 165–66 and Kannicht, *Helena*, vol. 1, 422–24.

14. In *Antiope*, Page restores a similarly abrupt intervention and command of Hermes, who enters to prevent Amphion from killing Lycus in revenge: Page, *Greek Literary Papyri* 68.

15. Thus, Way, *Tragedies of Euripides*, vol 3, xxi and Grube, *Drama of Euripides* 75–76.

16. Their entrance is all the more surprising because Teucer has suggested they may be dead (142).

17. Diggle follows Willink in deleting lines 1650–55.

18. In *Ion*, Athena explains both the parentage of Ion (1560–62) and the divine plan of Apollo (1566–68, 1595–1600); Apollo in *Orestes* explains both the disappearance of Helen (1629–34) and the designs of Zeus (1634, 1639–42); Athena in *Iphigenia among the Taurians* explains Orestes' mission to recover the statue (1440–41b) and Apollo's agency in sending him (1438–39); and the Dioscuri in *Electra* fail to explain either the matricide itself or the divine plan behind it (1244–48, 1301–2). In *Andromache* and *Suppliant Women*, no explanation is necessary and none is given.

19. There is nothing to support Spira's reference to "der großen Rückshau, die das ganze Geschehen als göttlichen Plan aufzeigt (1650ff.)": Spira, *Untersuchungen zum Deus* 122.

20. The unnecessary suffering of the many soldiers at Troy is a real but minor theme, and Papi goes too far in naming this the central message of the play: Papi, "Victors and Sufferers" 39, followed by Nicolai, *Euripides' Dramen* 29–30. However, it is not necessary to conclude that one or both lines are interpolated (Hartung, Kannicht) or corrupt (Dale, Diggle). Romilly interprets the inappropriate moral as implied mockery: "La justice divine n'est plus" ("La belle Hélène" 143, note 22).

21. Diggle reverses the order of lines 1682–83 (following A. Y. Campbell) and obelizes line 1685.

22. On Theoclymenus' sudden change of heart, compare Seidensticker, *Palintonos Harmonia* 196: "Der Genasführte schließt das Stück mit einem enthusiastischen Preis der Frau, die ihn genasführt hat," and Kannicht on 1642–87. Spira, however, claims that Theoclymenus has been converted by the gods, *Untersuchungen zum Deus* 122–23.

23. The simple epilogues are *Andromache* (1231–72, 1273–83, 1284–88), *Suppliant Women* (1183–1226, 1227–31, 1232–34), and *Helen* (1642–79, 1680–87, 1688–92).

24. Compare Kitto, *Greek Tragedy* 322 on *Helen*: "The entirely artificial *Deus* is a happy way of bringing to a close plots which were artificial, too, in their inception." Yet Kitto views such endings as empty and superficial (compare his p. 314).

25. As Stinton, *Euripides and Judgement* observes, the judgment of Paris was a favorite theme of Euripides, whose models for the εἴδωλον of Helen (Stesichorus, Herodotus) apparently make no mention of the judgment.

26. In Euripides, Hera is the agent who sets events in motion, while Zeus' inclinations coincide with her actions. In the *Cypria* (fr. 1), however, Zeus has a moral purpose in punishing mortals, and he is the agent of the war.

27. Compare Matthiessen, *Elektra, Taurische Iphigenie* 182: "Der Dichter unternimmt nicht einmal den Versuch, diese Gründe gegeneinander abzuwägen."

28. Hamilton nevertheless claims that the outcome of *Helen* shows "that Zeus's plan really was carried out," Hamilton, "Prologue Prophecy" 292; compare Burnett, *Catastrophe Survived* 99, and Erbse, *Studien zum Prolog* 213–15.

29. Theonoe is not claiming to be the arbiter between Hera and Aphrodite, *pace* Kitto, *Greek Tragedy* 324, nor is she simply making a personal choice, *pace* Zuntz, "On Euripides' *Helena*" 205–6, and Matthiessen, "Zur Theonoeszene" 689. She is deciding an issue disputed by the gods, as noted by Pohlenz, *Griechische Tragödie*, vol. 1, 388, and Conacher, *Euripidean Drama* 294–95 with note 10.

30. Theonoe's words, like those of most seers, are quite enigmatic. The many attempts to reconstruct Theonoe's philosophy are therefore misguided. Pippin, for example, recovers a Platonic theology: "the quarreling gods of mythology are split away from the true principle of divinity" ("Euripides' *Helen*" 162), while Dimock finds a moral imperative: "[Euripides] has attempted a demonstration that doing right is infallibly and totally rewarded with eternal

recognition in the light of truth" (*God, or Not God* 17). Theonoe, however, simply states certain personal beliefs without attempting to explain or justify them; the fact that she acts more justly than her brother does not make her knowledge less subjective.

31. Papi, "Victors and Sufferers" 32 observes that "Theonoe is completely independent of the Olympian gods since her choice to help Helen and Menelaus is the result of a personal decision (887) inspired by a higher code of justice that is not only different but even in opposition to that of Zeus." For the suggestion that Theonoe's views are traditional rather than enlightened, see Sansone, "Theonoe."

32. For example, Pohlenz, *Griechische Tragödie*, vol. 1, 436; Terzaghi, "Finali e prologhi" 309; Fritz, *Antike und moderne* 312. Compare discussion at the end of chapter 3.

33. Hamilton, "Prologue Prophecy" 283, however, regards the two "prophecies" as contradictory, since the dream is misinterpreted by Iphigenia.

34. On delayed fulfillment of the oracles, see Roberts, *Apollo and his oracle* 102–8. On the drama as a morality play, see Burnett, *Catastrophe survived* 47–72.

35. Likewise, the manner in which Theoclymenus falls for every detail of Helen's scheme is, or seems, fortuitous, and Theonoe's announcement of support is a happy surprise.

36. The special role of τύχη in *Helen* has not adequately been discussed. It has long been recognized that τύχη plays a greater role in the later plays of Euripides, for example in Schadewaldt, *Monolog* 256–57; Solmsen, "Euripides' *Ion*" 393 and 400; and Zürcher, *Darstellung des Menschen* 149–63; compare Meuss, "Tyche" 13–17. This role is denied by Busch, *Untersuchungen* 44–45 and by Spira, *Untersuchungen zum Deus* 132–38. Only Matthiessen, *Elektra, Taurische Iphigenie* 182, 184 draws attention to the special role of τύχη in *Helen*, although he prefers to call it "ernstes Lustspiel" rather than "τύχη-Drama." Occurrences of the word τύχη: twenty-four times in *Helen*, eighteen in *Ion*, sixteen in *Hippolytus*, fifteen times each in *Heracles* and *Iphigenia among the Taurians*.

37. Diggle deletes lines 713–19.

38. Diggle prints ὅτι in line 1137, and in 1142 emends to ἀμφιλόγοις, following Dobree.

39. These two passages contain striking echoes of Sophistic thought, in particular skepticism concerning knowledge (compare Gorgias DK 82B3, quoted later); the assertion that men cannot apprehend the gods (compare Protagoras DK 80B4, where ἀδηλότης may be echoed by ποικίλον καὶ δυστέκμαρτον in *Helen* 711–12); and the term ἀντιλόγοις (see Protagoras DK 80A1 and B5 on his two books of ἀντιλογίαι; this is the only example of this word or any of its cognates in Greek tragedy—Sophocles *Antigone* 377 ἀντιλογέω = ἀντιλέγω is not an exception). On the significance of these lines, compare Matthiessen, *Elektra, Taurische Iphigenie* 182.

40. Compare Hamilton, "Prologue Prophecy" 288: "Hermes' prophecy, like Apollo's oracle in the *Iphigenia*, is not set outside the action but is revealed to the audience by an actor fully conscious of its implications." See also Stuart, "Foreshadowing and Suspense."

41. Compare Seidensticker, *Palintonos Harmonia* 179–80, on the otherwise superfluous repetition of Theonoe's revelation. The comic effect of the recognition scene does not support a sustained parody, as argued by Steiger, "Wie entstand *Helena?*" or a critique of mythology, as argued by Schmiel, "Recognition Duo." However, the psychological seriousness of the scene is exaggerated by Alt, "Zur Anagnorisis."

42. Too often, Theoclymenus is regarded as one or the other: either "a pious and kindly man," Grube, *Drama of Euripides* 348, or an "impious" and "cruel despot," Pippin, "Euripides' *Helen*" 157.

43. If she has any reason of her own, she does not reveal it to the audience and apparently forgets it, since she exits at the end of the scene as abruptly as she entered (1029). If νόμον δὲ τὸν ἐμὸν θεοῖσιν ἀποδοῦσαι refers to purification of the air, we are not told what purpose the purification and procession serve.

44. If αἰθέρος μυχούς (Wecklein, followed by Dale, Kannicht, Diggle) or μυχόν (Pfluck, followed by Grégoire) in 866 is correct, the only parallel is αἰθέρος πτυχαί, which accompanies a deus ex machina (*Orestes* 1631[?] and 1636), a divine chariot (*Phaethon* fr. 779.7 Nauck), a spiriting-away by the gods (*Helen* 44 and 605) or the abode of the gods (*Ion* 1445). Yet Theonoe is hardly a conventional god; with her head in the clouds (ὡς πνεῦμα καθαρὸν οὐρανοῦ δεξώμεθα 867) and her talk of δίκη and γνώμη (1002–4, 1013–6), she could almost be a parody of Socrates; compare Aristophanes, *Clouds* 316–17 (οὐράνιαι Νεφέλαι . . . / αἵπερ γνώμην καὶ διάλεξιν καὶ νοῦν ἡμῖν παρέχουσιν), and Sansone, "Theonoe" 27 on "the eschatological mumbo jumbo of 1013–1016." The resemblance to Socrates is taken more seriously by Pohlenz, *Griechische Tragödie*, vol. 1, 387 and 430, and Ronnet, "Cas de conscience" 258–59.

45. This abruptness has caused scholars to assume corruption (Kannicht), a lacuna (Zuntz) or interpolation (Hartung, Wilamowitz, Diggle).

46. On ways in which Helen's effective role comments upon Athenian social values, see Foley, "*Anodos* Dramas" 148–51. On Helen's control of, or authority within, the narrative, see Holmberg, "Euripides *Helen*."

47. As with Theoclymenus, scholars tend to insist upon a single view of Menelaus, either a *miles gloriosus*: Kuiper, "De *Helena*" 184, and Grube, *Drama of Euripides* 339; or a Homeric hero: Dirat, "Personnage de Ménélas" and Podlecki, "Basic Seriousness" 402–5.

48. See Stesichorus 192, 193 *PMGF* and Herodotus 2.112–120. For a discussion of antecedents, see Conacher, *Euripidean Drama* 286–89 and Kannicht, *Helena*, vol. 1, 26–48. For an entertaining reading of different literary versions of the enigmatic Helen, see Austin, *Helen of Troy*.

49. Compare Brooks, *Reading for the Plot* 97–101.

50. Compare Page, *Medea* xxi–xxv; Bond, *Heracles* xxvi–xxx; Platnauer, *Iphigenia* xi–xii. Likewise the execution of Eurystheus in *Children of Heracles*, the reconciliation of Hippolytus and Theseus in *Hippolytus*, the murder by Orestes of Neoptolemus in *Andromache*, and Hecuba's revenge upon Polymestor in *Hecuba* all seem to be innovations by Euripides.

51. In *Trojan Women*, the fall of Troy is not the outcome of the action, but the background to the entire play, and *Phoenician Women* ends with at least two possible outcomes, the exile of Oedipus and the conflict over Polyneices' corpse.

52. On the likelihood of a revival of the *Oresteia* in the 420s, see Newiger, "Elektra in Wolken."

53. See Aristotle, *Poetics* 1451 b.21.

54. On free invention in *Ion* and *Iphigenia among the Taurians*, compare Howald, *Untersuchungen zur Technik* 57, *pace* Sansone, "Theonoe and Theoclymenus" 18.

55. It is possible that Creusa in *Ion* is largely an original creation; see Owen, *Ion* xii–xiii.

56. Dale, Kannicht, and Diggle follow Nauck in deleting parts of lines 9–10; Erbse, *Studien zum Prolog* 211 retains them, accepting Heel's emendation of ὅτι to οὔτι in line 9.

57. See *RE* s.v. Busiris, and compare Radermacher, "Ueber eine Scene" 281–82.

58. For echoes of the *Odyssey* in *Helen*, see Eisner, "Echoes of the *Odyssey*" and for the play as a parody of the *Odyssey*, see Steiger, "Wie entstand *Helena*."

59. On such portrayals of foreigners in Greek tragedy, see Hall, *Inventing the Barbarian*.

60. On formal handling of the suppliant scene in *Helen*, compare Strohm, *Euripides* 29–30.

61. For readings that emphasize the "tragic" seriousness of the play, see Podlecki, "Basic Seriousness" and Masaracchia, "Interpretazioni euripidee."

62. See especially Solmsen, "Zur Gestaltung." For other discussions of intrigue plays, see Radermacher, "Intrigenbildung"; Strohm, *Euripides* 64–92; and Diller, "Erwartung, Enttäuschung." Compare also Matthiessen, *Elektra, Taurische Iphigenie* 93–143.

63. On appearance and reality in *Helen*, see especially Solmsen, "Ὄνομα and πρᾶγμα" and C. Segal, "Two Worlds." On the play's philosophical content, see also J. Griffith, "Some Thoughts" and Ronnet, "Cas de conscience."

64. On new concepts of divinity and justice, see especially Pippin, "Euripides' *Helen*" and Dimock, *God or Not God* and compare Zuntz, "On Euripides' *Helena*."

65. Sextus Empiricus *ad. math.* 7.65 = Gorgias DK 82B3.

66. For example, Thucydides 2.51–53 and 3.82–84. For an extreme statement of the play's reflection of contemporary events, see Grégoire, pages 11–24 in Grégoire and Méridier, *Helen*, and Drew, "Political Purpose."

67. Thucydides, *History* 8.1.

68. "The play's reason for existing [was] to be a diversion to make the Athenians smile in the midst of suffering," Pippin, "Euripides' *Helen*" 155 or "an escape from the afflictions of the time," Lesky, *Greek Tragic Poetry* 315; compare Austin, *Helen of Troy* 139.

69. The play's comic qualities are emphasized by Grube, *Drama of Euripides* 332–52 and Maniet, "*Hélène* comédie," and its tragicomic qualities by Kitto, *Greek Tragedy* 311–29 and Seidensticker, *Palintonos Harmonia* 153–99. It has also been labelled parody by Steiger, "Wie entstand *Helena*" and satyric by Sutton, "Satyric Qualities." On the comic qualities of individual scenes, see especially Seidensticker.

70. For *Helen* as a comedy of ideas, see Pippin, "Euripides' *Helen*"; for the play as a philosophical romance, see Segal, "Two Worlds" 556.

71. Whitman, *Euripides* 35 despairs of defining the play's genre, while Wolff, "On Euripides' *Helen*" 61 describes it as "chameleon-like." Austin, *Helen of Troy* seems to imply that the play's ambiguous qualities all derive from the enigmatic character of the mythical Helen.

72. Compare note 62 of this chapter. On anticipations of New Comedy, see Post, "Menander and *Helen*" and compare Knox, "Euripidean Comedy."

73. The surviving plays of this type are usually placed shortly before *Helen* (412), *Ion* in 417 or 418 (Dale) or around 413 (Diggle), and *Iphigenia among the Taurians* around 413 (Platnauer) or 414 (Diggle); Sophocles' lost *Tyro* was produced before 414 (scholiast to Aristophanes, *Birds* 275). Euripides' lost *Antiope* and *Hypsipyle* were reportedly produced between 412 and 405 (scholiast to Aristophanes, *Frogs* 53) and share features with these plays (but see Cropp and Fick, *Resolutions* 74–76 for arguments suggesting a much earlier date for *Antiope*).

74. *Bacchant Women* might be considered an exception in which Euripides belatedly rediscovered his medium; for a brief discussion of the play, tending in a different direction, see the beginning of chapter 11.

Chapter 10

1. Just as Jason calls the savage Medea a lion, not a woman (λέαιναν, οὐ γυναῖκα 1342), Menelaus calls Orestes and Pylades lions, not men (δισσοῖν λεόντοιν· οὐ γὰρ ἄνδρ᾽ αὐτὼ καλῶ 1555). And just as Jason demands the bodies of his children for burial (θάψαι νεκρούς μοι τούσδε καὶ κλαῦσαι πάρες 1377), Menelaus demands to bury the body of Helen (ἀπόδος δάμαρτος νέκυν, ὅπως χώσω τάφῳ 1585). On similarities with *Medea*, compare G. Arnott, "Euripides and the Unexpected" 59–60 and Zeitlin, "Closet of Masks" 62.

2. On Medea as θεός, see Knox, "*Medea* of Euripides" 303–6, following Cunningham, "Medea."

3. Page's suggestion (*Actors' Interpolations* 41–42) that Helen did not appear onstage was promptly answered by Lesky ("Zum *Orestes*" 46) who pointed out that Menelaus ad-

dresses her at 1673–74 (compare τῆσδε 1639, and 1683–85). Lesky, following Bulle and followed by Willink, wants Apollo and Helen to appear on a θεολογεῖον rather than the μηχανή, but as Mastronarde, "Actors on High" 262–64 argues, use of the crane for Apollo and (the mute) Helen is more likely.

4. All that follows is the chorus' formulaic prayer for victory (1691–93). This extra-dramatic gesture stands outside the play and is elsewhere preceded by other recessional lines from the chorus: in *Iphigenia among the Taurians*, it is preceded by a farewell in anapests (1490–96), and in *Phoenician Women*, it is preceded by an echo of Oedipus' closing moral from *Oedipus the King* (1758–63). In *Orestes*, however, we pass at once from deus ex machina to prayer for victory with no comment upon the completion of the action.

5. Arrowsmith, Introduction to *Orestes* 106; compare Willink, *Orestes* xxii. For a partial list of scholarship on *Orestes*, see Willink, *Orestes* xi–xviii.

6. On spectacular effects in *Orestes*, see especially Arnott, "Tension, Frustration." On reflection of events in Athens, see Burkert, "Absurdität der Gewalt" and Longo, "Proposte di lettura." Less convincing is the thesis in Eucken, "Rechtsproblem" that the confusion conceals a dialectical argument about justice.

7. Much of the argument of this section was earlier presented in Dunn, "Comic and Tragic." I am grateful to the Regents of the University of California for permission to adapt this copyrighted material.

8. It is this combination of opposing impulses that defines for me the "tragicomic" quality of the play. Contrast Barnes' definition of *Orestes* as "tragicomedy" because it contains one or more of three specific elements: Barnes, "Greek Tragicomedy" 130. Compare Hall's passing remark that "The text itself seems to be locked in a battle between tragedy and comedy" in Hall, "Political and Cosmic Turbulence" 277.

9. Compare *Hippolytus* 421–23, *Ion* 672, 675, *Phoenician Women* 391; discussion in Bonner, *Aspects* 67–85 and Jones, *Athenian Democracy* 44. An earlier reference has passed unnoticed: Aeschylus, *Persians* 591–94.

10. Plato, Isocrates, and other fourth-century critics of democracy regarded παρρησία as a liability; see Bonner, *Aspects* 67–85. In an earlier age, free speech was not called παρρησία, and was not approved (e.g., Thersites in the *Iliad*).

11. There are nineteen occurrences of σιγή, σιγάω, and σῖγα (to those given in Allen and Italie, *Concordance* add σῖγα 182), and twenty-two including σιωπή and σιωπάω. Words for noise also occur with unusual frequency in *Orestes* (e.g., nine occurrences of κτύπος and κτυπέω).

12. Compare Whitman, *Aristophanes and the Comic Hero*, especially 21–26.

13. Some editors find her hesitations too illogical. Thus Klinkenberg deletes 12–15 and Nauck deletes 38, followed by di Benedetto (del. 15 and 38), Willink (del. 15 and obol. 38), and Diggle (del. 15).

14. Compare Grube, *Drama of Euripides* 375 on the visual impasse: "[Orestes] as it were, both is and yet is not before us; all we see is a shapeless heap of blankets."

15. On the amusing innovation compare Kitto, *Greek Tragedy* 348, and Winnington-Ingram, "Euripides" 131. Murray and di Benedetto delete 136–39, following Wilamowitz-Moellendorff.

16. The scene is also an amusing parody of Aeschylus' *Libation Bearers* and Sophocles' *Electra*, in which Clytemnestra sends Electra to make offerings to Agamemnon's tomb; here Helen would have Electra repeat the part at her mother's tomb, while Electra invites Helen to play Clytemnestra to her own daughter Hermione. In Helen's greeting, Diggle deletes lines 71 and 74.

17. On Euripides' original version, see *RE* s.v. Tantalos; on possible allusions to the teachings of Anaxagoras and Prodicus, see Scodel, "Tantalus and Anaxagoras" and Willink, "Prodikos."

18. At lines 5, 347, 350, 813, 986, and 1544. O'Brien, "Tantalus" connects mention of Tantalus instead with the threat of stoning in Argos and with Orestes' threat to throw masonry upon Menelaus.

19. At Sophocles, *Oedipus at Colonus* 42 and 486. The hypothesis to *Eumenides* may imply its mention in that play, but see A. Brown, "Eumenides" 267–76. Mention of Tantalus and the Eumenides recurs primarily in the lyric passages; on myth in the odes, compare Fuqua, "World of Myth."

20. With 551–56, compare *Eumenides* 657–61 and the outburst of a spectator reported by the scholiast on *Orestes* 554 ("and without a mother, you foul Euripides"); with 566–70, compare *Libation Bearers* 896–98. For a fuller discussion of parody in *Orestes*, see Olivieri, "Dell'*Oreste*."

21. On the characterization of Menelaus, see Greenberg, "Euripides' *Orestes*" 168, and Benedetto on *Orestes* 638–89.

22. Diggle places line 651 after 657, following Paley.

23. On "the frequent references to running, leaping and rushing," see Rawson, "Aspects of *Orestes*" 156. On reversal of Pylades' silent role, compare Nisetich, "Silencing of Pylades."

24. Compare Greenberg, "Euripides' *Orestes*" 180–81. Wecklein, followed by Diggle, deletes part of the following speech (938–42), and Willink deletes it all (932–42).

25. The same argument that failed to convince Tyndareus (564–71) is no more effective before the Assembly (931–37), as noted by Eucken, "Rechtsproblem" 163.

26. Three-way dialogue is used very effectively, building gradually (Orestes and Electra 1018–64; Orestes and Pylades 1065–1176; Orestes and Electra 1177–1206; Orestes, Pylades, and Electra 1207–45) and making repeated mention of the threesome (1178, 1190, 1243, 1244).

27. A surprising reversal; usually the chorus asks for silence (Aeschylus, *Agamemnon* 1344) or another asks the chorus for silence (Sophocles, *Electra* 1399; Euripides, *Hippolytus* 565–68) to hear what is happening inside. With κτύπον ἐγείρετε here, contrast μηδ᾽ ἔστω κτύπος 137.

28. On the shrill delivery of the Phrygian's ἁρμάτειον μέλος, see scholiast to line 1384.

29. Compare Hall, "Political and Cosmic Turbulence" 269–77 on the impasse between *philia* and *eris*.

30. *Electra* 1273–75 also alludes to this aition, without mentioning Παρράσιον or Ὀρέστειον by name.

31. Scholiast to line 279, who adds that the gaffe was parodied by Aristophanes, Strattis, and Sannurion. Compare the outburst at line 554 (note 20 in this chapter).

32. Diggle deletes these and the preceding lines (1556–60), following Oeri.

33. Parry, "Euripides' *Orestes*" 352.

34. Schein, "Mythical Illusion" 53.

35. On the moral depravity of Orestes and his companions, see Mullens, "Meaning of *Orestes*" followed by Boulter, "Theme of ἀγρία" and Smith, "Disease in *Orestes*." In defense of their character, see Krieg, *De Euripidis Oreste* 13–17, Erbse, "Zum *Orestes*," and (on Orestes in particular) Porter, *Studies,* especially 45–54 and 68–89. On the play's moral vacuum, see Burkert, "Absurdität der Gewalt," Wolff, "*Orestes*" 134; and Schein, "Mythical Illusion" 66.

36. Jekels, "On Psychology of Comedy" 174 and 179.

37. On questioning of values, see Reinhardt, "Sinneskrise bei Euripides," and Lanza, "Unità e significato" 71. On generational conflict, see Falkner, "Coming of Age." On violence see Burkert, "Absurdität der Gewalt" 106–8, and Longo, "Proposte di lettura" 282–86.

38. Thucydides, *History* 3.82.

39. Kott, "Ionesco" 100.

40. Goethe, *Italian Journey* 467–68.

41. Diggle obelizes lines 34–35, and in line 38 emends to φόβον.

42. Bloom, *Anxiety of Influence* 14, 49–73.

43. It likewise fills in gaps in the family past, looking back not to the crimes of Pelops, Atreus, and Thyestes, but to the earlier crime of Tantalus.

44. Scholiast to line 268; compare Stesichorus fr. 217 *PMGF* and discussion in Willink, *Orestes*, on 268–74.

45. As Willink, *Orestes* argues (on 268–74, 268, and 286–87), it is very unlikely that a real bow was used in staging the scene; the scholiast does not approve the practice of miming the scene, but nowhere implies that the practice is not Euripidean.

46. On mime in general, see Reich, *Der Mimus*.

47. On the similarities between Euripides and Timotheus, see Bassett, "Place and Date" 160–61 and Webster, *Tragedies of Euripides* 17–19.

48. For an excellent reconstruction of Timotheus' *Persians*, see Herington, *Poetry into Drama* 151–60.

49. Satyrus in his *Life* of Euripides reports that Euripides encouraged Timotheus and wrote the proem of *Persians*, and as a result Timotheus was victorious: *POxy* ix 1176, fr. 39, col. xxii. Porter, *Studies* 199–207 reminds us that the Phrygian's lyric narrative is more controlled in form and meter than the dithyramb of Timotheus.

50. ἀνάξια καὶ τραγῳδίας καὶ τῆς Ὀρέστου συμφορᾶς τὰ λεγόμενα (scholiast to 1512), ταῦτα κωμικώτερά ἐστι καὶ πεζά (scholiast to line 1521); for proposed deletion, see Gredley, "Is *Orestes*" and Reeve, "Interpolation I" 263–64.

51. Seidensticker, *Palintonos Harmonia* 102 and 109.

52. This expansion of horizons may also embrace satyr-drama. As Radermacher observed ("Ueber eine Scene"), the comic scene of a Greek hero running amok among cowardly barbarians was familiar in the legend of Heracles and Busiris in Egypt, and was dramatized in satyr-plays of Phrynichus and Euripides, as well as in comedy. Several critics go further, suggesting with Hartung that *Orestes* was originally staged in place of the satyr-play; this view is argued, e.g., by Luppe, "Zur Datierung" and is challenged by Sutton, "Supposed Evidence" and Porter, *Studies* 291–97.

Chapter 11

1. The play is securely dated to the period 411–407 by the scholiast to Aristophanes, *Frogs* 53, who cites *Phoenician Women* as one of several Euripidean tragedies closer in time to *Frogs* (405) than was his *Andromeda* (412). The expression "shortly before," πρὸ ὀλίγου narrows the most likely period to 409–407. In frequency of trimeter resolutions, *Phoenician Women* is closer to *Helen* (412) than to *Orestes* (408); see Cropp and Frick, *Resolutions* 23 and Mastronarde, *Phoenissae* 11 with note 1. A production in 407 should not be ruled out, since Euripides may have moved to Macedon later that year; see Bond, *Hypsipyle* 144. The conjecture that a tetralogy of *Antiope, Hypsipyle,* and *Phoenician Women* was produced with a "prosatyric" *Orestes* in 408, recently revived by Müller, "Zur Datierung" 66–69, Mueller-Goldingen, *Untersuchungen* 6–11, and Luppe, "Zur Datierung" is rightly rejected by Mastronarde, *Phoenissae* 11–12.

2. On the history of the text, see Mastronarde and Bremer, *Textual Tradition*.

3. Craik, *Phoenician Women* 39.

4. See, e.g., Xanthakis-Karamanos, *Studies* and Easterling, "End of an Era?"

5. See the discussion of West, "Tragica V."

6. *Oedipus the King* goes furthest in suggesting that the protagonist had (virtually) no choice in the past actions of murder and marriage.

7. Compare the discussion in Jones, *Aristotle and Tragedy* 247–52.

8. A majority of editors do not consider the prologue authentic, at least in its received form; Diggle would delete the entire prologue (1–162), as well as large portions from the rest of the play. For a defense of the prologue, see Knox, "Euripides' *Iphigenia*," who notes that in some ways the prologue of the lost *Andromeda* was "a much bolder experiment" (277).

9. Her change of heart has been criticized since Aristotle, *Poetics* 1454 a.31–33.

10. See Dodds, *Bacchae* xxxvi–viii.

11. See Segal, *Dionysiac Poetics* 215–71 on metatheater and Foley, *Ritual Irony* 205–58 on ritual motifs.

12. Apsines (Diggle p. 352) reports that Agave held and lamented his limbs one by one.

13. Hence, perhaps, the great popularity of *Orestes* and *Phoenician Women* in antiquity, and the relative neglect of *Bacchant Women*.

14. There is a vast literature on textual problems in the exodos. Those who argue for large-scale interpolation include Page, *Actors' Interpolations* 20–29; Friedrich, "Prolegomena"; Fraenkel, "Zu den *Phoenissen*"; Reeve, "Interpolation II"; and Dihle, "Prolog der *Bacchen*." Those who argue for its overall integrity include Valgiglio, *L'esodo delle Fenicie*; Diller, Review of Fraenkel; Erbse, "Beiträge"; Valk, *Studies in Euripides*; and Craik, *Phoenician Women*. The final scene as a whole, from 1581 on, has been rejected by Page, *Actors' Interpolations* 22, Willink, "Goddess εὐλάβεια," and Diggle. The closing section 1736–77 is frequently rejected, as, for example, by Mastronarde, *Phoenissae* 635–37 and Mueller-Goldingen *Untersuchungen* 258–62.

15. Craik, *Phoenician Women* 50. She marks as spurious 1613 and 1634, and notes as suspect 1604–7, 1744–46, and 1758–63. Compare the similar reservations voiced by Mastronarde, *Phoenissae* 43–48 on arguments often used in detecting interpolations.

16. I shall therefore let the reader know, in the notes, when passages I quote have been judged spurious, although I cannot address here individual arguments for and against.

17. Lyrics more often have a metrical structure of strophe and antistrophe that repeats meter (and presumably music and choreography) exactly, so that responsion provides an unambiguous point of completion.

18. Compare *Oedipus the King* 1524–25: ὦ πάτρας Θήβης ἔνοικοι, λεύσσετ', Οἰδίπους ὅδε, / ὃς τὰ κλείν' αἰνίγματ' ᾔδει καὶ κράτιστος ἦν ἀνήρ. Both passages have been judged spurious, in part because of this quotation. For deletion of *Oedipus the King* 1524–30, see Dawe, *Studies*, vol. 1, 266–73; for retention of the lines, see Arkins, "Final Lines" and Lloyd-Jones and Wilson, *Sophoclea* 113–14. *Phoenician Women* 1758–63 are rejected by many editors, including Mueller-Goldingen, *Untersuchungen* 262–66 and Mastronarde, *Phoenissae* 642–43; recent defenders of the lines include Erbse, *Studien* 245 and Valk, *Studies in Euripides* 51–56.

19. Many critics, including Mastronarde, *Phoenissae* 645 and Mueller-Goldingen, *Untersuchungen* 266 suspect these lines; see discussion in chapter 2.

20. Fraenkel, "Zu den *Phoenissen*" 98–100 and Kitto, "Final Scenes" 108–9 delete these lines; the passage is defended most recently by Mastronarde, *Phoenissae* 626 and Mueller-Goldingen, *Untersuchungen* 255–56 with his note 67.

21. Pausanias (1.30.4) mentions a herôon of Oedipus and Adrastus at Colonus, although elsewhere (1.28.7) he rejects the view that Oedipus was buried there. Androtion, so we are told (scholiast to *Odyssey* 11.271 = *FGrH* 324 F 62), said that Oedipus "dwelled" in Colonus, perhaps thus alluding to a hero cult. For discussion, see Kearns, *Heroes of Attica* 50–52, 208–9, and compare chapter 4, note 34 of this book.

22. Fraenkel, "Zu den *Phoenissen*" 86–88 deletes 1586b-90a (ἀρχὰς . . . σαφῶς γάρ); they are defended, on different grounds, by Mastronarde, *Phoenissae* 595–96 and Mueller-Goldingen, *Untersuchungen* 229.

23. Homer reports separately that Oedipus remained in Thebes when Jocasta died (*Odyssey* 11.271–80) and that he was buried at Thebes (*Iliad* 23.679–80); a scholiast on the latter passage reports that, according to Hesiod, Oedipus died at Thebes. The exile of Oedipus is not clearly described before *Phoenician Women* and Sophocles' *Oedipus at Colonus*, but the action of *Oedipus the King* presupposes the possibility of exile, and Pindar seems to allude to the exile of Oedipus (*Pythian* 4.263–69). March, *Creative Poet* 145–47 argues that the story of exile began with Aeschylus' *Oedipus*, but there are too many lost versions of the legend to hazard such speculation.

24. Compare Saïd, "Euripide" 522–23.

25. Fraenkel, "Zu den *Phoenissen*" 108–9 and Hose, "Überlegungen" 68–69 delete mention of Polyneices' burial; but see Mastronarde, *Phoenissae* 592–94 and 611–12.

26. Kitto, "Final Scenes" 108 wants to remove mention of Antigone's marriage by deleting 1664–82.

27. Scholiast to Sophocles, *Antigone* 1351: ὅτι διαφέρει τῆς Εὐριπίδου Ἀντιγόνης αὕτη ὅτι φωραθεῖσα ἐκείνη διὰ τὸν Αἵμονος ἔρωτα ἐξεδόθη πρὸς γάμον, ἐνταῦθα δὲ τοὐναντίον; compare hypothesis I to Sophocles, *Antigone*, and Euripides, *Antiope* fr. 164 Nauck: ἄριστον ἀνδρὶ κτῆμα συμπαθὴς γυνή.

28. See note 23 of this chapter.

29. To avoid such confusion, many editors delete lines 1737–57; see note 14 of this chapter.

30. Arg. 2: περιπαθεῖς ἄγαν αἱ Φοίνισσαι τῇ τραγῳδίᾳ· ἀπώλετο γὰρ ὁ Κρέοντος υἱὸς ἀπὸ τοῦ τείχους ὑπὲρ τῆς πόλεως ἀποθανών, ἀπέθανον δὲ καὶ οἱ δύο ἀδελφοὶ ὑπ' ἀλλήλων, καὶ Ἰοκάστη ἡ μήτηρ ἀνεῖλεν ἑαυτὴν ἐπὶ τοῖς παισί, καὶ οἱ ἐπὶ Θήβας στρατευσάμενοι Ἀργεῖοι ἀπώλοντο, καὶ ἄταφος Πολυνείκης πρόκειται, καὶ ὁ Οἰδίπους τῆς πατρίδος ἐκβάλλεται καὶ σὺν αὐτῷ ἡ θυγάτηρ Ἀντιγόνη.

31. See, for example, Conacher, *Euripidean Drama* 241–42. Foley, *Ritual Irony* 106–46, however, finds redemptive ritual power in Menoeceus' sacrifice.

32. Thus most recently Craik, *Phoenician Women* 244 and 249, who suggests that Creon's entrance with the body of his son provides "a tangible display of the tragedy of his branch of the family," but see Mastronarde, *Phoenissae* 514–15 and Mueller-Goldingen, *Untersuchungen* 208–9.

33. ματρὸς ἐμᾶς ἢ διδύμοις / γάλακτος παρὰ μαστοῖς / ἢ πρὸς ἀδελφῶν / οὐλόμεν' αἰκίσματα νεκρῶν; with an effective reversal of the expected pairing: twin bodies of her brothers, and outraged breast of her mother. Diggle emends to ἀγαλάκτοις, following Headlam.

34. Diggle deletes the exodos from 1582 to the end of the play; compare note 14 of this chapter.

35. Aristophanes in *Frogs* juxtaposes a quotation by "Euripides" of the opening line of his lost *Antigone* (1182) with a reply by "Aeschylus" that echoes details of this passage (1183–86); it is tempting to speculate that Oedipus' "prologue" here rewrites the earlier prologue of *Antigone* and that "Aeschylus" in *Frogs* cleverly uses Euripides' own words from *Phoenician Women* to attack the line his rival quotes from *Antigone*. On echoes of *Phoenician Women* in *Frogs*, compare Mastronarde, *Phoenissae* 599–600. The speech of Oedipus, at least as far as 1614, was rejected as spurious by Kitto, "Final Scenes" 110 and Fraenkel, "Zu den *Phoenissen*" 89–95.

36. Mastronarde, *Phoenissae* 3–4 has pertinent observations on the difference between "open" and "closed" form in drama, citing Pfister, *Theory and Analysis* 239–45. But Pfister, following Klotz, *Geschlossene und Offene* is chiefly interested in a general typology for a broad class of plays. It seems to me, however, that *Phoenician Women* does not belong to a more "open" class of Greek tragedies, but is in many ways entirely anomalous. In what follows, I attempt to describe this exceptional quality more fully.

37. For a complete list of references and discussion, see Rawson, "Family and Fatherland" 112–113 with note 11.

38. Saïd, "Euripide."

39. Contrast the elaborate and lengthy process of naming a Theban to stand against each Argive in Aeschylus, *Seven against Thebes* 407, 448, 474, 504, 555, 620, and 675. See also Mastronarde, *Phoenissae* 360–61.

40. Phrynichus *TrGF* I, 3 F9 = scholiast to Aristophanes *Wasps* 220; compare Kranz, *Stasimon* 111.

41. Stesichorus fr. 195 *PMGF* = scholiast to *Phoenician Women* 670.

42. Tangentially introduced just at the end, if the end of the play is genuine, but the final scene has long been suspect and the issue of burial may not belong. See discussion in Mellon, *Ending of Aeschylus*; Thalmann, *Dramatic Art* 137–41; and Hutchinson, *Septem* 209–11.

43. The "Lille Thebaid" ascribed to Stesichorus (fr. 222b *PMGF*), in which the boys' mother tries to resolve the quarrel before Polyneices leaves Thebes and raises the expedition. The mother has generally been identified as Jocasta, but March, *Creative Poet* 127–28 argues that she is Oedipus' second, nonincestuous wife. Mueller-Goldingen, *Untersuchungen* 34–35 argues that she is Jocasta and that Euripides echoes particular details from Stesichorus; see also Stephanopoulos, *Umgestaltung* 109.

44. By including Adrastus and not Eteocles among the Seven, Euripides seems to reject Aeschylus in favor of the *Thebaid*; compare Stephanopoulos, *Umgestaltung* 124.

45. Compare Saïd, "Euripide" 517.

46. The story is clearly cast as parallel to that of Erechtheus and his daughter, to which Teiresias alludes in 854–55, so Euripides' *Erechtheus* may also be a part of this intertextual web. On Euripides' invention of Menoeceus, see Mastronarde, *Phoenissae* 28–29; Stephanopoulos, *Umgestaltung* 116–22 argues that even if Menoeceus is to be equated with Megareus (Sophocles, *Antigone* 1303), the manner of his death is original with Euripides. Lines 1015–18 are deleted as superfluous by many scholars, Mastronarde and Diggle included, although retained by Craik, *Phoenician Women* and defended by Romilly, "*Phoenician Women* of Euripides" 128–30.

47. Earth, War, Furies, and curses are each discussed below; when a divine role is sought or conjectured, it is typically that of an unnamed θεός or θεοί (70, 155, 379, 382, 468, 586, 871, 873, 1031, 1198, 1200, 1202, 1426, 1614, 1763; compare 258, 637) or unnamed δαίμων or δαίμονες (18, 491, 1000, 1066, 1199, 1266, 1653, 1662; compare 352, 888). For a different view of the divine realm in this play, see Treves, "Le *Fenicie*" 194.

48. Arg. 3: Τὸ δρᾶμα ἔστι δὲ ταῖς σκηνικαῖς ὄψεσι καλόν, †ἐπεὶ† καὶ παραπληρωματικόν· ἥ τε ἀπὸ τῶν τειχέων Ἀντιγόνη θεωροῦσα μέρος οὐκ ἔστι δράματος, καὶ ὑπόσπονδος Πολυνείκης οὐδενὸς ἕνεκα παραγίνεται, ὅ τε ἐπὶ πᾶσι μετ᾽ ᾠδῆς ἀδολέσχου φυγαδευόμενος Οἰδίπους προσέρραπται διὰ κενῆς.

49. The authenticity of the whole "teichoskopia" has occasionally been challenged, most recently by Dihle, "Prolog der *Bacchen*" 60–71; for counter arguments, see Mastronarde, *Phoenissae* 168–73.

50. Foley, *Ritual Irony* 143, however, suggests that the repetition "may hint at the appropriate reordering of the disordered generations of the house of Laius."

51. Foley, *Ritual Irony* 126 has good observations on the "antimythical" nature of this play, in which "Euripides' tragic poetry threatens to descend from the realm of philosophy, where necessary and probable events cohere in a well-ordered *praxis*, to the randomness of history." She concludes, however, that the play is rescued from this "disaster" by the self-sacrifice of Menoeceus and by the devotion of Antigone.

52. The Telemachy, or travels of Telemachus in books 1–4 of the *Odyssey*, are clearly subordinated to the main narrative thread. On meanders and labyrinths as figures for the delays of the plot, see Barchiesi, "Endgames" and Miller, *Ariadne's Thread*.

53. Romilly, "*Phoenician Women* of Euripides" 122. For arguments connecting Polyneices more specifically to Alcibiades or to the democratic party, see Delebecque, *Euripide* 352–64 and Goosens, *Euripide et Athènes* 600–9.

54. Arthur, "Curse of Civilization" 184.

55. Saïd, "Euripide"; Goff, "Shields of *Phoenissae.*"

56. Foley, *Ritual Irony* 106–46 is thus especially useful in stressing various positive themes and developments; I cannot agree, however, that the action as a whole follows a positive and redemptive course.

57. On the nobler and more virile associations of death by the sword, see Loraux, *Tragic Ways* 12.

58. " Escape odes" include *Hippolytus* 732–775, *Iphigenia among the Taurians* 1089–1152, and *Helen* 1451–1511. The odes in *Hippolytus* and *Helen* are discussed by Padel, "Imagery of the Elsewhere."

59. See Morson, "For the Time Being" and the discussion of *Heracles* in chapter 8 of this book.

60. Bakhtin, *Dialogic Imagination* 7.

61. Compare Bakhtin, *Dialogic Imagination* 30. On ethical freedom in the narrative theory or "prosaics" of Bakhtin, see Morson, "For the Time Being" and Rubino, "Opening up."

62. "The last link in a long chain of Theban misfortunes," Grube, *Drama of Euripides* 371; compare Pohlenz, *Griechische Tragödie,* vol. 1, 380–81 and Podlecki, "Some Themes" 372–73 and, in a different vein, Arthur, "Curse of Civilization" on the inevitable violence inherent in human culture.

63. With eighty-seven (or eighty-five) lines, the only extant prologue speech that comes close is that of the rambling Hermes in *Ion* (eighty-one lines). The first two lines of the prologue may be later additions; see Haslam, "Authenticity" and Mastronarde, *Phoenissae* 139–41.

64. We might contrast with the charms of this wandering narrative the dangers of a linear path. In the opening lines (of suspect authenticity; see previous note), Jocasta invokes the sun, which cuts a path through the stars in heaven (Ὦ τὴν ἐν ἄστροις οὐρανοῦ τέμνων ὁδόν 1) as the author of misfortunes for Thebes; the oracle at Delphi echoes this invocation (compare Ὦ . . . Ἥλιε, θοαῖς ἵπποισιν 1–3 with Ὦ Θήβαισιν εὐίπποις ἄναξ 17) when it warns Oedipus not to sow the furrow of children (μὴ σπεῖρε τέκνων ἄλοκα δαιμόνων βίᾳ 18). The attempts to cut a straight path prove disastrous for the city and the family, and give way to the uncertain possibilities of blind wandering.

65. These lines point to the contrast between Helen who cannot see her brothers (lying dead in Sparta) and Antigone who cannot make out the shape of her brother (now distant, soon to die), as noted by Mastronarde, *Phoenissae* 168.

66. See Arthur, "Curse of Civilization."

67. The entire shield scene, 1104–40, has been considered an interpolation, most recently by Dihle, "Prolog der *Bacchen*" 73–84; Mueller-Goldingen, *Untersuchungen* 176–78; and Diggle. For a defense of the passage, see Mastronarde, "*Phoinissai* 1104–40"; for a good reading of the scene, see Goff, "Shields of *Phoenissae.*"

68. Although Arthur's article is excellent in many respects, I cannot agree that the image of Dionysus is a purely positive one, here corrupted and perverted by the unmusical Ares: Arthur, "Curse of Civilization" 176.

Works Cited

Journal citations employ the following standard abbreviations:

AJP	*American Journal of Philology*
BICS	*Bulletin of the Institute of Classical Studies*
CA	*Classical Antiquity*
CJ	*Classical Journal*
CP	*Classical Philology*
CQ	*Classical Quarterly*
CR	*Classical Review*
G&R	*Greece and Rome*
GRBS	*Greek, Roman and Byzantine Studies*
HSCP	*Harvard Studies in Classical Philology*
JHS	*Journal of Hellenic Studies*
MD	*Materiali e Discussioni per l'analisi dei testi classici*
RhM	*Rheinsiches Museum*
TAPA	*Transactions of the American Philological Association*
WS	*Wiener Studien*
YCS	*Yale Classical Studies*

Adams, Robert M. *Strains of Discord: Studies in Literary Openness* (Ithaca, 1958).

Aeschylus. *Septem quae supersunt tragoediae*, ed. D. Page (Oxford, 1972).

Allen, James T., and Gabriel Italie. *A Concordance to Euripides* (Berkeley, 1954).

Alt, Karin. "Zur Anagnorisis in der *Helena*." *Hermes* 90 (1962) 6–24.

Amandry, Pierre. "Chronique des fouilles et découvertes archéologiques en grèce en 1948, I." *Bulletin de Correspondance Hellénique* 73 (1949) 516–36.

Aristotle. *Nicomachean Ethics*, tr. D. Ross, rev. J. L. Ackrill and J. O. Urmson (Oxford, 1980).

Arkins, Brian. "The Final Lines of Sophocles, *King Oedipus* (1524–30)." *CQ* 38 (1988) 555–58.

Arnott, Peter. *Greek Scenic Conventions* (Oxford, 1962).

Arnott, W. Geoffrey. "Euripides and the Unexpected." *G&R* 20 (1973) 49–64.

———. "Tension, Frustration and Surprise: A Study of Theatrical Techniques in Some Scenes of Euripides' *Orestes*." *Antichthon* 17 (1983) 13–28.

Arrowsmith, William. Introduction to *Heracles*. Pages 44–59 in *Euripides*, vol. 2, ed. D. Grene and R. Lattimore (Chicago, 1956).

———. Introduction to *Orestes*. Pages 106–11 in *Euripides*, vol. 4, ed. D. Grene and R. Lattimore (Chicago, 1958).

Arthur, Marylin B. "The Curse of Civilization: The Choral Odes of the *Phoenissae*." *HSCP* 81 (1977) 163–85.

Austin, Colin. "De nouveaux fragments de l'*Erechthée* d'Euripide." *Recherches de Papyrologie* 4 (1967) 11–67.

———. *Nova Fragmenta Euripidea in Papyris Reperta* (Berlin, 1968).

Austin, Norman. *Helen of Troy and Her Shameless Phantom* (Ithaca, 1994).

Bain, David. *Actors and Audience* (Oxford, 1977).

Bakhtin, Mikhail M. *The Dialogic Imagination*, ed. M. Holquist, tr. C. Emerson and M. Holquist (Austin, 1981).

Barchiesi, Alessandro. "Endgames: Ovid's *Metamorphoses* 15 and *Fasti* 6." Forthcoming in Roberts, Dunn, and Fowler, *Classical Closure*.

Barlow, Shirley A., ed. Euripides, *Trojan Women* (Warminster, 1986).

Barnes, Hazel E. "Greek Tragicomedy." *CJ* 60 (1964) 125–31.

Barrett, W. S., ed. Euripides, *Hippolytos* (Oxford, 1964).

Bassett, S. E. "The Place and Date of the First Performance of the *Persians* of Timotheus." *CP* 26 (1931) 153–65.

Beckett, Samuel. *Waiting for Godot* (New York, 1954).

Benedetto, Vincenzo di, ed. Euripides, *Orestes* (Florence, 1965).

Beschi, Luigi. "Contributi di topografia ateniese." *Annuario della Scuola Archeologica di Atene* n.s. 29–30 (1967–68) 511–36.

Bieber, Margarete. "The Entrances and Exits of Actors and Chorus in Greek Plays." *American Journal of Archaeology* 58 (1954) 277–84.

Bloom, Harold. *The Anxiety of Influence: A Theory of Poetry* (Oxford, 1973).

Boardman, John. "Herakles, Peisistratos and Eleusis." *JHS* 95 (1975) 1–12.

Bond, Godfrey W., ed. Euripides, *Heracles* (Oxford, 1981).

———, ed. Euripides, *Hypsipyle* (Oxford, 1963).

Bonner, Robert J. *Aspects of Athenian Democracy* (Berkeley, 1933).

Boulter, Patricia N. "The Theme of ἀγρία in Euripides' *Orestes*." *Phoenix* 16 (1962) 102–6.

Brecht, Bertolt. *The Good Woman of Setzuan*, tr. E. Bentley (New York, 1965).

———. *The Threepenny Opera*. Pages 145–226 in *Collected Plays*, vol. 2, tr. R. Mannheim and J. Willett (New York, 1977).

Brelich, Angelo. *Paides e Parthenoi*, vol. 1 (Rome, 1969).

Brommer, Frank. *Herakles II: die unkanonischen Taten des Helden* (Darmstadt, 1984).

Brooks, Peter. *Reading for the Plot* (New York, 1984).

Brown, A. L. "Eumenides in Greek Tragedy." *CQ* 34 (1984) 260–81.

———. "Prometheus Pyrphoros." *BICS* 37 (1990) 50–56.

Brown, S. G. "A Contextual Analysis of Tragic Meter: The Anapest." Pages 45–77 in *Ancient and Modern: Essays in Honor of G. F. Else*, ed. by J. H. D'Arms and J. W. Eadie (Ann Arbor, 1977).

Brulé, Pierre. "Retour à Brauron: Repentirs, avancées, mises au point." *Dialogues d'Histoire Ancienne* 16 (1990) 61–90.

Burkert, Walter. "Die Absurdität der Gewalt und das Ende der Tragödie: Euripides' *Orestes*." *Antike und Abendland* 20 (1974) 97–109.

———. *Greek Religion*, tr. J. Raffan (Cambridge, 1985).

———. "Greek Tragedy and Sacrificial Ritual." *GRBS* 7 (1966) 87–121.

Burnett, Anne P. *Catastrophe Survived* (Oxford, 1971).

———. "Hekabe the Dog." *Arethusa* 27 (1994) 151–64.

Busch, Gerda. *Untersuchungen zum Wesen der τύχη in den Tragödien des Euripides* (Heidelberg, 1937).

Cacoyannis, Michael. *The Trojan Women* (film version, 1971).

Carroll, Lewis. *Sylvie and Bruno Concluded* (London, 1893).

Chalk, H. H. O. "ἀρετή and βία in Euripides' *Herakles*." *JHS* 82 (1962) 7–18.

Chapiro, Jose, ed. *Gespräche mit G. Hauptmann* (Berlin, 1932).

The Chester Mystery Cycle, 2 vols., ed. R. M. Lumiansky and D. Mills (Oxford, 1974–86).

Codrignani, Giancarla. "L' 'aition' nella poesia greca prima di Callimaco." *Convivium* 26 (1958) 527–45.

Collard, Christopher, ed. Euripides, *Supplices*, 2 vols (Groningen, 1975).

Conacher, D. J. *Aeschylus' Prometheus Bound* (Toronto, 1980).

———. *Euripidean Drama: Myth, Theme and Structure* (Toronto, 1967).

Craik, Elizabeth M. "Euripides' First *Hippolytos*." *Mnemosyne* 40 (1987) 137–39.

———, ed. Euripides, *Phoenician Women* (Warminster, 1988).

Croally, N. T. *Euripidean Polemic: The Trojan Women and the Function of Tragedy* (Cambridge, 1994).

Cropp, Martin, and Gordon Fick. *Resolutions and Chronology in Euripides* (London, 1985).

Cunningham, Maurice P. "Medea ἀπὸ μηχανῆς." *CP* 49 (1954) 151–60.

Dale, A. M., ed. Euripides, *Alcestis* (Oxford, 1961).

———, ed. Euripides, *Helen* (Oxford, 1967).

Davies, Malcolm, ed. Sophocles, *Trachiniae* (Oxford, 1991).

Davis, Lennard J. "A Social History of Fact and Fiction: Authorial Disavowal in the Early English Novel." Pages 120–48 in *Literature and Society*, ed. E. W. Said (Baltimore, 1980).

Dawe, R. D. *Studies in the Text of Sophocles*, 3 vols (Leiden, 1974–78).

Decharme, Paul. *Euripides and the Spirit of his Dramas*, tr. J. Loeb (New York, 1906).

Delebecque, Edouard. *Euripide et la guerre du Péloponnèse* (Paris, 1951).

Dewald, Carolyn. "Wanton Kings, Pickled Heroes, and Gnomic Founding Fathers: Strategies of Meaning at the End of Herodotus' *Histories*." Forthcoming in Roberts, Dunn, and Fowler, *Classical Closure*.

Dickens, Charles. *Posthumous Papers of the Pickwick Club*, ed. J. Kinsley (Oxford, 1986).

Dieterich, Albrecht. "Die Entstehung der Tragödie." *Archiv für Religionswissenschaft* 11 (1908) 163–96.

Dihle, Albrecht. "Der Prolog der *Bacchen* und die antike Überlieferungsphase des Euripides-Textes." *Sitzungsberichte der Heidelberger Akademie der Wissenschaften* 1981:2.

Diller, Hans. "Erwartung, Enttäuschung und Erfüllung in der griechischen Tragödie." Pages 93–115 in *Serta Philologica Aenipontana*, ed. R. Muth (Innsbruck, 1962).

———. Review of Fraenkel, "Zu den *Phoenissen*." *Gnomon* 36 (1964) 641–50.

Dimock, George E. "*God, or Not God, or between the Two?*"—*Euripides' Helen* (Northampton, 1977).

Dirat, Maurice. "Le personnage de Ménélas dans *Hélène*." *Pallas* 23 (1976) 3–17.

Dodds, E. R., ed. Euripides, *Bacchae*, 2nd ed. (Oxford, 1960).

Drew, D. L. "The Political Purpose in Euripides' *Helena*." *CP* 25 (1930) 187–89.

Drew-Bear, T. "The Trochaic Tetrameter in Greek Tragedy." *AJP* 89 (1968) 385–405.

Duncan, Thomas S. "The Deus ex Machina in Greek Tragedy." *Philological Quarterly* 14 (1935) 126–41.

Dunn, Francis M. "The Battle of the Sexes in Euripides' *Ion*." *Ramus* 19 (1990) 130–42.

———. "Beginning at Colonus." *YCS* 29 (1992) 1–12.

———. "Comic and Tragic License in Euripides' *Orestes*." *CA* 8 (1989) 238–51.

———. "Ends and Means in Euripides' *Heracles*." Forthcoming in Roberts, Dunn, and Fowler, *Classical Closure*.

———. "Euripidean Endings" (Ph.D. diss., Yale University, 1985).

———. "Euripides and the Rites of Hera Akraia." *GRBS* 35 (1994) 103–115.

———. "Fearful Symmetry: The Two Tombs of Hippolytus." *MD* 28 (1992) 103–11.

DuPlessis, Rachel Blau. *Writing beyond the Ending: Narrative Strategies in Twentieth-Century Women Writers* (Bloomington, 1985).

Easterling, Patricia E. "The End of an Era? Tragedy in the Early Fourth Century." Pages 559–69 in *Tragedy, Comedy and the Polis,* ed. A. H. Sommerstein et al. (Bari, 1993).

————. ed. Sophocles, *Trachiniae* (Cambridge, 1982).

Edmunds, Lowell. "The Cults and the Legend of Oedipus." *HSCP* 85 (1981) 221–38.

Eisner, Robert. "Echoes of the *Odyssey* in Euripides' *Helen.*" *Maia* 32 (1980) 31–37.

Eliade, Mircea. *The Myth of the Eternal Return,* tr. W. R. Trask (Princeton, 1954).

Eliot, George. *Middlemarch,* ed. D. Carroll (Oxford, 1986).

Erbse, Hartmut. "Beiträge zum Verständnis der euripideischen *Phoinissen.*" *Philologus* 110 (1966) 1–34.

————. *Studien zum Prolog der euripideischen Tragödie* (Berlin, 1984).

————. "Zum *Orestes* des Euripides." *Hermes* 103 (1975) 434–59.

Erp Taalman Kip, A. Maria van. "Euripides and Melos." *Mnemosyne* 40 (1987) 414–19.

Eucken, Christoph. "Das Rechtsproblem im euripideischen *Orest.*" *Museum Helveticum* 43 (1986) 155–68.

Euripides. *Fabulae,* 3 vols., ed. J. Diggle (Oxford, 1981–94).

Falkner, Thomas M. "Coming of Age in Argos: Physis and Paideia in Euripides' *Orestes.*" *CJ* 78 (1983) 289–300.

Foley, Helene P. "*Anodos* Dramas: Euripides' *Alcestis* and *Helen.*" Pages 133–60 in *Innovations of Antiquity,* ed. R. Hexter and D. Selden (New York, 1992).

————. *Ritual Irony: Poetry and Sacrifice in Euripides* (Ithaca, 1985).

Fowler, Don P. "First Thoughts on Closure: Problems and Prospects." *MD* 22 (1989) 75–122.

————. "Second Thoughts on Closure." Forthcoming in Roberts, Dunn, and Fowler, *Classical Closure.*

Fraenkel, Eduard. "Zu den *Phoenissen* des Euripides." *Sitzungsberichte der Bayerischen Akademie der Wissenschaften* 1963:1.

Friedrich, Claus. "Die dramatische Funktion der euripidischen Gnomen" (Ph.D. diss., University of Freiburg, 1955).

Friedrich, Wolf-H. "Prolegomena zu den *Phönissen.*" *Hermes* 74 (1939) 265–300.

Fritz, Kurt von. *Antike und moderne Tragödie* (Berlin, 1962).

Fuochi, Mario. "Le etimologie dei nomi propri nei tragici greci." *Studi Italiani di Filologia Classica* 6 (1898) 273–318.

Fuqua, Charles. "The World of Myth in Euripides' *Orestes.*" *Traditio* 34 (1978) 1–28.

Fusillo, Massimo. "Was ist eine romanhafte Tragödie? Überlegungen zu Euripides' Experimentalismus." *Poetica* 24 (1992) 270–99.

Gantz, Timothy. *Early Greek Myth* (Baltimore, 1993).

Gay, John. *The Beggar's Opera,* ed. P. E. Lewis (Edinburgh, 1973).

George, David B. "Euripides' *Heracles* 140–235: Staging and the Stage Iconography of Heracles' Bow." *GRBS* 35 (1994) 145–57.

Girard, René. *Violence and the Sacred,* tr. P. Gregory (Baltimore, 1977).

Giraudoux, Jean. *Plays,* tr. R. Gellert (New York, 1967).

Goethe, Johann W. *Italian Journey,* tr. W. H. Auden and E. Mayer (New York, 1968).

Goff, Barbara E. *The Noose of Words: Readings of Desire, Violence and Language in Euripides' Hippolytos* (Cambridge, 1990).

————. "The Shields of *Phoenissae.*" *GRBS* 29 (1988) 135–52.

Gollwitzer, Ingeborg. *Die Prolog- und Expositionstechnik der griechischen Tragödie* (Gunzenhausen, 1937).

Goossens, Roger. *Euripide et Athènes* (Brussels, 1962).

Gredley, B. "Is *Orestes* 1503–36 an Interpolation?" *GRBS* 9 (1968) 409–19.

Greenberg, Nathan A. "Euripides' *Orestes*: An Interpretation." *HSCP* 66 (1962) 157–92.

Grégoire, Henri, and L. Méridier, ed. Euripides, *Helen* (Paris, 1961).

Gregory, Justina. "Euripides' *Heracles*." *YCS* 25 (1977) 259–75.

Griffith, John G. "Some Thoughts on the *Helena* of Euripides." *JHS* 73 (1953) 36–41.

Griffith, Mark. *The Authenticity of Prometheus Bound* (Cambridge, 1977).

———, ed. Aeschylus, *Prometheus Bound* (Cambridge, 1983).

Grube, G. M. A. *The Drama of Euripides* (New York, 1961).

Haigh, A. E. *The Tragic Drama of the Greeks* (Oxford, 1896).

Hall, Edith. *Inventing the Barbarian* (Oxford, 1989).

———. "Political and Cosmic Turbulence in Euripides' *Orestes*." Pages 263–85 in *Tragedy, Comedy and the Polis*, ed. A. H. Sommerstein et al. (Bari, 1993).

Halleran, Michael R. "Rhetoric, Irony and the Ending of Euripides' *Herakles*." *CA* 5 (1986) 171–81.

Hamilton, Richard. *Choes and Anthesteria* (Ann Arbor, 1992).

———. "Neoptolemos' Story in the *Philoctetes*." *AJP* 96 (1975) 131–37.

———. "Prologue Prophecy and Plot in Four Plays of Euripides." *AJP* 99 (1978) 277–302.

———. "Slings and Arrows: The Debate with Lycus in the *Heracles*." *TAPA* 115 (1985) 19–25.

Hammond, N. G. L. "More on Conditions of Production to the Death of Aeschylus," *GRBS* 29 (1988) 5–33.

Hartung, J. A., ed. and tr. Euripides, *Alcestis* (Leipzig, 1850).

Haslam, Michael W. "The Authenticity of Euripides, *Phoenissae* 1–2 and Sophocles, *Electra* 1." *GRBS* 16 (1975) 149–74.

Heath, Malcolm. *Unity in Greek Poetics* (Oxford, 1989).

Herington, C. John. *The Author of the Prometheus Bound* (Austin, 1970).

———. "The Closure of Herodotus' *Histories*." *Illinois Classical Studies* 16 (1991) 149–60.

———. "Old Comedy and Aeschylus." *TAPA* 94 (1963) 113–125.

———. *Poetry into Drama* (Berkeley, 1985).

———. "A Study in the *Prometheia*." Parts I and II, *Phoenix* 17 (1963) 180–97, 236–43.

Hermann, Godfried, ed. Euripides, *Bacchae* (Leipzig, 1823).

Hodgdon, Barbara. *The End Crowns All: Closure and Contradiction in Shakespeare's History* (Princeton, 1991).

Holmberg, Ingrid E. "Euripides' *Helen*: Most Noble and Most Chaste." *AJP* 116 (1995) 19–42.

Holt, Philip. "The End of the *Trachiniai* and the Fate of Herakles." *JHS* 109 (1989) 69–80.

Hoppin, Meredith C. "Metrical Effects, Dramatic Illusion and the Two Endings of Sophocles' *Philoctetes*." *Arethusa* 23 (1990) 141–82.

Hose, Martin. "Überlegungen zur Exodos der *Phoinissai* des Euripides." *Würzburger Jahrbücher für die Altertumswissenschaft* 16 (1990) 63–74.

Hourmouziades, Nicolaos C. *Production and Imagination in Euripides* (Athens, 1965).

Howald, Ernst. *Untersuchungen zur Technik der euripideischen Tragödien* (Leipzig, 1914).

Hubbard, Thomas K. *The Mask of Comedy: Aristophanes and the Intertextual Parabasis* (Ithaca, 1991).

Hutchinson, G. O., ed. Aeschylus, *Septem contra Thebas* (Oxford, 1987).

Jagendorf, Zvi. *The Happy End of Comedy* (Newark, 1984).

James, Henry. "Preface to *Roderick Hudson*." Pages 3–19 in *The Art of the Novel*, ed. R. P. Blackmur (New York, 1934).

Jekels, Ludwig. "On the Psychology of Comedy." Pages 174–79 in *Comedy: Meaning and Form*, 2nd ed., ed. R. W. Corrigan (New York, 1981).

Johnson, Samuel. *Johnson on Shakespeare*, ed. W. Raleigh (Oxford, 1925).

Jones, A. H. M. *Athenian Democracy* (Oxford, 1957).

Jones, John. *On Aristotle and Greek Tragedy* (London, 1962).

Jonson, Ben. *Volpone, or, The Fox*, ed. R. B. Parker (Manchester, 1983).

Kamerbeek, J. C. "Prophecy and Tragedy." *Mnemosyne* 18 (1965) 29–40.

Kannicht, Richard, ed. Euripides, *Helena*, 2 vols (Heidelberg, 1969).

Katsouris, Andreas G. "The Formulaic End of the Menandrean Plays." *Dodone* 5 (1976) 243–56.

Kearns, Emily. *The Heroes of Attica, BICS* Supp. 57 (London, 1989).

Kermode, Frank. *The Sense of an Ending: Studies in the Theory of Fiction* (New York, 1967).

Kirk, Geoffrey S. "Methodological Reflections on the Myths of Heracles." Pages 285–97 in *Il Mito Greco*, ed. B. Gentili and G. Paione (Rome, 1977).

Kitto, H. D. F. "The Final Scenes of the *Phoenissae*." *CR* 53 (1939) 104–11.

———. *Greek Tragedy: A Literary Study*, 3rd ed. (London, 1961).

Klotz, Volker. *Geschlossene und offene Form im Drama*, 4th ed. (Munich, 1969).

Knox, Bernard M. W. "Euripidean Comedy." Pages 250–74 in *Word and Action* (Baltimore, 1979).

———. "Euripides' *Iphigenia in Aulide* 1–163 (in that Order)." Pages 275–94 in *Word and Action* (Baltimore, 1979).

———. *The Heroic Temper: Studies in Sophoclean Tragedy* (Berkeley, 1964).

———. "The *Hippolytus* of Euripides." Pages 205–30 in *Word and Action* (Baltimore, 1979).

———. "The *Medea* of Euripides." Pages 295–322 in *Word and Action* (Baltimore, 1979).

Koniaris, George L. "*Alexander, Palamedes, Troades, Sisyphus*—A Connected Tetralogy? A Connected Trilogy?" *HSCP* 77 (1973) 85–124.

Kott, Jan. "Ionesco, or a Pregnant Death." Pages 97–108 in *The Theater of Essence* (Evanston, 1984).

Kovacs, David. "Euripides, *Troades* 95–7: Is Sacking Cities Really Foolish?" *CQ* 33 (1983) 334–38.

———. *The Heroic Muse* (Baltimore, 1987).

———. "Treading the Circle Warily." *TAPA* 117 (1987) 257–70.

Kranz, Walther. *Stasimon: Untersuchungen zu Form und Gehalt der griechischen Tragödie* (Berlin, 1933).

Krieg, W. *De Euripidis Oreste* (Halle, 1934).

Krieger, Murray. *A Reopening of Closure: Organicism against Itself* (New York, 1989).

Kroeker, E. *Der Herakles des Euripides: Analyse des Dramas* (Giessen, 1938).

Kuiper, W. E. J. "De Euripidis *Helena*." *Mnemosyne* 54 (1926) 175–88.

Kuntz, Mary. "The Prodikean 'Choice of Herakles': A Reshaping of Myth." *CJ* 89 (1994) 163–81.

Lanza, Diego. "Redondances de mythes dans la tragédie." Pages 141–49 in *Métamorphoses du mythe en grèce antique*, ed. C. Calame (Geneva, 1988).

———. "Unità e significato dell'*Oreste* euripideo." *Dioniso* 35.1 (1961) 58–72.

Lattimore, Richard. Introduction to *The Trojan Women*. Pages 122–24 in *Euripides*, vol. 3, ed. D. Grene and R. Lattimore (Chicago, 1958).

Lee, Kevin H., ed. Euripides, *Troades* (London, 1976).

Lesky, Albin. *Greek Tragedy*, 2nd. ed., tr. H. A. Frankfort (London, 1967).

———. *Greek Tragic Poetry*, tr. M. Dillon (New Haven, 1983).

———. "Zum *Orestes* des Euripides." *WS* 53 (1935) 37–47.

Lewin, Arnold H. "A Study of the Prologoi of Four Plays of Euripides" (Ph.D. diss., Cornell University, 1971).

Linders, Tullia. *Studies in the Treasure Records of Artemis Brauronia Found in Athens* (Stockholm, 1972).

Lloyd-Jones, Hugh. "Artemis and Iphigenia." *JHS* 103 (1983) 87–102.

————. "Heracles at Eleusis: P.Oxy. 2622 and P.S.I. 1391." *Maia* 19 (1967) 206–29.

Lloyd-Jones, Hugh, and Nigel Wilson. *Sophoclea* (Oxford, 1990).

Longo, Oddone. "Proposte di lettura per l'*Oreste* di Euripide." *Maia* 27 (1975) 265–87.

Looy, Herman van. "Observations sur un passage de l'*Hippolyte* d'Euripide (vv. 29–33)." Pages 135–40 in *Studi filologici e storici in onore de Vittorio de Falco*, ed. F. Cupaiuolo et al. (Naples, 1971).

————. "Παρετυμολογεῖ ὁ Εὐριπίδης." Pages 345–66 in *Zetesis: Album amicorum door vrienden en collega's aangeboden aan Prof. Dr. E. de Strycker*, ed. E. Dhanis et al. (Antwerp, 1973).

Loraux, Nicole. "Herakles: The Super-Male and the Feminine." Pages 21–52 in *Before Sexuality: The Construction of Erotic Experience in the Ancient Greek World*, ed. D. M. Halperin et al. (Princeton, 1990).

————. *Tragic Ways of Killing a Woman*, tr. A. Forster (Cambridge 1987).

Ludwig, Walther. "Sapheneia: Ein Beitrag zur Formkunst im Spätwerk des Euripides" (Ph.D. diss., University of Tübingen, 1954).

Luppe, Wolfgang. "Zur Datierung der *Phoinissai* des Euripides." *RhM* 130 (1987) 29–34.

Maniet, A. "*Hélène*, 'comédie' d'Euripide." *Les Études Classiques* 15 (1947) 305–22.

Manuwald, Bernd. "μῶρος δὲ θνητῶν ὅστις ἐκπορθεῖ πόλεις: Zu Euripides, *Troerinnen* 95–97." *RhM* 132 (1989) 236–47.

March, Jennifer. *The Creative Poet: Studies on the Treatment of Myth in Greek Poetry*, BICS Supp. 49 (London, 1987).

Masaracchia, Emanuela. "Interpretazioni euripidee II: Per l'interpretazione dell'*Elena*." *Helikon* 17 (1977) 162–77.

Mason, P. G. "Kassandra." *JHS* 79 (1959) 80–93.

Mastronarde, Donald J. "Actors on High: The Skene Roof, the Crane, and the Gods in Attic Drama." *CA* 9 (1990) 247–94.

————. "Are Euripides *Phoinissai* 1104–40 Interpolated?" *Phoenix* 32 (1978) 105–28.

————, ed. Euripides, *Phoenissae* (Cambridge, 1994).

Mastronarde, Donald J., and Jan M. Bremer. *The Textual Tradition of Euripides' Phoinissai* (Berkeley, 1982).

Matthiessen, Kjeld. *Elektra, Taurische Iphigenie und Helena*. Hypomnemata 4 (Göttingen, 1964).

————. "Zur Theonoeszene der euripideischen *Helena*." *Hermes* 96 (1968) 685–704.

Mayerhoefer, Franz. "Ueber die Schlüsse der erhaltenen griechischen Tragödien" (Ph.D. diss., University of Erlangen, 1908).

Mellon, Peter S. "The Ending of Aeschylus' *Seven Against Thebes* and Its Relation to Sophocles'*Antigone* and Euripides'*Phoenissae*" (Ph.D. diss., Stanford University, 1974).

Meuss, Heinrich. "Tyche bei den attischen Tragikern." *Programm, Königliches Gymnasium zu Hirschberg* (1899) 3–17.

Mewaldt, Johann. "Heroische Weltanschauung der Hellenen." *WS* 54 (1936) 1–15.

Michelini, Ann N. *Euripides and the Tragic Tradition* (Madison, 1987).

Miller, J. Hillis. *Ariadne's Thread* (New Haven, 1992).

Mitchell, Robin N. "Miasma, Mimesis, and Scapegoating in Euripides' *Hippolytus*." *CA* 10 (1991) 97–122.

Morson, Gary Saul. "For the Time Being: Sideshadowing, Criticism, and the Russian Counter-Tradition." Pages 203–31 in *After Poststructuralism: Interdisciplinarity and Literary Theory*, ed. N. Easterlin and B. Riebling (Evanston, 1993).

Müller, Carl W. "Zur Datierung des sophokleischen Ödipus." *Akademie der Wissenschaften und der Literatur, Mainz, Abhandlungen der geistes- und sozialwissenschaflichen Klasse* 1984: 5.

Mueller-Goldingen, Christian. *Untersuchungen zu den Phönissen des Euripides* (Stuttgart, 1985).

Mullens, H. G. "The Meaning of Euripides' *Orestes*." *CQ* 34 (1940) 153–58.

Murnaghan, Sheila. "Trials of the Hero in Sophocles' *Ajax*." Pages 171–93 in *Images of Authority*, ed. M. M. MacKenzie and C. Roueché (Cambridge, 1989).

Murray, Gilbert. *Euripides and His Age*, 2nd ed. (London, 1946).

———. "Excursus on the Ritual Forms Presented in Greek Tragedy." Pages 341–63 in J. E. Harrison, *Themis: A Study of the Social Origins of Greek Religion* (Cambridge, 1912).

———. "Heracles, 'The Best of Men.'" Pages 106–26 in *Greek Studies* (Oxford, 1946).

———. "The *Trojan Women* of Euripides." *Living Age* 245 (1905) 37–52.

Newiger, H.-J. "Elektra in Aristophanes' *Wolken*." *Hermes* 89 (1961) 422–30.

Nicolai, Walter. *Euripides' Dramen mit rettendem Deus ex machina* (Heidelberg, 1990).

Nisetich, Frank J. "The Silencing of Pylades (*Orestes* 1591–92)." *AJP* 107 (1986) 46–54.

Norwood, Gilbert. *Essays on Euripidean Drama* (Berkeley, 1954).

O'Brien, M. J. "Tantalus in Euripides' *Orestes*." *RhM* 131 (1988) 30–45.

Olivieri, Alessandro. "Dell'*Oreste* di Euripide." *Rivista di Filologia e di Istruzione Classica* 28 (1900) 228–38.

O'Neill, Eugene G. Jr. "The Prologue of the *Troades* of Euripides." *TAPA* 72 (1941) 288–320.

Owen, A. S., ed. Euripides, *Ion* (Oxford, 1939).

Padel, Ruth. "'Imagery of the Elsewhere': Two Choral Odes of Euripides." *CQ* 24 (1974) 227–41.

Page, Denys L. *Actors' Interpolations in Greek Tragedy* (Oxford, 1934).

———, ed. Euripides, *Medea* (Oxford, 1952).

———, ed. *Greek Literary Papyri* (Cambridge, 1942).

Papi, Donatella G. "Victors and Sufferers in Euripides' *Helen*." *AJP* 108 (1987) 27–40.

Parmentier, Léon. "Notes sur les *Troyennes* d'Euripide." *Revue des Études Grecques* 36 (1923) 46–61.

Parry, Hugh. "Euripides' *Orestes*: The Quest for Salvation." *TAPA* 100 (1969) 337–53.

Pearson, A. C., ed. *Fragments of Sophocles*, 3 vols (Cambridge, 1917).

Peradotto, John J. *Man in the Middle Voice: Name and Narration in the Odyssey* (Princeton, 1990).

Perrotta, Gennaro. "Le *Troiane* di Euripide." *Dioniso* 15 (1952) 237–50.

Pfister, Max. *The Theory and Analysis of Drama*, tr. J. Halliday (Cambridge, 1988).

Pickard-Cambridge, A. W. *The Dramatic Festivals of Athens*, 2nd ed., rev. by J. Gould and D. M. Lewis (Oxford, 1968).

———. *The Theatre of Dionysus in Athens* (Oxford, 1946).

Pippin, Anne N. "Euripides' *Helen*: A Comedy of Ideas." *CP* 55 (1960) 151–63.

Platnauer, M., ed. Euripides, *Iphigenia in Tauris* (Oxford, 1938).

Podlecki, Anthony J. "The Basic Seriousness of Euripides' *Helen*." *TAPA* 101 (1970) 401–18.

———. "Some Themes in Euripides' *Phoenissae*." *TAPA* 93 (1962) 355–73.

Pohlenz, Max. *Die griechische Tragödie*, 2nd ed., 2 vols. (Göttingen, 1954).

Poole, Adrian. "Total Disaster: Euripides' *The Trojan Women*." *Arion* n.s. 3 (1976) 257–87.

Porter, John R. *Studies in Euripides' Orestes* (Leiden, 1994).

Post, L. A. "Menander and the *Helen* of Euripides." *HSCP* 68 (1964) 99–118.

Pucci, Pietro. "Euripides: The Monument and the Sacrifice." *Arethusa* 10 (1977) 165–95.

———. "Gods' Intervention and Epiphany in Sophocles." *AJP* 115 (1994) 15–46.

———. *The Violence of Pity in Euripides' Medea* (Ithaca, 1980).

Quint, David. *Epic and Empire* (Princeton, 1993).

Rabinowitz, Nancy S. *Anxiety Veiled: Euripides and the Traffic in Women* (Ithaca, 1993).

Radermacher, Ludwig. "Intrigenbildung in der attischen Tragödie." *Anzeiger der Akademie der Wissenschaften in Wien*, philosophisch-historische Klasse 69 (1932) 20–25.

———. *Das Jenseits im Mythos der Hellenen* (Bonn, 1903).

———. "Ueber eine Scene des euripideischen *Orestes*." *RhM* 57 (1902) 278–84.

Rawson, Elizabeth. "Aspects of Euripides' *Orestes*." *Arethusa* 5 (1972) 155–67.

———. "Family and Fatherland in Euripides' *Phoenissae*." *GRBS* 11 (1970) 109–127.

Reckford, Kenneth J. "Phaedra and Pasiphae: The Pull Backward." *TAPA* 104 (1974) 307–28.

Rees, B. R. "Euripides, *Medea* 1415–9." *AJP* 82 (1961) 176–81.

Reeve, Michael D. "Interpolation in Greek Tragedy, I." *GRBS* 13 (1972) 247–65.

———. "Interpolation in Greek Tragedy, II." *GRBS* 13 (1972) 451–74.

Rehm, Rush. *Marriage to Death: The Conflation of Wedding and Funeral Rituals in Greek Tragedy* (Princeton, 1994).

Reich, Hermann. *Der Mimus* (Berlin, 1903).

Reinhardt, Karl. "Das Parisurteil." Pages 16–36 in *Tradition und Geist: Gesammelte Essays zur Dichtung*, ed. C. Becker (Göttingen, 1960).

———. "Die Sinneskrise bei Euripides." Pages 227–56 in *Tradition und Geist* (Göttingen, 1960).

Richter, David. *Fable's End: Completeness and Closure in Rhetorical Fiction* (Chicago, 1974).

Roberts, Deborah H. *Apollo and His Oracle in the Oresteia*. Hypomnemata 78 (Göttingen, 1984).

———. "Different Stories: Sophoclean Narrative(s) in the *Philoctetes*." *TAPA* 119 (1989) 161–76.

——— . "Outside the Drama: The Limits of Tragedy in Aristotle's *Poetics*." Pages 133–53 in *Essays in Aristotle's Poetics*, ed. A. O. Rorty (Princeton, 1992).

———. "Parting Words: Final Lines in Sophocles and Euripides." *CQ* 37 (1987) 51–64.

———. "Sophoclean Endings: Another Story." *Arethusa* 21 (1988) 177–96.

Roberts, Deborah H., Francis M. Dunn, and Don P. Fowler, eds. *Classical Closure: Reading the End in Greek and Latin Literature* (Princeton, forthcoming).

Robertson, D. S. "The End of the Supplices Trilogy of Aeschylus." *CR* 38 (1924) 51–53.

Romilly, Jacqueline de. "La belle Hélène et l'évolution de la tragédie grecque." *Les Études Classiques* 56 (1988) 129–43.

———. "*Phoenician Women* of Euripides: Topicality in Greek Tragedy." *Bucknell Review* 15.3 (1967) 108–32.

Ronnet, Gilberte. "Le cas de conscience de Théonoé, ou Euripide et la sophistique face à l'idée de justice." *Revue de Philologie* 53 (1979) 251–59.

Rosenmeyer, Thomas G. *The Art of Aeschylus* (Berkeley, 1982).

Rubino, Carl A. "Opening up the Classical Past: Bakhtin, Aristotle, Literature, Life." *Arethusa* 26 (1993) 141–57.

Ruijgh, C. J. "Observations sur l'emploi onomastique de κεκλῆσθαι vis-à-vis celui de καλεῖσθαι, notamment dans la tragédie attique." Pages 333–35 in *Miscellanea Tragica in Honorem J. C. Kamerbeek*, ed. J. M. Bremer et al. (Amsterdam, 1976).

Saïd, Suzanne. "Euripide ou l'attente déçue: l'exemple des *Phéniciennes*." *Annali della Scuola Normale Superiore di Pisa* 15 (1985) 501–27.

Sansone, David. "Theonoe and Theoclymenus." *Symbolae Osloenses* 60 (1985) 17–36.

Sartre, Jean-Paul. *Les Troyennes* (Paris, 1966).

Schadewaldt, Wolfgang. *Monolog und Selbstgespräch* (Berlin, 1926).

Schein, Seth L. "Mythical Illusion and Historical Reality in Euripides' *Orestes*." *WS* n.s. 9 (1975) 49–66.

Schlesinger, Alfred C. *The Gods in Greek Tragedy: A Study of Ritual Survivals in Fifth-Century Drama* (Athens, 1927).

Schmid, Wilhelm. *Die klassische Periode der griechischen Literatur.* 5 vols in *Handbuch der Altertumswissenschaft,* ed. W. Otto (Munich, 1929–48).

Schmidt, Henry J. *How Dramas End: Essays on the German Sturm und Drang* (Ann Arbor, 1992).

Schmidt, Wieland. "Der Deus ex Machina bei Euripides" (Ph.D. diss.University of Tübingen, 1964).

Schmiel, Robert. "The Recognition Duo in Euripides' *Helen.*" *Hermes* 100 (1972) 274–94.

Schwyzer, E. *Dialectorum graecarum exempla epigraphica potiora* (Leipzig, 1923).

Scodel, Ruth. "Tantalus and Anaxagoras." *HSCP* 88 (1984) 13–24.

———. *The Trojan Trilogy of Euripides,* Hypomnemata 60 (Göttingen, 1980).

Segal, Charles P. *Dionysiac Poetics and Euripides' Bacchae* (Princeton, 1982).

———. *Euripides and the Poetics of Sorrow* (Durham, 1993).

———. "Shame and Purity in Euripides' *Hippolytus.*" *Hermes* 98 (1970) 278–99.

———. "Theatre, Ritual and Commemoration in Euripides' *Hippolytus.*" *Ramus* 17 (1988) 52–74.

———. "Tragic Beginnings: Narration, Voice and Authority in the Prologues of Greek Drama." *YCS* 29 (1992) 85–112.

———. "The Two Worlds of Euripides' *Helen.*" *TAPA* 102 (1971) 553–614.

Segal, Erich. *Roman Laughter,* 2nd ed. (Oxford, 1987).

Seidensticker, Bernd. *Palintonos Harmonia* (Göttingen, 1982).

Shakespeare, William. *Complete Works,* ed. W. J. Craig (Oxford, 1930).

Shaw, G. Bernard. *Pygmalion: A Romance in Five Acts* (New York, 1951).

Silk, M. S. "Heracles and Greek Tragedy." Pages 116–37 in *Greek Tragedy,* ed, I. McAuslan and P. Walcot (Oxford, 1993).

Smith, Barbara H. *Poetic Closure: A Study of How Poems End* (Chicago, 1968).

Smith, Wesley D. "Disease in Euripides' *Orestes.*" *Hermes* 95 (1967) 291–307.

Solmsen, Friedrich. "Euripides' *Ion* im Vergleich mit anderen Tragödien." *Hermes* 69 (1934) 390–419.

———. "Ὄνομα and πρᾶγμα in Euripides' *Helen.*" *CR* 48 (1934) 119–21.

———. "Zur Gestaltung des Intriguenmotivs in den Tragödien des Sophokles und Euripides." *Philologus* 87 (1932) 1–17.

Sophocles. *Fabulae,* ed. H. Lloyd-Jones and N. G. Wilson (Oxford, 1990).

Spira, Andreas. *Untersuchungen zum Deus ex Machina bei Sophokles und Euripides* (Kallmunz, 1960).

Stanley-Porter, D. P. "Who Opposes Theoclymenus?" *CP* 72 (1977) 45–48.

Steiger, Hugo. "Wie entstand die *Helena* des Euripides?" *Philologus* 67 (1908) 202–37.

Stephanopoulos, Theodoros K. *Umgestaltung des Mythos durch Euripides* (Athens, 1980).

Stinton, T. C. W. *Euripides and the Judgement of Paris* (London, 1965).

———. "The Scope and Limits of Allusion in Greek Tragedy." Pages 67–102 in *Greek Tragedy and its Legacy,* ed. M. Cropp, E. Fantham, and S. E. Scully (Calgary, 1986).

Strohm, Hans. *Euripides: Interpretationen zur dramatischen Form.* Zetemata 15 (Munich, 1957).

Stuart, Donald C. "Foreshadowing and Suspense in the Euripidean Prolog." *Studies in Philology* 15 (1918) 295–306.

Sutton, Dana F. *The Lost Sophocles* (Lanham, 1984).

———. "Satyric Qualities in Euripides' *Iphigeneia at Tauris* and *Helen.*" *Rivista di Studi Classici* 20 (1972) 321–30.

————. "Supposed Evidence that Euripides' *Orestes* and Sophocles' *Electra* were Prosatyric." *Rivista di Studi Classici* 21 (1973) 117–21.

————. *Two Lost Plays of Euripides* (New York, 1987).

Terzaghi, Nicolà. "Finali e prologhi Euripidei." *Dioniso* 6 (1937) 304–13.

Thalmann, William G. *Dramatic Art in Aeschylus's Seven Against Thebes* (New Haven, 1978).

Thomson, George, ed. Aeschylus, *Prometheus Bound* (Cambridge, 1932).

Thucydides. *History of the Peloponnesian War*, tr. R. Warner (Harmondsworth, 1972).

Torgovnick, Marianna. *Closure in the Novel* (Princeton, 1981).

Treves, P. "Le *Fenicie* di Euripide." *Atene e Roma* 11 (1930) 171–195.

Valgiglio, Ernesto. *L'esodo delle Fenicie di Euripide* (Turin, 1961).

Valk, M. van der. *Studies in Euripides: Phoenissae and Andromache* (Amsterdam, 1985).

Vernant, Jean-Pierre. "The Historical Moment of Tragedy in Greece." Pages 1–5 in J. P. Vernant and P. Vidal-Naquet, *Tragedy and Myth in Ancient Greece*, tr. J. Lloyd (Sussex, 1981).

Verrall, A. W. *Essays on Four Plays of Euripides* (Cambridge, 1905).

————. *Euripides the Rationalist* (Cambridge, 1895).

Vos, Maria F. *Scythian Archers in Archaic Attic Vase-painting* (Groningen, 1963).

Walker, S. "A Sanctuary of Isis on the South Slope of the Athenian Acropolis." *Annual of the British School at Athens* 74 (1979) 243–57.

Walsh, George B. "Public and Private in Three Plays of Euripides." *CP* 74 (1979) 294–309.

Way, A. S. *The Tragedies of Euripides in English Verse*, 3 vols. (London, 1898).

Webster, T. B. L. "The Order of Tragedies at the Great Dionysia." *Hermathena* 100 (1965) 21–28.

————. *The Tragedies of Euripides* (London, 1967).

West, M. L. "Tragica V." *BICS* 28 (1981) 61–78.

Westermann, Antonius. Μυθογράφοι: *Scriptores Poeticae Historicae Graeci* (Brunswick, 1843).

Whitman, Cedric H. *Aristophanes and the Comic Hero* (Cambridge, 1964).

————. *Euripides and the Full Circle of Myth* (Cambridge, 1974).

Wilamowitz-Moellendorff, U. von. *Aischylos Interpretationen* (Berlin, 1914).

————, ed. Euripides, *Herakles*, 3 vols (Berlin, 1895).

Willink, C. W., ed. Euripides, *Orestes* (Oxford, 1986).

————. "The Goddess εὐλάβεια and Pseudo-Euripides in Euripides' *Phoenissae*." *Proceedings of the Cambridge Philological Society* 36 (1990) 182–201.

————. "Prodikos, 'Meteorosophists' and the 'Tantalos' Paradigm." *CQ* 33 (1983) 25–33.

Willson, John R. "The Etymology in Euripides, *Troades* 13–14." *AJP* 89 (1968) 66–71.

————. "An Interpolation in the Prologue of Euripides' *Troades*." *GRBS* 8 (1967) 205–23.

Willson, Robert E. *Shakespeare's Reflexive Endings* (Lewiston, 1990).

Winkler, John J. "Aristotle's Theory of the Novel and the Best Tragedy." Unpublished manuscript.

Winnington-Ingram, R. P. "Euripides: Poiêtês Sophos." *Arethusa* 2 (1969) 127–42.

Wolff, Christian. "Euripides' *Iphigenia among the Taurians*: Aetiology, Ritual, and Myth." *CA* 11 (1992) 308–34.

————. "On Euripides' *Helen*." *HSCP* 77 (1973) 61–84.

————. "*Orestes*." Pages 132–49 in *Euripides: A Collection of Critical Essays*, ed. E. Segal (Englewood Cliffs, 1968).

Woodford, Susan. "Cults of Heracles in Attica." Pages 211–15 in *Studies Presented to G. M. A. Hanfmann*, ed. D. G. Mitten et al. (Mainz, 1971).

Yunis, Harvey. *A New Creed: Fundamental Religious Beliefs in the Athenian Polis and Euripidean Drama*. Hypomnemata 91 (Göttingen, 1988).

Xanthakis-Karamanos, G. *Studies in Fourth-Century Tragedy* (Athens, 1980).

Zeichner, Friedrich. "De deo ex machina Euripideo" (Diss., University of Göttingen 1924).

Zeitlin, Froma I. "The Closet of Masks: Role-Playing and Myth-Making in the *Orestes* of Euripides." *Ramus* 9 (1980) 51–77.

———. "The Power of Aphrodite: Eros and the Boundaries of the Self in the *Hippolytus*." Pages 52–111 in *Directions in Euripidean Criticism*, ed. P. Burian (Durham, 1985).

Zuntz, Gunther. "On Euripides' *Helena*: Theology and Irony." Pages 201–27 in *Euripide; sept exposés et discussions*. Entretiens sur l'Antiquité classique 6 (Geneva, 1960).

———. *The Political Plays of Euripides* (Manchester, 1955).

Zürcher, Walter. *Die Darstellung des Menschen im Drama des Euripides* (Basel, 1947).

Index of Euripidean Passages

Important citations are in bold.

General Index

Adams, Robert, 9
Aeschylus, 29, 48, 112, 152
  closing lines in, 21–22
  parodied or subverted, 165, 173, 176–77, 198
  Agamemnon, 78, 176, 181
  Danaids, 186, 208n28
  Eumenides, 13, 79
    aetiology in, 58–59
    authority figure in, 37–38
    revised by Euripides, 51, 56, 63, 165, 175
  Libation Bearers, 175, 176
    exit lines in, 21–22
  Persians, 5, 79–80, 102, 124, 181, 208n28
  Prometheus Bound
    aetiology in, 57–58
    prophecy in, 80
  Prometheus Unbound, 80
  Psychagogoi, 214n29
  Seven against Thebes, 59, 190
    revised in *Phoenician Women*, 191–92, 193
aetiology. *See* aition
Agathon, 152
aition, 46–63, 88–89, 104, 107
  ambivalent, 93–96, 117–18
  definition of, 48
  invented, 56–57, 63, 94–5
  irrelevant, 136–37
  and prophecy, 66, 73–76
  See also commemoration
Antiphanes, 27, 29
aperture, 128, 199–200
Aristophanes 29, 99, 124
  closing lines in, 21
  and comic hero, 7, 163, 171
Aristotle, 4, 15, 77
  on tragic unity, 64, 127
Arrowsmith, William, 120, 161
Arthur, Marylin, 198, 201

Bakhtin, Mikhail, 9, 127–28, 199
Barlow, Shirley, 101
Barrett, W. S., 24
Beckett, Samuel, 18
Bieber, Margarete, 88
Bloom, Harold, 175
Brecht, Bertolt, 43, 65
Brooks, Peter, 9, 98
burial, 55, 56–57, 60, 115–16
Burnett, Anne, 42

carnival, 174
Carroll, Lewis, 127
Chalk, H. H. O., 120, 123
chance, 147–51, 154, 156
choral exit, 14–25, 116, 183–84
  definition of, 14
  repeated, 17, 19, 24–25, 135–36
chorus, role of, 14–15
civic values, 121–22, 124
closure, approaches to, 8–9
comedy, 7, 156, 178–79
  and chance, 149
  and deus ex machina, 42–43
  and dramatic illusion, 19, 29, 65
  and license, 163, 168, 171, 173
commemoration, 73, 92–95
  of dead character, 52–54, 55–56
  of living character, 54, 55–56
Conacher, D. J., 7, 109
concluding prophecy, 29, 64–83, 104–5, 137
  definition of, 66
  See also epilogue
continuous action, 6, 24, 40, 67–68, 71
  and choral exit, 22
  not contained by drama, 45, 64, 76–78, 83
Craik, Elizabeth, 180, 183
Creophylus, 94
curtain, 13–14, 18–19, 21, 26
Cypria, 113, 175